growing australian natives

SECOND EDITION

John Mason

and the staff of

ACS Distance Education

Kangaroo Press

GROWING AUSTRALIAN NATIVES
First published in Australia in 1997 by Kangaroo Press
An imprint of Simon & Schuster (Australia) Pty Limited
Suite 2, Lower Ground Floor,
14-16 Suakin Street, Pymble NSW 2073

A CBS Company
Sydney New York London Toronto

Visit our website at www.simonsaysaustralia.com

This second edition published in 2007

Cataloguing-in-Publication data:

Mason, John, 1951–
Growing Australian natives.

2nd ed.
Includes index.
ISBN 9780731813100 (pbk.).

1. Native plant gardening - Australia. 2. Native plants for cultivation - Australia. I. Title.

635.95194

Internal design by Avril Makula
Cover design by Melissa Keogh
Cover image *Banksia praemorsa* © M. Fagg, Australian National Botanic Gardens
Typeset in 10.5 on 12.5 Berkeley Book
Printed in China through Colorcraft Ltd, Hong Kong

10 9 8 7 6 5 4 3 2 1

Contents

Preface
to the Second Edition

Growing Australian Natives is designed to help you develop a sound understanding of how to grow Australian native plants. It is easy to read, and draws upon the author's own experience of growing native plants and his extensive research into the subject. This book develops further the ideas and information provided in *Native Plant Expert*, first published by the Australian Horticultural Correspondence School, then later by Kangaroo Press in 1997. It is similar in format but covers many more plants and provides even more tips for successfully growing native plants.

In this new edition plant names have been thoroughly reviewed and updated. Where a particular species has been renamed, we refer to it by both its new and old Latin names, so that it can be easily found under either name.

I would like to thank all the following people who have contributed to the original edition and to the second edition of this book.

Tutors of the Australian Correspondence School and ACS Distance Education:
Iain Harrison, Dip.Hort.Sc, AHCS, Senior Tutor
Alison Bundock, Ass.Dip.Hort, BA, Grad.Dip.Hort
Alan Lewis, Cert.Eng, Cert.Hort, MAIH
Adriana Fraser, Cert.Hort., Adv.Cert.App.Mgt., Adv.Dip.Hort.
Margot Witnall, Dip.Hort.Sc, Dip.Ldsc.
Albert Filippa, Dip.Hort.
Lynette Hannan, Dip.Hort.Sc.
Paul Plant, B.App.Sc (Hort.Tech), MAIH
Tosca Zraikat, B.Ed.
Valeria Astorga, PhD.Biol

Part One

1. Introduction

What's so good about natives?

There are a number of reasons why Australian natives are worth growing.

First there is their enormous variety: at least 20,000 species, including around 700 species of acacias and over 500 species of eucalypts. One can find native plants for just about any situation, from deserts to rainforests to alpine regions. Many natives have evolved to withstand harsh conditions, including saline conditions, arid conditions, strong winds, pollution, and flooding. It is important to remember that the natives that naturally occur in your own area have evolved to cope and thrive under those local conditions.

Second, many Australian natives have extremely attractive flowers, fruit, foliage or habit, which are often unique to Australia. In fact, a large number of indigenous Australian plants are endemic — that is, they do not occur anywhere else in the world. By growing natives, we can help ensure that these species are preserved.

Third, the flora and fauna of Australia have evolved together over a long time, so by growing Australian natives we encourage the survival of native fauna as well.

Fourth, while some have been widely cultivated, many Australian native plants are new to the world of gardening, some so new that we are still learning how to grow them properly. Unlike plants from many other countries, relatively few Australian plant species have undergone extensive plant breeding or plant selection programs. Some exceptions are the kangaroo paws (*Anigozanthos* sp.) and the Geraldton wax (*Chamelaucium* sp.), which have been the focus of breeding and selection programs for the last few years. Often we are still working with raw material from the bush, whereas plants such as camellias and roses have been grown, hybridised and generally studied for hundreds of years. As yet, many horticulturally valuable species still haven't even been collected from the wild.

Three types of native flora

Australian native plants can be divided into three main groups:

- **INDO-MELANESIAN (OR ASIAN) FLORA**. Plants evolved from species originating in South-East Asia. These are typified by plants from tropical or subtropical rainforests in the north of the continent.
- **ANTARCTIC FLORA.** Plants which have evolved from species present when the Australian continent was linked with what is now called Antarctica. These plants are typified

by broad-leaved deciduous and evergreen species such as beeches, sassafras, conifers and other plants from southern (cold-climate) rainforests. Many of these plants have affinities with species in New Zealand, South America and South Africa.
- **SCLEROPHYLL FLORA.** Typified by eucalypt forests and woodlands, these plants clearly evolved inside Australia. They are more widespread than the other two types, dominating the majority of the continent, particularly in the more arid and semi-arid regions.

The main groups of cultivated plants

FERNS

Ferns are a primitive group of plants that do not have flowers. They are soft-wooded, and reproduce by developing spores (similar to seeds) on the undersurface of their fronds (like leaves). Ferns belong to the phyla Pteridophyta, a classification which groups together several related families.

GYMNOSPERMS

Gymnosperms are less complex than flowering plants but more complex than ferns. They produce seeds that are borne on the upper surface of a scale (such as the scales of a cone), and are born 'naked' (that is, they don't have a protective case such as an ovary around the seed). This group of plants includes the conifers, which bear their seeds in cones, and cycads.

ANGIOSPERMS (OR FLOWERING PLANTS)

These are the dominant plants of the world, which comprise most of our crop species and the majority of our ornamental plants. In angiosperms, the seeds are borne within a closed structure called the ovary which eventually becomes the fruit. There are two main groups of angiosperms:

1. **MONOCOTYLEDONS**. Monocots are flowering plants which have only one leaf emerge when their seed germinates. The veins on their leaves are parallel. They are sometimes called narrow-leaved plants. This group includes the grasses, orchids and the lilies.
2. **DICOTYLEDONS**. Dicots are flowering plants which have two leaves emerge from the germinating seed. The leaf veins are not parallel. They are often called broad-leaved plants. This group contains the largest percentage of our cultivated plant species and includes such families as the Myrtaceae, Asteraceae, Papilionaceae and Mimosaceae.

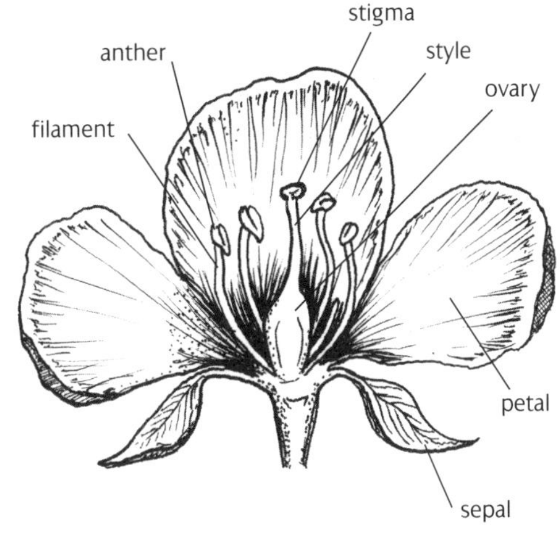

Parts of a flower

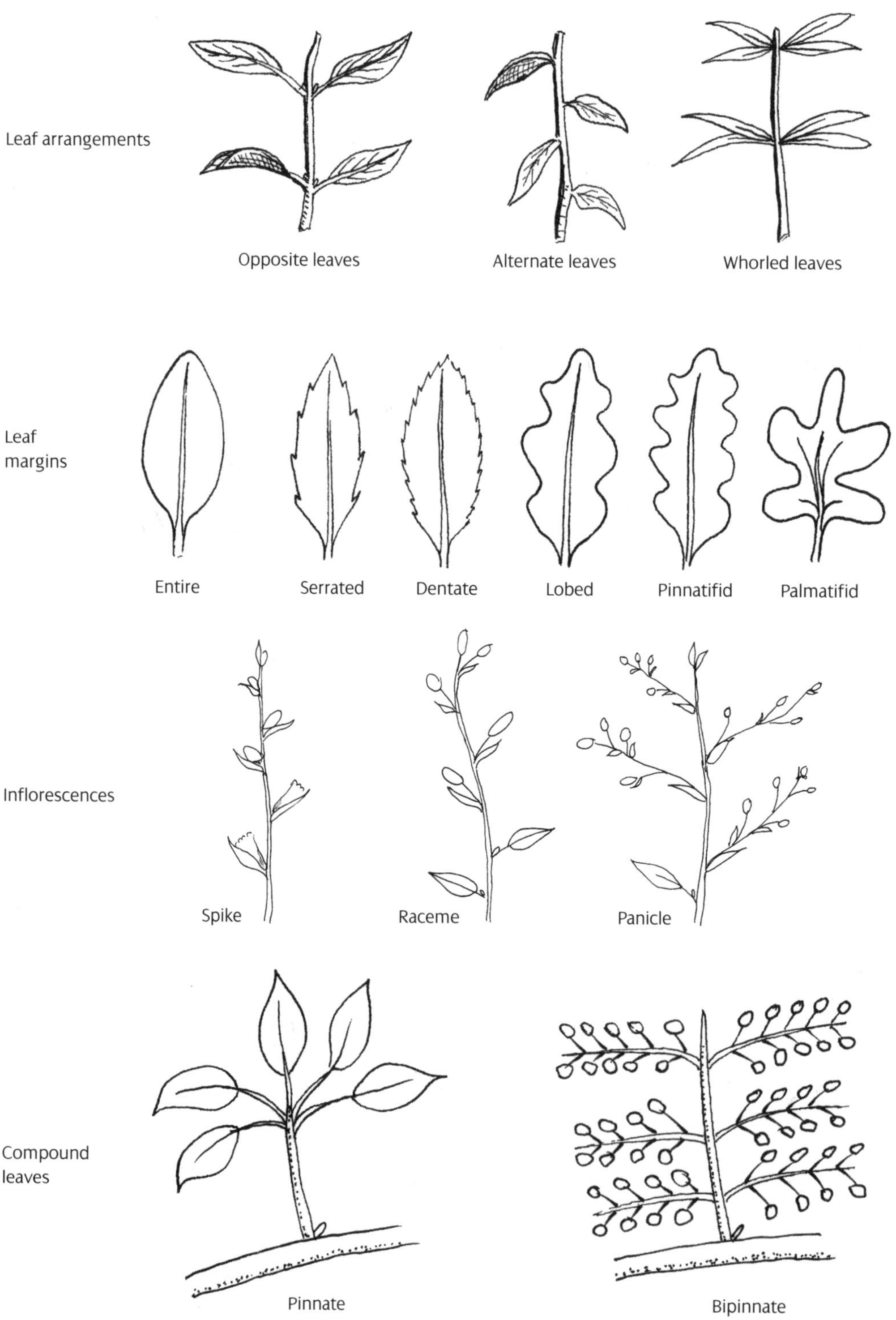
Leaf arrangements
Opposite leaves
Alternate leaves
Whorled leaves
Leaf margins
Entire
Serrated
Dentate
Lobed
Pinnatifid
Palmatifid
Inflorescences
Spike
Raceme
Panicle
Compound leaves
Pinnate
Bipinnate

Naming your native plants

When you grow or observe a particular plant it becomes very important to be able to clearly distinguish it from other plants. Plants have two different types of names.

COMMON NAMES

These are names given to plants generally by home gardeners. The names are not usually accurate and very often several different plants bear the same common name, for example, flame bush or spider flower.

SCIENTIFIC NAMES

Based on the Latin language, these are names given to plants by scientists, and allow for accurate identification of plants. Any one name will only be used for one plant, for example, *Acacia baileyana*.

Scientific names consist of two or more words. The first word indicates the **genus** (or group) to which that plant belongs, and the second word indicates the **species** which is specific to the plant. Sometimes there are different forms of a species. For example, *Acacia baileyana* can be obtained as a blue-leaved plant or as a blue-leaved plant with purple tips to the foliage. To distinguish one form from another, a third word is added to the name, for example, *Acacia baileyana* 'Purpurea'. The third word is a **variety** name.

Sometimes two different species breed with each other to produce a new type of plant. Such a plant is called a **hybrid**. For example, *Eucalyptus* 'Torwood' is a hybrid between *Eucalyptus torquata* and *Eucalyptus woodwardii*. Hybrids can also be listed by placing an 'x' sign between the names of the parents if they are known; for example, *Eucalyptus torquata* x *Eucalyptus woodwardii* signifies the same plant as the name *Eucalyptus* 'Torwood'.

Different plants that are similar to each other but are not of the same genus are grouped together to form plant families. A plant family is a collection of several similar genera (plural of genus).

It is most useful to become familiar with this system of plant naming. Plants within the same family tend to have similar likes and dislikes. By getting to know the characteristics of a family, you develop a basis for learning both how to identify and how to grow plants within that family.

You may notice some plant names are written with the words syn., sp. or spp. Syn. is an abbreviation for synonym, which is an alternative or outdated but still acceptable botanical name. For example, the red-flowering gum might be written as *Corymbia ficifolia* syn. *Eucalyptus ficifiolia* — the new genus is *Corymbia*, but the plant is more widely known by its old genus *Eucalyptus*.

The letters sp. are an abbreviation for the word species; for example, *Thryptomene* sp. The plural of sp. is spp.

Commonly grown native plant families

MYRTACEAE

The Myrtaceae family contains some of the most significant Australian native plant genera, including *Eucalyptus*, *Corymbia*, *Callistemon*, *Melaleuca*, *Lophostemon*, *Thryptomene*, *Angophora*, *Agonis*, *Baeckea*, *Leptospermum*, *Eugenia*, *Astartea* and *Micromyrtus*. Non-native genera in this family include *Myrtus* (myrtle) and *Feijoa*. Members of this family are generally hardy and adaptable to a wide range of conditions. Most can be readily propagated from seed, and many of the smaller shrub

Myrtaceae

types are often also propagated from cuttings.

The following three families were formerly included as subfamilies in the Leguminosae (the 'pea' family), but are now recognised as three separate families. They are characterised by their pod-type fruit or legumes. They are useful for improving soil fertility — colonies of bacteria on the roots convert nitrogen from the air to feed the plant. Most native legume species are propagated from seed which is first soaked in boiling water.

MIMOSACEAE

Flowers appear like a fluffy ball or cylinder (stamens are large and much more obvious than petals), and seeds develop in pods. Mimosaceae includes the genera *Acacia*, *Albizzia* and *Nepuntia*.

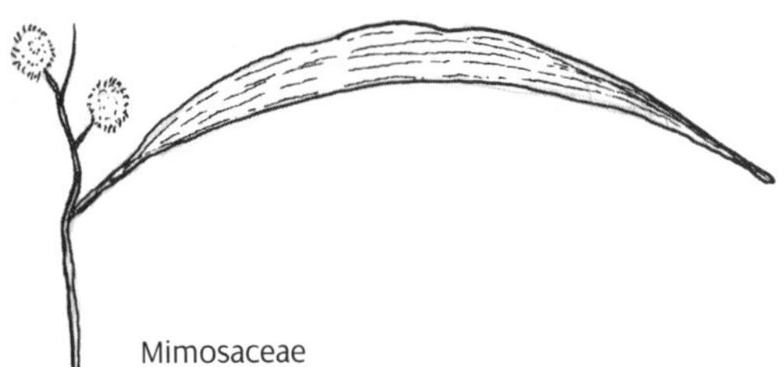
Mimosaceae

FABACEAE (SYN. PAPILIONACEAE)

These have a typical pea-like flower (there are five petals, two are joined and three are free), and seeds develop in pods. Fabaceae includes the genera *Aotus*, *Oxylobium*, *Pultenaea*, *Hardenbergia*, *Kennedia*, *Gompholobium* and *Swainsonia*.

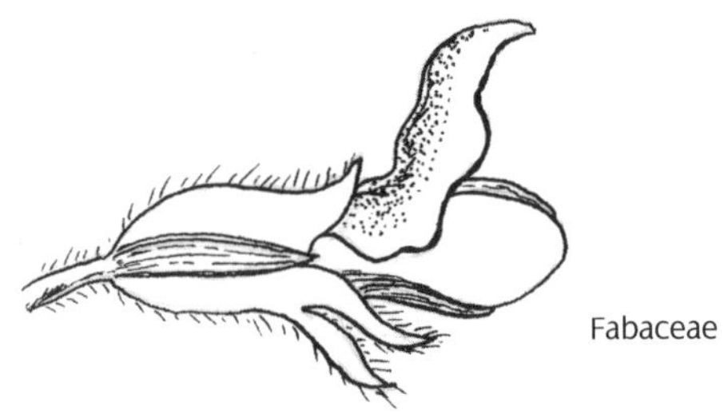
Fabaceae

CAESALPINACEAE

These plants have five petals, all obvious and free (not joined). Flowers are asymmetrical, and leaves are normally compound. This family includes the native cassia and non-Australian plants such as *Bauhinia* and *Gleditsia*.

Caesalpinaceae

PROTEACEAE

A diverse family with around 800 species and 38 genera in Australia. They are commonly known for the large, showy flowers which are borne on many species. Examples of Australian native genera in this family include *Grevillea*, *Banksia*, *Hakea*, *Stenocarpus*, *Isopogon*, *Telopea*, and *Dryandra*. Flowers are variable, although the petals tend to be insignificant. Leaves are often thick and dry in texture, and often with sharp tips. Seeds are large and woody.

Generally plants in this family require well-drained soils and commonly suffer from iron deficiency and phosphorus toxicity in cultivation. Some rainforest genera, including *Macadamia*, are an exception. They require more phosphorus than other genera in the family. Root rot is also a common problem. Propagation is commonly from seed for most species, with the notable exception of grevilleas, which are grown from cuttings. Many species from other genera have, however, been successfully grown by cuttings or grafting.

RUTACEAE

Twenty genera in Australia including *Asterolasia*, *Boronia*, *Correa*, *Crowea*, *Diplolaena*, *Eriostemon*, *Flindersia*, *Geijera*, *Microcitrus*, *Murraya*, *Phelabalium* and *Zieria*. Leaves of species from this family are covered with small dots (oil glands); flowers have either four or five petals. This family includes many small shrubs with attractive flowers.

PITTOSPORACEAE

Most of the plants in this family are native to Australia. Notable genera include *Pittosporum*, *Hymenosporum*, *Bursaria*, *Billardiera* and *Marianthus*. Flowers have five petals, leaves are simple (undivided) and arranged alternately on the stem, and fruits are either a berry or capsule (often attractive). Many varieties may be propagated from both seed and cuttings.

ASTERACEAE (COMPOSITAE)

The daisy family has a worldwide distribution of about 800 genera and 12,000 species. Australian genera include *Helichrysum*, *Bracteantha*, *Olearia*, *Rhodanthe* and *Brachyscome*. The flowers are actually a composite of many small flowers fused together to appear as one single flower. If the flower is pulled apart it can be seen that it is made up of many individual units, each one having its own set of floral parts (petal, stamen, stigma, ovary, etc). Some Asteraceae

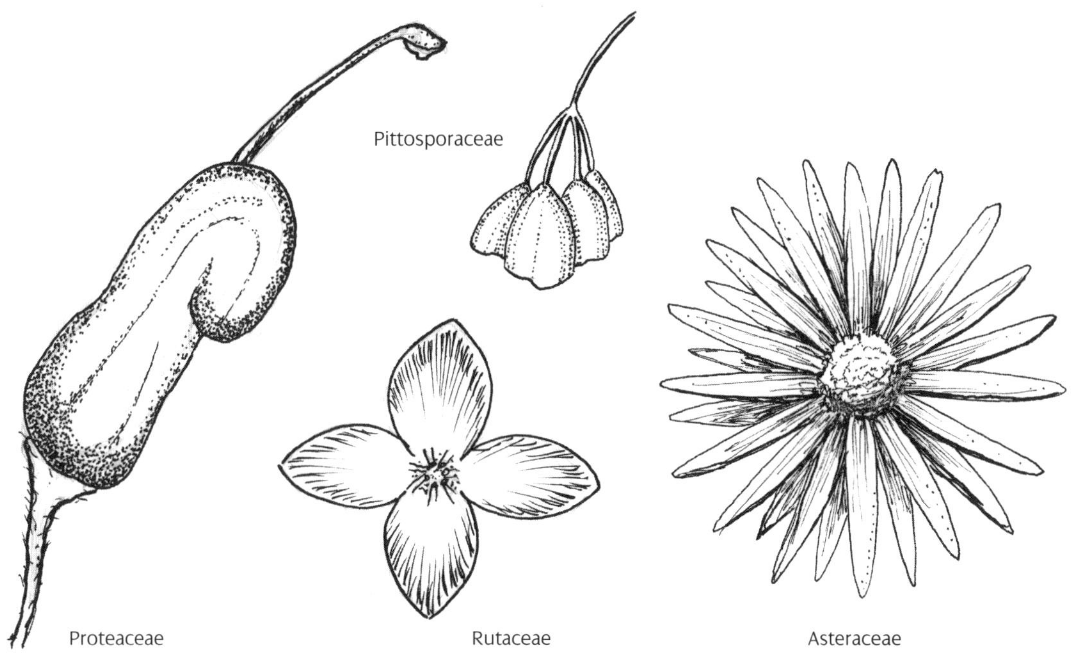

flowers are incomplete and have only some of the floral parts. Flowers in this family are generally fast growing, flower prolifically, and prefer well-drained soils. Many are excellent cut flowers or are used for dried floral arrangements.

LAMIACEAE (LABIATAE)

Commonly known as the mint family, genera in Australia include *Prostanthera*, *Westringia* and *Hemiandra*. The stems are roughly four-sided (similar to a square or rectangle in cross-section). The leaves are simple (not divided like a pinnate leaf), and are arranged in whorls around the stem. The flowers are two-lipped. Members of this family can often be identified by their pungent smell when the leaves are crushed. Most are relatively hardy and tolerate damp soils at least for a short period.

Lamiaceae

EPACRIDACEAE

Heath-like shrubs including *Epacris*, *Leucopogon*, *Sprengelia*, *Styphelia* and *Richea*. Flowers normally have five petals which are joined in the lower part of the flower to form a tube. Leaves are generally fine, stiff and often prickly. Most species have fine roots that are easily damaged if the soil around them is disturbed (that is, cultivated). Most prefer moist but well-drained soil.

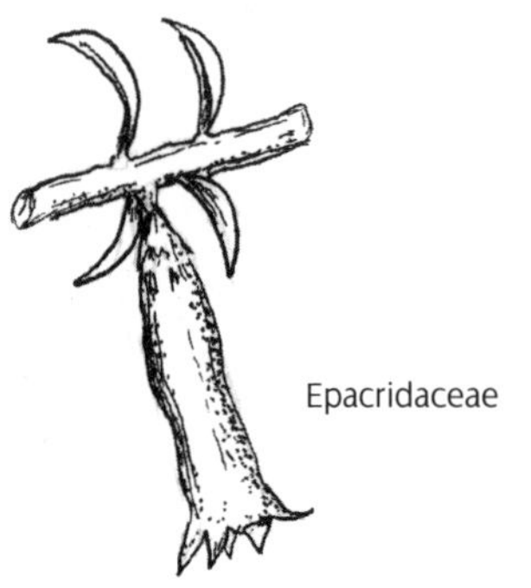
Epacridaceae

ORCHIDACEAE

There are around 15,000 species of orchids distributed worldwide, with 551 species in 91 genera in Australia. Most are found in the northern rainforests, although some extend into colder temperate regions. The majority of those found in the southern parts of Australia are terrestrial (growing in the ground), while many of those from subtropical and tropical areas (for example, *Dendrobium*) are epiphytic (growing on tree trunks, rocks and fallen logs). Flowers are complex, and often very showy. Five petals make up an irregular-shaped flower. The stamens unite with the pistil to form a structure called the column. All species are perennial and have thickened tuberous or bulbous roots.

Orchids are mainly propagated by division or tissue culture. Many of the showier tropical species have been widely hybridised, and many cultivars are known.

Orchidaceae

LILIACEAE

The lily family includes some 2000 species worldwide, many of which are bulbs cultivated for ornamental purposes. The flowers have six petals, usually separate, but sometimes fused. The ovary is superior (that is, it sits above the point where you find the base of the petals). Some Australian members of the Liliaceae are found in the genera *Asparagus*, *Bulbine*, *Blandfordia*, *Dianella* and *Thysanotus*. These are commonly found in heathlands and drier forests of south-east Australia. Exotic examples include onions (*Allium*), tulip, hyacinth, lilies and aloe.

Plants in this family generally require good drainage. Most Australian species are readily propagated by seed; some are propagated by division.

Liliaceae

2.
Growing natives

There are three main factors that affect the way a plant grows: environmental factors such as temperature, light and moisture; nutrition (that is, the supply of food to the plant); and the influence of pests and diseases on the plant's health. You should strive to gain a broad appreciation of these three factors. With such an understanding comes the ability to make your own decisions about how to grow a particular plant in a particular place.

ENVIRONMENTAL FACTORS

Consider where the plant grows naturally, as this may give you some idea of its requirements. For example, banksias tend to occur in well-drained soils, indicating that they need good drainage. Similarly, plants that grow above the snowline will probably tolerate very cold conditions. A plant may be grown successfully outside its natural environment but you could find that it grows differently; for example, tropical plants which are grown in the cooler southern states tend to be smaller in size (in other words, the plants may need more protection than they do in the north).

Consider light and temperature conditions. Characteristics such as foliage colour, flowering, fruiting, rate of growth, etc. are largely controlled by temperature and light conditions. It is helpful to think of plants as having 'optimum', 'tolerable' and 'intolerable' ranges of environmental conditions. For instance, for a particular *Grevillea* species optimum growth may be achieved if temperatures stay between 20°C and 30°C. The same plant may tolerate temperatures as low as –5°C and perhaps as high as 50°C but will not thrive and if the temperature goes beyond these extremes the plant will die. If light is insufficient many plants will lose the brilliant colour in their leaves, and flowering and subsequent fruit development could also be affected.

Similarly rainfall, wind, hail, frost, etc. will all affect plant growth.

NUTRITION

Both northern and southern rainforest species tend to require reasonably fertile soil conditions. However, sclerophyll plants which have evolved in relatively infertile soil conditions will grow better in soils that are not overly fertile.

Caring for native plants in the garden

When Australian bush gardens first became popular in the 1970s, it was believed that because native plants were hardy, they didn't require extra attention. As a result, many native gardens at that time ended up full of lanky, overgrown and unattractive plants. We now know that many native plants respond well to ongoing maintenance, such as fertilising, watering and pruning.

PESTS AND DISEASES

There are hundreds of pest and disease problems that commonly affect native plants. Insect attacks occur in the natural environment as well as in cultivation. For example, many *Eucalyptus* species often have anywhere from 15% to 50% of their foliage eaten by insects annually. If the plant is healthy, most pests and diseases will not be of any great concern and will probably not need treatment. For example, wasps lay their eggs in the flowers and leaves of wattles causing abnormal swellings and distortions (called galls) as the grub develops. Although the galls are unsightly, most plants will recover from the injury. For some plants though, a severe gall infestation will eventually lead to death.

The best way to fight pests and disease is to grow hardy and resistant species. When you propagate plants, discard the weaker growing ones. When you buy plants, buy the healthiest looking specimens, even if they are smaller or more expensive.

Some diseases are very damaging and almost impossible to combat. For example, *Phytophthora cinnamomi*, or cinnamon fungus, is a soil-borne disease that attacks the roots of a wide variety of plants, causing a thinning of foliage and eventual dieback of the plant. The disease moves in water in the soil and is more likely to occur if the ground is wet. It is virtually impossible to control, so if you suspect that you have it, take a soil sample to your Department of Agriculture for analysis. If your fears are confirmed, all you can do is improve the drainage in your soil, implement hygiene practices to prevent its spread, and try to stick to plant varieties which are resistant to the fungus.

Chemical sprays can be used in your native garden to control pests and diseases but you should be aware that:

- Some chemicals will kill *all* insects and soil organisms, including the beneficial insects that naturally eat your pests, the bees that pollinate your flowers, and the worms that carry rotting material into the lower levels of the soil.
- Some chemicals may harm wildlife, either as a result of direct feeding of sprayed plants or insects, or through contamination of water and soil.
- Some chemicals are very dangerous to humans; others are much less of a problem!

Know your chemical thoroughly before you use it!

Natives at a glance

The following points are general comments about natives and shouldn't be considered iron-clad rules. (There are exceptions.)

- Don't feed natives with fertilisers which contain a high percentage of phosphorus (including superphosphates).
- Don't break the tap root on native trees when planting them.
- Tall native shrubs and trees do not transplant well.
- Many natives require good drainage — it is a good idea to plant them on a raised mound of soil.
- Mulching is generally desirable, to keep roots cool and minimise water loss in summer.

Growing good-looking plants takes more effort than just planting and standing back! Even our so-called 'hardy natives' require ongoing care if you want to get the best from them.

Soils — the key to good plant growth

A plant is only as good as the soil it grows in. Soil provides plants with their nutrients, it holds them firm in the ground, and it provides air and water. The soil's physical structure and biological and chemical nature are critical to good plant growth.

PHYSICAL STRUCTURE

Soil is composed of solids and non-solids (pore spaces containing air and water). The solid component of soil is made up of four different types of particles in varying percentages:

- Sand and gravels — particles between 0.02 and 2 mm diameter
- Silts — particles between 0.02 and 0.002 mm diameter
- Clays — particles less than 0.002 mm diameter
- Organic matter, in varying stages of decomposition

The nature of a soil is mainly determined by how much of each of these four particle types goes to make up the soil. This will help determine how much pore space is present in the soil. Too much or too little of any one of these components will cause the soil to have undesirable characteristics; for example, a soil with a large proportion of small particles will have poor drainage, whereas soil with a large proportion of large particles will have poor water retention.

The physical structure of the soil can also be altered by human intervention; for example, heavy foot or machine traffic, or over-cultivation can result in compaction of the soil, causing a reduction in pore space between the soil particles.

CHEMICAL NATURE

- Plants obtain their food in the form of nutrients from the soil. There are around 50 different nutrients used by plants. Some are needed in large quantities (for example, nitrogen, potassium and phosphorus), whilst others are only needed in small amounts.
- Nutrients must be in the right balance in the soil — too much of one nutrient can stop the plant from using another nutrient.
- The acidity of the soil can affect the plant's ability to use nutrients, thus the acidity (or pH) must be at the right level for the plant to perform at its best.
- Each type of plant has a different set of chemical conditions that are ideal for it — what is best for one type of plant may not be best for another.

BIOLOGICAL NATURE

The presence of harmful or beneficial organisms in the soil can directly affect plant growth and health. For example, organisms such as nematodes can directly attack plant roots, mycorrhiza may increase the availability of nutrients to plant roots, nitrogen-fixing agents such as *Rhizobium* bacteria may help convert atmospheric nitrogen into a form

What type of soil do you have?

The type of soil can be determined by a simple test:

1. Take several large pinches of soil (about an eggcup full) in the palm of your hand and add just enough water to make it stick together (not too wet or dry). If it doesn't stain the fingers and feels coarse, it is a SAND.
2. If it can be rolled into a ball which holds together, while still feeling gritty, it is a LOAMY SAND.
3. If it can be rolled into a cylinder while still feeling gritty, but where the cylinder barely holds together, it is a SANDY LOAM.
4. If the cylinder is more solid and doesn't crack or feel gritty, but doesn't bend without cracking, it is a LOAM.
5. If it's like a loam except it's also sticky, it is a CLAY LOAM.
6. If it is very sticky and when bent, the cylinder doesn't crack at all, it is a CLAY.

suitable for uptake by plant roots, and earthworms will help improve soil structure and fertility by the digestion and movement of organic matter through the soil and by increasing pore space by the presence of their burrows.

SOIL PROFILE

Topsoil generally has a higher percentage of organic material and more nutrients than the lower layers. Topsoil generally drains better than deeper soil. The change from the topsoil to deeper layers is normally gradual, allowing roots to adapt to changes as they grow deeper. Plants tend not to like abrupt changes from one soil type to another, so thoroughly mix compost, sand or topsoil when adding to the planting hole to avoid sudden changes in the soil layers.

IMPROVING SOIL STRUCTURE

Soils which have poor structure may be fixed in the following ways:

Clay soils

Lime, gypsum and commercial soil improvers cause soil particles to clump together (aggregate) to form structured soil crumbs ('peds'). This makes the soil easier to dig, helps water to be absorbed, and assists earthworms and other small organisms to carry organic matter deeper into the soil.

Organic matter can be incorporated into the soil, and sand can be incorporated to improve drainage, but generally large amounts of sand would be required, so it is rarely done.

Sandy soils

Clay and organic matter will aid water retention. In both cases the addition of organic matter has extra benefits, including raising the soil's fertility, encouraging worms and beneficial soil micro-organisms, and improving the soil's ability to resist sudden or extreme changes in soil temperature or chemistry (termed a 'buffering effect').

HOW TO SOLVE DIFFERENT TYPES OF SOIL PROBLEMS

PROBLEM	SOLUTION
Poor drainage	Lay drainage pipes Plant in raised garden beds Treat clay soil with soil conditioners such as organic matter or gypsum
pH too low	Add lime or dolomite
pH too high	Add powdered sulphur Dig in manure or compost Use acidic fertilisers, such as ammonium sulphate
Moss or algae growing on pots	Repot plants into better draining soil Don't fertilise so often Reduce watering Sprinkle a layer of coarse sand on the surface of the soil
Soil getting too hot or cold	Mulch the surface Water in hot weather
Soil drying out too quickly	Mulch the surface Water more regularly (e.g. trickle systems)
Salt (white cake) on surface of the soil in pot plants	Leach out by heavy watering and ensure good drainage

Improving drainage

CREATING RAISED BEDS

Raised garden beds will enable many plants to be grown in areas where they would normally be difficult to grow. Beds raised to a height of around 0.5 m or more will have a significant effect on drainage. Raised beds and mounds will also add interest to an otherwise flat garden. There are two common ways of building raised beds:

1. **SHAPING THE EARTH.** Raised mounds are created by moving soil (preferably with a machine) from other parts of the property and pushed into mounds. Mounded areas created this way are preferred because there tends to be less impact on the soil structure.
2. **BUILDING A RETAINING WALL** (perhaps with railway sleepers or rocks), and filling in the area enclosed by the wall with imported soil. Be sure to allow for drainage holes in the bottom of the wall.

INSTALLING DRAINS

Since many Australian native plants are adapted to dry conditions, soil that drains freely will generally give better results in the garden than soil that remains damp for long periods.

An isolated patch of dampness or soggy soil which will suffocate plant roots may be corrected by making a simple soakaway pit. Dig a hole about 1 metre wide and 1.2 metres deep in the damp spot, or just below it. Fill the pit with coarse rubble (rock, bricks, broken tiles, or anything which will drain well) and replace the former topsoil. Drain holes such as this should be kept well away from buildings, as they can damage foundations.

Another method of drainage is sand slitting. This involves digging a narrow trench through the area to be drained to where the water will run into a soakaway pit or stormwater drain. There should be a drop along the length of the drain (as with any drainage line) of at least 2.5 cm for every 6 metres so the water will flow. Once the trench has been dug, it is then filled with coarse sand. A thin layer of topsoil can be placed on top of the sand. The trench should be about 30–60 cm below the surface.

The most permanent type of drain consists of PVC agricultural drainage pipes laid underground with an outlet into a stormwater drain, large soakaway pit or sump pit. Trenches should be dug through the topsoil layer into the harder subsoil layer (often clay). There should be a reasonable slope in the trench of at least 1 in 100, in other words for every 1 metre of pipe there should be a fall of 1 cm, so for a 6-metre length of pipe there would be a minimum fall of 6 cm. Trenches may penetrate the hard subsoil layers in places to achieve the required depth and slope. Trenches should be at least 10 cm below the surface, or they can be much deeper if you wish.

Once the trench is dug, line it with a layer of drainage cloth (geo fabric) then place a very thin layer of porous aggregate (1–2 cm stones) in the bottom. The drainage cloth and aggregate will prevent loose soil blocking the holes in the pipe. Once the pipes are laid, they should be covered to a depth at least equal to their diameter with coarse aggregate (that is, 1–2 cm screenings). Another layer of drainage cloth can then be placed on top of the screenings and topsoil or sand placed on top of this layer. This will allow good water penetration, and the layer of drainage cloth will prevent silt being washed into and blocking the pipe. The drain may be alternatively covered with coarse mulch for aesthetic effect.

LIMESTONE UNDERLAY TECHNIQUE

This method was developed after observations showed that many difficult-to-cultivate plants occurred naturally in soils with a calcium- or lime-rich layer below the surface.

The method involves laying 15 cm of crushed limestone or limestone chips about 30 cm below the topsoil. It is particularly useful for growing banksias, dryandras and other plants from Western Australia which have proven difficult to cultivate outside that state.

Experiments at the Australian National Botanic Gardens in Canberra have also shown that the technique may be useful in overcoming problems caused by the fungus *Phytophthora cinnamomi*, as the presence of calcium is thought to inhibit the growth of the fungus. At this stage the experiments have been inconclusive, but the indication is that it can be very helpful in growing members of the Proteaceae family, such as darwinias and verticordias.

Natives on low-fertility soil

Plants from the following genera have been recorded growing successfully on low-fertility soils in New South Wales and south-west Western Australia. This can be a useful guide in helping you to select plants for areas with low-fertility soils, or in helping you decide how much to fertilise particular plants. (Note: Some species from these genera may grow just as well or better on fertile soils.)

Myrtaceae family

Actinodium, Agonis, Angophora, Astartea, Baeckea, Beaufortia, Callistemon, Calothamnus, Calytrix, Chamelaucium, Darwinia, Eremaea, Hypocalymma, Kunzea, Leptospermum, Melaleuca, Micromyrtus, Regelia, Thryptomene, Verticordia

Proteaceae family

Banksia, Conospermum, Dryandra, Franklandia, Grevillea, Hakea, Isopogon, Lambertia, Lomatia, Persoonia, Petrophile, Stirlingia, Telopea

Rutaceae family

Astrolasia, Boronia, Correa, Crowea, Eriostemon, Phebalium, Zieria

Fabaceae family

Bossiaea, Brachysema, Burtonia, Chorizema, Daviesia, Dillwynia, Eutaxia, Gompholobium, Goodia, Hardenbergia, Hovea, Jacksonia, Kennedya, Mirbelia, Pultenaea, Templetonia, Viminaria

Epacridaceae family

Astroloma, Epacris, Leucopogon

Making compost

Compost is a valuable source of organic matter in various stages of decomposition that can be incorporated into your soil, or used as a mulch to improve moisture retention, soil structure and, to a lesser extent, improve fertility. Any organic material, if left long enough, will eventually rot down due to the action of micro-organisms. Composting is simply a way of speeding up the rate of decomposition and minimising nutrient loss.

CONDITIONS IN A COMPOST HEAP

Moisture should be between 40% and 60%. Outside this range the rate of decomposition will be slower. (*Note*: 50–55% moisture is when the material is about as wet as a squeezed sponge.) Keep the compost heap damp but not saturated.

OXYGEN — micro-organisms that decompose the organic matter require oxygen to survive. By turning your compost heap you mix oxygen into the material so that aeration is improved. Compost bins which are filled to the brim and sealed to the outside with a plastic lid can be very slow to decompose as there is little air available in the compost.

TEMPERATURE — decomposition occurs when the temperature is between 40°C and 60°C. If the temperature drops below 40°C the rate of decomposition decreases, if it goes over 60°C, many of the micro-organisms causing decomposition will die. Temperature conditions will vary from one part of a compost heap to another. Usually the centre of the heap is the warmest, and decomposition is therefore usually faster in the centre of the heap. For this reason, it is advisable to mix up the contents of a heap from time to time. A heap of 1 to 3 cubic metres volume maintains reasonable temperature conditions. A smaller heap will be too cold in the centre at times, while a larger heap will get so hot in the centre that micro-organisms die.

pH — the acidity of a compost heap will increase in the early stages of decomposition, but will return to normal as time progresses. Lime is sometimes added to offset this initial drop of pH. Tests have shown the addition of lime can lead to serious losses of nitrogen from compost.

WHAT TO USE IN COMPOST

The best type of compost will result from using the best type of organic material. You should aim to create compost with a carbon to nitrogen (C:N) ratio of between 25 and 30. You can achieve this average by mixing material with a low C:N ratio with material of a high C:N ratio. Below are some examples of C:N ratios:

Lawn clippings — 20
Weeds — 19
Chicken manure — 7
Leaves — 60
Fruit waste — 35
Cow manure — 10
Sawdust — 450
Straw — 100
Food waste — 15

By mixing materials with low C:N ratios with materials with high C:N ratios you can help speed up decomposition; for example, mixing chicken manure which is high in nitrogen with sawdust which is low in nitrogen. Despite this consideration for what is ideal, you can use absolutely anything organic on your compost heap if you wish. Just understand that if the C:N ratio is not right, it may take a very long time for decomposition to occur. If you are using a lot of material with a high C:N ratio such as sawdust, you should add a nitrogen fertiliser such as sulphate of ammonia or blood and bone. This will help reduce the C:N ratio.

WHAT CAN GO WRONG?

The main reasons for compost failing are as follows:

- It is too wet. The presence of a foul smell will indicate that this is probably the case. Extra turning or adding dry materials can overcome this problem.
- It is too dry. If the centre of the heap is dusty, it is far too dry.
- C:N ratio is incorrect. Lack of nitrogen because of too much high-ratio material is common. (To correct, add sulphate of ammonia.)
- Potash deficiency. Often the nutrient most lacking in compost is potash. Small amounts of sulphate of potash will correct this.

How to plant a native plant

The first step is to prepare the soil and to remove any weeds (see sections on improving soils and weed control).

BASIC PLANTING PROCEDURE

1. Thoroughly soak the plant in the pot and allow it to drain. This helps the plant come out of the pot more easily.
2. Dig a hole at least twice the width of the pot, and slightly deeper than the depth of the pot. Roughen the sides of the hole with the edge of the spade; this is especially important in hard-packed clay soils.
3. Fill in one-third of the hole, using the same soil dug from the hole.
4. Carefully remove the plant from the pot.
5. Loosen any exposed roots. (But if most of the roots are inside the soil ball, you might not need to do much. If there is a tight mass of roots on the outside of the soil ball you may need to break a centimetre or so into the ball all over; this is best done with a sharp knife or secateurs.) Cut into the root ball from the bottom to the top in four sections around the ball. A hose can also be used to wash some soil from the root ball, allowing you to gently free the roots. This is a particularly good method when the potting soil has become air-dry and no longer holds water, and roots have become more or less trapped within the dry root ball. Free any roots circling the bottom.
6. Place the plant in the hole, making sure it is at the same depth in the soil as it was in the pot. Backfill the hole with soil then firm the soil down gently using your hands. Don't bury the trunk/stem, as this can affect the success of some plants.
7. Make a lip of soil around the base of the plant to hold water.
8. Sprinkle slow-release native plant fertiliser at the recommended rate around the base of the plant.
9. Soak thoroughly with water.
10. Place a layer of organic mulch around the plant. Take care to keep the mulch away from direct contact with the plant stem.

FERTILISERS

You can use concentrated, fast-acting fertilisers, which will feed large amounts of nutrients to the plant quickly, or slower-acting, long-term fertilisers — there are many possibilities in between these two extremes. When using concentrated fertilisers, avoid direct contact with the roots of a young plant. Usually coated, slow-release fertilisers are more appropriate with natives, particularly in sandy soils where nutrients can be leached out very quickly.

Be sure to check the phosphorus content of any fertilisers you intend to use and, for most native plants, avoid using large amounts of fertilisers containing more than a small amount of phosphorus. The exception is rainforest plants, which are less sensitive to phosphorus. Commonly used fertilisers that have high phosphorus levels include superphosphate, hoof and horn, and blood and bone. The toxic effects of high phosphorus levels can be offset if balanced with high levels of nitrogen. Generally, phosphorus toxicity is more of a problem in container-grown plants than in the soil, where phosphorus is often immobile ('fixed') in the soil. The addition of fertilisers containing calcium (such as gypsum and lime) can make soil phosphorus more readily available. This can sometimes create toxicity problems.

TIME OF PLANTING

Planting is best timed to allow plants to settle in and to become established before facing the harshest time of the year. The harshest time of year will vary from place to place. Timing may also vary according to the species being planted.

In temperate climates, planting may be done at any time of the year providing the plant will receive adequate water. In the southern states planting is best done in autumn or spring when rainfall is high and there is adequate warmth in the soil to stimulate root growth. In tropical and subtropical climates planting may be better carried out after the hottest part of the year, but while the ground is still moist.

In areas with severe frosts, planting is best carried out in mid-spring after the threat of late frosts has passed. This will give the plants time to establish before the following winter.

Always avoid planting on hot or windy days as plants are more likely to dry out in these conditions.

STAKING

Staking is not always necessary, and in some cases stakes do more harm than good. When movement of a plant in the wind is stopped completely, it may not develop sufficient strength in the trunk to withstand the wind when the stake is finally removed.

Plants should only be staked if they are likely to fall over because they are exposed to severe winds, or if they are likely to suffer from vandalism or unintentional damage. A tree guard may alternatively be used (for example, surrounding the plant with a plastic tube), to protect it from wind, vandalism and foraging animals.

When you do tie a plant to a stake, the tie should be loose to allow the plant to move about in the wind. If movement is restricted, the tree may never develop proper strength at the point between its roots and trunk. Do not drive the stake next to the trunk, as this will damage the roots and will prevent proper trunk development. Instead, use a length of flexible non-abrasive material (such as thick, plastic-covered wires or nylon pantyhose) tied into a figure-of-eight between two stakes and the trunk of the plant. Be sure to check as the plant grows that the tie is not restricting its growth. Remove the tie after one season — by this stage the trunk will most likely be strong enough to support the plant.

Stakes can also be used simply as a marker (without ties) for small plants that may be overgrown by grass, before they have had a chance to get established and put on a spurt of growth. This makes them easy to locate when you are mowing, trimming, etc.

MULCHING

Organic mulches have several advantages as follows:

- They help control weeds.
- They conserve soil moisture.
- They improve soil structure as they decompose.
- They add nutrients to the soil.
- They reduce fluctuation in soil temperature.
- They can promote earthworms.
- They can reduce soil erosion.

Almost any organic material can be used as mulch. Here are just a few examples: woodchips, sawdust, tan bark, pine bark, leaf mould, paper, compost, straw, prunings, lawn clippings, cardboard. There are even some inorganic materials which are useful as mulches, including gravel, scoria, blue metal, coarse sand and river pebbles.

Wind can be a problem, blowing away lightweight mulches, such as wood shavings, when they are first laid down. Once thoroughly wet and settled, however, even these mulches tend to stay where they are.

All too often, the desired benefits of the mulches are not achieved. Some common mistakes are:

- Mulch is not thick enough. Different types of mulches should be applied at different thicknesses. For example, to control weed growth, the following mulches should be applied at the rates outlined below.

MATERIAL	DEPTH
Woodshavings	250 mm
Newspapers	10 sheets
Bagasse (sugar cane mulch)	200 mm
Pine bark	150–200 mm
Coarse sand	250 mm

- Black plastic placed under mulch will create an impermeable layer, causing plants to suffer from water stress. Sweating underneath may cause water to stagnate, creating foul smells and promotion of root diseases.
- Weeds need to be eradicated *before* the mulch is laid. A non-selective, non-residual herbicide, such as glyphosate, can be sprayed several weeks before laying the mulch.
- Maintenance is often ignored. Top up organic mulches regularly and remove weeds before they develop seed heads.
- Woodshavings and some other mulches need to be kept moist for the first month or two. This will allow the mulch to settle and prevent the wind blowing away large amounts of material.
- As organic materials decompose, they draw on nitrogen from the soil. Plants which are grown in mulches made from shavings, woodchips and paper may show nitrogen deficiency symptoms (i.e. the leaves will turn yellow). To counteract this, apply a small amount of sulphate of ammonia around the base of the plant, or some other nitrogenous fertiliser.
- Many organic materials actually repel water when they are dry. If mulch has not been thoroughly moistened when first laid down, rain can run off the surface to the sides of the plants. Dry grass clippings used as a mulch are particularly prone to repelling water.

Special planting techniques

Most home gardeners shouldn't have too much difficulty in establishing new plants. In some areas, however, problems such as severe soil erosion and arid climate will mean that special techniques are needed to enable the plants to establish in their new environment.

POCKET PLANTING

This is simply establishing a pocket or basin on a slope. The soil excavated from the pocket is used to form a wall enclosing the pocket on the downslope side. The wall will then retain water and help prevent soil erosion. An overflow spillway in the wall will prevent the pocket from being washed away in heavy rain. The pocket may need to be re-formed every now and then, until the plant is established.

SLOPE SERRATION

Sloping sites can be terraced to enable plant establishment and reduce erosion. Slopes are cut into steps, approximately 1 metre wide, with the steps sloping back towards the hill to retain water. Over time, the steps will erode; however, the plants will usually have become established by then. The loose soil from the eroded steps also provides favourable germination sites for seeds dropped from other nearby plants.

WATTLING

This technique relies on the use of bunches of branches placed on slopes to prevent erosion. Bundles of long, slender branches are tied into bundles and are partially buried in contoured trenches which have been cut across the slope, or cut branches and dried brush are simply spread across the surface of the slope. Chicken wire mesh or strands of fencing wire are sometimes pegged down on top of the branches to hold them in position. (Some types of wire mesh can lead to zinc toxicity, particularly on moist soils.) Layers of straw, or commercially available synthetic matting, can be used to similar effect.

This technique has been more commonly used overseas, although it can be used here on badly degraded sites to enable native species to regenerate. In Australia, dried brush (for example, *Leptospermum*) is more commonly used. This type of brush material often contains large quantities of capsules that release seed, which will often readily germinate on the newly stabilised slope.

PLANTING ARID SITES

Plant establishment in arid sites with no irrigation can be extremely difficult. Mulching, controlling competing weed growth, wide spacing of plants, and creating saucers of soil to retain water are simple ways of overcoming the water-shortage problem. Smaller-sized plants also have a better chance of becoming established.

Condensation trap

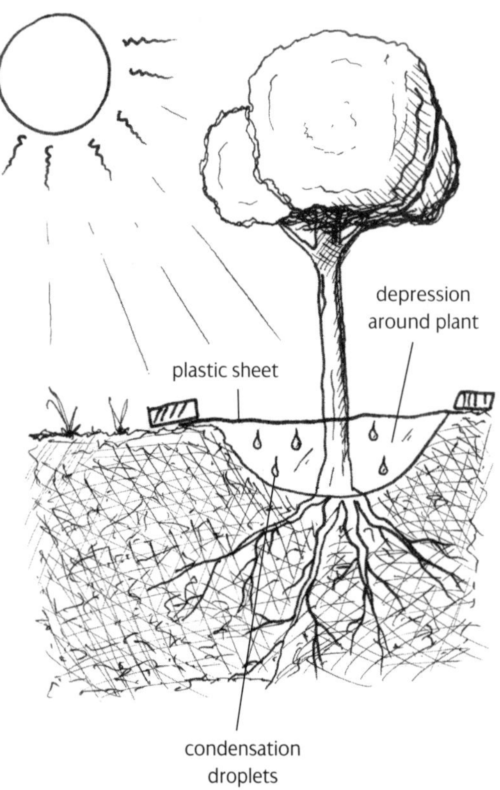

Condensation traps have also been used with some success in areas with clear night skies. One simple method of trapping the moisture from condensation is to construct a 1.5-metre diameter planting basin with a depth of 30 cm. The plant is placed on a mound in the centre, and a layer of polythene sheeting is used to line the basin to collect evaporating soil moisture, which condenses on the sheet and drips back to the ground.

DIRECT SEEDING

Direct seeding is a low-cost method of re-establishing vegetation, although the results are less predictable than transplanting established nursery-grown plants.

The most important factor is to eliminate the weeds before they seed so as to remove competition from the germinating weed seeds. An initial spray with chemical herbicides will give the best results; alternatively, cultivation can be used to encourage dormant weed seeds to germinate which can then be sprayed. A light cultivation of the soil will also provide favorable germination conditions for the native seeds.

Seed can then be broadcast either by hand on small sites, or by direct drilling or mechanical hoppers for larger areas. Fencing the site and follow-up weed control may also be required. Irrigation, or timing your seeding to make the best use of rainfall, will help the germinating seeds get a good start.

In areas where there is an existing cover of native vegetation, natural regeneration can give good results. The site should be fenced off, and the weeds on the windward side of the tree (where seeds are most likely to drop) should be removed.

Pruning native plants

PRUNING SHRUBS

Many native shrubs will take relatively hard cutting back, but some will not. If you don't know a plant, you may be taking a grave risk by heavily pruning it. In particular, many wattles tend to die back if pruned too heavily, though sometimes the same variety will re-grow rapidly after a heavy cut. You cannot always predict if the plant will recover from a heavy pruning.

In nature, shrubs tend to be nibbled constantly by native animals. Similarly, most natives in the garden respond well to frequent light pruning. The safest way to prune native shrubs is frequent light tip pruning, rather than occasional heavy pruning. One exception is the red boronia (*Boronia heterophylla*), which will actually live longer if the flowers are harvested in a heavy pruning every spring.

PRUNING TREES

Native trees are generally similar to most other trees in the way they should be pruned.

Native trees are best pruned when they are young to help them establish well-balanced forms which will be strong when they reach maturity. Be sure you know the appropriate growth habit for the tree you are pruning. Most mature trees have one main trunk, with major branches coming off that, although some species naturally have a multi-trunked habit.

Forked trunks and branches growing at narrow angles to the main trunk are undesirable, as they are likely to develop structural problems. When a forked trunk or two branches join at a narrow angle, the join is a weak union and there is a greater likelihood that a split will develop at some stage in the future, resulting in one branch falling. If this type of forking is seen on an established tree, then one side of the tree should be removed. Even if this looks unattractive in the short term, it will grow back into balance and the tree will be much stronger for the operation.

When a branch is cut from a tree, the cut should be made along a very precise line to minimise the chance of wood rot developing.

Eucalypts should not be pruned heavily. Pruning stimulates dormant buds (epicormic buds) to shoot; these shoots grow quickly but are only weakly attached to the main trunk or branches. The resulting growth is unattractive and, in the future, may develop into weak, unstable branches.

Pruning native shrubs

Most native shrubs require regular light pruning; indeed if they are not pruned, they soon become lanky and unattractive. Pruning improves the plant's shape and maintains the plant's vigour.

Prune native shrubs after flowering, removing up to one-third of the growth.

HOW TO CUT A BRANCH FROM A TREE

- First identify the branch bark ridge — this is the swelling or area of folding on the inside of the crotch where the two branches join.
- Identify the collar of the branch which is to be removed (a swelling at the base of the branch on the underside).
- Make a cut on the underside, 300 mm or so above the collar, 30% of the way through the branch.
- Make a cut on the top, 400 mm or so above the collar. Keep cutting until the branch drops, leaving only a stub.
- Now make a final cut to remove the remaining stub, cutting from a point on the outside of the branch bark ridge to a point on the outside edge of the collar.

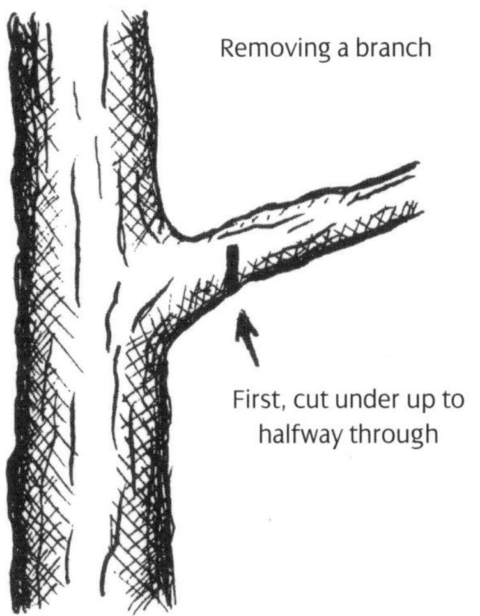

Removing a branch
First, cut under up to halfway through

Second, cut top further from trunk to avoid the bark tearing when it falls

Third, remove stump by cutting on outside of bark ridge (bulge away from trunk)

Pruning prevents problems

Most well-pruned trees and shrubs will never require extra support. Good pruning will promote a strong structure. A lack of or poor pruning can lead to real problems, creating forked trunks and weak joins in the branches. Without support these plants can be hazardous. Branches are more prone to breaking or tearing under excessive weight and splits can occur in the main trunk of the tree.

Watering natives

Australia is generally a very dry continent and wise usage of our water resources is critical. Most gardeners are now familiar with the need to use less water in the garden; indeed, water restrictions are now a way of life in many areas. Fortunately for native plant gardeners, once established most natives require less water than most exotics, and hence are the ideal choice for a waterwise garden.

How often you water will depend on a variety of factors including the type of plants you are growing; local climatic conditions such as the amount, frequency and timing of rainfall, winds, sunshine, etc.; and soil conditions.

The following points should be considered when deciding when and how to water your natives:

- Minimise your garden's water requirements by selecting plants that require little or no watering.
- A good deep watering is more effective than a lot of shallow watering. It encourages roots to travel deeper into the soil, and reduces the development of extensive surface roots that require frequent watering. This is very important when establishing young plants.

Waterwise native gardens

Waterwise gardens use minimal amounts of water, not just during droughts or periods of water restrictions, but all the time. Some tips for a waterwise native garden:

- Replace unused or surplus lawn areas with native grasses.
- Use hardy native groundcovers, such as *Grevillea* 'Royal Mantle' to cover open garden beds.
- Select plants that originate from arid and semi-arid regions. Desert plants, costal plants, and plants from sclerophyll forests generally require little water.
- Use organic mulch — aged woodchips and leaf litter are ideal.
- Install a rainwater tank.
- Use grey water from the shower and washing machine to water the garden.
- Condition clay soils with gypsum to improve water penetration.

- Water only when you need to. If there is moisture in the soil within 2–3cm of the surface (poke your finger into the soil to check) then there is generally no need to water. If new growth on your plants appears healthy and there is no evidence of wilting, burning, etc. during the warmer times of the day, this also indicates that there is adequate moisture present in the soil.
- Try and group plants with similar watering requirements together. This helps reduce the likelihood of under watering or over watering particular plants.
- Avoid watering plants from areas of low rainfall during hot weather. Wait till conditions cool down. In particular avoid watering the foliage of these plants as high humidity levels can help the spread of disease.

Fertilising established natives

Contrary to popular opinion, natives do need feeding. The main nutrients required are nitrogen (N), phosphorus (P) and potassium (K). The ideal ratio will depend on the particular types of plants you are growing. A suitable NPK ratio for a large number of natives is: 10% Nitrogen, 2–4% Phosphorus and 67% Potassium.

There is a large number of readymade 'native' fertilisers available from nurseries, garden centres and chain stores. Check the labels on the packets or containers to see what the NPK ratios are before deciding which one to use.

Problems may occur in gardens where native plants are growing in or around lawns. Lawns need regular feeding with fertilisers containing phosphorus, but natives may be adversely affected by the high concentration of phosphorus. In such situations be prepared to have a poor-quality lawn. Alternatively, use lawn fertilisers sparingly and be prepared for some deterioration in your native plant health. Lawn fertilisers containing rock phosphate are less damaging to natives than those containing superphosphate, but they should still only be used sparingly.

FERTILISER APPLICATION TIMES

AREA	TIME
Temperate areas	August/September
Cool climates	October, or after frosts have finished
Arid inland areas	March/April, or after good falls of rain
Subtropical and tropical areas	Year round providing adequate water is available

Controlling weeds

There are two broad categories of weeds: annuals and perennials. Annual weeds grow from seed to full maturity within 12 months. If you can stop seeds from being produced, then the old plant dies and there are no seeds for new plants to grow from. Perennial weeds persist from year to year. If you kill off the top but not the root, they are likely to re-grow from the root.

Weeds can be controlled in several ways:

- By physical methods, including mowing, cutting, chopping, digging them out, burning, mulching and weed mats.
- By chemical methods. Different types of chemicals have different effects on weeds. Translocated chemicals, such as glyphosate, move throughout the sap system of the weed, killing every part of the plant. This type of chemical needs to be used with particular care as it will kill plants you want to keep if you let it touch them. Other chemicals are more specific, killing only one type of weed (for example, broad-leaved weeds in lawns) without killing other types of plants (such as lawn grasses).
- By competition. If the desired plant is healthy and vigorous, it will naturally compete with the weeds.
- By biological control. Living organisms, such as grazing animals and certain insects, are used to attack or eat the weeds.

WEED CONTROL BEFORE PLANTING

All weed growth should be removed before planting to reduce competition while new plants are establishing. In particular all parts of creeping plants such as couch, kikuyu, bent and buffalo grasses, and bulbous plants such as oxalis, should be carefully removed by hand or killed with a translocated herbicide such as glyphosate; these move through all parts of the weed including roots. Chemical control should be done prior to disturbing the soil so that broken-off sections of weeds are not buried in the disturbed soil where they might strike as new plants.

WEED CONTROL AFTER PLANTING

Weed control after planting is best achieved by non-chemical means, unless the problem is really extensive, as you run the risk of damaging your natives. Heavy mulches or weed mats laid down at the time of planting and regularly maintained will greatly reduce the likelihood of weeds becoming established. Maintaining plants in a healthy condition through good fertilising, watering, pruning, etc. will allow them to out-compete any weed growth. As weeds develop, hand weeding, slashing, mowing, etc. can be used.

3. A guide to native plant problems

Two main steps are required for controlling problems that affect native plants. First, you must identify what the problem is. Second, you must treat the problem, either to cure it or to prevent the spread of the problem to other plants.

Problems

These usually fall into one of four categories: pests, diseases, weeds or environmental disorders. Your first step in dealing with any 'sick' plant, therefore, is to decide in which of these four categories the problem belongs.

PESTS

Pests are animals of various sizes and forms, from microscopic worms to dogs, birds, kangaroos and even humans. Insects are just one of many groups of animals that can cause damage to plants, although they are perhaps the most significant group of plant pests.

DISEASES

These are problems caused by living organisms other than animals. Fungi, bacteria and virus are the most common.

ENVIRONMENTAL DISORDERS

Problems caused by soils, inadequate nutrition and adverse weather conditions such as frost, wind, cold and heat are included in this category.

WEEDS

Weeds are plants that grow where you don't want them. It is not the type that makes a plant a weed, but the location of a plant. Weeds compete with your garden plants for nutrients, water, space and light, making it harder for the plants to grow well.

Preventative medicine in the garden

The best way to be sure that problems like those outlined above do not occur in the garden is to prevent problems from starting in the first place. To do this, follow the standard procedures listed below.

CONSIDER THE SITE

Are there any particular problems with the site that should be rectified? This could involve fixing up soil problems such as poor structure, fertility or drainage; removing weeds; providing windbreaks; providing adequate fencing to control grazing animals, etc.

USE HEALTHY PLANTS AND SEEDS

The roots and top growth should be well developed. There should be no deformed growths (twisted, distorted leaves, swellings on roots, etc). Avoid plants with badly marked leaves, or plants contaminated with insects. Seeds and bulbs should be fresh and free of abnormal markings or any rots.

Select varieties that are resistant to diseases or pests, and are known to be successful in your locality.

MAINTAIN CLEANLINESS

Remove and burn any diseased fruit, flowers or leaves. (Do not compost them or let them lie on the ground.) Wash soil off paths and other surfaces. Sit container plants on stones or paving, or on top of a couple of bricks (not directly on top of soil). This reduces movement of disease from the soil into the pot. Be careful not to wear dirty boots into a propagation area as they can carry disease from the general garden into the propagation area.

MAINTAIN NUTRITION AND WATER NEEDS OF THE PLANT

Do not over water or under water — one is as bad for the plant as the other! Over watering (waterlogging) is indicated by yellowing of the lower leaves, sometimes wilting and eventually dropping of lower leaves. Under watering is indicated by browning of tips and foliage generally and at times by severe wilting and leaf drop.

Lack of nutrients is indicated by slow rate of growth and, in severe cases, by discolouration on leaves.

INSPECT PLANTS REGULARLY

Act as soon as a problem is detected. Look at leaf tips first. The young growth will indicate general vigour (or lack of it). Look for dieback, discolouration of leaves or wood, distortion of growth, rots, eaten or broken tissue, or other signs that can indicate problems.

Common pest problems of natives

APHIS

Many different types, 1-mm long, in various colours, most commonly green. They inject their syringe-like mouthpiece into soft plant tissue, sucking nutrients out of the plant. They can transfer viruses or other diseases from plant to plant. They are normally found in colonies comprising dozens to thousands of individuals. Aphids are most likely to attack the more tender tissue on shoot tips, leaves or stems. Severe infestations can stop buds from opening. Aphis can also cause wilting, leaf curl and other foliage deformities. They prefer dry, warm weather. Extreme heat, cold or wet weather will reduce numbers.

Control

NATURAL — Use biological controls such as ladybirds and other antagonistic insects, or use a garlic spray. Spray small infestations with a strong jet of water. Sticky traps made from honey-coated pieces of bright yellow cardboard are also useful.
CHEMICAL — Spray with pyrethrum or other suitable insecticide.

BORERS

These grubs bore out cavities inside plant stems. Evidence is often found in the form of entry holes and coatings of webbed sawdust on affected branches. In some cases it may be possible to cut away a section of the plant to verify the presence of borers. Borers are most likely to attack already weakened trees, usually entering through tissues injured from pruning cuts, broken branches or grazed bark. Many plants are susceptible to borers, including acacia, callistemon and grevillea.

Control

NATURAL — Remove the infected parts and burn. Maintaining the plant's vigour by watering, feeding, etc will help the plant to recover.
CHEMICAL — Use a systemic insecticide containing Dimethoate or Omethoate.

BUGS

Many bugs have a similar appearance to beetles. One of the main differences is that bugs feed by piercing and sucking plant juices while beetles have chewing mouthparts.

Control

NATURAL — Remove by hand.
CHEMICAL — Dimethoate

CATERPILLARS

There are many different types of caterpillars. They normally eat the tender parts of a plant (leaves and young shoots). Some cluster together in colonies, forming a ball of crawling grubs, but most are solitary, each crawling around independent of the others.

Control

NATURAL — Spray with Dipel (a commercially available preparation containing bacteria which kills only caterpillars). Remove by hand.
CHEMICAL — Spray with chemicals such as Malathion, pyrethrum or Carbaryl.

DODDER

A parasitic twining plant that germinates in soil and spreads rapidly. When it comes into contact with a larger plant it sends invasive sucker-like projections into the host plant from which it obtains nutrients and water.

Control

Destroy as soon as possible by either physical removal or chemicals. Infested parts of the plant should be pruned off and destroyed.

LEAFHOPPERS

Small leaf-shaped sap-sucking insects which jump when disturbed.

Control

Spray with pyrethrum for mild infestations, Lebacyid or Rogor for heavy infestations.

LEAF MINERS

A small insect that eats long winding tunnels between the surfaces of leaves. Normally tunnels are white first and later turn brown. This group of pests can attack a wide variety of plants.

Control

NATURAL — Remove infected parts and burn.
CHEMICAL — Dimethoate or Omethoate, or white oil.

LERPS *see psyllids*

MEALY BUGS

The adult resembles a slater covered with white waxy powder and waxy cotton-like threads. Mealy bugs are generally 5–20 mm long, can live on roots, under bark, and move about on a plant according to seasonal conditions. They are related to scale insects.

Control

NATURAL — Spray with a strong stream of water to dislodge the insects from the plant, or touch insects with a swab of cotton wool dipped in alcohol.

CHEMICAL – Spray white oil, Dimethoate or Confidor directly on the insects.

MITES *see red spiders*

NEMATODES

Also called eelworms, nematodes are small worm-like organisms that attack and burrow into plant tissue, especially the roots or leaves. They can cause distortion in growth (such as swellings), yellowing foliage, dwarfing and dieback. They attack a wider range of plant types than many other pests.

Control

NATURAL — Use resistant plant varieties. Keep tools clean. Plant marigolds, mustard or asparagus as deterrents. Dig in organic matter to lower the pH to a level in which some nematodes find it difficult to breed.
CHEMICAL — Apply Nemacur.

PSYLLIDS

These small sap-sucking insects are commonly found on eucalypts. They have a protective covering (the lerp) which appears as a small lump on the leaf. The leaves become reddish-brown and blotchy, and eventually turn brown. Severe infestations will cause leaf drop and dieback of limbs.

Control

Spray young trees with Dimethoate.

RED SPIDERS

Small red-coloured mites (a type of spider), they are almost invisible to the naked eye. Infestations appear as a red haze, usually on the backs of leaves. Leaves can turn a bronze colour and die. Red spiders and several other types of mites can attack native plants, particularly ferns and soft-leaved plants.

Control

NATURAL — Introduce predatory spider mites, available from biological control companies. Plant repellent herbs such as onion, garlic and chives.
CHEMICAL — Apply derris dust.

SAWFLY *see caterpillars*

SCALES

These shield-like insects that fix themselves onto leaves, branches and stems, and feed by sucking sap from the plant, cause serious weakening of the plant. There are two main groups of scale: soft and hard.

Soft scale are covered with a waxy or mealy secretion. They usually feed on larger leaf veins. They don't normally cause a lot of direct damage, but the honeydew they excrete stimulates growth of sooty mould fungus. While the fungus is generally harmless, over a period of time it may reduce the vigour of the plant.

Hard scale are small flattened insects with soft bodies covered by a hard shell. They breed very fast and develop many generations in a year. They can cover fruit, leaves and other plant parts, causing more serious damage than soft scale.

Control

Spray with white oil. Remove smaller infestations by hand.

SNAILS AND SLUGS

These molluscs prefer damp situations, feeding at night on tender, juicy foliage. During the day, they shelter under broad leaves, stones or logs. The glistening mucus trail is a tell-tale symptom, even when the pests are not visible.

Control

NATURAL — Plant prostrate rosemary or wormwood to deter snails. Spread fresh sawdust on the ground. Improve drainage.
CHEMICAL — Use snail pellets or powder with care (these can be dangerous to pets).

SLATERS

Also called woodlice, slaters live under stones, amongst mulch, and other shady, moist places. They eat young, tender foliage, and prefer plants already damaged by another pest.

Control

NATURAL — Remove garden rubbish which may harbour slaters.
CHEMICAL — Apply suitable types of snail bait.

THRIP

Small, and often difficult to see, these sap-sucking insects swarm over leaves and flowers in summer. The usual symptom is flecking of leaves or flowers.

Control

Apply pyrethrum or derris dust.

WASP GALLS

These are swellings or bumps on leaves and stems caused by wasps laying eggs in the plant tissue. The unsightly galls form as the larvae develop.

Control

Remove and burn galls when they first appear on young plants.

WHITE FLY

There are many different types of white fly. The young six-legged insects are minute in size, feeding on the undersides of leaves.

Control

Use yellow cardboard sticky traps.

Common diseases of native plants

BLIGHT

A disease that suddenly causes parts of a plant, such as shoots and leaves, to stop growing and die.

Control

Remove and burn all infected tissue as soon as detected. Copper sprays will help control most blights.

BOTRYTIS

A grey mould that attacks flowers, fruits and seedlings. It occurs in humid weather and attacks a wide range of plants. Flowers become spotty at first, and later they rot and become covered with a fluffy mould. Badly diseased buds fail to open. Botrytis can also affect stems and leaves with mouldy rot and fluffy grey growth.

Control

NATURAL — Don't water the plant, water underneath the plant directly onto the soil. Any diseased flowers should be removed and burnt.
CHEMICAL — Apply Fongarid.

BRACKET FUNGUS

This fungus may be an indication of more serious wood rot inside a plant or tree. If this occurs at the tree base, and rot has progressed too far, the tree must be removed and burned.

CINNAMON FUNGUS

Phytophthora cinnamomi, otherwise known as cinnamon fungus, 'die back' or 'root rot', is a very serious fungus disease found in both commercial crops and home gardens. It infects the roots of plants and moves quickly through the plant tissue causing a thinning of the foliage, dieback, and in many cases, plant death. One of the worst aspects of this disease is that it affects a very wide variety of different plants: trees, shrubs, ornamentals, fruits, vegetables, natives, exotics; thousands of different plants are known to be susceptible.

The disease is commonly associated with wet soils and heavy clay sites. Infected soils often have a low pH, are poorly drained, and become waterlogged in wet seasons.

Eucalypts belonging to the subgenus *Renantherae* are susceptible; those belonging to the subgenus *Macrantherae* or *Poranthreae* are more tolerant. Species of *Prostanthera* are susceptible, but species of *Westringia* are tolerant. *Xanthorrhoea* are very susceptible.

Control

Very few fungicides have any effect. Soil sterilisation can be used to eradicate the fungus in an infected area before planting. Often, the best approach is simply to improve drainage in the infected area.

DAMPING OFF

There are several fungi species that cause damping off, including *Pythium*, *Phytopthora*, *Rhizoctonia* and *Sclerotium*. This disease occurs on young seedlings and is a serious nursery problem. The plant rots at the base and collapses.

Control

NATURAL — Cleanliness, hygiene and good drainage are very important, especially in humid greenhouses. Provide good ventilation; don't plant seedlings too close together.
CHEMICAL — Apply copper-based sprays.

DIEBACK

Kills the tips of the plant, and continues killing the stems and leaves as the disease spreads throughout the plant. There are different types of fungal diseases which can cause dieback. The most serious type of dieback is cinnamon fungus (see above) which can cause death of fully grown trees. Dieback can also be caused by waterlogging.

Control

NATURAL — Cut off infected parts and burn. Feed and water the plant if the infection is not bad.
CHEMICAL — You must identify the type of dieback and select the appropriate chemical. If unsure, try Fongarid.

DOWNY MILDEW

Often occurs in damp conditions. The upper leaf surface turns yellow, and a grey mould begins to develop underneath.

Control

NATURAL — Improve ventilation by removing or thinning surrounding foliage and avoid watering foliage.
CHEMICAL — Sulphur spray.

LEAF SPOT

Spots of dead or discoloured tissue on a leaf after wet and humid weather.

Control

NATURAL — Remove and burn infected leaves.
CHEMICAL — Spray the plant with a fungicide such as Zineb or Maneb.

POWDERY MILDEW

Causes a white powdery growth on the leaf surface.

Control

NATURAL — Do not overcrowd plants. In hot, humid or moist conditions, water from underneath.
CHEMICAL — Apply sulphur spray.

RUST

This fungus causes brown-orange spots or stripes, usually on leaves.

Control

CHEMICAL — Apply sulphur spray or a suitable fungicide.

SOOTY MOULD

A fungus that grows as a black sooty covering over the plant, normally associated with sugar secretion from sucking insects such as scale or aphis. Usually, removing the sucking insect will cause the sooty mould to disappear within a few weeks.

VIRUSES

Viruses are small microscopic organisms that live inside the bodies of other organisms. They are parasitic, and can cause a wide variety of different effects, including leaf variegation and distorted growth.

Control

Viruses are very difficult to control. Infected plants should be removed and burned. Control insects (in particular, aphis) that may contribute to its spread.

Problems of different native plants

The problems below have been either seen by the author or recorded in reliable references as occurring on at least some species of the respective genera.

PROBLEMS OF DIFFERENT NATIVE PLANTS

PLANT	PESTS	DISEASES	OTHER PROBLEMS
Acacia (wattle)	Borers, caterpillars, mealy bug scale, weevils, jassids, wasp galls	Cinnamon fungus, root rot, rust, leaf spot, powdery mildew	Mistletoe, poor drainage
Acmena (syn. *Eugenia*)	Passion vine hopper, scale, pimple gall	Black mildew, root rot, leaf spot	—
Albizzia (false wattle)	Caterpillars, scale	Root rot	Poor drainage
Allocasuarina (and *Casuarina*)	Borers, caterpillars, wasp and beetle galls, jassids, scale	Rot (*armillaria*)	Mistletoe
Alyogyne	Scale, aphids, thrip, white fly, psyllid, harlequin bug, root knot nematode	Botrytis, sooty mould	—
Angophora	Caterpillars	Shoot blight	—
Anigozanthus	Aphids, snails, leaf miners, leaf nematodes	Ink spot, botrytis, crown rot	Iron deficiency, poor drainage
Araucaria	Pine bark weevil, borer, scale	Crown gall, leaf spot, blight	—
Astroloma	Dogs, cats	Cinnamon fungus, botrytis	Excess wet or dry, iron deficiency
Atriplex	Scale, snails, mites	—	—
Baeckea	Thrip, caterpillar	Cinnamon fungus, tip blight	—
Banksia	Leaf galls, borers, white fly, stem galls	Cinnamon fungus, wood and root rots	Iron deficiency, phosphorus deficiency, over wet soil

PLANT	PESTS	DISEASES	OTHER PROBLEMS
Bauera	White fly	—	—
Beaufortia	Caterpillar	Cinnamon fungus	—
Billardiera	—	Botrytis	—
Boronia	Aphis, scale, snails, white fly, mealy bug	Sooty mould, collar rot	—
Brachychiton	Caterpillars, weevils, beetles, wasp galls	Crown gall	—
Brachyscome	Rutherglen bug	—	—
Brachysema	Caterpillars, white fly	—	—
Callistemon	Scale, borers, thrip, leafhoppers, sawfly	Botrytis	—
Callitris	Aphids, insect galls, borers, sawfly	—	—
Calothamnus	—	Cinnamon fungus, powdery mildew, botrytis	—
Calytrix	Caterpillars	Botrytis	—
Carpobrotus	Scale, snails, slugs	—	—
Cassia	Caterpillars, beetles, stem nematodes, crusader bugs	Leaf spot, wilt, root rot, powdery mildew	—
Chamaelaucium	Caterpillars, white fly, rabbits, possums	Cinnamon fungus, botrytis, powdery mildew	—
Clematis	Aphids, leafhopper, root nematodes	Crown gall, smut, leaf spot, rust, powdery mildew, leaf blight	—
Cordyline	Mealy bug	Ring spot virus, crown gall	—
Crowea	Aphids, white fly, mealy bug, scale	Cinnamon fungus, collar rot, sooty mould	—
Dampiera	Aphids	Botrytis	—
Darwinia	Leafhopper, aphids	Cinnamon fungus, powdery mildew, botrytis	—
Daviesia	Caterpillars (in seeds)	—	—
Dendrobium (king orchid)	Rodents, beetles	Virus	—
Diplolaena	White fly	Collar rot	—
Dodonaea	Scale	Sooty mould	—
Dryandra	Leaf miner	Cinnamon fungus	Iron deficiency, poor drainage
Epacris	Case moths	Cinnamon fungus	Drought
Eremophila	Aphids, scale, beetles, root nematodes	Alternaria, botrytis, sooty mould	—

PLANT	PESTS	DISEASES	OTHER PROBLEMS
Eriostemon	Scale, mealy bug, aphids, white fly	Collar rot, botrytis, sooty mould	—
Eucalyptus	Aphids, thrip, scale, caterpillars, borers, beetles, jassids, weevils, insect galls, nematodes, termites, leafhoppers, lerps, possums	Armillaria root rot, cinnamon fungus, root rots, shoot blight, crown gall, sooty mould	Mistletoe, dodder
Grevillea	Caterpillars, scale, mealy bug, mites, root nematode, psyllids, white fly, leaf miners	Alternaria leaf spot, cinnamon fungus, dieback, root rot	Poor drainage, iron deficiency
Hakea	Looper caterpillars, white fly, scale, borers, mites	Cinnamon fungus	—
Hardenbergia	Passion vine hopper, caterpillars (in seeds), web caterpillars, leafhoppers, thrips, root nematodes	Powdery mildew	—
Helichrysum	Caterpillars, aphids, slugs, snails, root nematodes, rutherglen bug	Crown rot	Poor drainage
Hemiandra	—	Botrytis	—
Hibbertia	Thrips	Cinnamon fungus	—
Hibiscus	Scale, white fly, harlequin bug, thrips, psyllid	Botrytis	—
Homoranthus	Web caterpillar	—	—
Hovea	Caterpillars (in seeds)	Cinnamon fungus	—
Hypocalymma	Caterpillars	Cinnamon fungus, powdery mildew	—
Indigofera	Caterpillars (in seeds)	—	—
Kennedia	Caterpillars (in seeds) passion vine hopper, leaf miner	Sooty mould	—
Kunzea	Web caterpillars	—	—
Lambertia	Leaf miners, loopers	—	—
Leschenaultia	Caterpillars	Cinnamon fungus	Poor drainage
Leptospermum	Scale, thrip, aphis, borers, beetles, weevils, caterpillars	Sooty mould, root rot	—
Lophostemon	Caterpillars, wasp galls, leaf miners, nematodes	—	Drought
Macropidia	As for anigozanthus	As for anigozanthus	—
Melaleuca	Caterpillars, scale, weevils, beetles, insect galls, psyllid	Cinnamon fungus, tip blight, powdery mildew	—
Melia	White cedar moth, leaf miners, beetles, slugs and snails	—	—

PLANT	PESTS	DISEASES	OTHER PROBLEMS
Myoporum	Scale, root nematode	Sooty mould	—
Olearia	Light brown apple moth, white fly, passion vine hopper	—	—
Phebalium	Scale, mealy bug, white fly	Sooty mould, collar rot	—
Pandorea	Leafhopper	—	—
Personnia	Hawk moth insect galls	—	—
Pimelea	White fly, light brown apple moth	Botrytis	—
Pittosporum	Scale, thrip, leaf miner, insect galls, borers, root nematodes	Sooty mould, blight, wilt, leaf spot, virus	—
Prostanthera (mint bush)	White fly, borers, passion vine hopper, snails, scale	Sooty mould, collar rot, cinnamon fungus	—
Pultenaea (egg and bacon)	Caterpillars (in seeds), insect galls	Cinnamon fungus	—
Rhodanthe	Slugs and snails, caterpillars, rutherglen bug	—	—
Scaevola	Snails and slugs	—	—
Solanum	Mites	Virus	—
Sollya	Aphis, leafhoppers	—	—
Stenocarpus	Leaf miner	Cinnamon fungus	Poor drainage, iron deficiency
Swainsonia	Caterpillars (in seeds), slugs, snails	Botrytis	—
Telopea (waratah)	—	Cinnamon fungus	Poor drainage
Tetratheca	White fly	—	—
Thryptomene	Web caterpillars	Cinnamon fungus, botrytis	—
Toona (*Cedrela*)	Beetles, red cedar tip moth	—	—
Verticordia	White fly	Cinnamon fungus, powdery mildew, botrytis	—
Viola (violet)	Slugs and snails	—	—
Westringia	White fly	—	—
Xanthorrhoea	Borers	Cinnamon fungus	—

Nutrient deficiencies and toxicities

Nitrogen deficiencies are the most common type of nutrient disorder in plants. Nitrogen deficiency is commonly caused by either a lack of nitrogen or by conditions restricting it being absorbed by the plant. For example, plants growing in excessively wet soil, very dry soil, or soil covered with rapidly decomposing organic matter can show signs of nitrogen deficiency, even when adequate nitrogen exists in the soil. Where problems like these occur, improving the plants' growing conditions — improving drainage, water availability or replacing the mulch (for example, using larger woodchips that break down slowly) — will allow better nitrogen uptake.

Iron deficiency is also common, but only on certain plants (for example, Proteaceae plants). Potassium and phosphorus deficiencies or toxicities may also occur. Most minor element problems are relatively rare.

Below is a guide to where different nutrient problems are most likely to occur:

- **NITROGEN** — Deficiencies and toxicities occur in all types of soils, but particularly in soil covered with fresh mulch, or in poorly drained soils.
- **POTASSIUM** — Problems are most common in acid or sandy soils.
- **PHOSPHORUS** — Deficiencies are more common with non-Australian plants. Toxicities are more common with Australian natives, particularly hakeas, banksias, grevilleas, telopeas and other Proteaceae plants.
- **CALCIUM** — Toxicity is associated with excessive liming.
- **MAGNESIUM** — Deficiency normally only occurs in sandy soils.
- **IRON** — Deficiency is more common in container-grown plants, or in sandy soils.

Water problems

Providing garden plants with adequate water is proving to be one of the most challenging problems for gardeners in the twenty-first century. Water quality is also an issue in many areas, where water used in the garden is adversely affected by salinity, groundwater contamination, algal blooms, or other contaminants.

All plants need water, but, once established in the garden, many native plants do not require additional watering. The main requirement for most plants is adequate water immediately after planting and during the first season of growth. By the end of the first season, the roots of most plants will have penetrated into the deeper, moister layers of the soil, and even during prolonged dry periods these plants will continue to grow.

There are exceptions, however. Some natives will not thrive and, indeed, may not survive in the garden without additional watering. These include:

- Natives that originate in moist habitats; for instance, in swamps and beside waterways, as well as those from subtropical and tropical regions in the north of Australia.
- Plants growing in very dry soil. Sandy soils that do not retain water are a particular problem, but other poor-quality soils may result from erosion, compaction or lack of sufficient organic matter, which reduce the soil's ability to support healthy plant life.
- Plants battling prolonged droughts. Even well-established, mature trees will suffer water stress and possible death if they are deprived of water for long periods.
- Plants suffering from saline contamination. High salt levels in water, soil or

> **Identifying water stress**
>
> Plants that are suffering water stress will show the following symptoms:
>
> - Wilting tips
> - Burnt and shrivelled leaves and flowers
> - Leaf drop and stem dieback.

concentrated fertilisers can prevent growth and, in severe cases, will poison the plant. Plants subjected to too much salt will show symptoms of water stress — burning, wilting, leaf drop and possibly death — because they are unable to maintain their internal water content. The only way to save saline-affected plants is to remove the source of salt and flush the soil with large quantities of water.

IDENTIFYING WATER-EFFICIENT PLANTS

Many natives have structural adaptations that allow them to grow in dry conditions. Water-efficient plants typically have the following features:

- **SMALL LEAVES** — Small rounded or needle-shaped leaves have a minimal surface area to reduce evaporation.
- **HAIRY LEAVES** — Hairs surrounding the leaf pores (stomata) slow down air movement, reducing water loss through the pores.
- **LIGHT LEAF COLOURS** — Blue-grey, silvery and grey-green leaf colours reflect the light and keep the leaves cooler.
- **TOUGH LEAVES** — Leaves are often leathery, thick, fleshy or waxy to prevent water loss.
- **WATER STORAGE ORGANS** — Water-efficient plants are often able to store water in the trunk (such as Baobab), and have fleshy leaves or swollen roots.
- **DEEP ROOTS** — Extensive deep-root systems enable plants to extract water held deep in the ground.

CATCHING AND CONSERVING WATER

Farmers have always known that fresh water is a precious resource, but, until recently, town gardeners connected to mains supplies have had seemingly limitless supplies of cheap, readily available water. We now know the importance of using less water in the garden, and also of becoming less reliant on external water supplies.

There are several ways of conserving water in the garden, apart from using mulch. These are:

Swales

Swales are an old farming practice used to catch and conserve water in many parts of the world. The concept can be adapted for both small and large gardens. It involves creating channels or furrows, and/or mounding the soil to create a barrier across a slope. Water flowing downhill is intercepted by the swale and held long enough for it to slowly infiltrate into the soil.

The swales are stabilised by plantings — dry-tolerant plants at the top of the swale and moisture-tolerant plants near the base of the furrow. Over time, the plants drop leaves and create a humus layer, which further increases the moisture-holding capacity of the swale.

Rainwater tanks

Rainwater tanks are used to catch and store runoff from house and shed roofs for domestic and garden use. Tanks used to be bulky and unsightly features in the yard, but innovations in tank design mean that now householders can enjoy the benefits of rainwater storage without sacrificing appearance. New water bladder systems allow water to be stored in unused cavities under the house or deck, while slim-line tanks can be positioned where space might be restricted; for example, in the passage between the house and the fence. Tanks are constructed from polyethylene, concrete or metal.

A 2000-litre tank is suitable for watering small gardens; for larger gardens and for non-drinking household use (for example, washing machines) the minimum practical size is a 5000-litre tank.

Grey water

This is waste water from the kitchen, laundry and bathroom (but not the toilet), and it can be used to water gardens, provided that garden-safe cleaning products are used. Most important, do not use laundry detergents containing phosphorus, as high levels of phosphorus are harmful to many commonly grown native plants. Other exceptions to using grey water include:

- kitchen waste water with a high grease content
- dishwasher water (too caustic)
- water containing high concentrations of bleaches, dyes, disinfectants or drain cleaners
- nappy/diaper bucket water
- rinse cycle from washing machines if softeners are used in the rinse.

Grey water is best used in subsurface irrigation systems that distribute the water 2–4 cm below the soil surface. Do not store grey water, and do not allow it to pool and stagnate in the garden.

Conserving water in the garden

- ➤ Match the plant to the environment.
- ➤ Plant at a suitable time of the year when natural rainfall is likely to fall.
- ➤ Create a slight depression around the plant to catch and retain water.
- ➤ Use mulch.
- ➤ Group plants with similar water requirements in the same areas of the garden.
- ➤ Install trickle irrigation.

For more information on grey water recycling visit the websites liste in the Appendices.

DEEP WATERING

Watering plants with a hand-held hose in the cool of the morning or at the end of a hot day is relaxing and enjoyable. However, spraying the garden with a hose every couple of days is not water efficient, and does little to promote growth in established plants. In fact, frequent light watering is detrimental to plants as it encourages surface roots, which are prone to drying out. Much of the water runs off the surface of the soil where it is quickly evaporates, and only a small amount soaks into the top few centimetres of soil.

The most efficient way to water plants is to water deeply and less frequently — once a week during dry periods is sufficient in most areas. A deep-watering regimen gives the plants much better drought tolerance as the roots are encouraged to grow downwards into the lower, moister soil layers.

- Water early in the morning, if possible. Plants watered in the evening are more prone to fungal diseases as the foliage stays wet overnight. Never water in the heat of the day — plants may be burnt and water is more likely to be lost through evaporation.
- Water the roots, not the leaves.
- Do not water beyond the plant's drip line (the area under the outer foliage).
- Do not over water. Over watering promotes soft, weak growth which is likely to suffer from the effects of wind, heat and other stresses.

AUTOMATIC WATERING SYSTEMS

A well-designed automatic watering system is water efficient and promotes drought tolerance in plants. The system can be controlled automatically by sensing devices which switch the water on or off when it is needed (see section below on Water-saving Products).

> **Watering new plants**
>
> One of the easiest ways to make sure new plants are getting enough water is to sink a piece of stormwater pipe or similar tube into the ground next to the plant, and fill it up once or twice a week during the first season.

In micro-irrigation systems, water is delivered directly to the plant roots via drippers or microsprays.

- In windy areas, use large drippers.
- Change the setting according to prevailing water conditions.
- Fit a sensor so that the system doesn't waste water during wet weather.
- Check the system regularly for blockages and to make sure foliage isn't blocking spray patterns.

WATER-SAVING PRODUCTS

- **SOIL MOISTURE SENSORS** — These are used with automatic watering systems to prevent them operating when the soil is already wet. The sensors are placed beneath the soil surface at a specified depth to determine the amount of moisture available to plants. When the moisture level drops below a predetermined amount, the sensor triggers the controller to operate the watering system.
- **WATER CRYSTALS** — These are made from synthetic material and absorb water many times their weight. When the crystals are mixed with water and incorporated into garden soil or potting mix, they provide a long-lasting reservoir for the plant roots during dry weather. It is claimed that water crystals can reduce watering frequency by up to 75% for pot plants, 15–40% in lawns, and 20–40% in vegetable beds.
- **SOIL WETTING AGENTS** — Granular and liquid soil wetting agents allow very dry soil to absorb moisture. Potting mixes, soils that have too much organic matter, and soils that have become extremely dry (such as garden beds under the eaves of houses) sometimes become 'hydrophobic'; that is, they become water repellent: the water rolls off the surface and is not absorbed into the soil. Plants growing in hydrophobic soil often exhibit water stress symptoms. Soil wetting agents help overcome the effect of organic waxy coatings.
- **ANTI-TRANSPIRANTS** — the coating left by anti-transpirants sprayed on leaves reflects sunlight and reduces moisture loss from the plant. Anti-transpirants are also useful for heat and frost protection.
- **GROW TUBES** — Plastic tubes placed over new plantings create a microclimate around the plant. Grow tubes are useful for conserving moisture, and also for protecting new plants from small animals, frost and wind.

USING HARD WATER

Some gardeners rely on water from underground aquifers (bores) to establish and maintain their plants. Bore water is often 'hard'; that is, it has a high degree of dissolved salts. The critical figure of total dissolved salts (TDS) is expressed as parts per million (ppm), and varies from area to area. Most plants will tolerate a TDS reading below 500 ppm; exceptions are ferns, orchids and some indoor plants. Many garden plants will tolerate TDS of 500 to 1500 ppm, while only a few plants can tolerate TDS readings above 1500 ppm.

If you must use hard water in the garden, the following methods may be helpful:

- Avoid wetting the foliage — use trickle irrigation or similar sprayers with a low trajectory.
- If trickle irrigation is used, make sure it delivers enough water to carry the salts well beyond the root area. Salts tend to accumulate at the edge of the water penetration area.

- Mulch heavily so that surface evaporation is reduced. As water evaporates it leaves salt deposits on the soil surface.
- Create mounded beds. Hard water can be safely directed in swales (channels) between the beds to moisten the lower soil layers. If better quality water (tank water, grey water) is available, it can be used to water the plants on top of the mounds. Heavy mulching will reduce salts being drawn to the surface.

4. Propagation

While most plants are produced by either seed or cutting propagation, there are many different ways of propagating native plants. These include tissue culture, budding and grafting onto seed or cutting-grown rootstocks, and division and separation of some bulbous and herbaceous perennial plants.

Other propagation techniques, such as layering and marcotting, may be important in the propagation of some specific types of exotic plants; however, they are relatively insignificant when propagating Australian natives.

There are normally three stages in producing a plant: propagation, transplanting and growing on.

Each of these stages may require specialised skills. Large nurseries have the luxury of being able to organise their staff to specialise in one or two of these stages of production. Smaller nurseries, however, may need to employ experienced staff, or to train staff in all stages of production. Amateur propagators, on the other hand, usually carry out all stages, perhaps not as quickly or easily as the professionals, but with practice and by focusing on particular kinds of plants amateurs often develop excellent propagation skills with one or two specific groups of plants.

Plants are either propagated from seed or vegetatively; that is, a new plant is grown from a piece of stem, leaf or root taken from another plant.

Propagating medium

Both cuttings and seeds can usually be planted into the same propagating medium. Appropriate media include:

- 75% coarse propagating sand (the same as aquarium sand) mixed with 25% peat moss, cocopeat or vermiculite.
- Rockwool propagating blocks — formed

A COMPARISON OF VEGETATIVE AND SEED PROPAGATION

VEGETATIVE	SEED
The new plant has *one* parent.	The new plant has *two* parents.
The new plant is exactly the same as the parent it is propagated from.	The new plant shares a mixture of characteristics from the two parents.
This is the most common method of growing native shrubs and creepers.	This is the most common method of growing native trees.

from a sponge-ike material made from fibres of molten rock. This is used extensively in the nursery industry.

Vegetative propagation

CUTTINGS

This involves taking a piece of stem, normally about 6 to 10 cm, from the growing tip of the plant, with about 75% of the leaf removed. Inserted in a suitable propagating mix and watered, this cutting will form roots and produce a new plant.

Semi-hardwood cuttings

Semi-hardwood cuttings are taken from the current season's growth that has begun to harden and brown. Most (but not all) broad-leaved native shrubs that grow less than 2.5 metres tall are propagated by 2- to 6-cm-long semi-hardwood cuttings taken in late summer or autumn. Cuttings are usually planted into pots or seedling trays. You should be able to plant 40 to 80 cuttings into a 200 mm-diameter pot, depending on the variety.

The normal procedure is as follows:

1. Fill the pot with your propagating medium (e.g. 75% coarse sand mixed with 25% peat). Dip the pot into a bucket of water and leave for a few minutes until thoroughly wet. Once all air bubbles have ceased rising from the pot, remove from the bucket and allow to stand and drain on a clean surface.
2. Take cuttings 2 to 6 cm long. Remove the bottom 70–80% of leaf from each cutting, and stand the cuttings in a jar of water to keep from drying out.
3. One by one, dip the bottom end of each cutting into a root promoting hormone (e.g. Seradix powder or IBA liquid — available from nurseries).
4. Insert the cuttings into the pot after treatment with hormone as follows:
   - Make a hole with a clean stick and place the cutting in the hole so that half to two-thirds of the cutting is below the surface.
   - Push the potting mix with the stick around the base of each cutting before moving onto the next. This reduces air pockets around the base of the cutting which might collect water and cause the cutting to rot.
   - Start at one side of the pot and systematically insert rows of cuttings moving towards the other side.

If you have difficulty getting cuttings to strike, the following tips could improve your chances:

- Use good-quality stock plants. Cuttings taken from healthy plants invariably strike better than those taken from less healthy plants. Often one variety of a plant species will produce a better result than another variety of the same species. If you repeatedly get poor results with cuttings from a particular plant, take cuttings of that species from a different plant — the results may be quite different.
- Use hormone treatments. Various powder and liquid chemicals are sold in nurseries and garden centres under names such as 'Seradix', 'IBA' and 'Rooting Hormone'. Cuttings are dipped in these to stimulate growth of roots. Difficult-to-root species often need such treatments for success.
- Use bottom heat to strike cuttings. Hot beds or propagating boxes provide a controlled source of heat. Warming the propagating mix encourages growth in the base of the cutting rather than in the leaves on top.
- Take cuttings from etiolated growth. Etiolated growth is plant growth which has occurred in very shaded or darkened conditions. This growth generally looks elongated and weak, but it often strikes

easier as cuttings. Some plants (e.g. *Astroloma*) are extremely difficult to produce in commercial nurseries because cuttings frequently fail. Placing a box over the plant for a few weeks before taking the cutting can improve the likelihood that the cuttings will succeed.

DIVISION

This involves breaking the roots of a plant apart so that each section retains some of the leaves and stems as well as roots. This should be done by gently pulling a clump apart by pushing two forks into a clump then rocking and pulling to gradually separate the two sections. This method minimises tearing. Any damaged or torn parts should be trimmed with a clean knife or secateurs.

Clumping plants, such as *Lomandra* and *Anigozanthus*, can be propagated by this method.

GRAFTING

This involves attaching a piece of stem (scion) from one plant onto another (rootstock) plant in such a way that the two different plants will grow together. Once they are growing, the top growth (leaves and stems) of the rootstock can be removed, allowing the scion to grow. The result is a plant which has the root system of one plant variety and the top of another variety. The advantage here is that a plant which has a weak or disease-susceptible root system can be grown on the roots of a more vigorous or hardy variety.

The most critical factor for success with grafting is to achieve contact between the cambium tissue in the scion. (That is, the layer between the bark and the wood.) If the two cambium layers touch, they will grow together; if not, the graft will fail.

There is increasing interest in grafting natives as many desirable plants from Western Australia have proven difficult to grow in other areas. Grafting varieties prone to root-rotting diseases onto hardy rootstocks means that gardeners can enjoy a wider range of plants. Grafted plants also flower earlier and, in the case of the red-flowering *Corymbia ficifolia* (also known as *Eucalpytus ficifolia*), which cannot grow from cuttings, grafting provides the only means of ensuring flower colour. However, grafting is a relatively new method of propagation with Australian plants and trials are being carried out to determine suitable rootstocks and techniques.

Top graft

This is done by cutting off the top of the rootstock and splitting the 'trunk' a couple of centimetres down the centre. The scion has a wedge cut at its base which is then pushed into the split rootstock. The two are then tied or sealed to hold the scion in place. Many native plant propagators use this technique because it can be done in a short amount of time, and with quick results.

Whip and tongue graft

This is perhaps the most common form of grafting general plants. It is usually performed in late winter when plants are beginning to enter a rapid growth period. This method is most commonly used in propagating new varieties onto the top of a one-year-old seedling or cutting-grown plant.

Approach graft

This technique is used in cases where you want to eliminate the risk of losing propagation material because a graft does not 'take'. The scion is grafted onto the side of the stock while it is still attached to its own root system. The scion is not cut away from its roots until the graft has taken. Though not commonly used with natives, this method may have an application in special situations.

Irrigated graft

Here the base of the scion is placed in a bottle

of water. This helps the scion to remain alive until the graft takes.

What can be grafted onto what?

Generally speaking, plants need to be very closely related to each other if they are to be successfully grafted.

- One variety of plant can usually be grafted onto another plant of the same species; for example, a variegated form of *Agonis flexuosa* can be grafted onto a plain green-leaved form of *Agonis flexuosa* grown from seed.
- In many cases a variety of plant can be grafted onto a plant of the same genus but a different species; for example, *Banksia prionotes* can be grafted onto *Banksia serrata*.
- In a few cases, a variety of plant can be grafted onto a plant of the same family but a different genus; for example, *Prostanthera* may be grafted onto a *Westringia* rootstock.

GRAFTING SELECTED NATIVES

Corymbia (syn. *Eucalyptus*)

Some gums (for example, *Corymbia ficifolia* (syn. *Eucalyptus ficifolia*) vary in flower colour when they are grown from seed. Grafting is one way to ensure the plant will have the flower colour you desire. *Corymbia ficifolia* has been successfully grafted onto *C. tessellaris*, *C. citriodora* and *C. maculata*. Approach grafting has been successful for several different eucalypts.

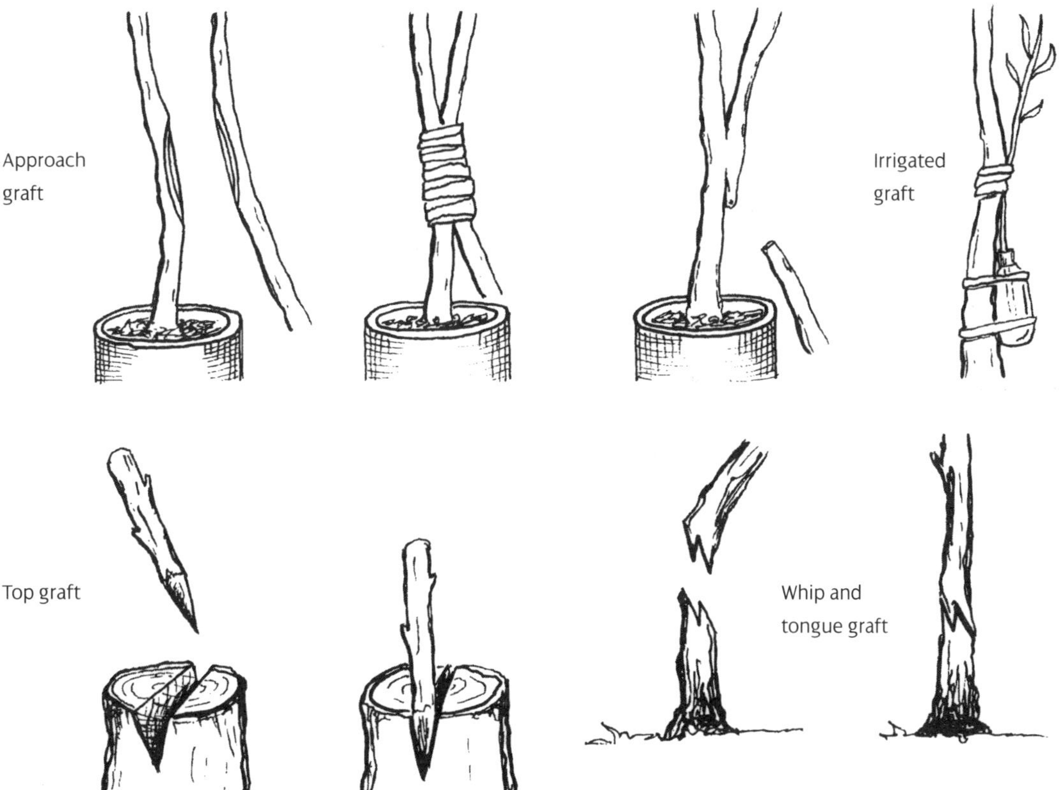

Different types of grafts

Swainsona

Swainsona formosus (Sturt's desert pea) (syn. *Clianthus puniceus*) is not a very hardy plant when grown on its own roots. The plant's chances of success can be greatly increased by grafting onto *Colutea puniceus* seedlings.

Correa

Various correas were successfully grafted onto *Correa alba* in the early twentieth century. *Correa alba*, being larger and hardier than some of the more attractive correas, can improve the plant's size and health.

Eremophila

Eremophila will graft successfully onto several species of *Myoporum*, which are generally hardier and easier to grow.

Grevillea

Prostrate grevilleas are grown grafted onto a tall stem of *Grevillea robusta* and sold in many nurseries as 'standards'. Over 200 species of *Grevillea* have been successfully grafted, though many grafts which initially take might fail some months later. The grevilleas with hairy leaves are generally much more difficult to graft successfully than those with smooth or shiny leaves.

Leschenaultia

Leschenaultias often die after heavy rain. Most don't tolerate wet soils very well. Horticulturists at Kings Park in Perth have been successful in growing some more difficult leschenaultias as grafted plants on top of *L. laricina*.

Prostanthera

Prostanthera is highly susceptible to cinnamon fungus. This disease will devastate these plants very fast. Grafting onto *Westringia fruticosa* rootstocks (which resist cinnamon fungus) has proven both easy and successful in controlling the problem.

Banksia

Many of the West Australian banksias have proven very difficult to grow in the eastern states of Australia and elsewhere. Grafting onto seedlings of *B. integrifolia*, *B. spinulosa* or *B. marginata* have produced good results.

Hakea

Some of the most attractive West Australian hakeas have been difficult to grow on their own roots outside of that state. Several nurserymen and native enthusiasts have been successful growing many of these species as grafts onto hardier eastern-state hakeas, such as *H. salicifolia* and *H. sericea*.

TISSUE CULTURE

Also called micropropagation, this relatively new technique involves taking small divisions from the parent plant and growing them in a sterile laboratory environment. After a period of time, as the microscopic sections of plants grow they are moved via a series of stages into the outside environment.

Tissue culture is used to grow very large numbers of genetically identical plants (clones) very quickly. Some species that have proven extremely difficult to grow in other ways are now propagated in large quantities via tissue culture.

Seed propagation

Most native trees and shrubs will grow fairly easily from seed. Many shrubs, however, are more commonly grown by cuttings because seed-grown shrubs may vary in shape, size, leaf colour and flower characteristics. Plants commonly grown from seed include *Acacia*, *Agonis*, *Allocasuarina*, *Angophora*, *Anigozanthos*, *Banksia*, *Callistemon*, *Callitris*, *Casuarina*, *Cordyline*, *Eucalyptus*, *Hakea*, *Lophostemon*, *Melaleuca*, *Pittosporum*, and most of the legume

BANKSIA SPECIES	GRAFT ONTO *B. integrifolia*	GRAFT ONTO *B. spinulosa*	GRAFT ONTO *B. marginata*
B. ashbyi	No	Yes	No
B. baueri	Yes	No	unknown
B. brownii	No	Yes	Yes
B. grandis	Yes	unknown	unknown
B. lemanniana	No	Yes	unknown
B. occidentalis	Yes	unknown	No
B. pilostylis	Yes	unknown	unknown
B. speciosa	Yes	No	unknown

EXAMPLES OF TECHNIQUES USED TO PROPAGATE NATIVES

CUTTINGS	DIVISION	SEED	GRAFTING	TISSUE CULTURE
Astartea	*Anigozanthus*	*Acacia*	*Banksia*	*Anigozanthus*
Astroloma	*Brachyscome*	*Agonis*	*Boronia*	Orchids
Bauera	*Conostylis*	*Allocasuarina*	*Corymbia*	Ferns
Boronia	*Lomandra*	*Angophora*	*Darwinia*	
Brachyscome	*Macropidia*	*Anigozanthus*	*Eremophila*	
Chamaelaucium	*Mazus*	*Banksia*	*Hakea*	
Correa	*Patersonia*	*Callistemon*	*Grevillea*	
Crowea	*Pratia*	*Chorizema*	*Leschenaultia*	
Epacris	*Scaevola*	*Dryandra*	*Macadamia*	
Grevillea	*Scleranthus*	*Eucalyptus/Corymbia*	*Prostanthera*	
Helichrysum	*Viola*	*Hardenbergia*		
Hibbertia		*Hovea*		
Hypocalymma		*Isopogon*		
Leschenaultia		*Kennedia*		
Leptospermum		*Leptospermum*		
Myoporum		*Melaleuca*		
Pimelia		*Pittosporum*		
Prostanthera		*Pultenaea*		
Thryptomene		*Xanthorrhoea*		
Tetratheca				
Westringia				

(pod-bearing) natives (for example, *Kennedia*, *Hardenbergia* and *Pultenaea*).

SEED COLLECTION

Many plants (such as melaleucas, eucalypts and hakeas) hold seeds in the fruits, seed cones or nuts for a long time while others (wattles and other legumes) drop seeds onto the ground as soon as mature. Seeds which drop need to be 'caught' before they are lost. This can be done either by watching them closely on a daily basis as they near maturity, or tying something such as a stocking over the fruit to catch the seeds.

How long does seed keep?

Some seeds will store for years and not deteriorate, even when stored in a light room. Most seed, however, is better stored in a dark, dry, cool environment. Acacia will store almost anywhere for a long time if kept dry. Eucalypt seed can keep for five to ten years, but is best kept in the dark and under low humidity and low temperature. If you are uncertain, seed is probably best stored in an airtight container in the dark at between 1°C and 3°C. Seeds from many of the warm rainforest plants must be used very soon after harvesting. Once they begin to dry out they lose viability fast.

SOWING SEEDS

Many seeds can be sown direct into sand–peat or sand–vermiculite propagation media then covered with a thin layer of coarse sand sprinkled over the surface. Some seeds, though, have physical or chemical inhibitors that ensure the seed only germinates in natural habitats when conditions are favourable for growth. Several treatments are used to stimulate seed germination prior to sowing:

Hot water treatment

Place seeds into a container and pour boiling water over them. Leave the seeds to soak in the water for about 24 hours, allowing the water to cool naturally, then remove the seed and sow it. Most native legumes benefit from this type of treatment; for example, *Acacia*, *Chorizema*, *Clianthus*, *Kennedia*, *Hardenbergia* and *Pultenaea*.

Scarification

Hard seed coats can be physically broken to allow water to penetrate and stimulate growth. This is done by either rubbing seed between sheets of sandpaper, or nicking seed with a razor blade or sharp knife. These operations must be done carefully to break the coat only without damaging the seed inside.

Leaching inhibitors

Some seeds (such as palms) have chemicals within the seed that prevent germination. In nature, these chemicals are washed out by heavy rains. Soaking or washing palm seeds continually for many days can increase the speed of germination.

Smoke treatment

Research has shown that many plants previously considered difficult to propagate can be stimulated to germinate by exposure to smoke or 'smoke water' prior to sowing. Smoke chemical treatments have been successfully applied in the following ways:

- Bubbling smoke through a container of water for about 60 minutes, and then applying that water to the seed (soaking, or watering sown seed).
- Channelling smoke into a tent containing trays of sown seed.

Success using smoke treatment has been achieved with *Calytrix*, *Conostylis*, *Dianella*, *Eriostemon*, *Geleznowia*, *Lechenaultia*, *Philotheca*, *Pimelea*, *Stylidium* and *Verticordia*.

PROPAGATING EUCALYPTS

There is considerable variation in the size and amount of seed produced by different

Eucalyptus species. Some species retain their seed for years while others shed their seed annually when the seed matures. Seed production will also differ from year to year. In some years there may be little or no seed while in others there may be a great quantity of seed. The extent to which this occurs once again depends on the characteristics of the individual species. Seed production may also differ considerably between trees of the same species both within a localised population and in separate populations of the same species. You should remember these characteristics when collecting seed. If one tree doesn't have mature, healthy seed, another one nearby or elsewhere might.

Only mature capsules should be collected. Capsules generally mature about 12 months after flowering and are hard, woody and dark brown in colour.

Eucalypts generally have a high germination percentage so it is important not to over sow. Germination usually occurs within two to four weeks. No germination treatments are required. Some species are prone to damping-off diseases so hygiene is important. Germinated seedlings should be potted on as soon as they are big enough to handle. Root pruning at this stage will help produce stronger, healthier plants. Root pruning involves trimming lateral roots to stimulate lateral root growth as well as cutting back tangled or coiled roots — you may need to gently tease the roots apart to do this. Without root pruning, the dominant vertical root tends to bend at the bottom of the pot and grow in circles. This leads to root spiralling, where the entire root ball remains in a tightly coiled mass even after planting. Some commercial growers use air-pruning cells (also called root training trays) to encourage both lateral and vertical seedling root growth.

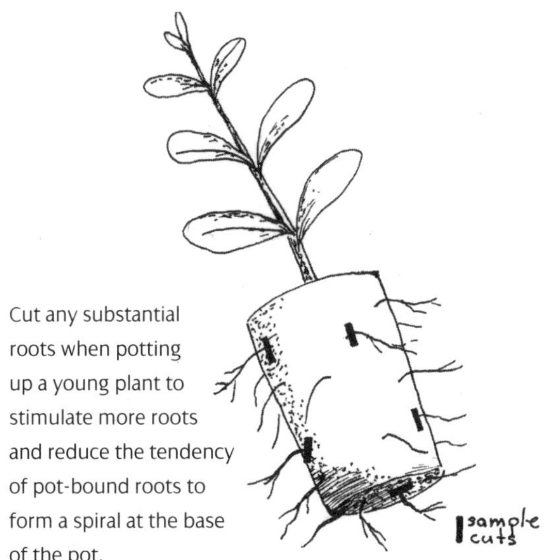

Cut any substantial roots when potting up a young plant to stimulate more roots and reduce the tendency of pot-bound roots to form a spiral at the base of the pot.

Once transplanted, care should be taken to disturb the roots as little as possible.

PROPAGATING ACACIAS

Acacias are generally prolific seeders, shedding their mature seed annually, with the pods often exploding. These seeds are hard coated and may remain viable for long periods of time. Germination percentages are high, particularly if the seed has had some pre-germination treatment. Germination may occur in as little as a few days, with the majority of seeds germinating within four weeks. A few species have a dormancy period which may be up to several months in duration before they will germinate. The seedlings should be transplanted when large enough to handle.

Pre-germination treatments for acacia seeds

1. Seeds are placed in a container and boiling water poured over them. They are left to soak for 12 to 24 hours. The seeds that have swollen up can be sown. Those that haven't can be retreated in the same way. Seeds that haven't swollen after three such treatments should be discarded.
2. Soak the seeds in a concentrated sulphuric acid solution for around 15 minutes. Care should be taken when handling the acid. The seed is drained and carefully washed

in water to remove all traces of the acid, and then sown.

3. The hard coat of the seeds can be abraded by sandpaper or nicked or cut by a sharp knife or razor blade, taking care not to damage the soft parts of the seed. Some legume seeds are more susceptible to rotting. These types are better to have the seed coat broken by abrasion or cutting with a knife than by hot water treatment which can leave them very moist inside.

Acacias should be planted out into their permanent position as soon as possible as they have strong, quick-growing root systems.

Where to put your planted seeds or cuttings

The ideal temperature for propagating most plants is around 18–27°C. Plants from warmer climates tend to prefer temperatures at the higher end of this scale, and from cooler climates, the lower end. Too much heat or cold can greatly reduce the chance of success.

Excessive moisture can cause fungal diseases that attack young plants, but with good drainage, adequate ventilation and hygienic conditions, the risk of disease is greatly reduced.

To achieve the above conditions, containers of seeds or cuttings are commonly placed in a greenhouse or propagating frame on a clean, well-drained raised surface.

If there is a risk of overheating, then shade, cooling or ventilation is necessary. If there is a risk of cold, it may be necessary to use artificial heat (such as heating cables below the pots), or an enclosure which can be closed up at night. Greenhouse suppliers can provide advice on a variety of products used for propagation.

If you are only growing a small quantity of plants, you can place pots on a sunny window ledge in the house (in cooler weather), or a well lit but cool part of the house (in warmer weather). The kitchen, laundry or bathroom are often preferred because of the higher humidity in these rooms.

Some plants (for example, banksias and dryandras) actually require low temperatures to germinate, and often do better if pots of seed are left outside until the plants begin to grow.

Transplanting

Transplanting is the process of taking newly propagated plants from the propagating media and placing them in a growing media, in a manner that minimises damage or reduces any setback in growth of the transplanted plant. It is not always as straightforward as might be expected, particularly with tissue-cultured plants. When plants are taken from one environment to a different one, they can experience a shock which, under extreme circumstances, can cause them to die. You need to pay careful attention to where plants come from and ease them into their new environment.

Tissue-cultured plants are the most difficult to transplant and establish in soil. Plants taken from a greenhouse, or propagated in a warm climate and moved into areas with cooler climates can also be difficult to establish and maintain. Two critical factors at this stage are cleanliness (so that you don't expose the plants unnecessarily to diseases or pests), and a good-quality growing medium.

TRANSPLANTING SEEDLINGS

Ideally, seedlings should be transplanted as soon as possible after they have emerged. This will vary to some degree according to the type of plant you are growing. Those with larger seedlings can generally be handled earlier than smaller ones. Normally, seedlings will be transplanted after the first or second true leaves have appeared.

Trays or flats of seedlings can be removed to a protected propagation area still in their containers. They should be well watered, and, if possible, allowed to drain for a short time prior to lifting seedlings. The seedlings can then be carefully lifted from their containers and gently pulled apart, taking care to minimise damage to roots. Retain as much of the propagating media as possible around the roots, and only remove small clumps or groups of seedlings at a time to prevent roots from drying out.

Seedlings that are grown in-ground or in large beds and are to be grown on in containers can be carefully lifted immediately prior to transplanting, then quickly transferred to a protected area for transplanting. Keep these seedlings moist by temporarily placing the roots in a container of water, a plastic bag, or covering them with moist newspaper. If possible, lift only small amounts of these seedlings at a time to ensure that they are not left lying around for any length of time.

Fill the containers (whether flats, pots or punnets) in which the seedlings will be grown on with a suitable growing medium, and make a hole or holes with a dibble stick. Insert the roots of the seedling into the hole, and gently press growing medium around the roots to ensure good contact. For large flats or containers, dibble boards can be used to make large numbers of holes at a time. Water the transplanted seedlings immediately, and place them as soon as possible in a protected growing-on environment.

TRANSPLANTING CUTTINGS

Carefully knock out the cuttings from the container. If root development is evident, then the cuttings can be carefully pulled apart, retaining as much propagation media as possible around the roots, and transplanted into suitable containers as with seedlings. Those cuttings that haven't struck — that is, there is little or no root development — should be placed back into the propagation medium. Discard cuttings with obvious rot at their base or stem. Thoroughly water all of the cuttings, struck or unstruck, straightaway.

Potting up plants

Plants are potted for the following reasons:

1. They are getting too big in the pot they are in and need more room to grow.
2. You want them to grow at a faster rate to produce a larger plant in less time.
3. You want the plant in a different container for aesthetic or functional reasons.
4. You want to root-prune the plant. This promotes the development of new healthy feeder roots.Root pruning may also be undertaken to remove diseased roots.
5. You want to put the plant into a better medium.

Growing on

As the plants grow they must be protected from harsh environments and the ravages of pests and diseases. Careful consideration must be given to where they are placed. The surface on which the pots are resting should be well drained, clean, and preferably slightly sloping concrete or asphalt; otherwise, use gravel or weed mat. Watering, fertilising, regular spraying, pruning, staking and any other actions needed to bring the plant to a suitable size are important components of this stage of production.

5.
Landscaping with natives

Creating a native garden involves more than just buying native plants and planting them. Understanding how to design a landscape will enable you to make the most of the space that you have available.

The design process

Before getting your hands dirty you need to follow a process of information gathering, planning and design.

INFORMATION GATHERING

The first step in designing any landscape is to collate information about your site and your landscaping requirements, as these will influence the decisions you make about your design.

First, you will need to survey your site and record its dimensions and existing features on a site plan. Often this work can largely be avoided if a plan of the site is available. Always double-check though, as official plans have been known to be wrong. The following details should be accurately recorded on your site plan:

- the dimensions and placement of boundaries and buildings
- the position of existing landscape components, such as paths, driveway, trees and clothesline
- the position of services such as drains, water and gas pipes, taps, meters, easements and power lines
- the location of doors and windows on buildings.

You should also have a record of the contours or slope of the site, and note badly drained areas, shaded areas, and good and bad views.

If you intend to incorporate a building in your design — for example, a shed or gazebo — you may need to consult your local council to find out whether there are building or planning restrictions that affect your proposed design. These vary from municipality to municipality; for example, the restrictions on the distance a building can be located from a boundary.

You will need to study the environment of your locality and your site. Climate, wind, temperature, frost, rainfall etc. can vary greatly from place to place, even in the same town or city. Drive around nearby areas and see what plants are growing successfully there.

Look closely at how temperature and weather extremes affect your site; for example, the direction of prevailing winds, and whether there are excessively shaded or sunny areas or low-lying frost pockets. What is the soil like? Be aware that the soil can vary in its character over very small distances. Do not rely on a single sample from one place. Dig holes, either with a spade or an auger and study changes in the soil as you progress through the profile (i.e. go deeper). Measure the pH and note the texture of each sample. Mark your findings down on the site plan.

Finally, consider your needs, preferences, priorities and budget. What functions does the design need to fulfil? For example, do you need a space for children's play, or for entertaining or relaxing? Make a list of all the essential functions and priorities. Also note any particular likes or dislikes that may influence your design; for example, particular plants or building materials. Consider how much time you will have to maintain the new landscape and also what resources are available to do the job. Can you do the work, or will you need to pay landscape constructors? What materials are readily available? Is it cost effective to do the work in stages, as money becomes available, or will the construction and planting be completed within a set time frame?

PLANNING

This stage involves deciding on an overall theme or garden style and broadly deciding the design concepts. You may choose a theme using plants that grow well in the area, which will give you good results easily and cheaply. This may be the wisest course and will usually be low maintenance. Or you may have your heart set on a rainforest or an alpine rockery — but you live in Alice Springs! To do this will be more difficult and costly, but fun. It will also require a lot of maintenance time and money. You will want to work out a sequence of carrying out tasks, such as ordering in soil, pavers, purchasing pond liner etc, and finally planting and mulching.

Deciding on the design concepts involves considering what might be included in the new design. You may find it useful to draw a rough sketch or concept plan that shows the broad activity areas and major traffic routes (driveways, footpaths) through the garden. You may be happy with just one concept plan or you may decide to prepare several sketches to help you decide how best to use the space in your garden.

DESIGN

The same basic principles and procedures apply whether you are designing a small home garden or a large area of public parkland.

1. Draw a scale plan of your site on tracing paper placed over graph paper. If you use graph paper that has 1-cm-wide lines, then consider 1 cm on the paper to be equal to 1 metre on the ground, which is a 1:100 scale. This may seem to be a waste of time, but the drawings don't have to be elaborate and it will help to clarify your thinking. It is also cheaper and less painful to make mistakes on paper than when you are making the garden.
2. Decide the location of each axis on the plan. An axis is an imaginary line along which a person's view or attention will be attracted. Usually the axis is the line between where a person is standing in the garden and a feature or point of interest towards which his or her attention is drawn. For example, an axis in a backyard might be from the back door where a person enters the garden to a feature tree in a back corner. Axes give a sense of balance to the design and aid purposeful movement in the garden.
3. Decide on the functions to be achieved and designate the broad areas to be incorporated in the design. This step could occur either before or after deciding on the axes.

   Areas which might be designated for a home garden are an entry area, work area, service area (that is, bins, clothes line and so on), vegetable garden, decorative garden, play area and outdoor living area. The approximate location for these areas needs to be determined on the plan in such a way that they fit into the axis and each axis must fit with them. They should also be arranged so that there is no conflict between each area; for example, a children's active play is best separated from passive, quiet relaxation areas.

4. Start to draw in some of the basic details of the new design. Concentrate first on locating features at the end of each axis if one doesn't already exist, and other components which enhance these features. At this point you should also draw in the essential components (for example, a fence, washing line or gate).
5. The final stage is to fill in the details of the new design. Draw in the plants and other components in a way that complements what has already been drawn. If the plan is becoming too cluttered, you might prepare a separate planting plan.

Review the total design when drawn, make any necessary changes, and then draft it onto the tracing paper for a final copy.

Creating landscape effects

- Close mowing tends to make an area seem larger.
- A smooth boundary will make an area seem larger.
- Shadows or openings at one side of an area will make it seem wider.
- Looking downhill makes a distance seem longer.
- Looking uphill makes a distance seem shorter.
- Too much repetition and harmony is monotonous.
- Too much contrast is chaotic.
- Spaces which are too small can be oppressive.
- Large spaces are empty and hollow unless there are a large number of people in those spaces.
- Long spaces, especially in large-scale public landscapes, can be overdone, becoming psychologically exhausting.
- To achieve harmony in a space that is enclosed, the ratio of building height to space width should be no less than 1:4.
- Introduced landforms, such as reshaping of land, should blend in with existing topography.
- Coarse textures decrease the apparent size of spaces.
- Fine textures will make small spaces look bigger.
- Flowing curved lines are passive, soft and pleasant.
- Geometric lines and shapes are solid, strong and formal.
- Sharp, straight irregular lines create an active, vigorous feeling in a garden.
- A garden can be made to appear larger by making trees and other features from adjoining gardens appear to be part of it.

Native garden styles

When most people think of growing natives, the 'bush garden' which features native plants in a 'natural bushland' setting is the landscape style that comes to mind. While this garden style remains popular, there are many other ways to grow natives in the garden. Today, native plants are grown in formal gardens, rainforest gardens, indigenous gardens, cottage gardens, contemporary gardens, eclectic gardens, courtyard gardens and oriental gardens. But regardless of the garden's theme or style, good plant selection is vital.

Choosing native plants for your garden style

Some native plant gardeners are happy to grow any plant as long as it is a 'native'; that is, it originates in Australia. Purists are more likely to choose species that are indigenous to their locality. Others consider the garden style first, then select natives that do the same job as exotics; for example, training lillypillies as hedges or topiaries, or edging garden beds with small-growing varieties of lomandras.

BUSH GARDENS

Bush gardens first became popular in the 1960s and today there are still many bush garden enthusiasts. Bush gardens typically are modelled on natural bush habitats, such as heathland or dry sclerophyll woodlands. The main plantings are usually woody flowering shrubs, such as grevilleas, hakeas, prostantheras and callistemons, interspersed with smaller shrubs and groundcovers, such as baueras, eriostomons and brachyscomes. Larger bush gardens might also feature an over-storey of eucalypts, casuarinas or angophoras. Mossy bush rocks, winding paths and leafy bark mulches add to the bushland effect.

Good bush gardens are not low maintenance

It is worth keeping in mind that because many native plants are fast growing and early flowering, most bush gardens look great in the first couple of years after planting — regardless of what you choose or how you look after them. But it is only the gardens that are carefully designed and maintained that remain looking attractive for years into the future. Bush gardens do need maintenance!

While this garden style aims to re-create nature, it is essential to approach the design and maintenance in the same way as any other garden style, otherwise the garden may end up as a meaningless assortment of straggly plants. Follow the principles of landscape design, so that the garden is not only pleasing to look at but is functional as well. Consider the plants' form, texture and colour. Also consider their longevity — some smaller bushland plants only live a season or two, so you must be prepared to replace them at regular intervals.

Maintenance is also critical. Most native shrubs in garden settings need regular tip pruning to maintain a compact shape and to promote flowering. Native plants also respond well to regular fertilising during the main growing season.

Designing a natural bush garden

A natural bush garden can be anything which attempts to simulate a natural environment. The design must be informal and to have considered the whole atmosphere, including scents and sounds. The garden should be alive with chattering birds, fluttering butterflies and lizards lounging on warm rocks. Underfoot should be spongy with mulch smelling of earth and eucalyptus. For reduced maintenance it should be an area where the created garden inhibits the growth of unwanted weeds through close planting and mulching. A bush garden is more than just trees and shrubs. Try to include as well all of the low-growing herbs, grasses, lilies and so on of the understorey.

Remember, designing a garden is much harder than decorating a house. You can't simply put any plant anywhere because it looks nice. Tree ferns planted next to a sunny west wall will cook. You are dealing with living, three-dimensional plants which will grow and change through the seasons.

Many of the best bush gardens re-create a specific natural habitat, such as:

- An open woodland with groundcovers, climbers, grasses, shrubs and trees. This is the quintessential bush garden, and is suited to many areas of Australia. The plants typically withstand dry conditions and poor soils, although they will respond well to water and native plant fertilisers. One drawback is the plants are naturally adapted to bushfires — some contain volatile oils; others contain flammable bark or have other strategies that promote the spread of fire — so this must be considered if you live in an area that experiences bushfires.
- An indigenous habitat featuring the full complement of available plants growing naturally in the local area.
- A heathland, comprising mainly shrubs and groundcovers with showy flowers. Many of these plants are from south-western Australia and require well-drained, infertile soils and low humidity. A heathland garden might include dryandras, isopogons, lambertias, epacris and grevilleas.
- A rainforest, with ferns, palms, orchids, trees and climbers. A rainforest garden requires a protected position, effective irrigation and improved soils.
- An alpine habitat. The higher peaks in Tasmania, Victoria and southern New South Wales contain many small-growing alpine gems. They need low humidity and cool to temperate conditions. Many need excellent drainage, while others are adapted to wet, boggy soils. In gardens, they are best grown in rockeries, where they can be appreciated up close, and where their required conditions can be easily maintained.

When designing a native garden consider:

- How things fit together in the bush — trees, shrubs, grasses, rocks, leaf litter and natural watercourses.
- What makes up a bush garden — not just the plants, but also the native birds and animals, and soil, rocks etc.
- How you will put it all together and maintain it over time.

FORMAL GARDENS

Some people may be surprised that native plants can be grown in formal gardens. Formal gardens are characterised by a symmetrical design, straight lines, artificial landscaping materials, and controlled, neat plantings — qualities we don't normally associate with natural bush gardens. But there are natives that are ideally suited to this classic and enduring garden style. The key is to use natives that look more like exotic species; for example, natives from the subtropics and tropics with dark green glossy leaves and a naturally compact shape. Plants that have a strong architectural shape, such as Doryanthes and tree ferns, also work well in formal gardens.

Suitable native plants

HEDGES — Lillypillies (*Acmena*), *Syzgium* spp., *Austomyrtus*, *Grevillea rosmarinifolia*

EDGES — Lomandras, dwarf lillypillies

GROUNDCOVERS — *Mazus pumilo*, native violets (*Viola hederacea*)

CLIMBERS — *Pandorea*

CONTAINER PLANTS — kangaroo paws, topiarised lillypillies, *Ficus*

FEATURE PLANTS — *Doryanthes*, tree ferns (*Dicksonia antarctica* and *Cyathea* spp.), cycads, palms

CONTEMPORARY GARDENS

Contemporary gardens are characterised by clean lines, modern landscaping materials, and bold colours and textures. This garden style is well suited to urban landscapes, with its use of hard materials and strong geometric lines. It is most often used in small outdoor areas, especially courtyards where the paving and walls create a hard-edged look, although the concept can be adapted to more open suburban gardens whose owners are looking for a simpler, less maintenance-intensive design.

Contemporary gardens typically feature lots of hard surfaces and not much greenery. Plants are used as 'soft architecture', usually in repeat plantings or in containers. Foliage, colour and form are more important than flowers.

Suitable native plants

CONTAINERS — sedges and grasses, kangaroo paws

EDGE PLANTINGS — lomandras, dianellas

ARCHITECTURAL FEATURE PLANTS such as *Doryanthes*, grass trees (*Xanthorrhoea*), *Eucalyptus caesia*

COURTYARD GARDENS

Essentially a courtyard is an enclosed outdoor space. Not only does a courtyard provide an invaluable extension of the indoor living area, it is a retreat from the outside world; a private, intimate space which is ideal for relaxing and entertaining.

Like other parts of the garden, the courtyard can be informal or formal in style, although in most cases they tend towards the formal. This is largely due to the predominance of hard surfaces, such as paving, walls, furniture and planter boxes at the expense of greenery, and the fact that most courtyards are built in a square or rectangular shape.

Because courtyard gardens are sheltered by walls and fences, they are ideal for growing plants that need protected conditions; for example, subtropical rainforest plants. Another advantage of courtyard gardening is that every plant can be seen up close, either growing in containers or in narrow beds.

A disadvantage of courtyards is that they are often hot and glary in summer as the heat is reflected off walls and paving. Coastal and inland plants that withstand dry, hot conditions will thrive in warm courtyards. Alternatively, a small shade tree and climbers covering the walls will help to cool and shade the courtyard.

Courtyard design

In a small, confined space every feature counts, so it's important to select and place plants and other items to their best effect:

- Keep the plantings simple. Clipped hedges and repeat plantings of the same species will give the courtyard a clean, uncluttered appearance.
- Create one focal point, such as an eye-catching sculpture or water feature, rather than cluttering the space with small pots.
- Keep the secondary features in scale, including plants, furniture and garden ornaments.
- Make sure there is ample room for comfortable garden furniture.
- Choose hard surfaces that link the house, courtyard and other garden areas.

COTTAGE GARDENS

Cottage gardens originated in seventeenth- and eighteenth-century England as practical and productive gardens around countryside cottages. Today's cottage gardens are more diverse, with an emphasis on colour and abundance. Spaces are generally small in scale, with a focus on curving lines. Hard surfaces are kept to a minimum and are generally made from natural materials.

Small-growing flowering natives are ideally suited to the colourful cottage garden style. Like the exotic annuals and herbaceous perennials traditionally used in cottage garden plantings, some of the smaller natives flower early and abundantly and, within the first season of growth, will grow rapidly enough to cover any bare patches in the garden bed.

Cottage-style natives can be mixed with traditional exotic plantings or grown purely in native beds.

Suitable native plants

Tetratheca, tea tree hybrids, *Indigofera australis*,

eriostemons, philothecas, hypocalymmas, baueras, kangaroo paws, grasses and sedges, daisies, *Leschenaultia*, and small grevilleas, callistemons and melaleucas.

ORIENTAL GARDENS

Oriental gardens attempt to reflect nature, but in a more orderly and artistic way. The images created are intended to be like a painting or other work of art, with a focus on beauty and meaning that is perhaps in some ways beyond nature.

They usually reflect a philosophy, and are designed as a place for contemplation — as such, they are largely free of distractions caused by excessive contrasts in texture or colour.

Balance is asymmetrical rather than symmetrical. Ponds, streams and other water features are common — these fit very well with the natural theme. Rocks (seen as pieces of natural sculpture) and stepping stones are also commonly used. Plants are not a significant component, although those used are carefully selected to harmonise with the landscape.

Natives with a sculptural appearance are best suited to this garden style. A contemplative retreat in the garden might feature a small group of tree ferns or a single grass tree. Plants with a pendulous or weeping habit might be used as waterside features; for example *Callistemon viminalis*, *Allocasuarina torulosa* or *Agonis flexuosa*.

RAINFOREST GARDENS

Rainforest gardens are a relatively new style which is gaining popularity in both cooler climates and in the more humid subtropics and tropical regions of the world. The main characteristic of this garden style is abundant 'tropical' or 'jungle' plantings with a focus on foliage textures and colours, rather than flowers. The interplay between light and shade is also important.

There is a huge choice of native plants suited to this garden style, many of which are relatively new to horticulture. Most plants are from the coastal rainforests of northern New South Wales and Queensland, but there are also many interesting species from the cool temperate rainforests and wet sclerophyll forests in Tasmania and southern Victoria. These cool-climate species can be grown in many parts of the world, including the United Kingdom, New Zealand and the United States.

The typical rainforest garden has the following characteristics:

- Lush, dense growth.
- Areas of shade as well as smaller, open glades.
- Layers of vegetation — a tall canopy of trees, a middle layer of small trees or large shrubs, and a low-growing layer of ground covers.
- Moist, organic soil.
- Humidity.
- Mulch as a groundcover.
- Rainforest plants including trees with distinctive trunks, palms, tree ferns, orchids, vines, epiphytes (ferns, bromeliads, etc. that grow on rocks and trees).
- Informal design with winding paths used to link areas of the garden.
- Natural materials, such as rocks and timber used for construction of garden features.
- Ornamental features often include things associated with rainforests, such as structures and sculptures from rainforest regions (Africa, Bali, India, South America, etc.). Also use natural features, such as large mossy rocks and old tree trunks.

Suitable native plants

FERNS — including tree ferns, staghorns and ground ferns

SMALL TO MEDIUM TREES — palms, macadamia, golden penda (*Xanthostemon chrysanthus*), *Lomatia fraxinifolia*, native frangipani (*Hymenosporum flavum*), *Evodiella muelleri*,

Buckinghamia celsissima, tree waratah (*Alloxylon flammeum*)
SHRUBS — lilly pillies, native rhododendron (*R. lochae*), native lasiandra (*Melastoma affine*), native fuchsia (*Graptophyllum thorogoodii*), native orchids, gingers and cordylines

ECLECTIC GARDENS

Eclectic gardens do not follow any particular theme or style. Eclectic gardeners tend to enjoy lots of different styles of gardens. Using a creative approach, they take their inspirations from all the garden traditions, combining plants, garden accessories and outdoor artworks to create distinctive and highly individual landscapes.

Some eclectic gardeners are plant collectors, seeking out bold and unusual plants. For others, the plants are merely part of an overall effect, a backdrop for the other elements of the garden. Regardless of their approach to plants, traits that all eclectic gardeners share are imagination, flair, and a willingness to step outside the boundaries of conventional gardening.

The best eclectic gardens tend to have some unifying elements and not too many excessive contrasts. For example, hedges or repeat plantings of a single species will help to tie the different parts of the garden together.

XERISCAPES

Xeriscapes are landscaped gardens that have low water requirements, and hence are ideal for gardeners looking to reduce their water usage. The typical xeriscape garden has lots of cactus and succulents, but dry-land Australian natives are also very suitable for this garden style.

When designing a dry-land garden, provide plenty of light for the plants. Avoid plants with dense foliage and do not place them too close together. Swales and mulches will help to conserve water in the soil. Choose native plants naturally adapted to dry conditions, such as eremophilas, darwinias, spinifex, mallee eucalypts and dry-land acacias.

Container gardens

Many gardeners prefer to grow their plants in containers. The advantages of containers are that you can see the plants up close, you can provide ideal conditions for fussy plants, and you can move them around to suit the season or your needs. They are ideal for gardeners who are renting or have restricted space — even the smallest outdoor spaces, such as courtyards, balconies, entranceways or side passages, can accommodate at least a few pot plants.

One drawback of container gardens is that pots only have a small amount of space for soil and water so they dry out quickly. This means that native plants that tolerate dry conditions are the ideal choice for growing in containers where water is in short supply, or for busy gardeners who do not have the time or inclination to water their pot plants every day or so.

To reduce the amount of water used by your pot plants:

- Add water crystals to the potting mix
- Use a moisture-retentive mix (i.e. the mix contains some peat, cocopeat or similar material)
- Use glazed pots in preference to terracotta pots. Terracotta pots are porous, which means that water evaporates through the pot itself
- Do not allow the plant to outgrow its pot — a large mass of roots will take up so much space in a small pot that there isn't room for potting mix or water
- Install a micro irrigation system
- Place the pot in a sheltered position, away from drying winds and full midday sun
- Cover the surface of the potting mix with a bark mulch

- If the potting mix dries out and doesn't absorb water, use a wetting agent which will improve water infiltration.

HOW TO POT-UP PLANTS

1. **POTTING UP NEWLY-PROPAGATED PLANTS (SEEDLINGS OR ROOTED CUTTINGS)**
   Young roots are tender, so be careful. Always hold the plant by the stem or the leaves, and gently fill the pot with potting mix. This will prevent kinked or girdled roots.
2. **POTTING PLANTS FROM A SMALLER TO A LARGER CONTAINER**
   Gently loosen the roots of most plants (there are exceptions…don't loosen the roots of acacias, banksias and grevilleas), and cut and remove any circling roots.
3. **REFRESHING A TIRED PLANT**
   When potting back into the same container (or the same size container) remove some of the old soil and trim the roots. Prune some of the foliage (in proportion) and replace with some new potting mix and fertiliser.

Successful pot plants rely on a good quality potting mix, adequate water and regular feeding. Feed the plants with slow-release native fertiliser. Additional liquid feeding can help boost the plant and green-up foliage during the growing season.

MATCH THE PLANT WITH THE POT

For the best effect, team your plant with the pot so they complement each other in terms of shape, proportion and colour. Also look at how the pot fits in with the surrounding gardening features. For example, in a bushland garden, a pot may be best placed in a garden bed next to a winding path; in a formal garden, you might put the pot against a plain backdrop, such as a wall or hedge.
Some typical pot shapes:

- Urn with a narrow neck — grasses and sedges
- Tall urn with a broader neck — plants with cascading or arching foliage
- Broad, shallow pot or dish — alpine plants
- Broad tub or half barrel — shrubs and small trees
- Large square containers — usually used as a matched pair or for repeat plantings; look good with formal clipped plants

Garden features

Every garden, no matter its style or size, is enhanced by a garden feature or two. Garden features act as focal points, drawing the eye to a certain part of the garden or enticing the viewer into the garden for a closer look. They give the garden a sense of the owner's personality, and keep the garden looking fresh and interesting, even when the plants are not looking their best.

The typical bush garden might feature a rustic pergola, arbour or bench, while classical statues and fountains might adorn a more formal garden. However, your choice of garden features does not need to be constrained by a particular style or theme — unexpected and surprising features sometimes make the most interesting and successful statements.

The secret to using garden features, especially statues and ornaments, is restraint — don't overdo it! If the garden is too cluttered with objects, the effect will be lost. Keep foliage clear of the feature — plants should frame the feature, not overwhelm it.

Garden ornaments should be located where people are most likely to see them — either from the house or as they walk through the garden. Consider the colour of the ornament and its background — a dark-coloured ornament will look better with the sky or a pale wall as its backdrop, whereas a light-coloured ornament will be more accentuated against a dark background such as a black or brown tree trunk or a green hedge.

Water in the garden

Water adds a new and unique dimension to gardens, and can be used in many different ways to create many different effects. Still water in a tranquil garden pond or pool creates a feeling of serenity and peace, while moving water in fountains, streams and small waterfalls gives a more dynamic feel to the garden, generating a sense of life, movement and sound.

While the most popular water features for native gardens are birdbaths, informal ponds and dry creek beds that complement the 'natural bushland' effect, there are many other ways water can be used in the garden. Depending on your garden style, you might consider a modern water sculpture, a fountain, a bog garden, a courtyard water wall or a formal pool — to name just a few possibilities.

BUSHLAND PONDS AND WATERCOURSES

A 'natural bushland' pond, dam, creek, waterfall or bog will not only greatly enhance the appearance of the garden, it will provide a welcome haven for other garden visitors and residents, such as butterflies, dragonflies, frogs, lizards, tortoises, small mammals and birds.

Other benefits of garden ponds include:

- Modifying the environment of the garden, providing a moist, cool micro-climate for tender plants, or providing welcome relief by lowering the temperature near the house or other garden areas on a hot day.
- Providing a home for fish, frogs, water snails and other interesting aquatic creatures. These will help control mosquitoes and other annoying insects, and help keep the pool clean.
- Adding interest in the garden by providing a contrast to other features in terms of texture, colour or form, and by providing a reflective surface that allows an ever-changing scene, as the sun moves, as clouds pass by, or the wind ripples the water surface.
- Providing an opportunity to grow a range of interesting and attractive aquatic or waterside plants in the garden.

Informal ponds are generally free form in shape, so that they appear to be a natural part of the landscape. This type of design relies heavily on mixed plantings and supporting features with a natural appearance, such as rocks, to integrate the pond with the surrounding garden.

Generally ponds work best sited at the lowest point in the garden, as this is where water would naturally collect in the landscape. The exceptions are formal pools or ponds, which do not attempt to emulate a natural landscape — in which case they can be sited anywhere, and raised above the general ground level.

Waterfalls and streams, in particular, need to look natural, and so should be sited along the natural contours.

EDGING

Pond edging is critical for integrating the feature with the surrounding garden. A properly edged water garden looks great, but a badly edged one will stand out like a sore thumb.

If you want a natural look, the edge must be ill-defined (i.e. the edge merges into the surrounding land). Plants growing along the edge, such as sedges and ferns, will spread a little from the water out onto the land, and plants on the land may spread into or hang over the water. When the edge is well defined, the look is less natural, but if it is curved it can still convey an informal effect.

Natural ponds, where fish and water plants form part of a self-regulating ecosystem, should be as large and deep as possible. Shallow ponds evaporate quickly and experience greater temperature fluctuations that can be harmful to plants and fish. If you want to grow waterlilies or keep fish, the pond needs to be around 60 cm deep.

An ideal backyard pond is one that looks good, is environmentally stable, has a depth of around 50–70 cm over most of its area, and has relatively steep sides.

POND DESIGN

There are many factors to bear in mind when designing a pond.

Safety

If children are to have access to the pond then it must be made safe. It is not enough to make the pond shallow, as drowning may occur in even very shallow water; it is better to make it inaccessible. This may be done by including a steel mesh frame set just below the edge of the pond, or by constructing a raised pond. The inclusion of fencing or hedging in the pond design may also serve this purpose. Verify with your local council if fencing is required around the perimeter or if other regulations apply.

Location

Ideally, construct the pond in a sunny area, clear of plants which will drop leaves or have roots which cause damage. Consider visibility, access to power (if using a pump), and drainage (for when you clean it and for overflow). Sun reflection on the water can lighten up a dark spot of the garden, but may also result in severe glare.

Size

If the pond isn't big enough or deep enough, temperatures will fluctuate too much, affecting pond life. You need a surface area of at least 4.5 square metres to minimise problems. The depth should be at least 50 cm, and deeper in very cold areas to protect fish from extreme cold in winter.

Shape

Mark the pond out on the ground with string or rope to see what it will look like. If your garden beds and paths are curved then pond sides need to be curved. If the garden is more formal, with straight borders, the pond is better to be square or rectangular. Gently sloping sides create areas of very shallow water at the edges that are more likely to grow algae.

Edging

Gentle sloping sides will create a natural look. The addition of river pebbles, rocks, reeds and other plants at the water's edge will enhance this appeal. Bricks, paving and other harsh materials will give a more formal look although again this effect can be softened if your pond design includes curved sides.

Components

The pond surrounds should be splash-proof, non-slipping, and wear-and-tear resistant. Construction material may range from concrete, compacted clay, preformed PVC mouldings or flexible liner. If the pond is to include a fountain or waterfall, then piping, pumping and filtration system will be needed.

Sun or shade

The location of the water feature is important to receive the best benefit and to provide optimum conditions for water life. If full shade is cast over the pond, algae will not grow (which may sound good at first) but would be bad for other life forms too. Placed beneath trees and shrubs, the pond will be subjected to continual leaf, fruit and flower drop. The rotting debris pollutes the water resulting in harmful, possibly fatal effects on the fish. Some tree species even contain toxic substances in their leaves.

Located in full sun, the water will be

warmed to the optimum temperature for water life. Surrounding vegetation and waterlilies will grow best in full sun, but unfortunately so will algae. However, as the water plants grow they will progressively block out the sun which in time will kill the algae or keep it to a minimum. A surface cover between half and two-thirds is a recommended ratio, and this figure should be kept in mind when planting waterlilies or other aquatic plants.

Access

A bridge or raised stepping stones will look decorative and provide ready access across the pond or watercourse. The bridge design and construction materials should complement the pond and surrounding landscape. For natural ponds, a bridge constructed from timber sleepers or non-slip boards is ideal.

A BOG GARDEN

A bog garden is another option for a natural-look water feature. Bogs occur naturally on low-lying heavy clay, peat or silty soils. The bogs are filled with moisture-retentive decaying humus, and provide a rich habitat for frogs, insects and plants.

In the garden, bogs are usually constructed next to a pond to provide moist, rich soil for waterside plantings, but they can be built as an individual feature if you don't want to be bothered with a pond.

Construction

1. Dig out a large shallow depression about 30 cm deep.
2. Line the depression with thick plastic sheeting, which has been punctured with small drainage holes.
3. Cover the drainage holes with gravel then fill the depression with garden soil.
4. The soil can be enriched with compost and/or peat, depending on the plants' requirements. (Many bog plants prefer acid soils.)
5. Thoroughly moisten the soil before adding the plants, and keep it moist at all times.

Suitable native plants

Restio tetraphyllus
Scleranthus biflorus
Patersonia spp.
Orthrosanthus laxus, O. multiflorus
Mosses and ferns
Mazus pumilo
Juncus spp.
Drosera macrantha, planchonii
Gahnia spp.
Dianella caerula, D. tasmanica
Stylidium soboliferum
Viola hederaceae

OTHER WATER FEATURES

Other water features include fountains, water walls, pot ponds, water barrels, troughs, birdbaths and even shallow dishes. How well they work in the garden often depends on where they are positioned. A birdbath, for example, will be particularly attractive to small birds if it is placed in a leafy corner of the garden (providing cats aren't a problem), while a trough or barrel will make an interesting courtyard feature.

A shallow dish, which is probably the least expensive water feature, can look charming placed at the edge of a garden bed or path. An urn with water at the entrance to a garden or house can signify that you are about to enter an Asian-style garden.

Where to put plants

TREES

Compared to other plants, trees have a major impact on the landscape. They generally take a long time to create the desired effect and once they reach maturity they can be troublesome, especially in small gardens or planted too close to buildings. Destructive roots, dangerous branches and messy leaves are just some of the problems associated with planting the wrong tree in the wrong spot. Additionally, fully grown trees are expensive and often difficult to remove. For these reasons, it is vital to choose and place trees carefully — if unsure, ask for advice from your local garden centre or nursery.

There are many good reasons though for planting native trees. They provide welcome shade in summer, they provide important bird and animal habitats, and they create a sense of permanence in the garden.

Before planting, consider the tree's growth rate and eventual size. How long will it be before an intended effect is achieved? What will the effect be in the meantime? (*Note*: with some slow-growing trees it may take 50 years for the eventual effect to be achieved). Also consider its foliage density and form. Will it provide heavy or light shade? Does it have a spreading canopy, or a compact upright habit?

For the best visual effect, select one feature tree (for example, a tree with interesting bark or an attractive shape) and place it where it can be easily seen from inside the house. Careful placement of trees can enhance or frame views or other garden features; for example, in a formal garden, placing two trees either side of the house.

Garden accents

Accent is achieved through a visual break in the sequence or pattern of planting. It is used to create a dramatic effect and focus attention upon one particular part of a landscape.

If an accent is to work properly, it must be strong. For example, a small gap in a row of plants will only create a weak accent, whereas a larger gap will create a stronger accent.

Native shrubs need pruning

Most native shrubs grow quickly and within a couple of years will effectively hide unsightly views and provide shelter to the garden. However, they do become leggy and, if left unpruned, will eventually become a mass of woody sticks at eye level, topped by a sparse covering of leaves. Lightly prune them each year after flowering to keep them dense and attractive.

Trees can be used to block distant views. They may also moderate the effect of winds and other environmental conditions.

SHRUBS

Shrubs are the 'middle' layer of the garden. Tall shrubs are often used as a garden backdrop, screening fences and buildings and other unwanted views. Smaller shrubs provide attractive eye-catching features in the foreground.

LOW PLANTS

Low-growing plants such as perennials and groundcovers don't provide shade, nor do they screen areas, but, being at eye level or lower, they can have a more obvious and dramatic effect than larger plants in the garden. It is generally the low-growing shrubs and flowering perennials that provide most of the obvious colourful flowers in a garden. These are the finishing touches that make your garden something special.

Repeat plantings of low plants can be used to define the edges of garden beds. For an informal garden, plant groups of small tufting plants interspersed with spreading ground-covers. In formal gardens, use dwarf clipped hedges.

Native plant rockeries

In European- and American-style gardens, rockeries aim to reproduce the effect seen in alpine areas where low-growing plants are found amongst rocky outcrops. In native bush gardens rocks are used in a number of additional ways.

- Rocky outcrops on sloping areas help to retain the soil and prevent soil erosion.
- Outcrops or clusters of rocks placed at focal points are used as visual features.
- Rocks are used around pools or ponds.
- Rocks are used to provide a seemingly natural all-weather walkway; for example, rocks in a watercourse or amongst a garden bed, allowing access to places which would otherwise be inaccessible without damaging plants.
- Sometimes plants which tend to be unstable can be planted alongside large rocks. This gives the plant stability as its roots grow under the rock. Also the area below a rock can remain moist for longer in dry weather and not dry out as fast as more exposed soil.

COPYING NATURE

A rockery should re-create what occurs naturally. To be able to reproduce a natural effect, the landscaper must grasp an understanding of the way rocks occur in nature. Basically there are three different types of natural rock groupings.

Outcrops

Outcrops are like the tip of the iceberg where most of each rock lies below the surface. Rocks should not lie at odd angles but should relate to each other, conforming to the stratification of the imaginary parent rock lying below. Only allow well-weathered surfaces to show.

Rock falls

Rock falls occur naturally at the base of cliffs and slopes, and they should be constructed in the same way in a garden. Since most gardens do not have cliffs or steep slopes, this style of rock formation has a comparatively limited application. If you do have suitable topography, arrange the rocks in a haphazard way at the base of the slope. They can be odd shapes and sizes, but they must be the same type of rock to be appear realistic.

Alluvials

These are rock formations that occur naturally in watercourses. A dry creek bed can be created using pebbles or larger, well-rounded rocks.

ARTIFICIAL ROCKS

It is possible to simulate the effect of rocks in a garden using concrete constructions. This type of work has the following advantages over working with real rocks.

1. You do not have the heavy work of moving heavy boulders about (though mixing concrete can be heavy work).
2. You are not damaging natural environments by removing rocks which may be an integral part of natural ecosystems.
3. You are not restricted to only using rocks of a size which are able to be moved.
4. You can create any shape and size you desire.
5. Crevices for planting, watercourses, pools, etc. can be created where and in the form you want.

Artificial rocks, if created properly, will look just as real as the 'real thing'. Components used in the surface layer will create both a texture and colour which simulates natural formations.

The procedure is as follows:

1. Shaping

Create a mound of sand or soil in the shape of the boulder or rock cluster which you plan to build. This is often done by filling plastic or hessian bags with sand or soil and stacking in the desired shape.

2. Reinforcing layer

A layer of wire mesh (for example, chicken wire) is spread over the surface of the shaped form.

3. Base cement layer

A layer of concrete 6 to 10 cm thick is spread over the chicken wire. This mix needs to be relatively dry so it remains firmly in place when applied. If the concrete begins to slump in vertical sections, it may be necessary to lean bags of sand or soil against those sections as support until the cement dries. If the concrete is being applied in hot weather, you will need to keep the concrete moist by either hosing or covering it with wet hessian, or it will dry too quickly and crack. Similarly, if heavy rain is expected the work should be covered with plastic for protection.

The cement is applied at this stage using a trowel (or cement worker's float) to spread the cement from the bottom of the structure upwards. When doing steep sections it may be necessary to do a small part at a time, allowing it to dry before returning to the section above. The surface should NOT BE SMOOTH. Leave a rough trowelled surface at this stage. This layer should be strong giving the necessary structural support required for the final 'rock'.

4. Final layer

A final layer is rendered (that is, spread over the base layer). First cover the base layer with a fine wire mesh (for example, a 12 mm mesh). Use a mortar mix of 1 part cement to 3–4 parts sand and spread it 2–3 cm thick over the fine wire mesh. The next day, before the surface is completely hardened but firm enough to withstand some knocks, scrub the surface with a steel brush to roughen it. After 3 to 4 days, pick over the surface with a sharp instrument such as a chisel or screwdriver to create further textured effects.

An alternative method is to include some gravel in the render. This can either be left to harden to give a pebbly granite-like appearance or the gravel can be scraped away before the surface has hardened to give a pitted sandstone-like appearance.

A third method is to include some rock-salt crystals in the mix, which can be dissolved out by water when the surface has hardened. Naturally coloured sands and gravels should be used to give the best results.

If you are going to plant close to the work, be aware that concrete is alkaline (has a high pH), and will affect the pH of the soil around it as chemical components leach out of the cement. In sandy soil, the effect may wash away through the soil after six months or so; however, it is wise to test the pH, and perhaps compensate for this problem by washing the surface of the rock a few times with a 50-50 solution of vinegar and water.

Plants to use in rockeries

- Plants with suckering roots that bind the soil
- Small tufting plants
- Alpine plants that need good drainage
- Dainty plants that are easily overlooked in a ground-level bed
- Small plants, such as sedges that tolerate heavy wet soil, for planting at the base of poorly drained rockeries

Retaining walls

You should consider the following when designing retaining walls.

1. Shape and substance of the wall

The wall must follow the shape of the embankment it is retaining as close as possible to avoid carting large quantities of soil either in or out of the work site. The substance which the wall is built from is largely determined by what materials are available. Dry walls (without cementing) need a solid base/foundation. A mortared wall needs a concrete strip foundation and weepholes for drainage.

2. Positioning of the wall to minimise soil movement

All walls should slope back into the embankment (this slope is called the 'batter'). A minimum batter should be approximately 1 cm for every 6 cm in height. Ideally, the ground at both the top and bottom of a wall should be fairly flat to minimise erosion.

3. Drainage both above and below the wall

This factor is obviously more critical in clay soils. A spoon drain may be built at both the top and bottom of the wall. Sub-surface drains might also be used in these positions. If surface drainage is allowed to run over the top of the wall, it can cause bad erosion behind and at the base of the wall *very quickly*.

TIMBER WALLS

Timber retaining walls should never be more than 1.2 metres tall. Wood should be either a type which resists decay (such as red gum or yellow box), or else treated with a chemical to prevent decay or damage by insects, fungus, etc.

The two methods of building timber walls are:

Horizontal timbers

Timbers are laid horizontally, one on top of another, usually behind upright timbers concreted in place at frequent intervals. This type of timber wall is usually easier to build, and more stable than a vertical wall.

Vertical timbers

Posts, logs, railway sleepers, etc. are set in concrete, in a trench dug along the bottom of the embankment. There must be one-third of the timber below ground, and there should be a very good batter (better than for other types of walls), to ensure the timbers do not move. This type of wall is best suited to low walls (i.e. up to 0.5 m tall).

MASONRY/ROCK WALLS

The two main methods of building masonry or stone walls are:

Dry walls

These are built by stacking rocks or blocks one on top of another without using concrete or any other joining material to stick them together. The individual units need to be stacked in a way that they interlock as much as possible, and with a decent batter a good deal of stability is achieved. The base of this type of wall should be twice as wide as the main section of the wall. This spreads the weight and helps prevent the wall sinking.

Wet walls

The stones or blocks in this wall are concreted together. A strip foundation should be laid first, with steel reinforcing set in concrete. The stones/blocks are then laid on top. To further strengthen the wall, sections of wall are run back into the embankment at occasional intervals. These walls can be effectively cemented with a mortar mix of 3 parts fine sand to 1 part cement.

Creating a rainforest garden

The rainforest is often seen as one of the ultimate environments to duplicate in the garden. It can provide a home for native animals or provide you with a quiet, pleasant place to escape to. It is easily 'constructed' provided a few requirements are met to satisfy plant growth. Protection from direct sunlight and strong wind and an abundant supply of mulch or leaf matter are three of the most important necessities for the establishment of a rainforest. Understandably, if you already have a shaded site it makes your rainforest garden one step closer to completion.

Many people do not realise that rainforest plants are very adaptable to suburban gardens. Let us look at some of the good points of rainforest landscaping:

- Large rainforest trees that grow to heights exceeding 20 metres will only grow to about half that height in sunny domestic gardens.
- Full shade is not essential for rainforest trees as many will grow in full sun; indeed, many species that typically have a spindly habit and sparse foliage in shaded forests grow into very attractive garden specimens with rounded canopies, spreading branches and spectacular floral displays. Some species (such as palms) need shade in the early years of growth but tolerate full sun as they mature.
- Large areas are not essential to develop a rainforest — many people have successfully developed miniature rainforests on domestic blocks.
- Any soil can be made suitable provided a bit of extra pre-planting preparation is carried out. The better your soil is to begin with, the easier and quicker it will be to establish your rainforest.
- With adequate compost or leaf litter, water is better retained in the soil, therefore less additional watering is needed.
- There are several types of rainforests throughout Australia ranging from the tip of Queensland to the mountains of Tasmania, so no matter where you live your climate can be assisted to produce a rainforest.
- Many rainforest plants are extremely easy to grow, so much so that many are used as indoor plants (e.g. blackbean, *Castanospermum australe*) and others have been available throughout nurseries for decades (e.g. Alexandra palm, *Archontophoenix alexandrae*).

PLANTING A RAINFOREST

A rainforest is made up of several levels or strata of vegetation. These are generally referred to as the upper storey, middle storey and the lower storey (or groundcover). In a typical domestic block it is important to realise that you should not plant rainforest species that will grow to 20 metres or those that have invading destructive roots like umbrella trees (*Schefflera actinophylla*). For most gardens middle-storey plants are best treated as the upper-storey plants, so that the rainforest landscape takes on a human scale.

Pioneer plants are usually fast growing with a spreading canopy. They are, however, relatively short-lived and may need removal at some later date. These plants provide necessary shade and leaf litter which helps retain moisture and improves the organic matter content of the soil. These plants also provide essential shade for ferns and groundcovers and protection for the slower-growing species.

Climax plants are those plants that require some shade while young but which eventually outgrow the shade of the pioneer plants, resulting in their deterioration. They are long-lived. These are planted after the pioneer plants are between one to two years old with variable spacing distances (for example,

1.5 metres to 3 metres apart). A reasonable canopy can be developed in about five years depending upon species suitability to your climatic region.

Middle-storey and groundcover plants require plenty of shade and shelter. They are best planted after the pioneer plants are well grown and the climax plants are well established. Understorey plants are mainly ferns, orchids, native lilies, gingers and small palms. These plants prefer moist but not waterlogged sites. As these plants are at eye level, you may wish to provide contrast to the all-green rainforest by adding colourful 'tropical' plants. If, however, you are a purest, you may prefer to keep with only native groundcovers.

MAINTENANCE

Watering

Once established, rainforests are self-sustaining but only in areas that receive at least 750 mm of rainfall per year. In other areas, additional watering will be needed in dry times to prevent plant death. Hosing the canopy reduces transpiration (that is, water loss from leaves) and also cleans the plants. The use of trickle hoses or sprinklers will place the necessary water exactly where it is required.

Mulching

An essential part of the rainforest that must be kept up is mulching. Continual leaf fall may supplement this mulch but if the site is steep, new mulch may need to be added to overcome erosion or wash off. A layer of mulch provides a cool environment for the roots, holds moisture and supplies a mild fertiliser. Maybe more importantly, it provides the home for countless microbes to make the ecosystem complete.

Fertilisers

A balanced fertiliser can be spread over the area and watered in. Fertilise at a rate of 1 kg per 5 square metres applied three or four times over the year is frequently suggested. Blood and bone and Dynamic Lifter are also suitable. Organically based fertilisers are the best for this ecosystem.

Weed control

With adequate mulch and reduced light, few weeds will grow in an established rainforest. As weeds compete for light, moisture and nutrients they are best pulled out upon sight or spot sprayed.

Future plantings

Future plantings may be necessary to replace dead or weak plants and to achieve the succession of rainforest development. Try not to transplant rainforest plants each season until a final site is decided — this only results in weak plants. Once a plant has been planted leave it there unless it is essential that it must be removed or transplanted.

Pests and diseases

It is best not to use toxic chemicals. Try to leave insects for their predators. If possible manually collect insects or disease-damaged plant parts and destroy elsewhere. If sprays must be used consider the use of organic sprays such as garlic, pyrethrum or Dipel.

6.
Choosing your plants

You should choose your plants carefully. Remember, every plant has its good points and bad points, so you will need to decide for yourself which characteristics are most important to you. Consider all of the following qualities, and balance the importance of one against another according to your preferences and priorities.

AESTHETICS

Consider how a plant looks, including its colour, texture and density of foliage, fruit and flowers and changes in appearance throughout the year (for example, period and time of flowering, leaf colour changes). What is the habit or form of the plant — prostrate, weeping, vase-shaped? Will it create the type of effect you want? Will its appearance complement other types of plants growing nearby?

FUNCTION

What will the plant be used for? For example, do you want the plant to screen unwanted views, to attract birds, provide shade or to bind exposed soil on a slope? Will it fulfil this function adequately?

GROWTH CHARACTERISTICS

How dense is the foliage? How will the plant affect the environment around it? Trees can grow large, shading their surrounding area, and eventually cause sun-loving plants around them to deteriorate. Do you want shade or not? Do you want the garden cooler or warmer? Do you want it more or less moist? Do you want the plant to redirect or to stop the wind? The plants you select can affect all of these, and more.

HARDINESS

Will the plant withstand any adverse conditions your garden is likely to experience; for example, frost, drought, excessive heat, flood, high winds, poor soil conditions, pest or disease attack, etc?

SUITABILITY TO THE LOCATION

Is the plant ideally suited to the soil and climate in which it is being planted, or will it barely tolerate these conditions?

SAFETY

Is the plant potentially dangerous? Plants that are likely to have falling branches, spiky or thorny foliage, poisonous plant parts, etc. should be avoided unless they are grown in a position where they will not be a problem. Plants that are known to burn easily should be avoided in fire-prone areas. Pollen of some plants, such as the grasses and acacias, can also create allergy problems.

LIFE SPAN

How long is the plant likely to live? Many wattles, boronias and some other natives are relatively short-lived. In some situations this can be used to advantage: short-lived, fast-growing species can be planted as 'nurse plants', providing shelter for slow-growing, tender plants. In this way the short-lived plants help the garden to mature and evolve.

BEWARE! The biggest trap you can fall into is to choose your plants on impulse. Just because a plant catches your eye in the nursery it doesn't mean that it's the best plant for the spot you want to fill in your garden.

Plant relationships — aim for compatibility

In nature, plants and animals live together in balanced relationships. Compatibility should be of prime consideration when grouping plants. If the plants in a particular area all like the same conditions, it is far easier to maintain them. For example, you won't be over watering some and under watering others. If their vigour is similar, you will avoid having some plants compete with and choke the growth of others. All of the species will survive, because none is stronger than another.

If there is too much of an imbalance in your selection of plants, then the garden becomes difficult to maintain. Plant associations in nature can provide some insights into what will work in a garden. By studying what grows with a particular plant in the wild, we can get an idea of what may grow successfully with the same plant in cultivation.

Plants in forests occur usually in four or five tiers or layers. Species typical of each layer are as follows.

The upper canopy (tall trees)
Examples: *Eucalyptus globulus*, *Eucalyptus mannifera*, *Eucalyptus regnans*

The middle storey (medium trees)
Examples: *Allocasuarina verticillata*, *Acacia floribunda*, *Acacia melanoxylon*

The understorey (small trees or large shrubs)
Examples: *Melaleuca armillaris*, *Callistemon viminalis*, *Leptospermum lavaegatum*

The ground storey 1 (small shrubs and groundcovers)
Examples: *Correa reflexa*, *Hardenbergia violacea*, *Bauera sessiliflora*

The ground storey 2 (grasses, perennials and herbs)
Examples: *Stylidium graminifolium*, *Burchardia umbellata*, *Poa australis*

When selecting plants, you should be conscious of the tiers you are creating and how they will affect other tiers (for example, shade, wind protection, falling leaves and branches, intercepting rainfall).

Buying plants — what to look for

You will usually have a better chance of success by using healthy plants that have been hardened to the environment. Avoid plants with tender growth or diseased tissue.

It is almost always better to pay more for a healthy plant that will thrive than to buy a cheap but sick one from a clearance sale. A healthy plant will soon provide vigorous new growth and become established a lot quicker.

Before buying a plant, consider all of the points on this checklist.

1. LOOK AT THE ROOTS. Take the plant out of the pot if necessary.

- Roots should be of a light colour and have healthy-looking tips.
- If roots are shrivelled, rotting or blackened at the end, the plant is possibly unhealthy.
- Is the plant pot bound? Look for significant root growth coming through the bottom of the pot.

2. LOOK AT THE TIPS OF THE FOLIAGE.

- If leaf tips are healthy, they will be lush and unmarked.
- If they are not growing (particularly during growth seasons) the plant is not in peak health.
- If they are very soft and lush, they may be susceptible to extremes, such as frost, wind or temperature fluctuations.

3. LOOK AT THE SOIL. It should be moist but not saturated. It should not be too hard; you should be able to dig into it readily with your fingers.

4. LOOK AT THE FOLIAGE AND STEMS. There should be little, if any, damage to leaves and stems. There should be no sign of diseases or pests.

Climate zones in Australia

Since Australia's climate varies considerably from place to place, it is impossible to cover every climate zone. The gardener must rely heavily on commonsense in using the information in this or any other book to determine which plants to select for their particular situation. For a general guideline, however, the main climate traits of the regions are outlined below.

MELBOURNE

Summers are warm to hot and humid with maximum temperatures averaging 35°C. Winters are cold with minimum temperatures on the coldest days around 3°C. There are two or three frosts per month in June, July and August. Average rainfalls are 650 mm (25 inches) in Melbourne's city centre; 450 mm (18 inches) in the outer western suburbs; and 750 mm (30 inches) in the outer eastern suburbs. Rainfall is generally even throughout the year, though droughts are not uncommon. A wide variety of plants grow well in this climate, though inland species can suffer through summer humidity.

SYDNEY

This area experiences hot, humid days from November to April. Maximum summer temperatures in the city are normally around 30°C, but the western suburbs frequently experience summer maximum temperatures much higher than this. Minimum temperatures during the coldest times in winter are around 6°C. Frosts occur mainly in June, July and August in the western suburbs; other parts rarely experience frosts. Winters are wet, but summers are wetter. Annual rainfall is over 1000 mm (40 inches) in the city centre. Richmond, in the outer western suburbs, has about 40% less rain than the city.

PERTH

Summers are dry and hot, with temperatures averaging 36°C. Winters are wet, 800 mm (32 inches), with rainfall mainly between June and November. Humidity is low over summer. Frosts are rare around the city but increase inland. Minimum temperatures in mid-winter are around 6°C.

INLAND ARID AREAS

Much of Australia's inland is dry, and has low rainfall. Summers can be very hot and in the south, in particular, winters can be very cold.

ADELAIDE

Summers are hot and dry with maximums of 36°C, with a minimum winter temperature of 6°C. Light frosts occur in June to September. The average rainfall of 525 mm (21 inches) falls mainly over winter months.

BRISBANE

Summers are hot and very humid, with most of the annual 950 mm (38 inches) rainfall falling between December and March. The remainder of the year is mild to warm and dry. Frosts may occur in the inland suburbs and areas surrounding Brisbane.

DARWIN

Annual rainfall is over 1500 mm (60 inches) and falls mainly in the hot humid summer. Winters are warm and very dry.

FAR NORTH QUEENSLAND

Coastal rainforest areas from central Queensland to Cape York have a high summer rainfall. The climate is hot and more humid than south-east Queensland. Winters are warm, and can be very dry.

HOBART

Summers are mild and sometimes wet with maximum temperatures around 27°C. Winters are cold with minimums around 2°C. Light to moderate frosts occur in the waterside suburbs; inland suburbs can experience heavier frosts.

Plants for different situations

HARDY AND COLD-TOLERANT PLANTS

The authors have witnessed all of these species growing successfully in inland and snow-prone areas of southern Australia, though some have also been seen to suffer frost damage at times.

Trees

Acacia dealbata, elata, pravissima
Allocasuarina (most species)
Angophora costata
Callitris (most species)
Eucalyptus alpina (some varieties), *botryoides, cinerea, dives, globulus, gunni, leucoxylon, mannifera, melliodora, nicholi, pauciflora, polyanthemos, regnans, saligna, sideroxylon, stoatei, torquata, viminalis*
Melaleuca linariifolia
Pittosporum undulatum

Shrubs

Astartea fascicularis
Bauera (most species)
Callistemon citrinus, viminalis
Correa alba, reflexa
Darwinia citriodora
Grevillea alpina, juniperina, 'Poorinda' varieties, *rosmarinifolia*
Hakea nodosa, sericea
Indigofera australis
Leptospermum polygalifolium (syn. *L. flavescens*), *juniperina, scoparium*
Melaleuca (most temperate species)
Myoporum floribundum
Pimelea ferruginea
Pomaderris (most species)
Prostanthera (most species)
Pultenaea flexilis, villosa

Thryptomene calycina, saxicola
Westringia (most species)

Groundcovers

Billardiera scandens
Gastrolobium celsianu (syn. *Brachysema celsianum*)
Grevillea gaudichaudii, juniperina (prostrate form)
Leptospermum rupestre
Micromyrtus ciliata
Muehlenbeckia axillaris
Scleranthus biflorus
Themeda australis

FROST-HARDY NATIVE PLANTS

Trees

Acacia baileyana, dealbata
Allocasuarina stricta, torulosa
Banksia integrifolia
Callistemon salignus
Callitris oblonga
Casuarina cunninghamiana, glauca
Eucalyptus cinerea, cladocalyx, crenulata, gunnii, leucoxylon, macrandra, melliodora, nicholii, pauciflora, polyanthemos, sideroxylon, stellulata
Pittosporum phyllyraeoides

Shrubs

Acacia cultriformis, pravissima
Banksia ericifolia, marginata, media, spinulosa
Bauera rubioides, sessiliflora
Boronia filifolia, megastigma, muelleri, pinnata
Callistemon citrinus, pallidus, rigidus, sieberi (syn. *C. paludosus*)
Cassia sturtii
Correa alba, 'Manni', *reflexa*
Grevillea alpina, aquifolium, baueri, capitellata, lanigera, lavandulaceae, Poorinda hybrids, *rosmarinifolia, sericea, steiglitziana, tridentifera*
Hakea elliptica, nodosa, petiolaris, purpurea, salicifolia (syn. *H. saligna*), *sericea*
Indigofera australis
Kunzea capitata, parvifolia
Leptospermum juniperinum, lanigerum, polygalifolium (syn. *L. flavescens*), *scoparium*
Melaleuca decussata, elliptica, incana, pungens, squarrosa, stypheloides, thymifolia, uncinata
Philotheca myoporoides (syn. *Eriostemon myoporoides*)
Philotheca verrucosus (syn. *Eriostemon verrucosus*)
Prostanthera aspalathioides, crenulata, lasianthos, nivea, rotundifolia
Senna artemisioides (syn. *Cassia artemisioides*)
Telopea oreades, speciosissima
Thryptomene calycina, saxicola
Westringia fruticosa

Groundcovers

Brachyscome multifida
Chrysocephalum apiculatum (syn. *Helichrysum apiculatum/ H. ramosissimum*)
Correa decumbens
Epacris impressa, microphylla, pulchella
Eremophila glabra, maculata
Grevillea confertifolia, juniperina (prostrate form), *laurifolia*
Helichrysum baxteri
Kunzea pomifera
Leptospermum humifusum
Melaleuca wilsonii
Myoporum parvifolium
Xerochrysum bracteatum (syn. *Bracteantha bracteata*)

PLANTS FOR DRY CONDITIONS

These grow well in soils that are normally dry.

Trees

Adansonia gregorii
Brachychiton populneus, rupestris
Callitris columellaris, drummondii, endlicheri, preissii, verrucosa
Eucalyptus calycogona, eremophila, forrestiana, spathulata, tetraptera, torquata, viridis
Melia azederach

Shrubs

Acacia aneura, argyrophylla, aspera, converta, hakeiodes, rigens
Alyogyne hakeifolia
Banksia (most Western Australian varieties)
Cassia nemophila, sturtii
Eremophila drummondii, glabra, maculata, serrulata
Grevillea rosmarinifolia
Lasiopetalum bauri, ferrugineum
Myoporum insulare
Senna artemisioides (syn. *Cassia artemisioides*)
Westringia eremicola, fruticosa, longifolia

Groundcovers and low shrubs

Atriplex rhagodiodes
Eutaxia microphylla
Grevillea aspera, ilicifolia
Eremophila debile
Helipterum albicans
Kunzea pomifera
Myoporum parvifolium
Phebalium sp.
Ptilotus erubescens, exaltatus
Rhagodia
Rhodanthe chlorocephala subsp. *rosea* (syn. *Helipterum roseum*)
Swainsonia canescens, stipularis

PLANTS THAT TOLERATE DROUGHTS

These grow well during dry periods.

Trees

Acacia aneura, pendula, spectabilis, stenophylla
Allocasuarina inophloia, verticillata
Brachychyton rupestre
Callistemon (most tree types)
Callitris columellaris, preissii
Eucalyptus caesia, calycogona, camaldulensis, campespe, crucis, diversifolia, forrestiana, globulus, macrocarpa, papuana, radiata, spathulata, stricklandii, tetraptera, torquata, viridis
Ficus rubiginosa
Geijera salicifolia
Melia azederach var. *australasicus*
Pittosporum phyllyraeoides
Pleiogynuim timoriense

Shrubs

Atriplex (most species)
Banksia ericifolia, ornata
Callistemon (most shrub types)
Cassia nemophila
Chenopodium nitrariaceum
Dodonaea (most species)
Doryanthes excelsa
Eremophila (most species)
Eucalyptus grossa, tetraptera
Grevillea aspera, banksii, lavandulaceae, pteridifolia, steiglitziana, wilsonii
Hakea bucculenta, elliptica, laurina, multilineata, salicifolia (syn. *H. Saligna*), *sericea*
Jacksonia scoparia
Melaleuca decussata, elliptica, huegelii, lanceolata, uncinata, wilsonii
Prostranthera aspalathoides
Scholtzia capitata
Senna artemisioides
Solanum brownii
Swainsonia (most species)

Groundcovers

Allocasuarina nana
Carpobrotus glaucescens
Chrysocephalum apiculatum (syn. *Helichrysum apiculatum/H.ramosissimum*
Convolvulus erubescens
Kunzea pomifera
Myoporum parvifolium
Rhagodia deltophylla

Plants that tolerate both wet and dry conditions

Acacia dealbata, floribunda, howittii, longifolia, pravissima, saligna, verticillata
Agonis
Allocasuarina stricta
Angophora costata, floribunda, hispida
Banksia marginata, spinulosa
Bursaria
Callistemon citrinis, sieberi, viminalis
Calothamnus quadrifidus
Casuarina cunninghamiana, equisitifolia, glauca, humilis, paludosa
Corymbia citriodora (syn. *Eucalyptus citriodora*), *C. maculata* (syn. *Eucalyptus maculata*)
Dianella revoluta, tasmanica
Eriostemon myoporoides
Eucalyptus camaldulensis, crenulata, elata, globulus, haemastoma, microcarpa, muellerana, parvifolia, pauciflora, perrinana, pulchella, risdonii, robusta, saligna, spathulata, vernicosa
Gahnia radula
Grevillea acanthifolia, australis
Hakea nodosa, petiolaris, salicifolia (syn. *H. saligna*), *sericea*
Hibbertia procumbens, serpyllifolia
Kunzea ambigua, parvifolia, recurva
Lambertia formosa
Leptospermum, juniperinum, lanigerum, petersonii, poligalifolium (syn. *L. flavescens*), *scoparium*
Lomatia fraseri, myricoides, polymorpha
Melalueca armillaris, bracteata, decussate, diosmifolia, ericifolia, globifera, hypericifolia, incana, lanceolata, laterita, linariifolia, nesophila, nodosa, pulchella, thymifolia, quinquenervia, violacacea, stypheloides
Pittosporum undulatum
Sollya heterophylla
Themeda australis
Westringia angustifolia, brevifolia, longifolia, raleighii

WINDBREAK PLANTS

Acacia floribunda, longifolia, mearnsii, pravissima, saligna
Acmena smithii (syn. *Eugenia smithii*)
Agonis flexuosa
Allocasuarina (most species)
Callistemon citrinus, pallidus, salignus, viminalis
Callitris (most species)
Correa alba
Eucalyptus alpina, camaldulensis, forrestiana, globulus compacta, leucoxylon, pauciflora, polyanthemos, viminalis, viridis
Grevillea rosmarinifolia
Kunzea ambigua, flavescens
Leptospermum laevigatum, lanigerum, scoparium
Melaleuca armillaris, elliptica, ericifolia, huegelii, hypericifolia, nesophila, squarrosa, stypheloides
Myoporum insulare
Pittosporum undulatum
Westringia fruiticosa

WINDBREAKS IN SUBTROPICAL AND TROPICAL CLIMATES

Acacia (various species)
Acmena smithii (syn. *Eugenia smithii*)
Allocasuarina (most species)
Angophora costata
Araucaria cunninghamii, heterophylla
Archontophoenix alexandrae
Backhousia citriodora, myrtifolia
Banksia integrifolia
Brachychyton acerifolius, populus
Buckinghamia celsissima
Callistemon formosus, viminalis
Callitris collumellaris
Castenospermum australe
Cupaniopsis anacardioides
Eucalyptus tereticornis, tessellaris
Flindersia
Grevillea robusta
Harpullia pendula

Hibiscus tiliaceus
Leptospermum polygalifolium (syn. *L.flavescens*
Melaleuca leucadendron, linariifolia
Melia azaderach
Pittosporum revolutum, rhombifolium, undulatum
Pleiogynuim timoriense
Podocarpus elatus
Syzygium (many species)
Vitex ovata

SCENTED NATIVE PLANTS

Trees

Actinostrobus pyramidalis
Albizzia lebbeck
Anetholea anisata (syn. *Backhousia anisata*)
Angophora hispida, subvelutina
Backhousia, angustifolia, citriodora
Buckinghamia celcissima
Cananga odorata
Choricarpia leptopetala
Doryphora sassafras
Eleocarpus reticulatus
Eucalyptus (most but some more so than others)
Hymenosporum flavum
Flindersia (most species)
Mimusops elengi
Pittosporum undulatum
Randia (all species)
Stenocarpus salignus
Toona ciliata (syn. *T. australis*)

Shrubs

Acacia cardiophylla, dealbata, floribunda, mearnsii, pendula, suaveolens
Boronia (most species)
Bursaria incana, spinosa
Callistemon (most species)
Calothamnus (most species)
Darwinia citriodora
Eremophila mitchellii
Eriostemon (most species)
Gardenia megasperma
Grevillea australis, buxifolia, leucopteris, prostrata, tridentifera
Hakea drupacea (syn. *H. suaveolens*), *nodosa, plurinervia, varia*
Homoranthus flavescens
Kunzea ambigua
Leptospermum petersonii (syn *L. citratum*)
Lomatia arborescens
Melaleuca (many species)
Murraya ovatifoliolata
Olearia (most but not always attractive)
Orites fragrans
Pavetta australiensis
Phaleria chermsideana, clerodendron
Prostanthera (most species)
Randia (all species)
Zieria (all)

Groundcovers and small shrubs

Centipeda minima
Cymbopogon ambiguus
Dendrobium kingianum
Dichopogon fimbriatus
Grevillea curviloba
Hibbertia scandens
Homoranthus flavescens
Hypocalymma angustifolium
Indigofera australis
Lomandra longifolia
Mentha diemenica, laxiflora
Plectranthus argenteus, parviflorus
Sowerbaea juncea

Climbers

Clematis aristata, glycinoides
Faradaya splendida
Jasminum calcareum, lineare, suavissimum, volubile
Hoya australis, macgillivrayi
Morinda jasminoides
Rauwenhoffia leichhardtii

SOME PLANTS THAT FLOWER FOR EXTENDED PERIODS

Astartea fascicularis
Boronia denticulata
Brachyscome multifida

Callistemon (selected species)
Chrysocephalum
Correa alba
Crowea exalata
Darwinia citriodora
Grevillea (many species)
Leschenaultia formosa
Viola hederacea
Xerochrysum

POPULAR NATIVE CLIMBING PLANTS

For cooler climates

Billardiera bicolor, scandens, cymosa
Clematis aristata, microphylla (not in Western Australia)
Desmodium varians
Hardenbergia violacea
Kennedya rubicunda, nigricans
Muehlenbeckia adpressa
Pandorea pandorana
Sollya heterophylla

For dry inland

Cassia retusa
Clematis microphylla (not in Western Australia)
Jasminum didymun, linare
Parsonsia eucalyptophylla
Ipomea mulleri

For northern Australia (moist conditions preferred)

Abelmoschus moschatus
Ceropigia cunninghamiana
Cissus antarctica
Dioscorea reticulata
Dischidia
Faradaya splendida
Hoya australis, macgillvrayii, rubida
Hibbertia scandens, dentata
Ipomea digitata
Jasminum suavissimum
Kennedya retorsa, procurrens
Passiflora herbertiana

PLANTS FOR COASTAL CONDITIONS

Small shrubs requiring moderate protection (up to 1.5 metres)

Agonis flexuosa 'Nana'
Anigozanthos flavidus
Brachyscome iberidifolia
Correa decumbens, reflexa
Crowea exalata
Dampiera hederacea
Dianella revoluta
Epacris longiflora
Grevillea banskii (prostrate form), *thelemanniana*
Hibbertia cuneata
Melaleuca incana, nana
Pimelea ferruginea
Thryptomene saxicola
Xanthorrhea minor
Xerochrysum bracteatum

Small plants for exposed coastal conditions (up to 1.5 metres)

Acacia terminalis (prostrate form)
Banskia marginata (small and large forms available), *robur, spinulosa*
Bauera rubiodes
Brachysema lanceolatum
Calocephalus brownii
Calothamnus quadrifidus (low-growing form)
Carprobrotus rossii
Cassia nemophila
Grevillea fasiculata, lanigera
Hardenbergia violacea (bushy form)
Hovea acutifolia
Ipomoea
Leptospermum juniperinum 'Horizontalis', *sericeum*
Myoporum parvifolium
Senna artemisioides (syn. *Cassia artemisioides*)
Westringia

Medium to large shrubs requiring moderate protection (1.5–5 metres)

Acacia aneura, floribunda, iteaphylla, littorea, myrtifolia, pravissima, saligna

1 *Acacia dealbata* (page 99)

2 *Acacia pycnantha* (page 100)

3 *Angonis flexuosa* (page 104)

4 *Anigozanthos pulcherrimus* (page 111)

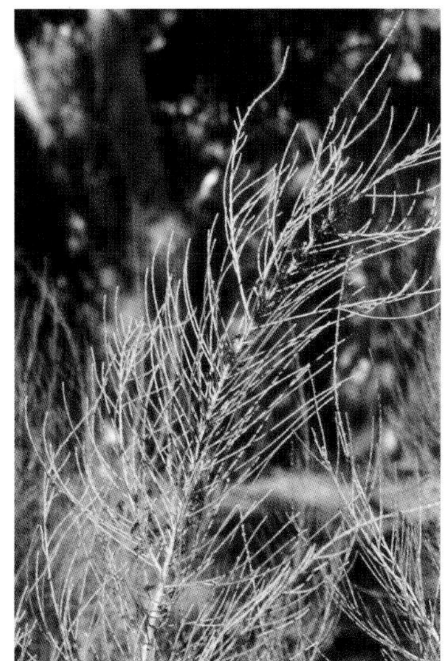

5 *Allocasuarina diminuta* (page 106)

6 *Astartea heteranthera* (page 112)

7 *Astrolasia asteriscophora* (page 113)

8 *Banksia menziesii* (page 118)

9 *Banksia conferta* (page 118)

10 *Banksia spinulosa* (page 118)

11 *Baeckea virgata* (page 117)

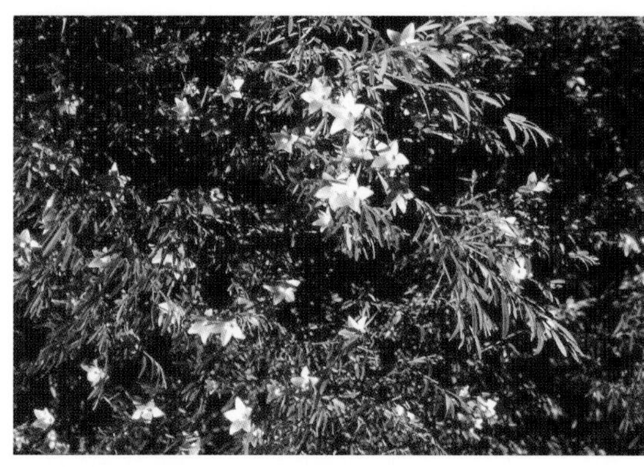

12 *Boronia crenulata* (page 121)

13 *Callistemon* 'Little John' (page 127)

14 *Callistemon comboynensis* (page 128)

15 *Chamelaucium axillare* (page 135)

16 *Choricarpia leptopetala* (page 136)

17 *Correa reflexa* (page 139)

18 *Crowea saligna* (page 141)

19 *Dampiera lavandulacea* (page 143)

20 *Dianella caerulea* (page 146)

21 *Dichondra repens* (page 146)

22 *Epacris impressa* (page 152)

23 *Eucalyptus ptychocarpa* (page 158)

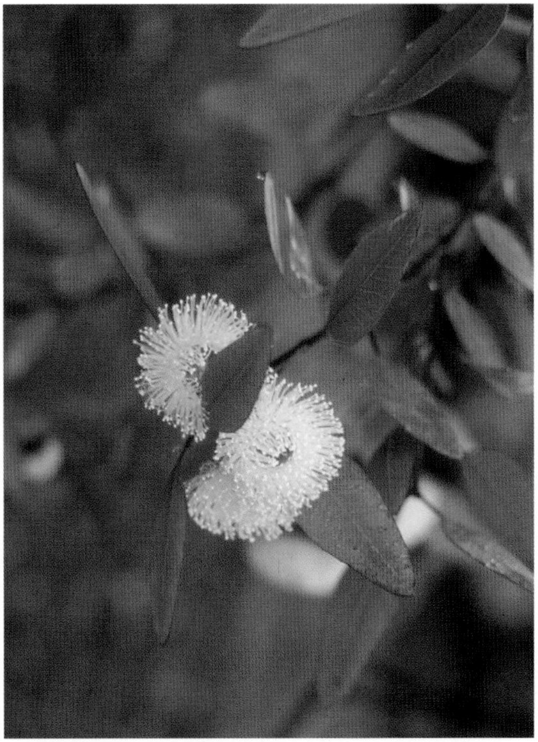

24 *Eucalyptus preissiana* (page 158)

25 *Eucalyptus torquata* (page 159)

27 *Grevillea bipinnatifida* (page 167)

26 *Eutaxia obovata* (page 161)

28 *Grevillea* 'Crosbie Morrison' (page 167)

29 *Grevillea* 'Poorinda Queen' (page 169)

30 *Hakea sericea* (page 172)

31 *Hakea petiolaris* (page 172)

32 *Helichrysum baxteri* (page 174)

33 *Hibbertia empetrifolia* (page 175)

34 *Hovea rosmarinifolia* (page 178)

35 *Hymenosporum flavum* (page 178)

36 *Kingia australis* (page 182)

37 *Kunzea ambigua* (page 183)

38 *Lambertia inermis* (page 184)

39 *Leptospermum laevigatum* (page 187)

40 *Leptospermum squarrosum* (page 188)

41 *Malaleuca elliptica* (page 194)

42 *Myoporum floribundum* (page 200)

43 *Olearia rudis* (page 201)

44 *Oxylobium ellipticum* (page 203)

45 *Phebalium elatius* (page 209)

46 *Prostanthera denticulata* (page 215)

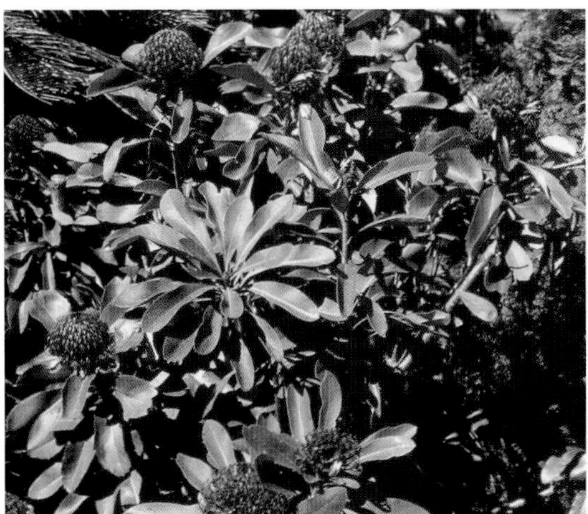

47 *Telopea speciosissima* (page 230)

48 *Tetratheca thymifolia* (page 231)

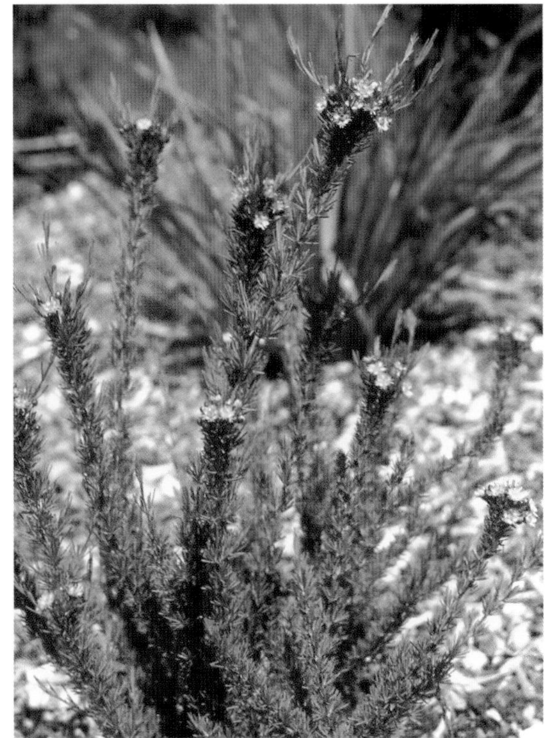

49 *Verticordia plumosa* (page 235)

50 *Xanthostemon chrysanthus* (page 238)

Banskia ericifolia, serrata
Callistemon 'Harkness', various species
Grevillea 'Clearview David', many species
Hakea bucculenta, laurina, salicifolia (syn. *H.saligna*), *victoriae*
Pittosporum tobira
Prostranthera ovalifolia

Medium to large shrubs for exposed coastal gardens (1.5–5 metres)

Acacia cyclops, suaveolens, truncata
Atriplex cinerea
Banskia media, praemorsa, verticillata
Callistemon 'Kings Park Special', *speciosus*
Correa alba
Grevillea 'Coastal Glow'
Hakea drupacea (syn *H. suaveolens*), *sericea*
Kunzea baxteri
Leptospermum
Melaleuca alternifolia, armillaris, bracteata, diosmifolia, hypericifolia, linariifolia, nesophila
Myoporum acuminatum
Westringia fruiticosa

Trees for coastal gardens (* requires moderate protection)

*Acacia baileyana *, crassicarpa, fimbriata *, floribunda *, longifolia* var. *sophorae*
Agonis flexuosa
Allocasuarina litoralis (syn. *Casuarina litoralis*)
Angophora costata, floribunda
Araucaria cunninghamii, heterophylla
Banskia integrifolia, serrata
Brachychyton populneus
Callitris preissii, columellaris
Casuarina glauca
Cassia brewsteri
Corymbia calophylla, citriodora* (syn. *Euclayptus citriodora*)*, *ficifolia* (syn. *Eucalyptus ficifolia*)*
Cupaniopsis anacardioides
Eucalyptus acmenoides, botryoides, camaldulensis, conferruminata (syn. *lehmannii*), *curtisii, diversifolia, kitsonia*, leucoxylon, punctata, robusta, rugosa, tereticornis, tessellaris*
Grevillea robusta
Hibiscus tiliaceus
Leptospermum laevigatum
Lothostemon confertus (syn. *Tristania confertus*)
Melaleuca styphelioides, viridiflora
Melia azaderach var. *australasica* (deciduous)
Pittosporum undulatum
Tristaniopsis laurina (syn. *Tristania laurina*)

Climbers (* requires moderate protection)

Clematis microphylla (not allowed in Western Australia)
Hardenbergia comptoniana
Hibbertia scandens
Hoya australis
Ipomea brasiliensis
Kennedia nigricans, rubicunda**
Muehlenbeckia adpressa
*Pandorea jasminoides**
*Sollya heterophylla**

PLANTS FOR LIME SOILS

Shrubs

Atriplex nummularia
Banksia ashbyi, ornata
Brachychiton populneus
Brachyscome iberidifolia, lanceolatum
Callistemon 'Harkness Hybrid'
Calothamnus quadrifidus
Casuarina humilis
Chamaelaucium uncinatum
Correa alba, decumbens, mannii
Diplolaena (most species)
Epacris impressa
Eremophila glabra
Grevillea ilicifolia (note: most grevilleas are not suitable), *leucopteris, pauciflora, vestita*
Leptospermum laevigatum
Leucophyta brownii (syn. *Calocephalus brownii*)
Melaleuca armillaris, hypericifolia, nesophila, nodosa, wilsonii
Myoporum insulare
Pittosporum

Rhagodia sp.
Swainsonia formosa (formerly *Clianthus formosus*)

Trees

Acacia aneura, baileyana, crassicarpa, pendula
Allocasuarina cristata, equisetifolia
Araucaria heterophylla
Banksia (most Western Australian species)
Brachychyton populneus, rupestris
Cassia brewsteri
Casuarina cristata, glauca
Eucalyptus camaldulensis, cladocalyx nana, conica, crebra, forrestiana, gomphocephala, lehmannii, leucoxylon rosea, melliodora, moluccana, papuana, platypus, tereticornis, tessellaris
Hibiscus tiliaceus
Lysiphyllum hookeri
Meleleuca leucadendra
Melia azaderach var. *australasicus*
Pittosporum phillyraeoides

PLANTS RESISTANT TO INNER-CITY POLLUTION

Trees

Acacia floribunda, longifolia, melanoxylon, pycnantha
Allocasuarina (many species)
Corymbia ficifolia (syn. *Eucalyptus ficifolia*)
Eucalyptus globulus compacta, ovata, torquata
Ficus macrophylla
Flindersia australis
Harpullia pendula
Melaleuca linariifolia, styphelioides
Pittosporum phyllyraeoides, undulatum
Pleiogynuim timoriense
Syzygium luehmannii

Shrubs

Acacia iteaphylla, retinoides
Actinostrobus pyramidalis
Callistemon citrinus, salignus
Calothamnus quadrifidus
Casuarina distyla
Grevillea rosmarinifolia
Hakea drupacea (syn. *H.suaveolens*), *sericea, salicifolia* (syn. *H. saligna*),
Leptospermum scoparium
Melaleuca armillaris, decussata, incana, wilsonii
Myoporum insulare

Native conifers

Conifers are not a major component of Australian flora; nevertheless there are some important native conifers. There are 9 genera and about 35 species of conifers, to be precise. Habitat preferences for these conifers are quite diverse, ranging from dry inland areas (such as *Callitris* sp.) to temperate coastal regions (*Araucaria* sp.), to cold mountain climates (*Podocarpus* sp.). Australian conifers are grouped in the following genera:

FROM THE CUPPRESSACEAE FAMILY:
Callitris (16 species), *Actinostrobus* (3 species) and *Diselma* (1 species)

FROM THE ARAUCARIACEAE FAMILY:
Araucaria (2 species) and *Agathis* (3 species) Australian species of these two genera are found in Queensland and northern New South Wales.

FROM THE PODOCARPACEAE FAMILY:
Around 11 species in the genera *Lagarostrobus* (syn. *Dacrydium*), *Microcachrys*, *Microstrobus*, *Phyllocladus* (these genera are principally found in Tasmania) and *Podocarpus* (eastern states).

FROM THE TAXODIACEAE FAMILY:
Three species of *Athrotaxus*, all from Tasmania.

The only genus that occurs naturally over a large part of Australia is *Callitris*. *Araucaria* and *Callitris* are the only native conifers that are grown widely in gardens around Australia.

Some native conifers to grow

Actinostrobus ❧ Cupressaceae

Small trees and shrubs from south-west Western Australia. They are densely branched and leaves are small and scale-like. They occur naturally on sandy soils, though *A. pyramidalis* adapts well to a much wider variety of soils and climates. Normally they are propagated by seed. Remove cones when ripe, put in a warm dry place and they will open naturally dropping their seed. Plant the seeds straightaway. Cuttings and grafting are also possible.

A. acuminatus Shrub 1–3-metre tall, green foliage; can be grown on a wide variety of soils; particularly suited to arid areas.

A. arenarius Shrub or small tree up to 5 metres tall; blue-green foliage; grows well on sandy soil in full or filtered sun.

A. pyramidalis Small tree or shrub up to 8 metres tall; by far the most commonly grown species; adapts to most soils; tolerates mild frosts, withstands periods of wet soil.

Athrotaxus ❧ Taxodiaceae

Slow growing, medium to tall trees with attractive foliage. When young, a cool temperate climate is preferred, with moist fertile soil with compost or mulch. Propagate from cuttings, soaked 24 hours in very weak solution of IBA hormone, or by seed.

A. cupressoides Narrow tree, up to 15 metres tall; small leaves.

A. laxifolia Tree up to 10 metres tall; more spreading than *A. cupressoides*.

A. selaginoides Tree up to 40 metres tall; cone-shaped.

Agathis ❧ Araucariaceae

There are 3 endemic species in this genus. They are large trees with distinctive scaly, dark brown bark. They are attractive specimen trees in frost-free coastal areas.

A. robusta (Queensland kauri) A tall, straight tree up to 50 metres tall. This is the most commonly grown species. Bark is dark brown and well marked. Often used in parks and large gardens in Queensland; also makes an attractive indoor pot specimen when young.

Araucaria ❧ Araucariaceae

Araucarias come from Australia, South America and the Pacific islands. Two species occur naturally on the Australian mainland: *A. cunninghamii* and *A. bidwilli*. The most commonly grown species is *Araucaria heterophylla*, the well-known native pine of Norfolk Island.

All are large majestic, symmetrical trees, best suited to large gardens or parks. They are hardy and tolerate moist soil and salt spray (they are particularly suited to coastal planting). Their timber is commercially valued. They respond well to fertile soils and watering during dry periods. They are slow growing but will survive in poor conditions. Propagation is by seed but the seed should be fresh.

A. bidwilli (bunya pine) A tall, erect tree to 40 metres. Branch arrangement is very symmetrical; bark is rough and dark-coloured. Cones are very large, 30 x 20 cm. Seeds are edible. Natural distribution is coastal districts in Queensland.

An imposing tree for coastal plantings, although care needs to be taken in choosing planting positions as the tree sheds prickly leaves and branchlets, which can be a nuisance, and the large cones can be dangerous when they fall. It is frost hardy.

A. cunninghamii (hoop pine) A tall, straight tree to 40 m. Leaves are narrow and inward curving to 1 cm. Cones are about 8 cm long. It is distributed in rainforests from northern New South Wales to Cape York in Queensland. A fast-growing tree, it is often used in forestry plantations which receive high rainfall. Also frequently used as indoor pot specimens.

Callitris ✻ Cupressaceae

Hardy large shrubs to medium-sized trees which typically have a compact column-shaped habit (very similar to the exotic cypress pines). There are 16 species in Australia, which are largely distributed in the drier inland areas of the continent. They are faster growing than most conifers and are hardy and generally drought tolerant. They are often used to create a more formal effect in native gardens.

Most grow in dry conditions, some in wetter coastal areas. Soils must be well drained; most tolerate frost and prefer filtered sun. Propagated easily by seed — cuttings are very slow to strike.

C. baileyi Up to 5 metres tall, bright green foliage, native to coastal rainforests of northern New South Wales and Queensland.

C. canescens Up to 6 metres tall, hardy, best suited to poor soils and coastal areas.

C. columellaris (coastal or white cypress) Up to 20 metres tall, one of the more commonly grown varieties; dark bluish-green foliage, brown-grey furrowed bark, pyramid shape, hardy. Found in all states except Tasmania.

C. endlicheri (black cypress pine) Small upright conical tree 5–20 metres tall, green or blue-green foliage, very hardy, occurring naturally on sandy or stony soils from Victoria to Queensland. The timber is commercially valuable.

C. hugelii (syn. *C. glauca*) (Murray pine) Tree 15–30 metres tall, varies in shape and foliage colour, very hardy shade or windbreak tree, but must have good drainage.

C. oblonga Tall shrub 2–7 metres tall, blue-green foliage, hardy, but best suited to cooler climates.

C. preissii Slender tree 10–20 metres tall, grey bark, best on sandy soils, tolerates calcareous soils and salt winds.

C. rhomboidea (Port Jackson pine) Erect columnar habit up to 6 metres tall; hardy, tolerating poor soils and coastal conditions. Occurs naturally in South Australia, Tasmania, Victoria, New South Wales and Queensland. It prefers moist conditions.

Podocarpus ✻ Podocarpaceae

There are over 100 species in this genus, most of which are found in the Southern Hemisphere. Seven species occur in Australia, ranging in size from small shrubs to trees. Their appearance is quite different to the typical conifer: bark is fibrous, leaves are simple with a prominent mid-vein, and the female plants bear showy fruit.

P. lawrencei (mountain plum pine) Size is very variable, depending on habitat. Tree-sized plants are found in lower mountain altitudes, but above the tree-line they appear as sprawling shrubs. They prefer well-mulched soils in sun or part shade.

Native ferns

Ferns have been around for millions of years. They do not have flowers or fruits but they do have stems, roots and leaves (fronds). The stem (rhizome) is often below the ground and insignificant. From the stem grow numerous leaves and wiry roots. They reproduce from spores.

About 450 Australian fern species are found, predominantly in the moister parts of the continent, with the largest percentage along the eastern coast, in the south-east and Tasmania, with a few extending to drier inland areas. They are found in a variety of situations, such as tropical rainforests (often growing as epiphytes on trees and rocks), in gullies in cool southern forests, in sub-alpine areas, in exposed coastal areas and tropical mangrove swamps, and in crevices in rocky outcrops in dry inland areas.

They can be found growing as epiphytes, as aquatics (floating ferns such as *Azolla*) and as terrestrials (growing in the ground). They vary in form from tiny filmy ferns, such as *Hymenophyllum*, to tall, woody-trunked species, such as *Cyathea* and *Dicksonia*, from spreading plants that form large colonies (*Pteridium*, *Culcita*, *Histiopteris*) to single tuft-like plants, and to climbers and scramblers (*Gleichenia*).

GROWING FERNS

As a general guide consider the following:

- Provide protection from direct sun and wind.
- Keep moist on hot or windy days
- Mulch the soil to reduce drying out.
- Soil should have high content of organic matter. Avoid sands. Heavy subsoil or clay must be mixed with organic matter and sand to become friable (i.e. loose).
- Eastern or southerly aspects are preferred with plants planted beside a wall or fence. In hot northern or inland areas full shade and frequent watering (several times each day) may be necessary to achieve success with even the hardier varieties.
- Severe frosts can burn unprotected fronds.
- The most common pest and disease problems are aphis, scale, mealy bug, white fly, slugs and snails, leafhoppers and caterpillars.
- Spreading ferns may need to be kept contained in a container of some sort to prevent them taking over parts of your garden.
- Most ferns prefer slightly acidic to acidic soils — only a few actually prefer alkaline conditions.

HINTS

- Some ferns, such as maidenhairs, commonly die back to ground level. Don't throw them away; they will regrow.
- Ferns are ideal in hanging baskets. Some epiphytic types can be grown on tree trunks or timber slabs hung on a wall. Ferns grown these ways are highly susceptible to drying out and should be taken down and placed amongst other plants during warm periods.
- Ferns grown in tubs, baskets or pots should be potted up in fresh soil each spring. An ideal soil would be:
  1 part coarse sand
  1 part peat moss
  1 part well-rotted manure.

Adiantum (maidenhair fern)
Adiantaceae

Generally delicate-looking ferns from moist areas, such as stream banks, amongst rocks and rainforests. They are creeping ferns forming small clumps, sometimes spreading over large areas. They are generally hardy, sometimes drought tolerant and fast growers under suitable conditions. Tropical species require warm conditions and high humidity. Most prefer ample water during warm months

ADIANTUM SPECIES	HEIGHT	FRONDS
A. aethiopicum Common maidenhair	Up to 0.8 m	3–4 pinnate
A. capillus-veneris European maidenhair	0.3–0.6 m	2–3 pinnate
A. cunninhamii Large maidenhair	Up to 1 m	2–3 pinnate
A. diaphanum Filmy maidenhair	Up to 0.3 m	1–2 pinnate
A. formosum Giant maidenhair	Up to 1.5 m	3–4 pinnate
A. hispidulum Rough maidenhair	Up to 0.5 m	2–3 pinnate

but should have little water during winter. They are usually heavy feeders and respond well to regular small doses of fertiliser. Many make excellent pot plants but potting mixes should be well drained, with an acid pH.

Asplenium (spleenwort) Aspleniaceae

The spleenworts are a widespread and varied group of ferns from a variety of habitats. They can be epiphytes or terrestrials and form clumps of various sizes. Fronds are usually simple or 1–3 times divided, usually green, often shiny. Some produce bulbils on mature fronds. They are generally fast growing, some are very hardy. Excess moisture can cause yellowing in periods of slow growth, and direct sun should be avoided.

Azolla (water ferns) Salviniaceae

Small aquatic ferns from mainly warm climates that float freely on the surface of water. They are hardy, often very fast growing and can become a weed. Their small moss-like fronds can turn reddish in full sun. They live in a symbiotic relationship with a blue-green algae

ASPLENIUM SPECIES	HEIGHT	FRONDS	COMMENTS
A. aethiopicum Shredded spleenwort	0.3–1 m	Semi-erect, bipinnate	Resents disturbance; protected, shady position
A. australasicum Birds nest fern	Up to 2 m	Long, broad	Popular garden specimen for shaded positions
Mother spleenwort	1.2 m	2–3 pinnate	Bulblets form on tips of leaves
A. falcatum Sickle spleenwort	Up to 1 m	1–2 pinnate	Also known as *A. polyodon*
A. flaccidum Weeping spleenwort	Up to 1 m	2 pinnate	Excellent in hanging basket
A. flabellifolium Necklace fern	0.3 m	1 pinnate	Normally pale green; a drooping habit
A. hookerianum Maidenhair spleenwort	0.2 m	1–2 pinnate	Very cold resistant
A. nidus Birds-nest fern	2 m	Simple	Tropical species sometimes confused with the more commonly grown *A. australasicum*
A. obtusatum Shore spleenwort	0.3 m	1 pinnate, fleshy	Grows on coast among rocks
A. trichomanes Common spleenwort	0.2 m	1 pinnate	Grows at higher altitudes
Note: Hybrids are common			

BLECHNUM SPECIES	HEIGHT	HARDINESS	GENERAL
B. articulatum Rosy water fern	0.5–1 m	Hardy	Slow growing, needs mulching
B. capense Palm leaf fern	Up to 3 m	Very	Needs wet acidic soil
B. cartilagineum Gristle fern	1.5 m	Very	Young growth bronze
B. fluviatile Ray water fern	Up to 0.5 m	Hardy	Needs shaded moist position
B. minus Soft water fern	2 m	Very hardy if wet	Tuft forming, needs wet soil, tolerates cold and direct sun
B. nudum Fishbone fern	1.2 m	Medium	Needs shade, moisture and acidic soil
B. orientale Tropical water fern	1.2 m	Very	Needs warm moist conditions
B. patersonii Strap water fern	0.5 m	Medium	Needs shade and water
B. watsii Soft water fern	1.2 m	Very	Semi-protected site

(*Anabaera azolla*). They will grow in mild temperate climates and can be grown as a water plant in ornamental ponds. They won't grow in fresh water (for example, tap water) as there will be none of the blue-green algae required for symbiosis present.

A. filiculoides Frequently reddish, occur commonly, fragment easily; hardy and easily grown.

A. pinnata Moss-like, occur commonly, free floating, not so hardy in the cold.

Blechnum (water ferns) Blechnaceae

Widespread, hardy clump-forming ferns from tropical and temperate regions. Some spread by rhizomes, most are terrestrial. Fronds are normally pinnate resembling the fronds of fishbone ferns, but can be lobed or undivided. New growth on some species is often an attractive bronze or pink in colour. Most are easy to cultivate, preferring shade, moist root zones, dry atmospheres and mild to warm conditions. They are suited to growing in containers.

Cheilanthes (rock ferns) Adiantaceae

Rock ferns are small, hardy, drought-resistant ferns from warm climates in inland areas, preferring rocky situations. They have creeping rhizomes and small finely divided fronds with a covering of scales or hairs. Their growth rate is medium to fast and they prefer moist soil while growing and good drainage. Some withstand, or even prefer, dryness during a dormant period, and many prefer lower humidity than the average fern.

CHEILANTHES SPECIES	HEIGHT	FRONDS
C. distans	Up to 0.3 m	2 pinnate, hairy
C. hirsute	Up to 0.1 m	2 pinnate thin fronds
C. lasiophylla	Up to 0.2 m	Very hairy
C. sieberi	Up to 0.4 m	2 to 3 pinnate, hairless

Davallia (hare's foot/rabbit's foot) Davalliaceae

Small ferns with long, scale-covered rhizomes that are mainly epiphytic. They make an excellent pot, slab or hanging basket fern. They are generally hardy, but usually require frost protection. They prefer mild to warm conditions and need heavy watering during active growth periods, but greatly reduced watering over winter.

DAVALLIA SPECIES	HEIGHT	FRONDS	GENERAL
D. denticulata	To 1 m	3 pinnate	Needs greenhouse in cool climates, deciduous over winter
D. pyxidata	To 0.8 m	2–3 pinnate	Easy to grow
D. solida	To 1 m	3–4 pinnate	Needs greenhouse in cool climates

Doodia (rasp ferns) Polypodiaceae

These are dwarf ferns with short scaly rhizomes from wet forests in tropical and temperate areas. They are hardy and generally medium to fast growing. Fronds are normally rough textured and often an attractive pink sheen when young. They prefer shaded, moist, cool to mild conditions and grow well among rocks.

D. aspera (prickly rasp fern) New growth attractive pink

D. caudata (small rasp fern) Hardy, attractive young pink fronds

D. media (common rasp fern) New growth attractive red colour

D.s quarrosa Easily grown in protected moist situations.

Marattia (potato fern) Marrattiaceae

Marattia salicina is a large, impressive fern up to 4 metres tall with thick fleshy bipinnate fronds from tropical Queensland. It is hardy but can be damaged by frost when young. It needs a sheltered, moist position, preferring warmth and high humidity, and can be grown as far south as Melbourne.

Marsilea (water clover or nardoo) Marsileaceae

Marsileas are hardy aquatic and bog ferns from the tropics and subtropics that float in deep water or root into the mud in shallow water. They have fronds like a four-leaved clover. They can be readily grown in mud in a pond or in a pot immersed in water. *M. drummondii* is the most commonly grown variety.

Microsorium Polypodiaceae

Microsoriums are small creeping ferns that grow generally as epiphytes on trees, rocks or other ferns. Their fronds are simple, generally strap-like or lobed, and glossy green. They grow in tropical to cool climates, generally preferring warm conditions although varieties from southern Australia will withstand much cooler conditions. They like good ventilation and medium to high humidity. They are easy to grow and are widely grown as basket or pot plants.

M. diversifolium (kangaroo fern) For cool to temperate climates

M. punctatum For tropical and subtropical conditions

M. scandens (fragrant fern) Scrambling fern for cool to mild conditions.

Nephrolepis (sword fern/fishbone) Oleandraceae

Nephrolepis are generally hardy ferns with creeping rhizomes that produce masses of tufts. They are generally fast growing, hardy terrestrial growers with some epiphytes. Found in the tropics and subtropics in dry open forests or on the edge of rainforests. They prefer lots of water in warmer months and protection from frosts. Some make excellent indoor plants.

N. cordifolia Up to 1 metre, very hardy, adapts to most situations

N. hirsutula Up to 1.8 metres, large fronds, frost tender.

Pellaea (sickle fern) ❧ Adiantaceae

Pelleae falcata is a hardy, small creeping fern that prefers rocky places in open forests, often forming large colonies. It is sometimes found in coastal dune areas. It has leathery green pinnate fronds that are often hooked like a shepherd's crook when young. It is easily grown in a pot or in the ground, and will withstand fairly sunny conditions.

Platycerium (staghorn/elkhorn) ❧ Polypodiaceae

Platyceriums are small epiphytes from tropical and subtropical areas that often produce big clumps of generally drooping but sometimes upright fronds. They are generally hardy, medium to fast growers, preferring warm conditions, filtered light and protection from frost. They can be grown as far south as Melbourne. In cool climates, they should be kept fairly dry.

P. bifurcatum The elkorn fern has a brown or green sheath (shield-like) of infertile fronds covering the roots. The fertile grey-green fronds are strap-like with a Y-shaped tip, up to 1 metre in length.

P. superbum The staghorn fern has a green sheath of infertile fronds covering the roots and broader lobed fertile fronds.

These are the two most commonly grown ferns in Australia. They are also two of the most cold-hardy species, being able to survive temperatures to 0°C or even lower.

Polystichum (shield fern) ❧ Aspidiaceae

Polystichum proliferum is a hardy tuft-like fern of cool regions in the south-eastern parts of the mainland and Tasmania. It does best in moist soils with partial shade, but will tolerate sunny conditions. It is easily propagated by the plantlets that form on mature fronds.

Pteris (brake/dish fern/table fern) ❧ Pteridaceae or Polypodiaceae

Generally fast growing, hardy, adaptable, clump-forming terrestrial ferns with pinnate fronds from mainly tropical regions. They grow under a wide variety of conditions. They need lots of water while actively growing and shouldn't be allowed to become pot bound.

P. comans Up to 2 metres tall, likes cool, moist fernery

P. tremula Up to 2 metres tall, hardy fern indoors or out

P. umbrosa Up to 2 metres tall, likes moist, shady conditions and large amounts of mulch

P. vittata Up to 1 metre tall, hardy, likes sunny well-drained position.

Sticherus (fan fern) ❧ Gleicheniaceae

Creeping ferns with long, thin rhizomes, mainly from watercourses or dry embankments in warm rainforests to dry forests. They are moderately hardy and slow growing. Their fronds are fan-shaped. They grow best in wet, semi-exposed conditions, but shouldn't be fertilised. They resent root disturbance.

S. flabellatus 1–4 tiers of umbrella-like pinnae, up to 2 metres tall, prefers semi-shade

S. lobatus Fan-shaped fronds, up to 2 metres tall, takes some sun

S. tener 1–4 tiers of umbrella-like pinnae, up to 2 metres tall, dislikes disturbance.

Todea (king fern) ❧ Osmundaceae

Todea barbara is an attractive, hardy, clump-like fern that forms short, often massive trunks. It has tough leathery fronds and is found in very wet sites, such as rainforests, gullies and streams. It grows well in moist garden sites or in well-watered containers, and will tolerate some sun.

Tree ferns

Tree ferns are best obtained as spore-grown plants. These can be transplanted easily from containers and will readily establish. *Dicksonia antarctica* (soft tree fern) supplied as sawn-off trunks are generally easy to establish. *Cyathea australis* (rough tree fern) does not easily establish by sawn-off trunks. Only transplant large tree ferns when absolutely necessary, and try to retain as much of the roots as possible. Trim back the fronds at transplanting to compensate for the loss of roots.

Tree ferns must be kept moist by watering with a slowly dripping hose in the crown of the plant. Do not allow them to dry out.

Cyathea ❧ Cyatheaceae

Cyathea australis (rough tree fern)
Up to 15 metres tall, common in southern and eastern Australia, in shaded fern gullies.

Cyathea cunninghamii (slender tree fern)
Up to 20 metres tall, with lots of roots coming from lower parts of trunk, small crown, usually grows only in deep wet gullies.

Dicksonia ❧ Dicksoniaceae

Dicksonia antarctica (soft tree fern)
From 2 to 12 metres tall, with tall, large crown, and dark thick trunk. Requires deep, fertile moist soil, shaded gullies or wet slopes. Less tolerant of dry spells than *Cyathea*.

Palms and cycads

Palms are narrow-leafed flowering plants belonging to the Palmae family.

Cycads are primitive cone-bearing plants which look similar to palms in their growth, but are in fact related to conifers. They have generally straight unbranched trunks terminating in a crown of pinnate leaves or fronds. Flowers and fruit are borne in cones, with male and female flowers found in separate cones, which may be on separate plants or in different locations on the same plant.

AUSTRALIAN CYCADS

Australian cycads belong to two related families. The Cycadacea family contains 11 Australian species in the genus *Cycas*. The Zamiaceae family contains 16 species in the genus *Macrozamia*, two species in the Bowenia genus, and two species in the Lepidozamia genus. They are found throughout the northern and central parts of Australia.

Macrozamia ❧ Zamiaceae

All need good drainage, are very slow growing, but live for hundreds, even thousands of years. All are propagated by seed. They may be attacked by scale insects on the leaves, and borers in the trunks. They make excellent feature plants in your garden or excellent tub plants.

M. communis Up to 3 metres in diameter and 2 metres tall, needs some shade.

M. peroffskyana Reaches 5 metres high after about 500 years.

M. readlei Up to 2 metres in diameter, the only species from Western Australia.

M. spiralis Little or no trunk, up to 2 metres in diameter, full sun or part shade.

M. suaveolens Height and spread varies greatly. Adapts to most soils, but needs moisture.

Cycas ❧ Cycadaceae

Slender to thick woody trunks with spreading palm-like crowns at the apex of the trunk. Popular as specimen plants and as tub plants. They are hardy but slow growing. Propagation from seed, which may be slow to germinate. Fresh seed and bottom heat generally give better results.

C. media Thick fire-resistant trunk, up to 2 metres or more tall. Seeds are poisonous. Good feature plant. Hardy, drought resistant and adaptable but needs good drainage and preferably full sun. It is frost hardy and can be grown in southern Australia.

AUSTRALIAN PALMS

Generally from the warmer parts of Australia, palms usually require heat and humidity. Most prefer moist but well-drained soil. Many can be grown in full sun if given adequate moisture, although most prefer filtered or dappled sunlight. Some adapt well to growing in the southern states. Propagation is by seed.

Many palms are adaptable to indoor environments for short periods. They must, however, at some time be taken outdoors to rest and recoup.

With over 40 species of palms native to Australia, the following list provides a small selection.

Many of the palms listed below are readily available at nurseries, although some species may only be available through specialist growers.

Other natives

The list on the next page provides a quick thumbnail sketch of a range of additional Australian plant genera that are not described elsewhere in this book, but which are in cultivation.

PALM VARIETIES	NATIVE TO	HEIGHT	COMMENTS
Archontophoenix alexandrae Alexander palm	Qld	5–20 m	Tapers in from a thick base
A. cunninghamiana Bangalow palm or Piccabean	NSW and Qld	4–20 m	Smooth and straight
Arenga australasica Native sugar palm	Qld	Up to 10 m	Elegant multiple trunks
Calamus (many sp.) Lawyer cane palms	Qld	Climbing	Spiny foliage
Carpentaria acuminata Carpentaria palm	NT	Up to 12 m	Slender single trunk
Howea forsteriana Kentia palm	Lord Howe Island	Up to 8 m	Elegant smooth trunk
Laccospadix australasica Atherton palm	Qld	1–3 m	Slim and delicate, single or multiple
Licuala ramsayi Queensland fan palm	Qld and NSW	4–10 m	Beautiful large fan-shaped leaves
Linospadix monostachys Walking stick palm	Qld and NSW	1.5–2 m	Graceful, small single stem
Livistonia australis Cabbage tree palm	Vic to Qld	6–30 m	Slender
Livistonia mariae Red cabbage palm	Central Aust.	5–15 m	Retains old fronds
Normanbya normanbyi Black palm	Qld	15–25 m	Tall slender palm
Ptychosperma elegans Solitaire palm	Qld	Up to 10 m	Slim with 3 m-long fronds

KEY

Soils: W = well drained F = fertile Mo = moist P = tolerates poor soils M = most soil types
Size: 2 x 3 m = 2 metres tall, 3 metres in diameter
Growth habit: T = tree ST = small tree SSh = spreading shrub Sh = shrub Cr = creeper Cl = climber Cp = clump
Hardiness: VH = very hardy H = hardy NH = not generally hardy Fr = frost tender D = drought tolerant
BD = tolerates bad drainage Shd = requires shade
Propagation: C = cuttings G = Grafting D = Division S = Seed S (hot) = seed treated with boiling water
S (scarify) = break seed coat with knife or sandpaper

PLANT (GENUS)	FAMILY	GENERAL	CULTURE
Abarema	Mimosaceae	Fluffy flowers, woody pods	W, Mo, 5–20 m, Fr, H, S (Hot)
Alectryon	Sapindaceae	Small to medium trees, pinnate leaves, showy fruits, occurs naturally in NSW and Qld	W, 6–15 m, M, T ,H, S
Alocasia	Araceae	Large spade-shaped leaves, large flower similar to an arum lily, occurs naturally in rainforests in NSW and Qld	F, Mo, to 1.5 m, Cp, R, S
Anopterus	Escalloniaceae	Toothed glossy green leaves, white or pink flowers in spring	T, 5–13 m, F, Shd, C, S
Aotus	Fabaceae	Yellow pea flowers	M, to 1 m, Sh, S (hot)
Archidendron	Mimosaceae	Large attractive flowers	Mo, T, H, S (scarify)
Archirhodomyrtus	Myrtaceae	Fragrant foliage, attractive berries	Mo, T or S, C or S
Argyrodendron	Sterculiaceae	Tall trees, usually buttressed, occurs naturally in NSW and Qld	T, to 40 m, F, S
Athertonia	Proteaceae	Large numbers of small brown flowers	W, F, Mo, Fr, to 20 m
Barklya	Caesalpiniaceae	Yellow pea flowers	M, to 20 m, ST, H, S and G
Bauhinia	Caesalpiniaceae	Red pea flowers, best in subtropics.	W, T, H, Fr, S (hot)
Celmisia	Asteraceae	Small plants with large daisy flowers	W, Mo, Cp, H, S or D
Chorilaena	Rutaceae	Medium shrubs with attractive flowers	Mo, Sh, Shd, H, C
Cinnamomum	Lauraceae	Dense trees, rough bark often fragrant, rainforest areas	T, to 30 x 15 m, F, M, Fr, S
Cissus	Vitaceae	Attractive foliage, used as indoor plants	Mo, Cl, Shd, Fr, C
Commersonia	Sterculiaceae	About 8 native species, starting to be grown	T, ST, Sh, H, S, C
Cryptandra	Rhamnaceae	Small white or pink flowers	Mo, Sh, H, C
Dendrobium	Orchidaceae	Usually epiphytic orchids forming clumps on tree trunks	W, Mo, to 1 m, Cp, H, Fr, Shd, D
Dichopogon	Liliaceae	Perennial tuberous herbs, tufts of soft linear leaves, small lily-like flowers	Cp, H, to 50 x 80 cm, S
Doryphora (Sassafras)	Athero-spermataceae	Tall straight grey trunk, compact crown, dominant in moist forest, a rainforest tree	to 25 x 10 m, Mo, T, Shd, S

Ehretia	Ehretiaceae	Tropical plant with fragrant flowers and attractive fruits	W, Mo, T and Sh
Eupomatia	Eupomatiaceae	Good garden subjects with glossy green leaves and red young growth	ST, Sh, Shd, M, C
Geijera	Rutaceae	Species from arid and wet climates	H, ST and Sh, S and C (often difficult)
Helmholtzia	Philydraceae	Flax-like plant with tall flower spike, occurs naturally in northern rainforests	1.5 m, Cp, F, Mo, S
Hemigenia	Lamiaceae	Very similar to *Hemiandra*, susceptible to cinnamon fungus	W, H to NH, C or G (on Westringia)
Hicksbeachia	Proteaceae	Multi-stemmed, sprays of cream flowers and red fruits, seed is edible, a rainforest tree	ST, F, Mo, 10 m, S
Hoya	Asclepiadaceae	Six Australian species, fragrant flowers	Mo, H, Fr, Cl, C
Isotoma	Lobeliaceae	One creeping species, several annual or perennial (in mild climates), small bushy species	Mo, Cr, annuals, Fr, D, S
Jasminum	Oleaceae	Climbing and semi-climbing plants, mostly yellow or white fragrant flowers	Mo, Cl, H, C
Mackinlaya	Araliaceae	Rainforest shrub, large glossy leaves, yellow flower heads, fleshy blue-grey berries	F, Mo, 1–3 m, Sh, Fr, C
Mentha	Lamiaceae	Suckering plants with aromatic foliage, small white or mauve flowers	M, Mo, 10–50 cm, D or C
Microcitrus	Rutaceae	Fragrant flowers, edible citrus fruits	W, to 8 m, ST or Sh, H, Fr, S, C or G
Orites	Proteaceae	Slow growing, white or cream flowers	W, Mo, Sh or T, S
Parsonsia	Apocynaceae	25 Australian species, fragrant flowers, tropical areas	Mo and S to M, Cl, H, Fr, S (fresh)
Philotheca	Rutaceae	Star-like flowers	W, Sh, H (needs cool roots), C
Poa	Poaceae	Ornamental grasses	M, Cp, H, D
Spyridium	Rhamnaceae	Attractive white leaves occur with tiny flowers	W, SSh or Sh, H to VH, C
Templetonia	Fabaceae	Attractive pea flowers, divided leaves	W, Sh, H, S (scarify)
Zieria	Rutaceae	White or pink flowers, scented leaves	W, Mo, to 4 m, H, Shd, C

7. Using natives

We mostly grow native plants as garden specimens but they have many other valuable domestic and commercial uses. In the home garden, we also grow native plants to attract birds and wildlife. Commercially, native plants are grown for their distinctive flowers, foliage and fruits for the floral industry and for craftspeople. Other useful products from native plants include essential oils, bush tucker and timber.

Bringing wildlife into the garden

Most native gardeners welcome wildlife in their garden. Whether the animals, birds and insects are just passers-by or long-term residents, they add beauty to the garden and create a sense of movement and life.

Of course, they are not just there for our enjoyment. Our wildlife needs native plants for food, shelter, nesting and perching. Native gardens provide a welcome refuge for wildlife and help to redress the loss of habitats in their natural environments.

HOW TO ATTRACT BIRDS

Beyond the obvious entertainment we derive from birds, there is the less obvious advantage that they help control insects and other pests. In order to attract birds to the garden, you need to provide the following:

- A desirable habitat — places to perch and safe places to get away from predators, such as cats.
- Water and food — a birdbath or shallow pond is ideal. For nectar-feeding birds, grow grevilleas, banksias and other nectar-rich native plants that flower a lot and for long periods of time.
- A wide variety of plants — a diverse garden will attract many different types of birds.
- Plants that provide nesting places, particularly shrubby plants and trees.

Bird shelters

An established garden with a diverse range of plants, including mature trees and shrubby plants, will most likely have suitable places for birds to perch and nest. Newer gardens will benefit from nesting boxes — these can be made or purchased from pet suppliers. The box should be securely attached to a tree trunk or fence post. A good bird shelter provides:

- a place to perch
- a clear view and access on all sides, to get in and out and not be cornered by predators
- a place which has restricted access for predators. To deter climbing animals such as rats and possums getting into the box or shelter, put a wide band of metal around the tree trunk or pole, below the shelter.

HOW TO ATTRACT BUTTERFLIES AND NATIVE BEES

Australia has almost 400 species of native butterflies, most of which occur in the subtropics and tropics. They are most active during the daytime in spring and summer. They flit from bush to bush, feeding on nectar-rich plants, searching for a mate, and looking for suitable plants on which to lay eggs.

While the adult butterflies feed on nectar from a wide range of flowering plants, the caterpillars (the larval stage of butterflies) only feed on the leaves of a specific range of food plants — these are sometimes called host plants. The female butterfly lays her eggs on a host plant; when the eggs hatch, the caterpillars eat the leaves on that plant. Most plants quickly recover from caterpillar attack; some even benefit from being 'pruned'.

A butterfly-friendly garden has the following characteristics:

- A wide variety of butterfly-attracting plants, including nectar-rich flowers and specialised caterpillar food plants
- One or more glades or open, sunny spaces, with butterfly food plants around the edges
- Plants flowering in spring, summer and autumn to provide a continuous food supply
- Informal or relatively undisturbed areas in the garden
- White or cream night-scented plants (e.g. *Pittosporum undulatum*) to attract moths
- Avoid the use of chemical insecticides which harm butterflies and their larvae

Some butterfly-attracting plants that can be grown in most areas are:
Brachyscome multifida
Olearia spp.
Pimelia spp.
Thryptomene saxicola
Dianella spp.
Gahnia spp.
Lomandra spp.
Leptospermum lanigerum
Westringia glabra, longifolia
Xerochrysum bracteatum (syn. *Bracteantha bracteata*)

Most people would be surprised to know that Australia is home to more than 1500 species of native bees. Unlike the more visible European honey bees, many native bees are small (the smallest is just 1.5 mm long) and their nests are difficult to find. Native bees play an important role in gardens, pollinating native plants, ornamentals, and fruit and vegetable plants as they collect nectar.

Some native bee-attractive plants are:
Angophora spp.
Brachyscome spp.
Epacris spp.
Grevillea spp.
Persoonia spp.
Hovea spp.
Pultenaea spp.
Goodenia spp.
Leucopogon spp.
Leptospermum spp.
Tristaniopsis laurina
Westringia spp.

ATTRACTING LIZARDS AND OTHER SMALL NATIVE ANIMALS

Diversity and informality are the key ingredients for attracting lizards, insects and small native mammals into the garden. No specific species need to be planted; it is more important to grow a wide range of trees, shrubs and groundcovers for their nectar, food and sap. In addition, provide sunny rocks, leafy bark mulch and hollow logs as basking and hiding places for lizards.

Natives as cut flowers

While kangaroo paws and Geraldton wax have been used as cut flowers for a number of years, there are numerous other native species that are ideally suited as cut flowers. Many Australian plants have unique flower and foliage forms, quite unlike any of the traditional flowers used by florists. Plants with extraordinary flowers like the Gymea lily, waratahs, grevilleas, dryandras and banksias are now in demand for both local and overseas flower markets. The fact that many species have long flowering periods, extended vase life, strong stems, and are excellent bouquet 'fillers', also makes them valuable as cut flowers.

The most commonly grown native plants for the local cut flower industry are kangaroo paws, Geraldton wax, *Thryptomene*, *Boronia*, *Banksia* and *Waratah*. Other plants that are in demand for flower export are stirlingia, koala fern (*Caustis blakei*), *Scholtzia*, Christmas bells (*Blandfordia*), Christmas bush (*Ceratopetalum gummiferum*), flannel flower, *Eriostemon*, riceflower, *Cryptandra* and *Eucalyptus* foliage.

Until fairly recently, most native flowers were cut straight from the bush. As natural populations have dwindled and demand for reliable supplies have grown, many cut flower varieties are now cultivated in plantations. A few species that have shown promise as cut flowers have undergone intensive development to create improved cultivars; for example, there are more than fifty named cultivars of Geraldton wax.

GROWING NATIVE PLANTS FOR CUT FLOWERS

Native plants that are grown specifically for their flowers and foliage need the following conditions:

- Adequate good quality water, especially as buds are forming
- Shelter from extreme weather conditions, especially wind and frost
- Well-drained soil, with a pH of 5.0 to 7.0 (for most species)
- Full sun (for most species), ideally planted in a site that faces north or north-east
- Adequate fertiliser, especially during peak growing periods.

Plants grown commercially are planted in rows that allow good access for machinery. Plants must be monitored and treated for pests and diseases, as only top quality, blemish-free flowers and foliage are acceptable for the florist trade.

USING NATIVE FLOWERS IN FLORAL ARRANGEMENTS

Focal flowers

These are the large colourful flowers that form the centrepiece of an arrangement:
Gymea lily (*Doryanthes excelsa*)
Waratahs (*Telopea* spp. and varieties)
Banksias (*Banksia* spp.)
Christmas bells (*Blandfordia grandiflora*)
Kangaroo paws (*Anigozanthos* spp. and varieties)

Flower fillers

Usually (but not always) flower fillers have branches with many small flowers:
Geraldton wax in bud and open flower (*Chamelaucium uncinatum*)
Crowea
Cryptandra
Thryptomene
Eriostemon
Christmas bush (*Ceratopetalum gummiferum*)
Flannel flower (*Actinotus helianthi*)
Hypocalymma
Bauera
Verticordia

How to prepare, arrange and preserve cut flowers

To ensure the best results from cut flowers:

- Strip all foliage from the lower stems that are to be immersed in water.
- Recut the woody stems and immediately place the stems in cold water. Cut the stems cleanly and at an angle.
- Arrange the prepared stems in a vase filled with water. As a general rule, plants with strong, rounded flowers like the banksias are best placed in towards the centre and base of an arrangement. Smaller, lighter flowers look better as support pieces placed higher in the arrangement.
- Do not put the vase in direct hot sunlight.
- Preservative can be added to the vase water, but is not essential.
- Change the water frequently — at least every second day.

Rice flower (*Ozothamnus diosmifolius* syn. *Helichrysum diosmifolius*)
Scholtzia
Stirlingia

Foliage fillers

Foliage fillers are plants with unusual, attractive, and long leaves:
Maidenhair fern (*Adiantum* spp.)
Lomatia
Juvenile foliage of *Eucalyptus cineria, globulus, pulverulenta, gunni*
Koala fern (*Caustis blakei*)
Persoonia
Xanthorrhea
Grevillea

Woody or unusual seed capsules

Hakeas
Banksias
Eucalyptus (especially the large urn-shaped fruits of *Corymbia ficifolia*)
Isopogon
Lambertia
Petrophile

DRIED NATIVE FLOWERS

Some native cut flowers are dried and even dyed to enhance their longevity and usefulness in floral arrangements and in craft.

Most dried flowers are produced in Western Australia. These include Banksias, *Verticordia*, *Stirlingia* and *Dryandra*. After harvesting they are processed by a variety of means, including air drying, bleaching, dyeing, preserving and freeze drying.

Edible natives

Hundreds of different plant species were used as a food source by Australian Aborigines. Nowadays we are familiar with just a few of those plants, although interest in bush tucker is undergoing a revival as both home gardeners and commercial growers are discovering the diverse range of edible native plants.

The best-known edible native plants are macadamias and Davidson's plums, both of which grow naturally in subtropical rainforests along the northern coast. The 'bush nuts' (*Macadamia integrifolia* and *M. tetraphylla*) once gathered by Aborigines are now rare in the wild but have been bred for a number of years (mainly in Hawaii) to produce superior varieties that are grown in large commercial plantations. Trees grow 12 to 15 metres but smaller grafted varieties are available. The trees are slow-growing and require deep, well-drained and enriched soil. They need a protected position as they are sensitive to frost, winds and drying out. The nuts can be eaten raw or roasted.

Davidson's plum (*Davidsonia pruriens*) is an

attractive small tree that produces a sour plum-like fruit. The fruit is used to make jam, conserves and wine, and as a flavouring in sauces and drinks. The tree requires shelter from winds and frost, and adequate water during the growing season.

BUSH TUCKER PLANTS

Some bush tucker plants are harvested from the wild but as demand is increasing more varieties are being cultivated. Most bush tucker is minimally processed or value-added (for example, as dried spices or in sauces); only very small volumes are sold and consumed as fresh produce.

QUANDONG (*Santalum acuminatum*): A shrub or small tree with a wide distribution in semi-arid regions of southern Australia. The tart-tasting fruit can be eaten fresh although it is more commonly dried and then reconstituted for use in sauces, preserves, chutneys, liqueurs and dipping sauces.

LEMON MYRTLE (*Backhousia citriodora*): A rainforest tree that grows to 15 metres in its natural environment. The leaves have a strong lemon scent and are used to flavour a wide range of sweet and savoury foods. They are also used in non-food products, such as cosmetics and household cleaners.

NATIVE LIMES: There are 6 species of true native citrus, as well as a number of hybrids. Until recently most native limes were harvested from wild populations of the desert lime, although commercial orchards are now starting to meet the growing demand from restaurants and food processors. These include the following:

- ***Desert lime*** (*Citrus glauca*): A small tree 2–4 metres tall with small green to yellow fruit.
- ***Finger lime*** (*Citrus australasica*): A rainforest tree that gows up to 10 metres tall bearing oval green to yellow fruit.
- ***Round lime*** (*Citrus australis*):A rainforest tree that grows 3–10 metres tall, with rough-skinned green to yellow fruit.

BUSH TOMATOES (*Solanum centrale*): Also called the desert raisin or desert tomato, this small shrub occurs naturally in central Australia. The green fruit is toxic and must not be eaten. The ripe fruit is dark brown and has a globular raisin-like appearance. The fruit is usually dried, either on or off the bush, then used sparingly to impart an intense piquant flavour to sauces, marinades and chutneys.

WATTLE SEEDS: Although a large number of wattle species have edible seeds, the elegant wattle or Gundabluey (*Acacia victoriae*) is the most commonly harvested species for the bush tucker industry. *A. victoriae* is a spiny-stemmed shrub or multi-stemmed tree that grows 3–4 metres tall. The glossy, dark brown seeds have a nutty flavour after roasting*. They are high in protein and are gluten-free, which makes them suitable for speciality diets. The roasted seeds are normally ground to a powder then added to breads, biscuits, cakes, sauces and icecreams.

* Many raw acacia seeds contain toxic compounds and have properties that inhibit enzymes in the digestive system. Seeds that are known to be edible should be roasted before consumption.

RIBERRY (*Syzgium leuhmannii* syn. *Eugenia leuhmannii*): A rainforest tree that grows to 30 metres in its natural environment but in cultivation rarely exceeds 10 metres. The red-pink berry-like fruit has a strong spicy flavour. The fruit is used in icecreams and sauces for meat dishes.

MOUNTAIN PEPPER (*Tasmannia lanceolata*): A medium to tall shrub from cool, moist forests in Tasmania, Victoria and southern New South Wales. Both the glossy, dark green leaves and the small dark berries are used as a hot, savoury spice in mustards, cheeses, sauces, breads and other savoury foods. Separate male and female trees are needed to produce berries. The berries, produced only on the female trees, can be dried, ground or preserved in brine.

WARRIGAL GREENS (*Tetragonia tetragonoides*): Also known as New Zealand spinach, this rambling green prostrate herb grows in many parts of Australia. It is regarded as an agricultural weed in some parts of Queensland. The plant grows quickly and is short-lived. The arrow-shaped leaves have a spinach-like flavour and are used in the same way as traditional spinach and Asian greens. However, they must be used with caution as the leaves contain high levels of oxalates. Only eat the leaves and young stems, and blanch them for 3 minutes before use to remove the soluble oxalates. The water should be discarded.

MUNTRIES (*Kunzea pomifera*): A prostrate or semi-upright shrub from drier regions of southern Australia. The greenish-purple fruit, up to 1cm in diameter, have a spicy apple flavour. Fresh fruit is used to make jams, added to fruit salads, and in sweet and savoury sauces. Trellising is used in commercial plantations to overcome problems caused by the plant's prostrate growth habit.

Growing natives for timber

Native trees are grown and harvested to provide building and furniture timber, fencing and pole timber, pulpwood, firewood and fodder.

The best-known Australian native trees, the eucalypts, are grown extensively for timber and paper pulp production, both in Australian and overseas plantations. Their main disadvantage is the long period of time required to produce a harvestable crop. For example, mountain ash (*Eucalyptus regnans*) typically takes more than 50 years before it can be harvested. Other species, though, can produce commercial timber in a shorter period; for example, spotted gum (*Eucalyptus maculata*) can be harvested in less than 20 years.

Blackwood (*Acacia melanoxylon*) and black wattle (*A. mearnsii*) have potential as timber for furniture, joinery and pulp. They are also excellent for controlling erosion. Both require adequate rainfall to be suitable for use as timber.

In subtropical and tropical areas, the main plantation timber is the hoop pine (*Auracaria cunninghamii*), although other rainforest trees, such as red cedar (*Toona ciliata* syn. *T. australis*), coachwood (*Ceratopetalum apetalum*) and crows ash (*Flindersia australis*), are also regarded as important timber species.

In drier inland areas, valuable native timber species include Callitris, Casuarina, ironbark (*Eucalyptus sideroxylon*), river red gum (*Eucalyptus camaldulensis*) and Acacia.

Extracting essential oils from native plants

The flavour and fragrance of scented plants, such as lemon myrtle, eucalypts and boronias are due to the aromatic compounds in their flowers, leaves and bark. When these are extracted by distillation, the resulting product is a volatile, colourless, oil-like material. Essential oils are used in food flavouring, and in the cosmetics, pharmaceutical and fragrance industries.

Two native plants are harvested

commercially for their essential oils: eucalypts and tea trees. Eucalyptus oil is mainly extracted from the blue mallee gum (*Eucalyptus polybractea*), a deep-rooted tree from the mallee regions of Victoria and New South Wales. The oil from this tree is used in inhalants, soaps, lozenges and other medicinal products. Other species used to produce medicinal oils include *E. globulus*, *E. dives*, *E. sideroxylon*, *E. viridis* and *E. leucoxylon*. Eucalypts used to produce industrial oils (to make disinfectants and industrial cleaners) include *E. dives*, *E. radiata* and *E. elata*. The lemon-scented gum (*Corymbia citriodora* syn. *Eucalyptus citriodora*) has been used to supply citronella oil. The production of eucalyptus oil has a long history — the first eucalypt distilleries were operating in the early days of colonial settlement.

Tea tree oil is mainly extracted from a small paperbark tree (*Melaleuca alternifolia*) that grows naturally in damp soils in northern New South Wales and Queensland. Oil production commences 12–18 months after planting, and the harvest continues on a 12–18 month cycle for up to 10 years.

Other native plants that yield essential oils include the brown boronia (*Boronia megastigma*), mountain pepper (*Tasmannia lanceolata*), lemon myrtle (*Backhousia citriodora*) and native frangipani (*Hymenosporum flavum*).

The yield of essential oil is usually very low in relation to the amount of plant material used. Depending on the quality of the plant and the distillation method used, yields of between 0.005% and 5% may be obtained. For most plants, the oil is extracted by stem distillation, which involves placing the plant material on a mesh surface in a closed still. Steam pumped into the still 'boils' the plant material very quickly and releases the aromatic compounds as vaporised oil. The vapour is rapidly cooled in a condensation chamber, causing the vapour and steam to liquidise and separate. Modern essential oil producers may perform this process under a partial vacuum. This reduces the boiling point of the steam, allowing a 'cooler' distillation which does less harm to the more fragile fragrance components.

Part Two

Plant Encyclopaedia

Terms explained

GROWTH RATE

Plant growth rates vary both according to species and the conditions the plant is growing in. All plants have optimum soil, temperature and light conditions under which they will grow faster than if conditions are not optimum. If temperature increases or decreases from the optimum, growth slows. The optimum temperature for plants from tropical places is generally higher than for plants from colder places.

Rate of growth also tends to be relative to the eventual height of the plant. For example, a rapid-growing plant may reach its eventual height in 2-4 years, whereas a slow-growing plant may take decades. For a 1-metre shrub the actual growth per year to reach full size might be much slower than for a 50-metre tall tree.

Any plant in poor soil and cold conditions might grow at a much slower pace than in ideal conditions, so a rapid grower under bad conditions may take 10 years to grow to full size, instead of the possible 2-4 years.

LIFESPAN

Lifespan, like growth rate, is also relative to conditions. A long-lived plant under ideal conditions might live hundreds of years. Under poor conditions, long-lived plants can have a vastly diminished lifespan.

Some short-lived plants may only live around 5-7 years even in good conditions, and there are even some that rarely last more than a year or two in the very best conditions.

ACACIA ❧ Wattles ❧ Mimosaceae

At a glance

NUMBER OF SPECIES 1200; about 1000 occur in Australia. It is the largest genus in Australia.
NATURAL HABITAT Throughout Australia in a wide variety of climatic and soil conditions (though only a few from tropical rainforests).
FLOWERING There will be a species flowering somewhere in Australia at any time of the year with the heaviest concentration of flowering times occurring between late autumn and late spring, depending on the species and where it is planted. Some Acacias are amongst the most spectacular flowering native plants. Flower colours are almost universally shades of yellow, ranging from pale through to golden.
HARDINESS Most are very hardy.
HABIT Ground covers, shrubs and trees.
FOLIAGE Varies greatly in shape and size. Colours are generally green to bluish–silver. Acacias may have either:

1. Bipinnate true leaves
2. Phyllodes, which are modified leaf stems that carry out the functions of the true leaves, once the true leaves become absent at maturity
3. Cladodes, which are stems that carry out the functions of the leaves. Both true leaves and phyllodes are absent.

GROWTH RATE Usually rapid.
LIFESPAN Generally short-lived (about 5–12 years) though some of the larger woody types (e.g. *A. decurrens* and *A. elata*) can live a lot longer.

Culture

- Suited to most soils. Some are sensitive to high phosphorus levels. *A. spectabilis* is sensitive to boron deficiency. Many are sensitive to over-wet soils.
- Borers are a major pest. Crusader bugs can also be a serious problem.
- Caterpillars are a problem on some feather-leaved types.

ACACIA SPECIES	SIZE	FOLIAGE	FLOWERING
A. acanthoclada	0.5–2 x 2 m	Green and hairy	Gold yellow, June–Jan
A. acinacea	0.5–2 x 2 m	Green	Gold yellow, Aug–Dec
A. aculeatissima	0.2–1 x 2 m	Green and narrow	Pale yellow, June–Nov
A. acuminata	6–10 x 3–5 m	Bright green	Bright yellow, Aug–Sept
A. adunca	8 x 3–5 m	Dark green	Bright orange-yellow, Aug–Oct
A. alata	1–2 x 1–2 m	Green and triangular	Cream yellow, May–Sept
A. anceps	3–4 x 3–4 m	Silver-grey	Bright yellow, Sept–Feb
A. aneura	4–15 x 2–6 m	Silver-green	Golden yellow, June–Oct
A. argrophylla	3–5 x 2–6 m	Silver-grey	Golden yellow, Aug–Nov
A. ausfeldii	1–4 x 1–3 m	Bright green	Golden yellow, Aug–Sept
A. baileyana	5–8 x 5 m	Blue-green	Yellow, July–Sept
A. beckleri	2–4 x 1–5 m	Dull green	Bright yellow, May–Oct
A. bidentata	0.3–1 x 1 m	Dark green	Cream, Aug–Dec
A. boormanii	3–5 x 2–4 m	Grey-green	Bright yellow, Sept
A. brachybotrya	1–5 x 3–6 m	Grey-green	Bright yellow, July–Nov
A. brachystacha	3–6 x 2–6 m	Grey-green	Yellow, July–Oct
A. buxifolia	2–4 x 2–3 m	Grey-green	Gold yellow, July–Dec
A. calamifolia	2–10 x 2–4 m	Grey-green	Gold yellow, Aug–Nov
A. cardiophylla	2–3 x 2–3 m	Light green	Bright yellow, July–Jan
A. cognata	4–6 x 3–6 m	Light green	Cream, Aug–Dec
A. colletiodes	2–3 x 2–3 m	Dull green	Bright yellow, July–Oct
A. cometes	0.2–0.4 x 0.5–0.9 m	Blue-green	Bright yellow, Sept–Nov
A. conferta	2–4 x 2–4 m	Grey-green	Gold yellow, May–Aug
A. cultriformis	3–4 x 3 m	Blue-green	Golden, Aug–Oct
A. cyanophylla = *A. saligna*	4–10 x 5 m	Green	Yellow, Aug–Nov
A. dealbata	5–20 x 8 m	Blue-green	Bright yellow, July–Sept
A. deanei	5–10 x 3–5 m	Green	Pale yellow, all year
A. decora	3–5 x 4 m	Grey-green	Golden yellow, Sept
A. decurrens	8–15 x 4 m	Dark green	Golden yellow, spring
A. dentifera	2–4 x 3 m	Blue-green	Cream yellow, Sept–Oct
A.disparrima (syn. *A aulacocarpa*)	6–25 x 6 m	Dark green	Pale yellow, Feb–June
A. drummondii	1.5 x 1 m	Green	Golden, July–Oct
A. elata	10–20 x 8 m	Brown-green	Cream, summer
A. fimbriata	3–7 x 3–6 m	Olive-green	Yellow, spring

ACACIA SPECIES	SIZE	FOLIAGE	FLOWERING
A. floribunda	4–8 x 4–6 m	Green	Yellow, July–Sept
A. howitii	4–8 x 4 m	Green	Pale yellow, spring
A. iteaphylla	4–5 x 4 m	Blue-green	Pale yellow, Mar–Aug
A. longifolia	4–10 x 4–8 m	Green	Yellow, July–Sept
A. mearnsii	1–25 x 10 m	Grey-green	Pale yellow, spring
A. melanoxylon	5–30 x 5–15 m	Grey-green	Cream, July–Oct
A. paradoxa (syn. *A. armata*)	2 x 2 m	Green	Gold balls, spring
A. pendula	5–10 x 3–4 m	Grey-green	Yellow, spring
A. perangusta	4–6 x 4 m	Olive-green	Yellow, late winter–spring
A. podalyriifolia	4 x 3 m	Blue	Golden, July–Oct
A. pravissima	4–8 x 5–7 m	Olive-green	Yellow, Sept
A. prominens	5–15 x 7 m	Blue-green	Lemon, Sept
A. pycnantha	4–10 x 4 m	Green	Yellow, July–Oct
A. saligna	4–10 x 5 m	Green	Yellow, Aug–Nov
A. sophorae	1–3 x 4 m	Green	Golden, spring
A. suaveolens	3 x 4 m	Blue-green	Pale, April–Sept
A. ulcifolia	1–2 x 1–2 m	Green	Cream, Mar–Sept
A. verticillate	2–7 x 1–3 m	Green	Yellow, June–Dec

- Pruning is risky, often resulting in dieback, although many species will react well to light pruning immediately after flowering.
- Responds well to watering in dry periods.

Propagation

Propagation is by pre-treated seed; that is, prior to sowing, pour boiling water over the seeds to soften the seed coat. Allow the water to cool before removing the seeds then immediately sow. The germination rate of seed after treatment is generally good. Seeds can be sown in propagating mix or directly seeded into the soil or open ground. Seeds stored in dry conditions will last for many years, but may require protection from insect and fungus attack. (See the section on seed propagation earlier in this text for more information on seed-raising and germination techniques.)

Some Acacias have also been successfully propagated by cuttings; this method is generally difficult, however. Usually those species with smaller leaves and phyllodes strike better than species with the large bipinnate leaves.

ACMENA ❧ Myrtaceae

Note: Was previously included in *Eugenia*

At a glance

NUMBER OF SPECIES About 15; 6 occur in Australia (undergoing reclassification).
NATURAL HABITAT Rainforests beside watercourses.
FLOWERING Flowers generally insignificant, but attractive berries ripen over autumn–winter.
HARDINESS Can be frost tender.

ACMENA SPECIES	HEIGHT	COMMENTS
A. brachyandra	8–20 m	Can be slow growing, best in subtropics
A. divaricate	5–12 m	Best in tropical climates
A. graveolens	10–20 m	Soil must be constantly moist but well drained, needs protection in cool areas
A. hemilampra	10–15 m	Will grow in cool climates despite coming from the subtropics
A. smithii	10–20 m	Most commonly grown species
Note: Dwarf varieties are also available.		

HABIT Well-formed trees, generally growing smaller in cooler climates.
FOLIAGE Dense, leaves have a smooth, shiny surface.
GROWTH RATE Moderate to rapid.
LIFESPAN Long-lived.
COMMENTS *A. smithii* berries are edible.

Culture

- Prefers cool, well-drained, moist and fertile soil.
- Likes to be mulched and fertilised regularly.
- Few pests, though scale can occur.
- Propagate from seed and sow seed fresh. Some can be grown from cuttings.

ACRONYCHIA ❧ Rutaceae

At a glance

NUMBER OF SPECIES 42; 16 found in Australia.
NATURAL HABITAT Open forests to rainforests.
FLOWERING White to cream.
HABIT Trees with spreading dense or thin crown.
HARDINESS Adapts well to southern states.
FOLIAGE Scented due to oil dots. Dark green.
GROWTH RATE Fast growing provided water is present.
LIFESPAN Long-lived.
COMMENTS Flowers attractive to butterflies. Excellent shade trees.

Culture

- Free-draining soils high in organic matter.
- Additional irrigation required in dry periods.
- Sunny position.
- Propagation: seed germination is erratic and difficult.

Species

A. acidula lemon aspen

- 10–20 m
- Edible fruit. Handsome tree with a dense canopy. From the Atherton Tablelands.

A. imperforata logan apple

- 3–10 m
- Yellow to orange edible fruit (Oct–Dec), suitable for jam making.

A. oblongifolia common acronychia

- Up to 25 m but usually only 12 m when domesticated
- Acidic edible fruit, varies in colour. A handsome tree with shiny foliage. Native habitat from Vic to Gympie.

ACTINODIUM ❧ Myrtaceae

At a glance

NUMBER OF SPECIES 2; both endemic to Australia.
NATURAL HABITAT South-western WA.
FLOWERING August to January.
HABIT Small shrubs.
HARDINESS Hardy.

FOLIAGE Small, aromatic.
GROWTH RATE Fast.
LIFESPAN Short-lived.

Culture

- Adapts to most soils, provided well drained.
- Prefers filtered sun.
- Withstands light frosts.
- Needs light pruning after flowering.
- Propagate from cuttings which strike easily at all times of the year, but best in Feb–March.

Species

A. cunninghamii
- 0.5 x 0.5 m, green foliage
- Flowers daisy-like, white and red.

A. spp.
- 0.3 x 0.2 m, green foliage
- Flowers as above, but flowering is more prolific. (This unnamed species is the species commonly cultivated in eastern Australia, and previously thought to be a form of *A. cunninghamii*).

ACTINOSTROBUS ❧ *see Conifers*

ACTINOTUS ❧ Flannel Flower ❧ Apiaceae

At a glance

NUMBER OF SPECIES About 17; 11 occur in Australia, 1 in New Zealand.
NATURAL HABITAT Varied.
FLOWERING Similar to a daisy or strawflower.
HABIT Small herbs.
HARDINESS Varies.
FOLIAGE Usually hairy and divided.
LIFESPAN Reported to be short-lived in cultivation.

Culture

- Generally requires good drainage.
- Prefers filtered sun, though some (not all) tolerate full sun.
- Propagate by seed or cuttings, but can be difficult to grow.

Species

A. forsythia
- 0.4 m. Flowers pink-white.
- Seed is slow to germinate.

A. helanthii
- 0.5–1.5 m. Flowers cream-white.
- Soft woolly foliage.

A. leucocephalus
- 0.4–1 m. Flowers white.
- Upright bush.

A. minor
- 0.4 m. Flowers white–cream.
- Wiry, spreading plant.

ADANSONIA ❧ Baobab ❧ Bombaceae

At a glance

NUMBER OF SPECIES About 12; 1 occurs in north-western Australia.
NATURAL HABITAT Tropics.
FLOWERING Large, normally white.
HABIT A tree with a fat swollen trunk and small branches.
HARDINESS Drought hardy, frost sensitive.
FOLIAGE Divided leaves.
GROWTH RATE Slow.
LIFESPAN Long-lived.
COMMENTS Large scented flowers.

Culture

- Well-drained soil.
- Warm climate. Tropics best, though they have grown in temperate climates.
- Propagate from seed. Seeds remain viable for 1 to 2 years.

Species

A. gregorii is the only Australian species. It is best grown in the tropics; even Brisbane is too far south for good results. Leaves drop during drought then flowering occurs before foliage regrows when the drought finishes.

ADENANTHERA ❧ Mimosaceae

At a glance

NUMBER OF SPECIES 8; 2 endemic to Australia.
NATURAL HABITAT Open forest, along streams and rainforest margins.
FLOWERING Small cream or yellow flowers.
HABIT Spreading tree.
HARDINESS Cold sensitive.
FOLIAGE Bipinnate leaves.
GROWTH RATE Medium growth.
LIFESPAN Medium.
COMMENTS *A. abrosperma* — seeds eaten by Aborigines after roasting, bark used as a fish poison. *A. pavonia* — seeds eaten by Aborigines after roasting. Flowers are attractive to butterflies.

Culture

- Well-drained soil.
- Sun to part-sun position.
- Propagate by seed.

Species

A. abrosperma

- 5–15 m
- Very ornamental Qld tree for domestic use. Drops leaves in dry season.

A. pavonia red sandalwood

- 5–15 m
- Very ornamental spreading tree from Qld and NT. Bright scarlet seeds used for ornaments and necklaces. Becomes deciduous in dry season.

ADENANTHOS ❧ Jug Flower ❧ Proteaceae

At a glance

NUMBER OF SPECIES 33; all endemic to Australia, mainly from south-western WA.
NATURAL HABITAT Mostly on well-drained, often poor soils, some come from swampy sites.
FLOWERING Usually small, tubular-shaped with an elongated style. Colour varies from white to yellow and red in late winter to summer.
HABIT Small shrubs.
HARDINESS Varies, some tolerate frosts.
FOLIAGE Normally small, variable in shape.
GROWTH RATE Medium to fast.
LIFESPAN Normally short-lived in cultivation.

Culture

- Must have good drainage.
- Prefers full sun or lightly filtered sunlight.
- Benefits from tip pruning after flowering.
- Only apply small amounts of slow-release organic fertilisers.
- Propagate by semi-hardwood cuttings in late summer.

ADENANTHOS SPECIES	HEIGHT	FLOWERS	COMMENTS
A. barbigerus	0.5–1 m	Red	Prefers gravelly soil, frost hardy.
A. cuneatus	0.5–3 m	Pink-purple	Tolerates frost and alkaline soils.
A. detmoldii	2–4 m	Yellow-orange	Prefers moist, sandy soils.
A. linearis	0.3–1 m	Cream-red	Prefers sandy well-drained soil.
A. obovatus	1 m	Red	Adapts well to cultivation.
A. pungens	2.5 m	Pink	Strongly scented leaves.
A. sericeus	2–7 m	Red to yellow	Attractive grey woolly foliage.

AGATHIS ❧ *see Conifers*

AGONIS ❧ Myrtaceae

At a glance

NUMBER OF SPECIES 11; all endemic to Australia.
NATURAL HABITAT South-western WA.
FLOWERING Globular heads or spikes. Time of flowering varies with variety.
HABIT Shrubs and small trees.
HARDINESS Once established very hardy, and drought tolerant.
FOLIAGE Small or large, undivided leaves.
GROWTH RATE Normally fast.
LIFESPAN Usually long-lived.
COMMENTS *A. parviceps* is excellent as a cut flower.

Culture

- Highly adaptable to different soils and climates.
- Responds to feeding with slow-release fertilisers or well-rotted manure.
- Grows well on wet soils.
- Grows in full sun or filtered shade.
- Young growing tips susceptible to frost.
- Minimal pest and disease problems.
- Responds to light tip pruning.
- Propagate by seed.

ALBIZIA ❧ Mimosaceae (syn Paraserianthes)

At a glance

NUMBER OF SPECIES 150; 10 occur in Australia.
NATURAL HABITAT Open dry forests to rainforest.
FLOWERING Mainly spring, some other times.
HABIT Shrubs and small trees.
HARDINESS Generally hardy.
FOLIAGE Feathery (bipinnate, some deciduous).
GROWTH RATE Very fast.
LIFESPAN Some short (e.g. *A. lophantha* rarely lasts longer than 3 to 7 years), others are medium-lived.

Culture

- Adapts to most soils provided well drained.
- Often dies back after pruning.

AGONIS SPECIES	SIZE	FOLIAGE	FLOWERING
A. flexuosa	6 x 5 m	Weeping, red tips	White, tea-tree-like in spring.
A. flexuosa 'Nana'	1 x 1 m	Attractive red tips	Rarely flowers.
A. flexuosa variegata	4 x 2.5 m	Slow growing	White.
A. juniperina	10 x 5 m	Narrow, silky when young	White with brown centre.
A. parviceps	3 x 2 m	Narrow and dense	Small, white.

ALBIZIA SPECIES	SIZE	FOLIAGE	FLOWERING	HABITAT
A. basaltica	3–6 x 2 m	Leathery	Yellow	Arid areas
A. lebbek	5–10 x 5 m	Dull green, light underside	White, green or brown brushes	Mild to warm areas
A. lophantha	3–7 x 2 m	Light green	Yellow-green, can flower all year	Most places
A. procera	Up to 20 x 5–8 m	Semi-deciduous	Cream or green	Warm areas

- Susceptible to waterlogging, caterpillars and borers.
- Propagate from seed which is first treated with boiling water or other methods (as for Acacia). Tropical types may rot with boiling water and are better nicked with a knife to break the seed coat.

ALLOCASUARINA ❧ Casuarinaceae

Note: *Allocasuarina* was previously part of the genus *Casuarina*.

At a glance

NUMBER OF SPECIES About 60; all endemic to Australia.
NATURAL HABITAT Widespread arid inland to coastal.
FLOWERING Varies over whole year.
HARDINESS Generally very hardy. Some not as tolerant to extended drought.
HABIT Mainly trees, a few shrubs.
FOLIAGE Tiny whorls of reduced scale-like leaves on modified pine needle-like stems (that carry out photosynthesis), often weeping fine-leaved appearance.
GROWTH RATE Usually rapid.
LIFESPAN Long-lived.
COMMENT Nitrogen-fixing plants.

Culture

- Suited to most soils if not waterlogged.
- Root system is vigorous. They are best planted out when young. Do not grow advanced trees in containers.
- Will tolerate some pruning of young plants for shaping.
- Propagation is normally from seed (no pre-germination treatment needed). Collect older cones as seed takes 12 months to mature on plant. Place cones in a paper bag and leave in sun, or warm place. They will open in time, releasing large quantities of seed.

ALLOXYLON ❧ Tree Waratah ❧ Proteaceae

At a glance

NUMBER OF SPECIES 4, 3 endemic to Australia.
NATURAL HABITAT Wet rainforests in the Atherton Tablelands to northern NSW.
FLOWERING Large clusters of red or pink.
HABIT Large shrubs to tall trees.
HARDINESS Frost sensitive. Prone to wind damage. Easy to grow if requirements are met.
FOLIAGE Immature foliage is lobed. Mature foliage is green and simple.
GROWTH RATE Slow growing out of natural habitat.
LIFESPAN Medium to long.
COMMENTS Seed-propagated plants grow better with a stronger root system, but take longer to flower. Regular pruning will encourage bushiness. Very good bird-attracting specimen. In nature the trees will reach greater heights. In domestic gardens they will be much smaller and usually with a better shape.

Culture

- Part sun in early years, then full sun.
- Provide irrigation when rainfall is inadequate.
- Provide wind protection.
- Mulch well.
- Propagation by seed (sown fresh) or semi-hardwood cuttings.

Species

A. flammeum (syn. *Oreocallis wickhamii*)

- 4–8 m
- Spectacular red flowers in spring. Slender tree with brittle wood. Green new growth tips. From northern Qld.

A. pinnatum (syn. *O. pinnata*, *Embothrium pinnatum*, *E. wickhamii* var. *pinnatum*)

- 10–20 m
- Pinkish-red terminal flower clusters from October to January. Can be difficult to establish in the domestic garden. From NSW.

ALLOCASUARINA SPECIES	HEIGHT	COMMENTS
A. brachystachya	1–3 m	Open spreading shrub, grows on infertile sandy soil.
A. campestris	1–3 m	Grows extensively in WA on sand plains and laterite.
A. crassa	1–2 m	Smooth-bark shrub from Tasman Peninsula and Cape Pillar growing on rocky outcrops.
A. decaisneana	5–15 m	Elegant slow-growing weeping foliage tree when adult. Flowers inconspicuous. Frost tolerant. Difficult to establish in gardens.
A. defungens	0.5 – 2m	Erect or sub-erect shrub with smooth bark. Grows in tall heath in sand. Central Australia.
A. diminuta	1–5 m	Shrub or small tree with smooth bark. Found in NSW on the tablelands, slopes and coastal ranges, sandstone ridges and hillsides in heath and low open woodland.
A. distyla	2–4 m	Bark mainly smooth. Grows in tall heath on sandstone ridgetops of mountain areas, grows well under eucalypts.
A. emuina	0.5–1.5 m	Spreading shrub with smooth bark found only in parts of Coolum and Caloundra in Qld. Grows in low heath in acid volcanic soil.
A. filidens	1.5–3 m	Shrub with roughish bark found growing in crevices of rocks, along with other shrubs, only on summits and exposed upper slopes of the Glasshouse Montains, Qld.
A. fraseriana	5–15 m	Tree from WA, grows in lateritic soil in jarrah forest near the coast. Grows in sand in woodland and open forest.
A. glareicola	1–2 m	Erect shrub with smooth bark from NSW, grows in open forest gravel soils over clay.
A. grampiana	1.5–4 m	Restricted to growing on sandy outcrops in the Grampians, Vic.
A. gymnanthera	2–5 m	Shrub or tree with smooth or fissured bark. Grows on sandy soil on sandstone ridges in low open woodland of NSW.
A. helmsii	1–5 m	Found in mallee woodland and tall heath, in a wide range of soils in WA and SA.
A. humilis	0.2–2 m	Erect and spreading shrub. Grows in heath in sand.
A. inophloia	5–7 m	Fibrous stringy brown bark. Generally seen growing in an open forest environment amongst species such as *Eucalyptus, Xanthorrhea* and a mixed understorey of shrubs and grasses. Commonly found on ironstone and sandstone ridges; adapts to a range of soil conditions but needs good drainage capacity if in areas of high moisture content.
A. lehmaniana	1–5 m	Shrub from parts of WA. Often grows near the sea in woodland and tall scrub, in sandy and sandy-loam soil.
A. luehmannii	Up to 15 m	A leafless tree, with fine, twisted, grey-green branchlets, found scattered in woodland on non-calcareous soils in Vic, NSW, Qld, SA.
A. littoralis	6–10 m	Intolerant of bad drainage but tolerant of salt spray. Most soils. A fast-growing tree with black trunk, hence the name, black she-oak. The branch ends often have an attractive pendulous habit. Frost tolerant down to about –7°C.

ALLOCASUARINA SPECIES	HEIGHT	COMMENTS
A. mackliniana	1–2 m	Shrub, endangered, found in western Vic.
A. media	1–3 m	Shrub with smooth bark. Found only in the low sandy woodlands of northern Wilsons Promontory, Vic.
A. misera	0.5–2 m	Shrub with smooth bark that occurs only in isolated locations in Vic.
A. monilifera	1.5–4 m	Shrub from northern and eastern Tas, Flinders Island, and Kent Group in Bass Strait. Grows in sandy soil in lowland heath and open woodland.
A. muelleriana	0.5–3 m.	Smooth-bark shrub that grows from Ceduna and the Flinders Ranges to eastern SA and north-western Vic, also on Kangaroo Island. Grows in scrub and heath, in rocky siliceous soils.
A. ophiolitica	1–3 m	This shrub only occurs in NSW in the southern end of the New England Region and adjoining coastal ranges from Bralga Tops to Curricabark and Glenrock. Grows on serpentine outcrops in tall heath and low open woodland.
A. paludosa	0.3–3 m	Spreading smooth-bark shrub that occurs along some coastal parts and adjoining tablelands of southern NSW, also in north-eastern Tas, Flinders Island, and parts of SA. Grows in heath and in poorly drained soils above swamps at edge of woodland.
A. paradoxa	0.5–2 m	Occurs in the Grampians and from the Melbourne area to Wilsons Promontory, Vic. Often grows in tall heath in sandy soil.
A. pinaster	1–3 m	Shrub restricted to parts of WA. Grows in tall shrubland and heathland in lateritic soils.
A. portuensis	3–5 m	Slender dioecious shrub with smooth bark from Sydney, NSW. Found in tall shrubland on slopes of sandstone headlands.
A. pusilla	0.2–2 m	Spreading shrub with smooth bark found growing in heath on sandy soils in Yorke Peninsula, SA, and both the Big and Little Deserts of Vic.
A. nana	2–4 m	Low-spreading shrub. Hardy in most soils but grows naturally in heath on sandstone, exposed situations, such as ridges on the eastern highlands, coast and tablelands of NSW and Vic.
A. rigida	0.5–4	Shrub with smooth bark. Grows in poor sandy soils on acid granite in parts of NSW and Qld.
A. robusta	0.5–2 m	Shrub that grows in the southern Lofty Ranges, SA, in upland heath and open woodland with an understorey of heath.
A. rupicola	1–3 m	Shrub that is restricted to certain parts of NSW and Qld, growing along rocky creeks and in granite clefts on mountain slopes.
A. simulans	0.5–4 m	Grows in heath on sandy soil in parts of NSW.
A. striata	1–5 m	Shrub grows in sandy clay in rocky areas and is frost tolerant.
A. thalassoscopica	1 m	Low-growing shrub growing only on south-facing upper slopes of Mt Coolum, Qld. Forms a dense, low closed heath.
A. torulosa	7–10 m	Popular ornamental tree, brownish weeping foliage.
A. verticillata	5–10 m	Drooping she-oak, tolerates salty soils, wind and some waterlogging.
A. zephyrea	0.5–2 m	Shrub that grows on rocky outcrops and heath in Tasmania's western lowlands, central and south-eastern highlands as well as on King Island.

wickhamii (syn. *O. wickhamii, E. wickhamii*)
- 15–25 m
- Pinkish-red flowers from September to November. Young shoots have pinkish tone. Leathery leaves. From northern Qld.

ALPHITONIA ⁕ Rhamnaceae

At a glance

NUMBER OF SPECIES 20; 6 endemic to Australia.
NATURAL HABITAT Fringe tree to rainforests and open forests, from NSW to Qld to NT.
FLOWERING Small insignificant flowers in large inflorescence.
HABIT Variable depending on sunlight exposure.
HARDINESS Very hardy in southern states. Adaptable to a variety of sites.
FOLIAGE Glossy dark green leaves.
GROWTH RATE Very fast growing.
LIFESPAN Medium.
COMMENTS An excellent pioneer tree. Large insect populations in these trees attract birds. Attractive trees for the garden or street.

Culture

- Full sun to part sun.
- Adapted to a range of soil types.
- Warmth, fertiliser and water encourages vigorous growth.
- Propagate by fresh seed.

Species

A. excelsa Red ash, soap tree
- 7–25 m
- Fragrant flowers (Feb–April). Tough timber.

A. petriei Pink ash, white ash
- 20 m
- Small fragrant flowers (Sept–Nov). Young branches smell like sarsparilla.

A. philippinensis
- 10–20 m
- Attractive spreading tree which flowers from October to March. Cold sensitive.

A. whitei
- 3–12 m
- Ornamental rainforest specimen with spreading habit.

ALPINIA ⁕ Zingiberaceae

At a glance

NUMBER OF SPECIES 250; 6 occur in Australia.
NATURAL HABITAT Fringe forests to rainforests.
FLOWERING White flowers in terminal erect inflorescences.
HABIT Fleshy tuberous clumping plant.
HARDINESS Sensitive to drought and frost.
FOLIAGE Soft fleshy light to dark green, borne on pseudostem.
GROWTH RATE Vigorous during wet season.
LIFESPAN Medium.
COMMENTS Good for understorey planting.

ALPINIA SPECIES	HEIGHT	COMMENTS
A. arctiflora	3–4 m	Dense panicles with pink bracts. Hairy foliage beneath. From tropical Qld.
A. arundelliana	1–1.5 m	Undulated leaf margins. Flowers have a reddish lip. Blue fruit when ripe. From Qld and NSW.
A. caerulea	1–3 m	Leaves may have red undersides. Purple lips on the flowers. Grows in tight clumps. Qld.
A. hylandii	0.5–1 m	Pinkish-white flowers. Bright shiny green leaves with wavy edges. From highland tropical areas of north Qld.
A. modesta	1–1.5 m	Leaves dark red-green above and deep red beneath. Pale pink flowers with red markings. Tropical Qld.

Culture

- Prefers part sun.
- Irrigation needed in dry periods.
- Propagation by seed or division.

ALSTONIA ❧ Apocynaceae

At a glance

NUMBER OF SPECIES 40–60, 6 recognised in Australia, and 2 subspecies.
NATURAL HABITAT Temperate, subtropical–tropical, some from rainforest areas.
FLOWERING Small white or cream, some species are fragrant, bearing long thin white fruit.
HABIT Ranging from small to tall trees.
HARDINESS Hardy.
FOLIAGE Varies with species.
GROWTH RATE Generally moderate.
LIFE SPAN Long-lived.

Culture

- Excellent park or street tree
- Warm conditions
- Most soils are suitable, some species tolerate drier conditions.

ALYOGYNE ❧ Malvaceae

At a glance

NUMBER OF SPECIES 4; all endemic to Australia.
NATURAL HABITAT Widespread, various habitats.
FLOWERING Profuse white, mauve or red hibiscus-like flowers. Flowering usually begins in the first year.
HABIT Shrubs.
HARDINESS Medium.
FOLIAGE Usually lobed and hairy.
GROWTH RATE Generally very fast growing.
LIFESPAN Short to medium.

Culture

- Usually needs some protection. Can be damaged by frosts or winds.
- Prefers well-drained but moist soils.
- Responds to annual feeding.
- Withstands heavy pruning (often needed to keep plants compact).
- Propagate from seed or cuttings.

Species

A. cuneiformis

- 2 x 2 m

ALSTONIA SPECIES	SIZE	COMMENTS
A. actinophylla	15 x 5 m	Erect tree with rough bark and open crown, blunt green lanceolate leaves, cream flowers, prefers light to medium soils and an open sunny position. NT and Qld.
A. constricta	12 x 4 m	(Australian quinine). Evergreen erect tree with rusty brown rough bark and milky sap, produces a yellow dye. Lanceolate leaves with long petioles. Profuse small yellow flowers. NSW.
A. linearis	3–10 x 1–5 m	Tree or shrub with white flowers late summer to late autumn. Sandstone hills and ridges of WA.
A. muelleriana	Up to 20 m high	(Hard milk-wood) Fast-growing large tree that produces a milky sap, tropical and subtropical areas. White decorative flowers. Excellent shade tree in fertile soils. Hardy species.
A. scholaris	Up to 38 x 10 m	(Milky pine) Erect tree with spongy furrowed, brown-grey bark, oblong dark green, glossy leaves to 15 cm long. Greenish-white tubular flowers in dense terminal clusters. Also occurs in India where the bark is used to treat bowel complaints. Very light timber.
A. spectabilis	10–15 x 8 m	Erect tree. Bears clusters of fragrant white flowers in spring.

- Thick dark leaves, flowers white with red spot in centre, best suited to warm dry climates or coastal areas.

A. hakeifolia

- 2 x 2 m
- Mauve flowers with dark red centres, suit warm dry climate.

A. huegelii

- 1–3 x 1–3 m
- Mauve flowers Oct-March, straggly unless pruned.

A. pinoniana

- 2 x 3 m
- From dry north, inland and coastal, mauve flowers with red centres.

ALYXIA ✻ Apocynaceae

At a glance

NUMBER OF SPECIES 80; 8 endemic to Australia — some rare.
NATURAL HABITAT Cool, temperate, tropical and subtropical, mainly in coastal areas.
FLOWERING Small white flowers with 5 overlapping petals. Decorative orange or red fruits.
HABIT Bushy shrubs or climbers.
HARDINESS Hardy species, tolerant of salt spray.
FOLIAGE Leathery, fleshy simple leaves.
GROWTH RATE Slow to moderate.
LIFESPAN Medium.
COMMENTS Shrubs can be trained as a hedge.

Culture

- Prefers partial shade.
- Some species need water during summer.
- Propagation is by fresh seed or cuttings.

Species

A. buxifolia

- 1.2 x 1.5 m
- Stiff glossy leaves, 1 cm white flowers in spring–summer followed by attractive red fruits. Slow-growing but hardy.

A. ruscifolia

- 3 x 1.5 m
- Erect shrub with sharp pointed, glossy, dark green leaves. White flowers in summer followed by orange autumn fruit. Full sun to heavy shade, well-composted soil.

A. tentanifolia

- 1–2 x 2.5 m
- Erect, rigid, pungent shrub, white-cream flowers in late autumn–winter and again in mid-spring. Prefers sandy clay, loam or gravel. Damp areas.

ANGOPHORA ✻ Myrtaceae

At a glance

NUMBER OF SPECIES 8; all from the east coast of Australia.
NATURAL HABITAT Mainly open forest, often in coastal areas.
FLOWERING Dense clusters of cream flowers in spring and summer. Very similar in appearance to eucalypt flowers. Flowers are followed by attractive ribbed fruits.
HABIT Trees.
HARDINESS Hardy once established.
FOLIAGE Like eucalypts, reddish tinge to new growth.
GROWTH RATE Rapid.
LIFESPAN Long-lived (over 100 yrs).
COMMENTS Closely related to eucalypts; flower buds and leaf arrangements are slightly different.

Culture

- Tolerates wide range of soils and climates (does not occur at high altitudes).
- Generally respond to the same cultural treatment required by eucalypts.
- Propagate from fresh seed.

ANGOPHERA SPECIES	HEIGHT	FLOWERS	COMMENTS
A. bakeri	to 20 m	Cream	Adapts to most soils, tolerates light frosts.
A. costata	to 30 m	Cream	Frost sensitive when young, very attractive bark.
A. floribunda	to 25 m	White	Withstands pruning, very adaptable.
A. hispida	to 10 m	Cream	Needs good drainage, suitable for coastal areas.
A. melanoxylon	to 12 m	Yellow	Frost hardy, tolerates heavy soils.
A. woodsiana	to 15 m	Cream	Appearance like *A. floribunda* but with larger leaves and fruits.

ANIGOZANTHOS ❧ Haemodoraceae

At a glance

NUMBER OF SPECIES 11; all endemic to Australia, many cultivars.

NATURAL HABITAT Generally sandy or gravelly well-drained soils in south-western WA.

FLOWERING Distinctive paw-shaped flowers in a range of colours and combinations (mostly shades of green, red, yellow or pink). Long flowering with main flush in spring.

HABIT Clumps with strap-like leaves and erect flowering stems.

HARDINESS Most are not hardy, a few are relatively hardy (e.g. *A. flavidus*).

LIFESPAN Often no more than 10 years.

GROWTH RATE Can be fast.

COMMENTS Very popular landscape plant due to the attractive habit and unusual flowers. Popularity amongst the cut-flower industry is also increasing.

Culture

- Generally requires well-drained soils in full sun.
- Most are at least partly frost tender.
- Highly susceptible to 'inkspot' (a fungal disease). Some hybrid varieties and *A. flavidus* are exceptions.
- Snails and slugs can be a serious problem.
- Some species lose their leaves during a period of dormancy.
- Propagation is by seed, division or tissue culture.

ANIGOZANTHOS SPECIES	SIZE	COMMENTS
A. flavidus	2 x 1 m	Flowers are variable, usually yellowish-green. Used as a parent species to increase vigour in modern hybrid varieties.
A. humilis (cat's paw)	0.5 x 0.2 m	Cream, yellow, orange, red or pink flowers in late winter to summer.
A. manglesii	0.5 x 1 m	Spreading clump. Green flowers with red base. WA floral emblem.
A. pulcherrimus	1 x 0.3 m	Yellow flowers in spring or summer. Requires excellent drainage; best in sandy or gravel soils; drought tolerant; needs full or filtered sun.
A. preissii	0.3 x 0.3 m	Yellow, orange and red flowers. Generally vigorous but short-lived in cultivation.
A. rufus	0.7 x 0.5 m	Small clump around tall, rich red spring–summer flowers; prefers sandy or gravel soils and lots of sun.
A. viridis	0.5 x 0.3 m	Hardier than some other species if well drained, tolerates some shade, iridescent green flowers in winter–spring

ANTHOCERCIS ❧ Solanaceae

At a glance

NUMBER OF SPECIES About 20; all endemic to Australia (10 from WA).
NATURAL HABITAT Variable, including coastal areas.
FLOWERING Mostly white tubular or bell-shaped flowers.
HABIT Small to medium woody shrubs.
HARDINESS Generally hardy.
FOLIAGE Variable, some species have thick-textured leaves.
GROWTH RATE Fast.
LIFESPAN Medium.
COMMENTS Not widely cultivated, but have great potential. Some have a strong pungent smell when in flower.

Culture

- Best on well-drained soil but most tolerate wet or dry periods.
- Grow in full or filtered sunlight.
- Propagate from cuttings with rooting hormone.

Species

A. albicans

- Adapts to cultivation; tolerates some frost and drought. Susceptible to botrytis.

A. frondosa

- Requires well-drained soil, probably relatively frost and drought resistant. Not extensively grown.

ARAUCARIA ❧ *see Conifers*

ASTARTEA ❧ Myrtaceae

At a glance

NUMBER OF SPECIES 5; all endemic to Australia, 4 in WA. Classification of this genus is currently being reviewed.
NATURAL HABITAT Varied.
FLOWERING Small white or pink flowers. Most species flower for extended periods.
HABIT Small bushes.
HARDINESS Very hardy.
FOLIAGE Fine, heath-like.
GROWTH RATE Fast.
LIFESPAN With regular light pruning they can be long-lived.
COMMENTS Closely related to the genus Baeckea. Sold as a ‘filler’ in the cut-flower industry.

Culture

- Withstands periods of waterlogging.
- Withstands some dry periods.
- Prune lightly and often to prevent legginess.
- Responds to light feeding.
- Responds to watering in dry periods.
- Propagate by tip cuttings, Feb/Mar.

Species

A. fascicularis

- 2 x 2 m
- White or pink flowers, leaves are longer than the flower stalks.

A. heteranthera

- 1 x 1 m
- White flowers, flower stalks are longer than the leaves.

A. intratropica

- 3 x 2 m
- White to pink flowers, tropical shrub, prefers some shade and good drainage.

ASTEROLASIA Rutaceae

At a glance

NUMBER OF SPECIES 5; all endemic to the eastern states of Australia.
NATURAL HABITAT Usually moist gullies and mountain areas.
FLOWERING White or yellow flowers, generally occurring in spring.
HABIT Small shrubs.
HARDINESS Hardy if soil very well drained.
FOLIAGE Hairy, undivided (simple) leaves.
GROWTH RATE Medium to fast.
LIFESPAN Medium.

Culture

- Well-drained but moist soil.
- Some shade.
- Tolerates some frost.
- Mulching is beneficial, but keep deep mulch away from the base of the plants to avoid collar rot.
- Scale and sooty mould can be serious problems.
- Propagates best from semi-hardwood cuttings in late summer.

ASTEROMYRTUS Myrtaceae

At a glance

NUMBER OF SPECIES 6
NATURAL HABITAT Tropical, open forests near streams.
FLOWERING Globes of brilliant colour.
HABIT Mostly weeping, but a few upright forms present.
HARDINESS Hardy and adaptable to southern parts of Qld.
FOLIAGE Weeping shiny dark green, spatulate to lineal leaves.
GROWTH RATE Medium growth.
LIFESPAN Long-lived.
COMMENTS Flower looks similar to the sun, bright and round. Fruit capsules produce round ball similar to an asteroid or meteor. Use to be classified under Melaleuca.

Culture

- Full sun to part sun.
- Good drainage important.
- May need irrigation in dry periods.
- Propagation by seed.

Species

A. angustifolia
- 3–4 m
- Narrow-shaped tree, white, cream, pink colour flower forms.

A. arnhemica
- Little-known species.

A. brassii (syn. *Melaleuca brassii*)
- Variable height
- Low weeping and tall upright forms exist. Variable in flower and leaf colour and features. Can be propagated by suckers. From Cape York.

A. lysicephala
- 2 m
- White flowers.

ASTEROLASIA SPECIES	SIZE	FLOWERS	COMMENTS
A. asteriscophora	1.5 x 1 m	Lemon	Filtered sunlight
A. correifolia	2 x 1.5 m	White	Shade
A. hexapetala	Up to 2 x 2 m	Cream	Filtered sun
A. phebalioides	1 x 1 m	Gold	Filtered sun
A. trymalioides	0.3 x 0.7m	Yellow	Full to part sun

A. magnifica

- 2 m
- Upright plant. Large white terminal flowers. From Arnhem Land.

A. symphyocarpa

- 3 m
- Extremely attractive weeping tree. Large orange globes are produced along the entire weeping branch. From Cape York. Deserves wider cultivation.
- Ideal in containers or hanging baskets.
- Roots do not like disturbance (don't cultivate near them).
- Difficult to propagate. Etiolated growth (i.e. elongated shoots grown in dark conditions) makes the best cuttings.

ASTROLOMA Epacridaceae

At a glance

NUMBER OF SPECIES 20; all endemic to Australia.
NATURAL HABITAT Both coastal and inland areas in temperate Australia.
FLOWERING Tubular flowers in a range of colours, including red, pink, green, orange, yellow and cream.
HABIT Low shrubs, some species are prostrate.
HARDINESS Most are very hardy.
FOLIAGE Fine, heath-like.
GROWTH RATE Medium to fast.
LIFESPAN Generally medium- to long-lived.

Culture

- Will adapt to most climates if protected from extremes.
- Scale, aphis and some other insects are an occasional problem.
- Prefers very good drainage.

ASTROLOMA SPECIES	HEIGHT	FLOWERS	COMMENTS
A. ciliatum	0.2– 0.8m	Red/green/black	Suits full or part sun, grows best in open position.
A. compactum	0.1–0.5 m	Bright red	Suits container growing.
A. conostephioides	0.5–1 m	Red	Suits part or full sun.
A. epacridis	0.4–1 m	Pink to red	Adaptable, suits pots or any well-drained soil.
A. humifusum	0.1–0.5 m	Red	Very adaptable as long as soil well drained.
A. pinifolium	0.3–1 m	Red or yellow	Best in pots in semi-shade.
A. stomarrhena	Up to 0.5 m	Pink or red	Sandy, moist, well-drained soil.

ATRIPLEX Salt Bush Chenopodiaceae

At a glance

NUMBER OF SPECIES About 60; all endemic to Australia.
NATURAL HABITAT Mainly arid or salt-affected areas.
FLOWERING Flowers occur most of the year. They tend to be insignificant although the fleshy fruits are bright-coloured and showy.
HARDINESS Very hardy.
HABIT Shrubs or herbs.
FOLIAGE Mainly grey and slightly thickened.
GROWTH RATE Fast.
LIFESPAN Variable, some can be long-lived.
COMMENTS The foliage and fruit of some species have ornamental value. They are also widely used as forage plants in arid areas, and in revegetation projects in areas with salt-affected and eroded soils.

Culture

- Salt and drought tolerant.
- Thrives in hot, dry conditions, in full sun.

- Some are frost tender.
- Prune to keep growth dense and well shaped.
- Propagate from cuttings at any time. Some germinate easily from seed, but others are both difficult and slow.

Species

A. cinerea

- Shrub 3 x 3 m
- Grey leaves and purple-green flowers in spring.

A. nummularia

- Low to medium shrub
- Attractive whitish stems and hairy silver-white leaves. Very hardy.

A. rhagodiodes

- Small shrub
- Silvery foliage. Resistant to frost.

A. semibaccata

- Prostrate shrub
- Useful groundcover species.

AUSTOMYRTUS Myrtaceae

At a glance

NUMBER OF SPECIES About 15; all endemic to Australia.

NATURAL HABITAT Northern Qld to northern NSW.

FLOWERING White flowers in profusion in spring

HABIT Bush shrubs.

HARDINESS Some species are very tolerant to frost.

FOLIAGE Normally glossy green elliptical. Semi-weeping foliage.

LIFESPAN Medium.

COMMENTS Some new varieties are available with new foliage colour and texture. A good plant to use in windbreaks. Good for planting under powerlines. Berries are attractive to birds.

Culture

- Full to part sun.
- Good drainage essential.
- Regular pruning, mulching and watering ensures a healthy well-shaped plant.
- Propagation by seeds or cuttings.

AUSTOMYRTUS SPECIES	HEIGHT	COMMENTS
A. acmenioides (scrub ironwood)	Up to 8 m	Slender small tree with attractive trunk. Slow growing.
A. bidwillii (python tree)	Up to 10 m	Slender tree with colourful trunk. Flowers and leaves are scented. In full sun the shape of the tree becomes more spreading. Can be slow growing.
A. dallachiana (lignum)	Up to 6 m	Large leaves with very attractive trunk.
A. floribunda (cape ironwood)	2–4 x 2–3 m	Retains foliage to the ground.
A. fragrantissima (sweet myrtle)	Up to 5 m	Attractive new growth. Very slow growing.
A. hillii (scaly myrtle)	Up to 6 m	Very dense growth and shiny leaves. Attractive new growth.
A. inophoia (thread-barked myrtle)	2 x 2 m	Graceful arching habit. Attractive new growth. Excellent for cultivation.
A. lasioclada (velvety myrtle)	Up to 5 m	Furry tips give plant a soft appearance.
A. metrosideros	Up to 4 m	Bushy shrub with attractive new growth. Very ornamental.

BACKHOUSIA ❧ Myrtaceae

At a glance

NUMBER OF SPECIES 7; 6 endemic to Australia.
NATURAL HABITAT Ranges from rainforests to dry forests, predominantly in NSW and Qld.
FLOWERING Five-petalled, small, generally white flowers. Most species flower in summer.
HABIT Medium to tall woody trees. Generally self-shaping.
HARDINESS Generally hardy to very hardy in cultivation. Few pests and diseases.
FOLIAGE Hairy or slightly glossy leaves, often pointed.
GROWTH RATE Generally fast.
LIFESPAN Generally long-lived.
COMMENTS Most species adapt very well to cultivation. Some of the taller species are good as screening plants. Provide some shade when young, but full sun produces a better shaped mature tree.

Culture

- Prune after flowering to maintain bushy growth, if desired.

Species

B. anisata (now known as *Anetholea anisata*)

- 10–25 m
- Fluffy flowers in summer.
- Foliage and flowers smell of aniseed. Rare tree. Excellent shade tree. From subtropical rainforests.

B. citriodora

- 6–13 m
- Fluffy flowers in spring–summer.
- Lemon-scented, slightly hairy foliage. Good street or specimen tree. From Qld forests.

B. myrtifolia

- 4–7 m
- Fluffy flowers in spring–summer.
- Smaller shiny leaves. Scented foliage. Excellent shade tree. From rainforests and gullies in Qld and NSW.

B. sciadophora

- 12 m
- Fluffy flowers in winter.
- Shiny foliage. Flowers and foliage have spicy scent. Good shade tree. From dry forests of NSW and Qld.

BAECKEA ❧ Myrtaceae

At a glance

NUMBER OF SPECIES About 72; 70 occur in Australia.
NATURAL HABITAT Found in all states but principally from south-western WA, growing in a large variety of climatic conditions.
FLOWERING Five-petalled, small, generally white flowers similar to Leptospermum. Most species flower in summer.
HABIT Prostrate to tall woody shrubs.
HARDINESS Generally hardy to very hardy in cultivation. Few pests and diseases.
FOLIAGE Small fine leaves variable in shape, oppositely arranged and sometimes pointed.
GROWTH RATE Generally fast, although some species may be slow.
LIFESPAN Generally medium- to long-lived, although some can be difficult to keep going in cultivation.
COMMENTS Some species tolerate wet conditions well. Some of the taller species are good as screening plants. Some varieties are being trialled for cut flower production.

Culture

- Prune after flowering to maintain bushy growth.
- Slow-release fertilisers and mulches are beneficial.

BAECKEA SPECIES	SIZE	FLOWERS	COMMENTS
B. astarteoides	1 x 1.5 m	Pink	Profuse flowers on arching branches.
B. behrii	1 x 0.5 m	White/pink	Slender, drought-resistant shrub.
B. benthamii	1–3 x 1–2m	White	Grows on the flat sand-plains of WA.
B. camphorata	1–3 x 1–2 m	White	Open shrub; very hardy.
B. camphorosmae	1 x 1–2 m	White/pink	Very attractive in flower; requires some protection.
B. crassifolia	30 cm x 1.3 m	white, pink or purple	Flowers autumn and again in late winter–spring. Grows on sandy soils. NSW, Vic, SA, WA.
B. densifolia	1 x 0.5 m	White	Bushy shrub; attractive and hardy.
B. diosmofolia	1 x 1 m	White	Flowers spring to summer. Well-drained soils. Qld, NSW.
B. gunniana	0.5–2 x 0.5 m	White	Semi-shade, moist soil in cold areas.
B. imbricata	0.5 x 0.3 m	White	Low growing shrub; very hardy.
B. linifolia	1–3 x 1 m	White	Weeping habit; very attractive and adaptable.
B. ramosissima (now known as *Euromyrtus ramomosissima*)	1 x 1 m	White/pink	Variable habit with a number of named varieties.
B. stenophylla	0.5–3 x 1 m	White	Weeping small to medium shrub.
B. utilis	1 x 1 m	White	Tolerant of wet soil and frosts.
B. virgata (now known as *Babingtonia virgata*)	1–4 x 1–4 m	White	Variable habit including prostrate, compact dwarf, weeping and silver-leafed forms.

BANKSIA ❧ Proteaceae

At a glance

NUMBER OF SPECIES About 73; all endemic to Australia, except for *B. dentata*, which is also found in Papua New Guinea; 58 come from WA.

NATURAL HABITAT Varies but usually well-drained soils. In WA mostly in the south-west. In the eastern states mainly along the east and south-east coasts and tablelands.

FLOWERING Varies but it is possible to find banksias in flower at all times of the year.

HABIT Bushes and trees.

HARDINESS Varies, but WA types are often difficult to grow in the east.

FOLIAGE Variable, mostly serrated.

LIFESPAN Long-lived

Culture

- Soil must be well drained for most varieties, particularly those from Western Australia. Plant on slopes, in raised beds or sandy soils. Most popular varieties prefer sandy soils.
- Do not feed with fertilisers containing phosphorus.
- Respond well to iron (place some rusty nails around plants).
- Do not over-water.
- Most are highly susceptible to cinnamon fungus (i.e. *Phytopthera cinnamomi*).
- Limestone underlay technique has proven useful to enable more difficult WA species to grow outside of their natural habitat.
- Propagation is normally by seed. Collect seed cones when seeds are ripe, but before

BANKSIA SPECIES	SIZE	FLOWERING AND GENERAL COMMENTS
B. aemula (syn. *B. serratifolia*)	2–6 x 2–6 m	Cream-yellow flowers in winter.
B. ashbyii	5 x 4 m	Orange flowers, normally in winter.
B. attenuata	Up to 15 x 6 m	Yellow flowers in spring–summer.
B. baueri	2 x 2 m	Large furry orange flowers in winter–spring.
B. baxteri	3 x 2 m	Yellow flowers in summer.
B. brownii	2 x 3 m	Red-gold flowers in autumn–winter.
B. burdettii	3–6 x 3–5 m	Orange and white flowers in spring–summer.
B. caleyi	2 x 3 m	Prickly foliage; yellow or red flowers in spring–summer.
B. candolleana	1.5 x 3 m	Bright yellow flowers in autumn–winter.
B. coccinea	4 x 2 m	Red-grey flowers in spring–summer.
B. conferta	3 x 3 m	Yellow flowers in summer–autumn.
B. dentata	3–8 x 5 m	Yellow flowers in autumn–spring, suits hot areas.
B. dryandroides	1 x 1–2 m	Brown flowers in spring–summer.
B. ericifolia	4 x 4 m	Gold, orange or red flowers, hardy.
B. grandis	7 x 3 m	Green-yellow flowers in spring–summer.
B. integrifolia	10–15 m	Yellow flowers in autumn–spring, very hardy.
B. ilicifolia	5–12 m	Yellow to green flowers in autumn or spring.
B. laevigata	3 x 3–4 m	Shades of yellow flowers from spring to summer, hardy and adaptable, prefers semi-arid areas.
B. laricina	2 x 3 m	Yellow flowers in winter, needs well-drained spot, very decorative sought-after cones.
B. littoralis	Up to 15 x 6–8 m	Bright yellow flowers in autumn–winter, suits coastal areas, wind tolerant.
B. marginata	4–10 x 4–6 m	Yellow flowers in late summer through to winter, very hardy in most areas.
B. menziesii	5 x 4 m	Pink tips with yellow base, flowers mainly in winter, hardy if well drained.
B. nutans	1–2 x 2 m	Brown to purple–brown flowers in spring and summer.
B. occidentalis	3 x 1.5 m	Red-gold flowers in late summer–autumn.
B. praemorsa	Up to 5 x 2.5 m	Yellow flowers with tinges of red to purple in summer to mid-winter.
B. prionotes	5–10 x 5 m	Flowers greyish turning orange-white in autumn–winter.
B. quercifolia	Up to 4 x 2.5 m	Brown flowers turning orange-brown.
B. robur	2 x 2 m	Green-yellow flowers in winter–spring.
B. serrata	6 x 4 m	Yellow flowers in winter–summer, very hardy and adapts to most areas.
B. spinulosa	3 x 3 m	Rich yellow and black flowers.
B. victoriae	4 x 4 m	Orange flowers in summer–autumn, difficult to grow.

seeds drop (for some varieties this is easy; for others, there is a relatively short period when seeds can be collected). Seeds remain viable longer if stored in cones (but cones can be prone to insect attack and may need to be treated with a pesticide). Store seed cones in a cool place. When ready to plant, place cones in a warm place for them to open and release their seeds. If seeds do not release easily, soak the cone in water for 2 days then plut in a warm place immediately. Day temperatures of 20°C to 25°C are best for seed germination. They are best left in a pot of seed-raising mix in the open or an unheated greenhouse (do not place in a heated greenhouse). Damping-off diseases can be a problem during early growth, and should be closely watched. Germination can take from 3 weeks to 3 months. Some species can be grown from cuttings (mainly the fine-leaved types such as *Banksia ericifolia*).

BARKLYA Caesalpiniaceae

At a glance

NUMBER OF SPECIES 1; endemic to Australia.
NATURAL HABITAT Dry rainforest environment preferred.
FLOWERING Profusion of golden narrow spikes in early summer.
HABIT Tree-like, but can be pruned to thicken the specimen.
HARDINESS Generally hardy in subtropical districts.
FOLIAGE Glossy heart-shaped leaves produce a dense canopy.
GROWTH RATE Slow.
LIFESPAN Medium.

Culture

- Responds well to pruning.
- Prefers moist but well-drained soils.
- Can tolerate short drought situations.
- Best in filtered sunlight or full sun.
- Propagates from seed, but takes many years to flower.

Species

B. syringifolia (crown of gold tree)

- Can reach 10 m but much less in cultivation. Native to districts around Brisbane but adaptable as far south as Sydney. Mulching and fertilising will speed up growth.

BAUERA Baueraceae

At a glance

NUMBER OF SPECIES 3; endemic to eastern Australia.
NATURAL HABITAT Moist sheltered sites.
FLOWERING White or pink flowers. Some flower all year.
HABIT Bushes.
HARDINESS Generally hardy. Hardy to frost.
FOLIAGE Small stalkless leaflets arranged in whorls.
GROWTH RATE Fast.
LIFESPAN Medium.

Culture

- Respond well to pruning.
- Prefer acid soils, but will grow in most types of soil.
- Tolerate wet or dry periods.
- Best in filtered sunlight.
- Scale is sometimes a problem.
- Propagates easily from cuttings.

Species

B. rubioides

- 1–2 x 3 m
- White to pink flowers all year, frost tolerant, flowers occur on stalks longer than leaves.

B. sessiliflora

- 2 x 4 m
- Rose to purple flowers in spring, a white-flowering form is also available, flowers occur in clusters not on stalks.

BEAUFORTIA ❧ Myrtaceae

At a glance

NUMBER OF SPECIES 18; all endemic to Australia mainly south-western WA.
NATURAL HABITAT Variable.
FLOWERING Mauve to red flowers, in brushes or globular heads.
HABIT Small bushes.
HARDINESS Hardy, but young plants susceptible to frost.
FOLIAGE Small leaves tight on stem.
GROWTH RATE Relatively fast.
LIFESPAN Medium.

Culture

- Prefers moist soils with good drainage, but withstands dry and wet periods.
- Prefers full sun or filtered sunlight.
- Prune lightly throughout the year except when flowering.
- Normally propagate by semi-hardwood cuttings or seed.

Species

B. decussate
- 3 x 1–2 m
- Rich red flowers in summer–autumn.

B. heterophylla
- 1 x 1 m
- Grey foliage, red flowers in spring.

B. incana
- 3 x 3 m
- Grey-green foliage, yellow flowers with red tips; hardy species.

B. orbifolia
- 2 x 1 m
- Green and red flowers turning bright red, very adaptable and hardy.

B. sparsa
- 2 x 1.5 m
- Orange-red flowers in autumn, hardy, good as a cut flower.

B. squarrose
- 1 x 2 m
- Orange-red flowers in summer–autumn.

BILLARDIERA ❧ Pittosporaceae

At a glance

NUMBER OF SPECIES 25; all endemic to Australia, mainly WA.
NATURAL HABITAT Mainly woodland and forest.
FLOWERING Tubular flowers with petals which curl back, fruits are a berry.
HARDINESS Most are hardy to very hardy.
HABIT Most are climbers, generally open.
FOLIAGE Lobed or simple undivided leaves.
LIFESPAN Long-lived.

Culture

- Best grown below or among other plants.
- Prefers moist but well-drained soil.
- Most need watering in dry weather.
- Seed propagation can be difficult, cuttings are generally easy.

Species

B. bicolour
- Cream or yellow with purple stripes.
- Avoid hot afternoon sun, best with filtered sun.

B. cymosa
- Greenish-white or purplish.
- Very hardy, from semi-arid areas, prefers sunny position.

B. longiflora
- Green–yellow.
- Cool moist spot, but tolerates sun.

B. scandens
- Greenish-yellow.
- Adapts to full sun or heavy shade.

BLANCOA ❧ Haemodoraceae

At a glance

NUMBER OF SPECIES 1 (*B. canescens*); endemic to WA.
NATURAL HABITAT Sandy plains.
FLOWERING Tubular pink flowers.
HARDINESS Hardy.
HABIT Small clumping herb.
FOLIAGE Grey-green leaves up to 25 x 0.5 cm.
LIFESPAN Five years or more if in good conditions.

Culture

- Prefers well-drained soil in full sun or semi-shade.
- Propagate by dividing clumps or from fresh seed, although germination can be unreliable.

BLANDFORDIA ❧ Christmas Bells ❧ Liliaceae

At a glance

NUMBER OF SPECIES 4; all endemic to eastern Australia.
NATURAL HABITAT Heaths and swamps, mostly in sandstone areas.
FLOWERING Red and yellow bell-shaped flowers which are borne on erect stems. Flowering occurs in summer.
HARDINESS Generally hardy once established.
HABIT Tufted perennial herb.
FOLIAGE Strap-like leaves.
GROWTH RATE Slow, plants can take up to 4 years before they commence flowering.
LIFESPAN Short to medium.

Culture

- Will grow best in acidic, moist, sandy soils, although considered difficult in cultivation.
- Prefer semi-shaded positions.
- Tolerant of frost.
- Can tolerate periods of waterlogging.
- Propagation is from seed, although they may be slow to germinate. Ripe seed is sown in spring and autumn.

Species

B. grandiflora

- Waxy red tubular flowers, with yellow edging.
- Will grow in a range of conditions but prefers moist, sandy soils in semi-shaded position. Frost tolerant.

B. nobilis

- Cylindrical red-yellow flowers.
- Naturally occurs on sandstone around Sydney. Full sun to part shade. Good drainage required.

BORONIA ❧ Rutaceae

At a glance

NUMBER OF SPECIES 95; 49 species in WA, 45 of which are endemic.
NATURAL HABITAT Coastal heaths, open woodland.
FLOWERING Mainly late winter and spring, some throughout the year.
HARDINESS Medium; some not very hardy.
HABIT Bushes and small trees.
FOLIAGE Varies in colour and shape; normally scented.
GROWTH RATE Normally fast.
LIFESPAN Often limited to 5–8 years.
COMMENTS Some can be difficult to get to survive in a 'mixed' garden (i.e. when grown among non-native plants).

Culture

- Prune hard in first year as this can significantly extend the plant's life.
- Scale can be a problem.
- Root protection is important, so grow beside log, rock or mulch.
- Feeding with well-rotted manure or compost is advantageous.

BORONIA SPECIES	SIZE	FLOWERS	COMMENTS
B. anemonifolia	0.4–1 x 1 m	Pink-white	Difficult to establish.
B. citriodora	0.5 x 1 m	Pale pink	Keep roots cool.
B. clavata	1.5 x 1.5 m	Green	Scented leaves and flowers.
B. denticulata	2 x 1 m	Pink, all year	One of the hardiest.
B. fastigata	0.5 x 1 m	Mauve-pink	Best under taller plants.
B. filifolia	0.5 x 1 m	Pink, all year	Cool, sunny spot.
B. floribunda	1.5 x 1 m	Pink	Scented foliage.
B. heterophylla	2 x 1 m	Red, spring	Well drained, mulched.
B. ledifolia	1.5 x 1.5 m	Rich pink	Often short-lived.
B. megastigma	1 x 1 m	Brown, spring	Short-lived.
B. megastigma lutea	1 x 1 m	Yellow	Can be short-lived.
B. mollis	1.5 x 1 m	Bright pink	Soft, divided foliage.
B. muelleri	0.5 x 1 m	Pink, spring	Fern-like foliage
B. pilosa	0.5–1 x 0.6 m	Pink, spring	Soft foliage.
B. pinnata	1.5 x 1 m	Bright pink	Divided foliage.
B. serrulata	0.5–1 x 1 m	Rich pink	Scented foliage.
B. spathulata	0.3 x 0.5 m	Pink	Suckering.
B. viminea	1 x 1 m	Pink	Adaptable, long flowering.

- Boronias will grow in both clay and sand; they tend to grow better in infertile soils.
- There is a wide variation within each species to tolerance of different soils (e.g. one *B. heterophylla* may grow better on a clay soil than another *B. heterophylla*).
- Boronias do not like temperature fluctuations, soil temperatures over 24°C or sudden changes in the water content of the soil.
- They prefer an acid soil (pH around 5.5) so do not add lime to soil.
- Propagate by semi-hardwood cuttings in late summer or early autumn, treated with hormone powder and placed under glass. Seedlings can take a long time to flower.

BOSSIAEA — Fabaceae

At a glance

NUMBER OF SPECIES About 50; all endemic to Australia.

NATURAL HABITAT Variable, ranging from coastal to inland areas.

FLOWERING Yellow-red pea-shaped flowers in spring.

HARDINESS Hardy in preferred conditions.

HABIT Small to medium shrubs.

FOLIAGE Variable.

GROWTH RATE Fast.

LIFESPAN Some are short-lived.

Culture

- Prefer moist, well-drained soil; some species tolerate clay soil.
- Grow in semi-shade.

- Place mulch around plants.
- Prune after flowering.
- Propagate from pre-treated (boiling water) seed (see Propagation section).

Species

B. cordigera

- To 0.5 m. Red and yellow flowers.
- Sprawling to over 2 m diameter.

B. dentata

- 1–2 m. Orange-red flowers.
- Triangular leaves, neat shrub.

B. linophylla

- 1.5 m. Golden-yellow flowers.
- Weeping shrub, bronze-green leaves.

BRACHYCHITON ❀ Sterculiaceae

At a glance

NUMBER OF SPECIES About 30; all endemic to tropical areas in Australia, except 1 which occurs in Papua New Guinea.

NATURAL HABITAT Ranges from rainforests to inland areas.

FLOWERING Showy clusters followed by large woody seed pods.

HARDINESS Some are extremely hardy.

HABIT Partially deciduous trees.

FOLIAGE Varies, some lobed and glossy, others entire (undivided) with a dull texture.

GROWTH RATE Slow, especially when young.

LIFESPAN Long-lived.

COMMENTS Rainforest species are less hardy.

Culture

- Grow best in warm climates.
- Soils should be well drained.
- Once established will withstand dry periods.
- Propagate with seeds collected from current season's capsules. These may take several months to germinate.

BRACHYCHITON SPECIES	HEIGHT	FLOWERS	COMMENTS
B. acerifolius (flame tree)	5–15 m	Brilliant red	Summer flowers. Leaves are shed before flowering. Amount of flowers varies year to year. Best in fertile soils and warm areas, but grows as far south as Melbourne.
B. bidwillii (little kurrajong)	5 m	Bright red	Hairy foliage and flowers. Excellent size for domestic gardens. From rainforests in south-east Qld.
B. discolour (lacebark)	10–20 m	Pink or red	Hairy leaves. Felt-like pink flowers in spring and summer. From NSW to Qld.
B. gregorii (desert kurrajong)	5–8 m	Cream to brown	Flowers after rain, drought tolerant, best in arid climates.
B. populneus (kurrajong)	10–15 m	Cream-pink	Adapts to dry inland areas, flecked. Frost tolerant.
B. rupestris (bottle tree)	5–20 m	Cream	Suits moist or dry soils, good in hot, arid areas; slow growing.

BRACHYSCOME ❀ Asteraceae

At a glance

NUMBER OF SPECIES About 90; most are endemic to Australia, some occur in New Zealand and Papua New Guinea.

NATURAL HABITAT Wide range, from coast to alpine areas.

FLOWERING Daisy flowers at varying times of the year.

HARDINESS Hardy.
HABIT Herbs and small shrubs.
FOLIAGE Divided leaves.
GROWTH RATE Fast.
LIFESPAN Short-lived.

Culture

- Tolerate a wide range of soils.
- Propagate by seed, cuttings or division.

Species

B. angustifolia

- 0.1 x 1.5 m. Small grey leaves carry pink or mauve flowers all year.

B. diversifolia

- 0.3 x 1.5 m. White flowers all year.

B. iberidifolia

- 0.3 x 1 m. White, pink, blue or mauve flowers most of the year.

B. multifida

- 0.3 x 1 m. Native of Qld, NSW and Vic, ground cover or tiny shrub with blue daisy flowers all year. Very hardy. Several varieties of this species are available.

BRACHYSEMA

see also Gastrolobium

At a glance

NUMBER OF SPECIES About 16, mainly from south-west WA. All *Brachysema* species have been transferred to *Gastrolobium*.
NATURAL HABITAT Varied, mainly south-western WA.
FLOWERING Elongated pea-shaped flowers, usually red coloured.
HARDINESS Generally very hardy.
HABIT Groundcovers and shrubs.
FOLIAGE Variable.
GROWTH RATE Medium to fast.
LIFESPAN Long-lived under good conditions.

Culture

- Tolerate most soils and conditions.
- Prune to keep bushy and promote flowering.
- Propagate by cuttings in late summer.

Species

G. lanceolatum* syn. *Brachysema lanceolatum
(Swan River pea)

- 1.5 x 3 m, red pea flowers for several months winter to spring; withstands some waterlogging and light frosts.

G. latifolium* syn. *Brachysema latifolium

- 2–3 x 3 m, creeping plant with red flowers May–Sept; grows on most soils in full sun or filtered sunlight (not shade).

G. praemorsum* syn. *Brachysema praemorsum

- 1.5 x 1.5 m, creeping plant. Flowers cream at first but change to red; tolerates only light frosts.

BRACTEANTHA *see Helichrysum*

BREYNIA Euphorbiaceae

At a glance

NUMBER OF SPECIES 25; 5 occur in Australia.
NATURAL HABITAT Open forests, stream banks and coastal districts.
FLOWERING Male and female flowers borne on the same tree.
HARDINESS Easily grown in warm climates from NSW to the tropics and into WA. May become deciduous in cold temperatures.
HABIT Graceful weeping habit. Can grow into a drab plant if not cared for.
FOLIAGE Usually green alternating leaves. Varieties now exist with very ornamental coloured forms.
GROWTH RATE Fast in warm climates.
LIFESPAN Long-lived.
COMMENTS Red fruits are decorative and eaten by birds.

Culture
- Full sun to part shade.
- Well-drained soil important.
- Propagate by seeds, root suckers or cuttings.

Species
B. cernua
- 2–4 x 1–2 m
- Ornamental graceful shrub.

B. oblongifolia coffee bush
- 2–4 x 1–2 m
- Graceful shrub but may become straggly, pruning is then required.

B. stipitate fart bush
- 2–5 x 1–3 m
- Glossy attractive leaves release unpleasant smell when crushed.

BUCKINGHAMIA ❧ Protaceae

At a glance
NUMBER OF SPECIES 1; endemic to north Qld.
NATURAL HABITAT Wet rainforest.
FLOWERING Pendulous cream flowers spring to summer.
HARDINESS Hardy if well drained.
HABIT Medium tree.
FOLIAGE Variable, lobed to entire.
GROWTH RATE Fast in warm humid climates.
LIFESPAN Long-lived.

Culture
- Well-drained soil in semi-shade or full sun.
- Can be hardy in temperate climates, but frost tender when young.
- Propagate from fresh seed, kept moist and barely covered.

Species
B. celsissima
- Up to 20 m tall and 10 m wide; much smaller in domestic gardens than in more open positions. Excellent street tree and specimen tree in gardens.

BULBINE ❧ Liliaceae

At a glance
NUMBER OF SPECIES 30; 3 occur in Australia.
NATURAL HABITAT Wide range, including coasts and forests.
FLOWERING Yellow flowers, mostly from spring to summer.
HARDINESS Hardy in moist, well-drained soils.
HABIT Small perennial herb.
FOLIAGE Succulent grass-like leaves similar in appearance to onion leaves.
GROWTH RATE Fast.
LIFESPAN Short-lived.

Culture
- Well-drained soil in full sun or semi-shade.
- Propagate from seed or by division.

Species
B. bulbosa
- Small, yellow-flowering herb growing from bulb-like tuber. Adaptable to a range of conditions.

B. semibarbata
- Yellow flowers; fibrous roots; prefers sandy soils.

BURSARIA ❧ Pittosporaceae

At a glance
NUMBER OF SPECIES 6; all endemic to Australia.
NATURAL HABITAT Varied, all states.
FLOWERING Small white flowers in terminal sprays.
HARDINESS Very hardy.
HABIT Shrubs and small trees.
FOLIAGE Small entire leaves.
GROWTH RATE Medium to fast.
LIFESPAN Medium.

Culture
- Prune to maintain shape.
- Most prefer well-drained soil.

- Most tolerate hot exposed positions.
- Propagate from seed or semi-hardwood cuttings.

Species

B. lasiophylla

- 2.5 x 1.5 m
- Variable shrub; leaves hairy underneath. Adapts to most soils, is frost hardy with white flowers spring and summer.

B. spinosa

- 2–10 x 0.5–5 m
- Variable shrub, with fragrant cream to white flowers followed by attractive clusters of brown seed capsules. Several named forms, some with spiny branches. Responds to pruning. Widespread in cultivation.

CAESIA ❧ Anthericaceae ❧ Liliaceae

At a glance

NUMBER OF SPECIES 2; distributed throughout Vic, Qld, NSW and Tas.
NATURAL HABITAT Plains grassland, woodland, valley sclerophyll forests
FLOWERING White through to pale blue flowers along the slender stems, spring to late summer.
HARDINESS Generally fairly hardy but will flower longer with summer moisture.
HABIT Tufted perennial grass-like herb.
FOLIAGE Grassy basal leafed tufts.
GROWTH RATE Medium–fast.
LIFESPAN Short-lived.

Culture

- Moist well-drained soils which tend to dry out in summer preferred.
- Propagate by seed or division.

Species

C. calliantha blue grass-lily

- 10–50 x 10–50 cm
- Useful rockery plant.
- Lilac to deep blue flowers.

C. parviflora* var. *parviflora (syn. *C. vittata*) pale grass-lily

- 10–30 x 10–25 cm
- White to pale lavender flowers.

C. parviflora* var. *minor

- 10–20 cm
- White flowers tinged with blue.

CALECTASIA ❧ Xanthorrhoeaceae ❧ Dasypogonaceae

At a glance

NUMBER OF SPECIES 11; all but one endemic to WA.
NATURAL HABITAT Varies according to species from damp areas to roadside and dryer plains.
FLOWERING Blue to purple flowers with yellow bracts occurring singly.
HARDINESS Moderate to hardy.
HABIT Rhizomatous, tufted, spreading, woody perennial, herbs or shrubs.
FOLIAGE Alternate small, flat linear leaves with entire margins, spirally or irregularly crowded.
GROWTH RATE Moderate once established.
LIFESPAN Short to medium.

Culture

- Well-drained soils.
- Sun to part shade.
- Drought and frost resistant.
- Propagation from seed; is very difficult and slow.

Species

C. cynea

- 0.3 x 0.3 m
- Wiry, stiff-tufted stem, crowded hairy, heath- like leaves, flowers metallic blue or purple with 3 star-shaped sepals in spring. WA.

C. intermedia

- 0.3 x 0.3 m
- Similar to *C. cynea*, purple, papery flowers. WA, SA, Vic.

CALLICOMA ⁂ Cunoniaceae

At a glance

NUMBER OF SPECIES 1; endemic to Australia.
NATURAL HABITAT Mainly rainforest and its margins, common along creeks and rocky gullies; NSW.
HARDINESS Hardy.
HABIT Tall shrub or tree to 20 m with reddish, hairy young stems.
FOLIAGE To 12 cm elliptic, dark green leaves, smooth on the upper surface but silvery and hairy underneath, serrated margins.
FLOWERING Round yellowish-brown flowers, on long peduncles, appear in clustered heads in spring.
GROWTH RATE Fast.
COMMENTS Early settlers made wattle and daub houses from the wood.

Culture

- Well-drained fertile soil.
- Shade.

Species

C. serratifolia

CALLISTEMON ⁂ Myrtaceae

At a glance

NUMBER OF SPECIES About 30; all except 4 endemic to Australia.
NATURAL HABITAT Usually in areas of high rainfall.
FLOWERING Showy bottlebrush-shaped spikes. Colours vary, including white, cream, yellow, green, pink, mauve and red.
HARDINESS Generally very hardy, tolerates some waterlogging and some drought.
HABIT Shrubs and small trees.
FOLIAGE Often leathery, undivided, lanc-shaped or oval leaves, young growth often attractive pink or red tinge.
GROWTH RATE Slow and sporadic at times, fast if properly treated.
LIFESPAN Long-lived.

Culture

- Appreciates watering during dry periods.
- Tip-prune regularly throughout year. Do not prune hard.
- Tolerates wide range of soils.
- Young foliage can be burnt a little by frost.
- Feeding with slow-release fertiliser can cause two flowering periods.
- Sometimes attacked by tip borers killing the ends of branches.
- Caterpillars are occasionally a problem.
- Propagate by seed, or selected varieties by cuttings.

CALOCEPHALUS ⁂ *see Leucophyta*

CALOSTEMMA ⁂ Amaryllidaceae

At a glance

NUMBER OF SPECIES 4; all endemic to Australia.
NATURAL HABITAT Open forest country to flood plains.
FLOWERING cluster (umbel) of flowers on a tall stalk.
HARDINESS Generally very hardy. Choose a species suitable for local climate.
HABIT Bulbous plant.
FOLIAGE Usually lineal shiny green leaves.
GROWTH RATE Medium.
LIFESPAN Medium.
COMMENTS Bulbs multiply with time. Flowers best after dry periods. Slow-release fertiliser improves plant growth.

Culture

- Does not tolerate cold, wet soils.
- Propagation is by seed which germinates readily, or division.

CALLISTEMON SPECIES	SIZE	COMMENTS
C. brachyandrus	1–4 x 1–2 m	Prickly, orange brush flowers.
C. citrinus	2–7 x 2–5 m	Has been hybridised to produce many cultivars. Green to red flowers in spring and autumn; best in full sun.
C. comboynensis	1.5–2 x 2–3 m	Crimson brushes intermittently throughout the year.
C. flavovirens	1–1.5 x 1–1.5 m	Yellowish-green flowers in late spring and early summer with sporadic flowering at other times.
C. formosus	3–6 x 2–4 m	Narrow stiff leaves, red spring flowers.
C. glaucus	Up to 2 m	Red terminal brushes from spring to early summer.
C. linearifolius	2–3 x 3 m	Red flowers in spring–summer.
C. linearis	3 x 4 m	Flowers in spring and summer, dull red with gold flecks, narrow-thin leaves.
C. lilacinus	4 x 4 m	*C. citrinus* hybrid, large purple flowers in late spring–early summer.
C. montanus	Up to 2 x 2 m	Squat red brushes several times throughout the year.
C. pachyphyllus	1–2 x 0.5–1.5 m	Dark red throughout the year.
C. pallidus	3 x 3 m	Cream-yellow flowers in Sept–Dec, very hardy, good for windbreaks.
C. pearsonii	0.7 x 1.5 m	Bright red-gold-tipped flowers in spring.
C. phoeniceus	2–4 x 3–5 m	Narrow grey–green twisted leaves, red flowers throughout spring–early summer.
C. pinifolius (syn. *C. paludosus*)	1.5 x 1.5 m	Narrow 7 cm-long leaves, green or red summer flowers.
C. pityoides (old name *C. sibieri*)	3 x 3 m	Cream to yellow brushes in late spring to late summer.
C. polandii	2–4 x 2 m	Thick stiff leaves. Large 10 cm-thick red brushes tipped with gold anthers in summer.
C. recurvis (syn. *C.* 'Tinaroo')	1–7 x 1–4 m	Crimson brushes with yellow anthers in spring.
C. rigidis	3 x 2 m	Red brushes in summer.
C. rugulosus (syn *C. macropunctatus*)	4 x 4 m	Red brushes with yellow anthers in summer and autumn.
C. salignus	5–10 x 4 m	White papery bark, flower colour varies from green through to cream, pink, red to purple; very hardy to drought resistant, green foliage with pink tips on new growth.
C. shiressii	3 x 1.5 m	White flowers in summer.
C. sieberi (syn *C. paludosus*)	3 x 2 m	Narrow leaves up to 6 cm long, pink flowers in summer.
C. subulatus	1–2 x 1–2 m	Crimson brushes during summer.
C. viminalis	10–12 x 2–6 m	Weeping foliage, bright red flowers in spring, hardy, excellent windbreak plant.
C. viridiflorus	3 x 2 m	Greenish-yellow brushes in summer.

Note: Many new hybrids are available with a range of flower colours and growth heights. Many of these new varieties are suitable to most districts and soil types.

Species

C. luteum (yellow garland lily)

- Late summer flowering plant from Qld, NSW and SA.

C. scott-sellickiana

- Summer white flowers. Very attractive. Qld, NT. Needs a heated house to be grown in southern states.

C. purpureum (garland lily)

- Late summer reddish-flowering plant. Natural populations subject to flooding but will tolerate dry conditions. Adapted to cultivation.

CALOTHAMNUS Myrtaceae

At a glance

NUMBER OF SPECIES 36; all endemic to WA.
NATURAL HABITAT Varying, from coastal to inland areas.
FLOWERING Red one-sided spike or cluster on older wood (looks similar to a one-sided bottlebrush flower).
HARDINESS Generally hardy, reasonably frost tolerant.
HABIT Shrubs.
FOLIAGE Narrow leaves, often fairly sparse covering.
GROWTH RATE Medium to fast.
LIFESPAN Can be long-lived.
COMMENTS Useful bird attractants.

Culture

- Adaptable to a range of soils and climatic conditions.
- Generally very few pest and disease problems, apart from scale.
- Prone to leggy growth; regular tip pruning will prevent this.
- Propagate by seed or semi-hardwood cuttings.

Species

C. gilesii

- 2 x 4 m
- Spreading shrub, grows best in full sun; red flowers in winter and spring, very hardy.

C. gracilis

- 0.6 x 0.5 m
- Red flowers from spring to summer.

C. graniticus

- 1–2.5 m tall
- Shrub with soft pine-like foliage and red flowers.

C. homalophyllus

- 2 x 2 m
- Red or cream spring flowers.

C.quadrifidus (common net bush)

- 3 x 4 m
- Red flowers, best in well-drained soil and full sun at least part of the day, very hardy. Prostrate form available.

C. villosus

- 2 x 2 m
- Grows in part or full sun, a little less hardy than the above.

CALOTIS Asteraceae

At a glance

NUMBER OF SPECIES 26; 24 endemic to Australia.
NATURAL HABITAT Grassland, woodland, wet grassland, plains grassland.
FLOWERING Daisy flowers, white, yellow, lilac
HARDINESS Hardy.
HABIT Annual or perennial herbs or small shrubs.
FOLIAGE Basal, alternate, flat, margins usually toothed or lobed.
LIFESPAN Varies, depending on species.
GROWTH RATE Fast.

Culture

- Well-drained soil.
- Some are drought resistant.
- Propagate by seeds or cuttings.

CALOTIS SPECIES	SIZE	COMMENTS
C. anthemoides	20 x 30 cm	Erect, smooth, perennial tufted herb; leaves are finely divided, flowers are white or lilac and showy in spring. Moist soils. Rare. NSW, Vic.
C. cymbacantha	10–30 cm H	Annual herb, erect and branching oblong 3–7-lobed leaves. Yellow flowers in late summer and again in late winter to spring. NSW, Qld, Vic, WA, SA.
C. dentex	Up to 80 cm H	Erect, hairy perennial shrub. Oblong leaves 2–9 cm long, upper leaves have entire margins, lower leaves serrated margins. Flowers brownish-yellow from spring to mid-autumn. NSW, Qld.
C. erinacea	Up to 90 cm H	Erect or prostrate spreading perennial, woody shrub, with toothed margins. Yellowish-brown flowers in late autumn to early spring. NSW, Qld, Vic, WA, SA, NT.
C. lappulacea	0.50 x up to 0.50 m	Perennial herb or small shrub. Wedge-shaped lower leaves. Yellow flowers most of the year. NSW, Qld, Vic, WA, SA.
C. scabiosifolia var. *scaiosifolia*	Up to 45 cm	Perennial hairy herb, spreads by stolons forming tufts. Lower leaves are lance-shaped and toothed or lobed, upper leaves narrower. Flowers white or lilac in late winter to mid-spring.
C. scapigera	Up to 35 cm	Smooth, suckering, perennial herb with tufts of narrow 100 mm leaves. White or lilac flowers from mid-spring to late autumn. NSW, Qld, SA, Vic.

CALYTRIX — Fringe Myrtle — Myrtaceae

At a glance

NUMBER OF SPECIES About 70; all endemic to Australia, mainly WA.
NATURAL HABITAT Mostly heathlands, some from cool climates, others warm.
FLOWERING Showy, small star-shaped flowers with elongated calyxes. Colours include white, cream, yellow, pink, mauve and blue.
HARDINESS Hardy.
HABIT Shrubs.
FOLIAGE Small entire leaves.
LIFESPAN Medium.
GROWTH RATE Medium to fast.

Culture

- Well-drained soils in full sun or semi-shade.
- Prune lightly after flowering.
- Excellent in containers.
- Some withstand extremes of shade or sun, most are best in light shade or filtered sunlight.
- Frost hardiness varies.
- Most need routine pruning to keep dense and bushy.
- Scale and grey mould are the only real insect and disease problems that are likely to affect growth.
- Propagate from tip cuttings, normally in early autumn.

CANANGA — Annonaceae

At a glance

NUMBER OF SPECIES 2; 1 endemic to Australia.
NATURAL HABITAT Low altitudes, rainforest districts in northern Qld.
FLOWERING Large yellow drooping petals from spring to early autumn. Very fragrant.
HARDINESS Hardy as far south as south-eastern Qld, possibly suitable to northern NSW. Not tolerant of frosts.
HABIT Large medium tree with weeping habit.
FOLIAGE Large alternate lime green.
GROWTH RATE Very fast during growing season. May stop growing during winter.
LIFESPAN Long-lived.

CALYTRIX SPECIES	SIZE	COMMENTS
C. alpestris	2 x 2–3 m	Attractive pink buds, opening to white flowers; fine foliage; spreading habit, commonly grown species.
C. amethystina	Up to 60 x 60 cm	Flowers blue-purple or violet in winter to spring.
C. asperula	Up to 20–60 cm	Small shrub. Creamy yellow flowers from spring to autumn.
C. aurea	1–2 x 1 m	Small yellow flowers in dense clusters; fragrant.
C. birdii	Up to 1 x to 1 m	Purple flowers in early to mid-spring.
C. brevifolia	Up to 2 x to 5 m	Pale green flowers, from warm climates, best suited to well-drained soil and filtered sunlight in a hot climate.
C. breviseta	Up to 1 x to 1 m	Purple-blue flowers in late winter to mid-spring.
C. brownii	3 x 2–3 m	Erect shrub. Whitish-cream flowers all year round. WA, NT, Qld.
C. decussata	50 cm x 1 m	Small spreading shrub; pale mauve flowers from summer to mid-winter.
C. carinata	Up to 3 m	Variable small straggly to large erect shrub. Pinkish-purple flowers in autumn–mid-spring.
C. decandra	Up to 1 x 1 m	Semi-prostrate shrub of variable height. Pink-purple flowers from mid-winter to early summer.
C. depressa	1 x 1–2 m	Pale yellow flowers.
C. desolata	Up to 1.5 x 1 m	Small to medium shrub. Pink or purplish-blue flowers from mid-autumn to mid-spring.
C. exstipulata	5 x 3 m	Tree-like shrub, mauve-pink flowers, prolific all year round.
C. flavescens	80 cm x 1 m	Scented yellow flowers, tolerates light frosts, best in a container.
C. fraseri	1 x 1–1.5 m	Purple flowers in summer–autumn.
C. glutinosa	1 x 1.5 m	Lilac-pink star flowers.
C. gracilis	60 cm to 1.5 m	Small shrub of variable size. Violet-blue flowers in mid-winter to mid-spring.
C. habrantha	Up to 1 x to 1 m	Small shrub. Pink-purple flowers mid-spring to mid-summer.
C. leschenaultii	Up to 1 x to 1 m	Beautiful small shrub. Purplish-violet-blue flowers marked with pink from winter to late spring.
C. longiflora	2 x 2.5 m	Deep pink flowers, good in warm climates; roots should be mulched to keep cool.
C. oldfeldii	1 x 1.5 m	Pink and violet flowers, resists light frosts and some drought, soils must be well drained.
C. strigosa	1 x 1 m	Purple to pink flowers, attractive fruits; needs warmth and good drainage to do well. Tolerates light frosts.
C. sullivana	3–4 x 2–3 m	White flowers, prefers some shade, otherwise quite hardy.
C. sylvana	Up to 1 x 1 m	Purple-blue and pink flowers in late winter–mid-spring.
C. tetragonal (syn. *C. sullivanii*)	1–2 x 1–2 m	Pink flowers; tolerates frosts and dry periods; a commonly grown species.
C. violaceae	To 45 x 45 cm	Small shrub. Purple-blue to violet flowers in late winter–mid-spring.

COMMENTS Source of the essence for Macassar oil, believed to be a male aphrodisiac.

Culture

- Full sun.
- Protect from winds.
- Irrigate in periods of low rainfall.
- Requires well-drained soils.
- Propagate by fresh seed.

Species

B. odorata Ylang Ylang

- Grows to approximately 10 metres in tropical areas, less in the subtropics. Can reach 5 metres wide. Has brittle branches.

CAREX ❧ Cyperaceae

At a glance

NUMBER OF SPECIES About 45 species; throughout Australia and some in New Zealand.
NATURAL HABITAT Common in moist to wet sites such as watercourses and swamps, but also in open forest.
FLOWERING Plume-like flowers on terminal spikes.
HARDINESS Hardy in moist conditions.
HABIT Perennial, grass-like sedges to 1 m high depending on species.
FOLIAGE Varies with species.
GROWTH RATE Rapid.
COMMENTS Some species used by Aborigines to make baskets.

Culture:

- Moist soils, some tolerate heavy clay.
- Some species will tolerate periods of dryness.
- Propagate by seed or division.
- Good rockery plants.

CAREX SPECIES	SIZE	COMMENTS
C. appressa	0.5–1.2 x 0.5–1 m	Bright green arching leaves up to 6 mm wide in dense tufts. Slow growing. Used for basket-making by Aborigines.
C. bichenoviana	25–50 cm H	Purple-brown plumes. Long creeping rhizomes. Tufted plant. Heavy clay.
C. breviculmis	Up to 15 cm	Adaptable grass-like plant with dense tufts of flat leaves and short creeping rhizomes.
C. fascicularis	0.5–1 m	Flowers arch gracefully above coarse bright green leaves. Moist conditions.
C. gaudichaudiana	0.1–0.6 m	Blue-green flat, erect leaves in coarse spreading tufts. Best in permanently moist soil.
C. incomitata	0.5–0.7 m	Pale green leaves up to 8 mm wide in diffuse tufts. Prefers well-drained soil.
C. inversa	10–30 cm	Bright green leaves form spreading clumps. Prefers moist, well-drained soils. Can become a weed.
C. iynx	Up to 40 cm	Coarse leaves form large clumps. Dense flower spikes. Moist soils.
C. pumila	10–30 cm	Flat leaves in tufts with reddish-brown flower spikes. Coastal dunes, sandy soils.
C. tasmanica	Up to 0.4 cm	Strongly veined leaves in tufts; grows on heavy wet soils.
C. tereticaulis	1 x 1 m	Leaves usually sheaths, hollow flower stems in dense clumps.

CASSIA ❧ Caesalpiniaceae

At a glance

NUMBER OF SPECIES About 600; 40 occur in Australia.

NATURAL HABITAT Wide range, including deserts and coastal areas.
FLOWERING Yellow buttercup-shaped flowers, often in sprays.
HARDINESS Very hardy.
HABIT Shrubs and small trees.
FOLIAGE Pinnate leaves or phyllodes.
GROWTH RATE Very rapid.
LIFESPAN Short to medium.

Culture

- Prefer sunny position with well-drained soil.
- Pruning will help prevent straggly growth.
- Propagate from scarified seed or seed that has been treated with boiling water (as for Acacias).

CASSINIA Asteraceae

At a glance

NUMBER OF SPECIES 28; 20 endemic to Australia.
NATURAL HABITAT Forests on the east coast.
FLOWERING Small white daisy flowers in dense terminal clusters.
HARDINESS Hardy.
HABIT Shrubs.
FOLIAGE Small alternate leaves; fragrant.
GROWTH RATE Fast.
LIFESPAN Short to medium.

Culture

- Tolerance to soil types and position is variable, most are adaptable to a range of conditions.
- Most prefer reasonable drainage and filtered sunlight or part shade.
- Frost tolerant.
- Prune heavily after flowering.

Species

C. compacta

- 3 x 2 m. Suits most well-drained soils, yellow or cream flowers in winter and spring.

C. longifolia

- 6 x 4 m. Prefers moist but well-drained soils; frost hardy; white flowers; prune regularly to keep in shape.

CASSIA SPECIES	SIZE	COMMENTS
C. artemisioides (Silver Cassia) (syn. *Senna artemisioides*)	1–2 x 1 m	Silvery-foliaged small shrub, 1–2 m tall and 1 m wide. Produces gold flowers for most of the year. Very hardy, tolerating coastal and inland conditions.
C. desolata	2 x 1–2 m	Originally named by von Muller, but thought to be a hybrid of *C. sturtii*, from hot arid areas. Open bush with blue-grey foliage and yellow flowers.
C. helmsii	1.5 x 0.5 m	Very hardy shrub from arid inland Australia; best in well-drained soil, full sun and low humidity.
C. nemophila	3 x 1–2 m	Yellow winter-spring flowers; frost hardy; best in dry climates; drought tolerant. Many varieties and hybrids exist. These comprise the most commonly grown varieties.
C. odorata (syn. *Senna odorata*)	1–2 x 1 m	Small hardy shrub.
C. sturtii	1.5 x 1 m	Woolly grey foliage, yellow-orange flowers can occur all year, easily grown, many hybrid forms exist.
C. surattensis	1.5–2 x 1–1.5 m	Soft green foliage and yellow flowers, from hot climates.
C. tomentilla	1.5–2 x 1–1.5 m	Soft new green growth, bright yellow racemes in summer; has a slightly weeping habit.

CASTANOSPERMUM ❧ Black Bean ❧ Fabaceae

At a glance

NUMBER OF SPECIES 1; endemic to the subtropics and tropics in eastern Australia.
NATURAL HABITAT Rainforests in northern NSW and Qld.
FLOWERING Pea-shaped red flowers, followed by large woody seed pods.
HARDINESS Hardy once established.
HABIT Large tree.
FOLIAGE Glossy pinnate leaves.
GROWTH RATE Rapid at first, then usually slows down before taking off again.
LIFESPAN Long-lived.
COMMENTS Very handsome shade tree for large gardens or parks. The large seeds are poisonous.

Culture

- Requires deep, moist and fertile soil.
- Grown as far south as Melbourne.
- Propagate from seed, which can be sown direct into large pots.

Species

Castonospermum australe is the only species in this genus. Flowers are normally red but a yellow-flowering variety is also known.

CASUARINA ❧ Casuarinaceae

(Also see *Allocasuarina*)

At a glance

NUMBER OF SPECIES 5 (in 1982 the *Casuarina* genus was split into 4 genera; most species are now placed in the *Allocasuarina* genus).
NATURAL HABITAT Widespread, including coastal and inland areas.
FLOWERING Separate male and female flowers are produced; these may be produced on the same plant or on separate plants, depending on the species. Attractive woody fruits are produced on the female plants.
HARDINESS Hardy.
HABIT Small to medium trees.
FOLIAGE Fine pine needle-like foliage; often with a weeping habit.
GROWTH RATE Fast.
LIFESPAN Long-lived.
COMMENTS See *Allocasuarina*.

Culture

- Same as *Allocasuarina*.

Species

C. cristata

- 12 x 7 m. Conical shape; suited to dry areas but will tolerate wet periods.

C. cunninghamiana

- 20 x 10 m. Grows along riverbanks; will also tolerate dry conditions.

C. equisetifolia

- 10 x 7 m. Sparse weeping habit; coastal plantings.

C. glauca

- 20 x 8 m. Tolerates swamps and coastal conditions.

C. obesa

- 8–20 x 6 m. Excellent in salt-contaminated soils.

CERATOPETALUM ❧ Cunoniaceae

At a glance

NUMBER OF SPECIES 5; all occurring in Australia and New Guinea.
NATURAL HABITAT Moist forests, rainforests.
FLOWERING Insignificant flowers; however, the surrounding bracts (i.e. showy, leaf-like structures) are often mistakenly thought to be the flowers.
HARDINESS Reasonably hardy.
HABIT Shrubs and trees.
FOLIAGE Opposite dark green leaves.

GROWTH RATE Medium to fast.
LIFESPAN Long-lived.
COMMENTS *C. gummiferum* is sold as a cut flower.

Culture

- Prefer well-drained soil in full sun or semi-shade.
- Water well in dry periods.
- Propagate from seed. Selected forms of *C. gummiferum* can be grown from cuttings.

Species

C. apetalum (coachwood)

- 10 m
- Greenish insignificant flowers, colourful red sepals.

C. gummiferum (NSW Christmas bush)

- 6 m
- Large shrub or small tree with attractive red sepals in December. Popular garden ornamental. Resistant to frost and tolerates heavy pruning. Several forms available.

CHAMELAUCIUM ❧ Wax Plants ❧
Myrtaceae

At a glance

NUMBER OF SPECIES About 30; all endemic to south-western Australia.
NATURAL HABITAT Varying, but most commonly sandy heath country, some from dry, arid areas.
FLOWERING Five-petalled, open, white, pink and red flowers. Texture of the petals is waxy.
HARDINESS Some can tolerate very harsh conditions, including drought, heat and frost.
HABIT Small shrubs.
FOLIAGE Narrow aromatic leaves.
GROWTH RATE Fast to very fast.
LIFESPAN Medium- to long-lived if pruned regularly.
COMMENTS Some species are grown widely as a cut flower for both domestic and export markets.

Culture

- Well-drained soil in sunny position.
- Do not like humidity.
- Most tolerate some frost and dryness.
- Main problems are scale insects and root rot fungi.
- Propagation is normally by cuttings as seed set is usually poor quality.

CHAMELAUCIUM SPECIES	SIZE	COMMENTS
C. axillare (Esperance wax plant)	2 x 2 m	White flowers in late spring and summer.
C. ciliatum	0.7 x 0.3–0.5 m	Small compact shrub with pink and white flowers turning red; best in dry soils.
C. megalopetalum	2 x 1 m	Cream–white flowers change to red with a green centre; a very hardy drought-tolerant garden plant if given excellent drainage.
C. paucifloraum	0.5–2 x 0.3–0.5 m	Upright shrub; flowers start white and turn pink; grows well in part or full sun; drought-tolerant.
C. uncinatum (Geraldton wax)	2–5 x 0.5–2 m	Normally open growth unless pruned, this is the most horticulturally important species. Pink flowers in spring. Several forms available with differing shades of pink to mauve flowers.

CHORICARPIA ❧ Myrtaceae

At a glance

NUMBER OF SPECIES 2; endemic to eastern Australia.
NATURAL HABITAT Moist forests.
FLOWERING White ball-shaped flowers in dense clusters.
HARDINESS Hardy.
HABIT Trees.
FOLIAGE Opposite simple leaves.
GROWTH RATE Medium growth rate.
LIFESPAN Long-lived.

Culture

- Deep, fertile, moist soil. Mulch or spread compost annually.
- Frost hardy.
- Avoid heavy shade.
- Propagate from seed.

Species

C. leptopetala
- 8–12 m
- Will grow as far south as Melbourne, this is the better species for home gardens.

C. subargentea
- Up to 40 m
- Confined to subtropics; flowers on young growth are brownish.

CHORIZEMA ❧ Fabaceae

At a glance

NUMBER OF SPECIES 18; all endemic to Australia, mainly occurring in south-western WA.
NATURAL HABITAT Usually grow beneath shrubs or trees, mainly on sand.
FLOWERING Spring.
HARDINESS Very hardy.
HABIT Small shrubs and ground covers.
GROWTH RATE Normally rapid grower.
LIFESPAN Medium- to long-lived.

Culture

- Require well-drained but moist soil. A mulched sandy soil or mounded area in heavier soils is ideal.
- Prefers filtered sunlight.
- Some will tolerate light frost, others are frost tender.
- They respond well to pruning after flowering.
- Propagate by cuttings or from seed treated with boiling water.

Species

C. aciculare
- 0.5–1 m. Pink and yellow flowers.

C. cordatum
- 0.5–1 m. Orange, red, purple and yellow flowers.

C. dicksonii
- Up to 1 m. Red, yellow and orange flowers.

C. diversifolium
- Climber. Pink, yellow and orange flowers.

C. ilicifolium
- 1–3 m. Red, yellow and orange flowers.

CLEMATIS ❧ Ranunculaceae

At a glance

NUMBER OF SPECIES 250; 5 endemic to eastern Australia.
NATURAL HABITAT Occurs in a wide range of habitats, including open forests and rainforests.
FLOWERING Spring.
HARDINESS Hardy.
HABIT Climbing plants.
FOLIAGE Pinnate leaves.
GROWTH RATE Can be fast under preferred conditions.
LIFESPAN Medium- to long-lived.

Culture

- Will grow well in sun or semi-shade.
- Requires support to climb on.
- Some species will tolerate dry conditions.

Most prefer ample moisture.

- Propagate by cuttings or fresh seed.

Species

C. aristata

- White flowers. Tolerates either dry or moist soils, prefers semi-shade or filtered sun.

C. glycinoides

- Green-white flowers. Sometimes frost tender, needs cool moist position.

C. microphylla

- Cream-green flowers. Good drainage and well-lit position.

C. pubescens

- White flowers. Hardy and adaptable.

CONOSPERMUM ✥ Smoke Bush ✥ Proteaceae

At a glance

NUMBER OF SPECIES About 50; all endemic to Australia, mainly occurring in south WA.
NATURAL HABITAT Sandy heaths and plains.
FLOWERING Tubular in spring.
HARDINESS Not hardy in eastern states.
HABIT Small shrubs.
FOLIAGE Undivided, sometimes crowded on the stem.
LIFESPAN Medium lifespan.
COMMENTS Excellent as cut flowers.

Culture

- Requires well-drained soils.
- Best suited to dry climates.
- Prefers full sun or only slight shade.
- Dislikes humidity.
- Seed propagation can be difficult, semi-hardwood cuttings have been successful.

Species

C. longifolium

- 1–2 x 1.5–2 m. White flowers.

C. mitchellii

- 1–2.5 x 1–1.8 m. Grey or white flowers.

C. patens

- 0.5–1 x 0.5–1.2 m. Grey-blue flowers.

C. stoechadis

- 1–1.8 x 1–2 m. Silver and woolly flowers.

C. taxifolium

- 0.5–2 x 1–2 m. Cream to white flowers.

C. triplinervium

- 2–3.5 x 2–4 m. Woolly and white flowers.

CONOSTYLIS ✥ Haemodoraceae

At a glance

NUMBER OF SPECIES Over 20, all from WA.
NATURAL HABITAT Open shrub or woodland.
FLOWERING Woolly yellow, white or pink flower heads.
HARDINESS Generally hardy.
HABIT Small tufted clumps.
FOLIAGE Strap-like leaves.
GROWTH RATE Generally rapid.
LIFESPAN 5 years or more if conditions are good.
COMMENTS Flowers can be dried.

Culture

- Tolerates some shade, but requires good light to flower well.
- Grows in most soils provided they are not waterlogged.
- Prefers some protection; e.g. grows well next to a rock or wall.
- Propagate by division in winter. Seeds do not set well.

CORDYLINE ✥ Agavaceae

(Previously placed in the Liliaceae family)

At a glance

NUMBER OF SPECIES About 20; 8 occur in Australia.
NATURAL HABITAT High rainfall areas.
FLOWERING Spring to summer.
HARDINESS Most are hardy.

CONOSTYLIS SPECIES	HABIT	COMMENTS
C. aculeata	Spreading clump up to 0.4 m tall	Leaves have spines, yellow flowers in spring and summer. Particularly hardy, frost and drought tolerant. Several varieties available.
C. bealiana	Compact clump up to 0.2 m tall	Requires good drainage, light and shading. Usually yellow-orange flowers.
C. candicans	Clumping plant up to 0.5 m tall	Grey-white leaves, yellow flowers in winter and spring.
C. preisii	0.3 x 1 m	Long narrow green leaves, yellow flowers in spring.
C. prolifera	Tiny clump up to 0.1 m tall	Cream to pale yellow flowers. Needs good drainage and partial shade.
C. robusta	Clump up to 0.5 m tall	Golden flowers from winter to summer. Prefers well-drained soil, good light and heat, though it tolerates light frosts.
C. stylidioides	Spreading clump, 0.1–0.3 m tall	Prefers warm temperate, arid climate. Golden flowers can occur most of the year. Sometimes confused with *C. prolifera.*

HABIT Spreading clumps, with slender, upright stems.
FOLIAGE Strap-like leaves.
GROWTH RATE Usually rapid.
LIFESPAN Long–lived.
COMMENTS Several species make hardy indoor plants. Sometimes confused with *Dracaena*. Roots of *Cordyline* are usually white while *Dracaena* roots are yellow.

Culture

- Prefers well-drained fertile soil.
- Propagate by seed. Some species also propagate by division or stem cuttings.

Species

C. australis

- Up to 4 m tall
- A New Zealand species, often mistakenly called Australian. Hardy, several forms available. Has become an environmental weed in some areas.

C. rubra

- Up to 4 m tall
- Light purple flowers and red berries. Requires wet, shady conditions, warm to mild climate.

C. stricta

- 2–5 m tall
- An upright suckering plant that prefers some shade, will tolerate dark conditions and is drought resistant.

C. terminalis

- Hardy upright plant that grows best in the subtropics in well-drained soils. There are several coloured leaf forms available.

CORREA ⁂ Native Fuchsia ⁂ Rutaceae

At a glance

NUMBER OF SPECIES 11; all endemic to the eastern states and SA.
NATURAL HABITAT Coastal to mountain areas, not arid regions.
FLOWERING Mainly winter and spring.
HARDINESS Hardy.
HABIT Small shrubs.
FLOWERING Bell-shaped, similar to fuchsias.
FOLIAGE Simple, elongated leaves.

GROWTH RATE Fast.
LIFESPAN Medium- to long-lived.

Culture

- Prefers moist, drained soils and filtered sun.
- Prune lightly.
- Usually no need to water or feed if mulched.
- Propagate by cuttings at most times of the year.

CORYMBIA *see Eucalyptus*

CRINUM Amaryllidaceae

At a glance

NUMBER OF SPECIES 110; 12 occur in Australia.
NATURAL HABITAT Stream banks and flood plains.
FLOWERING Large clusters of white flowers over summer.
HARDINESS Generally very hardy to cultivation. Frost sensitive.
HABIT Fleshy, clumping low plant.
FOLIAGE Strappy, glossy green.
LIFESPAN Many years.
GROWTH RATE Vigorous in growing season.
COMMENTS Very adapatable to cultivation.

Culture

- Tolerant of full or part sun.
- Irrigate in dry periods.
- Leaves may be eaten by common garden pests.
- Propagate by seed or division.

CORREA SPECIES	SIZE	COMMENTS
C. alba	Nearly prostrate up to 1.5 x 2.5 m	Bushy variable shrub, with grey-green foliage. White flowers throughout the year but mostly in spring. A good plant for coastal gardens.
C. backhousiana	Spreading shrub 1–2 m tall	Green- to rust-coloured flowers in winter or spring.
C. decumbens	Prostrate up to 0.6 m	A small shrub with green foliage, and red flowers in summer.
C. glabra	Shrub up to 2.5 x 2 m	Green to red flowers winter to spring.
C. 'Mannii'	Shrub to 1 x 1 m	Green foliage with grey underside, and red flowers in winter and spring.
C. reflexa	Variable; 0.3–2 x 1–3 m	Green to blue-green foliage and red flowers with yellow tips in winter. Several cultivars available.

CRINUM SPECIES	SIZE	COMMENTS
C. asiaticam	1 m tall	White to pink flowers, dark red stamens, cold sensitive.
C. brisbanicum	0.5 m tall	White with green tips.
C. flaccidum	0.5–1 m tall	White or yellow broad petals, strongly scented at dusk.
C. pedunculatum	1–50 cm tall	White with slender petals, pleasant fragrance. Qld and NSW.
C. uniflorum	3 m tall	White or pinkish narrow petals, red stamens, cold sensitive but good for cultivation, tolerates clay soils.

CROWEA ❧ Rutaceae

At a glance

NUMBER OF SPECIES 3; all endemic to Australia (1 from WA, 2 from NSW and Vic.)
NATURAL HABITAT Normally moist, high rainfall sites.
FLOWERING Star-shaped flowers.
HARDINESS Hardy.
HABIT Small shrubs.
FOLIAGE Small undivided, elongated, light green.
LIFESPAN Medium to long.

Culture

- Adapts to most soils if well drained.
- Prefers part shade.
- Root system must be kept cool.
- Propagate by semi-hardwood cuttings.
- Keep bushy with light tip pruning.

CRYPTOCARYA ❧ Lauraceae

At a glance

NUMBER OF SPECIES 200–250; 44 endemic to Australia.
NATURAL HABITAT Tropical and subtropical dry rainforests and vine-scrubs of NSW, Qld, NT.
FLOWERING Usually small and insignificant, colour varies according to species.
HABIT Large shrubs to tall trees with attractive foliage.
HARDINESS Hardy.
GROWTH RATE Often slow to moderate.
LIFESPAN Medium- to long-lived.
COMMENTS Birds are attracted to the fruits.

Culture

- Well-composted soils.
- Frost-free areas.
- Medium–high rainfall.
- Propagation is by seed.

CRYSOCEPHALUM ❧ *see Helichrysum*

CUPANIOPSIS ❧ Sapindaceae

At a glance

NUMBER OF SPECIES 7 endemic to Australia.
NATURAL HABITAT Rainforests.
FLOWERING Almost all year depending on species. Inconspicuous flowers.
HARDINESS Adaptable to cultivation.
HABIT Small to large spreading trees.
FOLIAGE Pinnate glossy leaves, usually with attractive new foliage colour.
LIFESPAN Long-lived.
GROWTH RATE Slow growing in early stages.
COMMENTS All have horticultural merit. Plants will respond to mulching, watering and fertilising.

Culture

- Full to part sun. Full sun will achieve a thicker, rounded specimen.
- Irrigation may be needed in dry conditions, but some species have proven to be very tough.
- Excellent drainage needed.
- Propagate by seed.

Species

C. anacardioides (tuckeroo)

- 10 m tall. NSW, Qld, NT. Added fertiliser and watering will speed up growth dramatically. Grown throughout Brisbane.

C. flagelliformis (brown tuckeroo)

- 6 m. NSW, Qld, NT. Attractive new dark brown growth. Slender habit.

C. serrata (rusty tuckeroo)

- 10 m. Qld, NSW. Attractive toothed foliage. Slender in shape. Moderately fast growing.

CROWEA SPECIES	SIZE	COMMENTS
C. angustifolia var. *dentata*	0.3 m to 0.8m high	Wide with narrow leaves and pale pink or white flowers in spring.
C. angustifolia var. *angustifolia*	To 3 m high	Pale pink or white flowers in spring.
C. exalata	Rounded shrub to 0.7 m	Bright green leaves and many pink flowers in summer and autumn. This is the most commonly grown *Crowea*.
C. saligna	Open spreading shrub to 0.5 m high	Large dark pink or white flowers mainly in winter.

CRYPTOCARYA SPECIES	SIZE	COMMENTS
C. bidwillii	To 20 m	Small tree, often shooting from the base, hairy young leaves becoming smooth, green and shiny. Yellow-green bell-shaped flowers from spring to midsummer, followed by dark purple-black fruits. Well-drained to dry soil and dappled light.
C. cunninghamii	To 25 m	Fragrant, glossy, oblong leaves, cream-green small flowers in spring, followed by purple-black fruit.
C. erythroxylon	To 35 m	Glossy green leaves, paler underneath, small green-cream flowers followed by black fruit.
C. foetida	10–20 m	Small to medium tree. Smooth green leaves have prominent yellow veins. Flowers have an unpleasant fragrance. Fruit purple-black.
C. foveolata	20–35 m	Tough, rigid green leaves. Green-yellow flowers followed by round black fruit.
C. glaucescens	15–30 x 4 m	Shiny dark green leaves, numerous creamy-pale green scented flowers from mid-spring to mid-summer followed by black fruit. Valuable timber tree.
C. laevigata	Up to 6 m	Simple, narrow, dark green glossy leaves with 3 veins. Panicles of flowers appear in the leaf axils in spring–summer followed by red-orange fruit. Slow-growing understorey plant.
C. mackinnoniana	Up to 18 m	Young new growth limp and red-brown. Long, broad, glossy green leaves up to 30 cm long. Small purple flowers.
C. meissneriana	6 m	Shrub or small tree with hairy new growth becoming smooth and glossy with paler green to bluish-green underside. Small yellowish flowers followed by black fruit.
C. triplinervis	6–10 m	Small tree with dense crown of 3-veined glossy, dark green leaves. Pale green slightly fragrant flowers in spring followed by bird-attracting purplish-black fruit.
C. williwilliana	6–10 m	Shrub to small tree often shooting from the base. Broad, dark green, smooth, glossy leaves. White silky flowers in spring followed by black fruit.

CURCUMA ✣ Zingiberaceae

At a glance

NUMBER OF SPECIES 80; 1 endemic to Australia.
NATURAL HABITAT Rainforest margins.
FLOWERING December to March.
HARDINESS Excellent in tropical and subtropical districts.
HABIT Fleshy herb with subterranean rhizome.
FOLIAGE Light green pleated leaves up to 2 m.
LIFESPAN Long-lived. Generally dies down in dry season.
GROWTH First signs of growth in the season are the flowers then the foliage.
COMMENTS Aborigines roasted the tubers or used them to flavour food.

Culture

- Rich well-drained soil.
- Sunny position.

Species

C. australasica

- Large conspicuous pinkish spreading bracts. Small yellow flowers are tucked between the bracts.

CYPERUS ✣ Cyperaceae

At a glance

NUMBER OF SPECIES About 600; 130 endemic to Australia.
NATURAL HABITAT Swamps, along edges of lakes and in waterways.
FLOWERING Spring–summer.
HARDINESS Usually hardy in most conditions depending on species.
HABIT Annual or perennial grass-like herbs, tufted or rhizomatous
FOLIAGE Attractive, usually bright green, grass-like strappy leaves that are often reduced to sheaths.
GROWTH RATE Slow-spreading.
COMMENTS Some species are useful as ornamental poolside plantings.

Culture

- Moist to wet soil.
- Semi-shade or full sun.

Species

C. gunnii

- 0.6–1 m. Dense tufts; rigid stems same length as leaves. Bright brown flower spikes. Moist, boggy soil.

C. ihotskyanus

- 0.1–0.6 m. Tufted herb with creeping rhizome. Reddish-brown flower spikes. Wet conditions.

C. lucidus

- 0.6–1.5 m. Shiny dark green channelled leaves, rough margins.

C. mirus

- 40–60 cm. Dense tufts, leaves shorter than brownish flowering stems.

C. vaginatus

- 0.7–1 m. Short basal leaves; 1 m erect flowering stems, brown spikes.

DAMPIERA ✣ Goodeniaceae

At a glance

NUMBER OF SPECIES About 60; all endemic to Australia, many from south-western WA.
NATURAL HABITAT Variable, ranging from coastal heaths to forests.
FLOWERING Mainly blue or purple flowers in spring and summer.
HARDINESS Variable, some very hardy.
HABIT Mainly small herbaceous shrubs, some groundcover species.
FOLIAGE Undivided leaves, sometimes with a toothed or wavy margin.
LIFESPAN Medium.

Culture

- Prefers moist but not waterlogged soil.

DAMPIERA SPECIES	SIZE	FLOWERS	PREFERRED CONDITIONS
D. alata	Prostrate	Dark purple-blue with light centres	Good drainage, full sun or slight shading.
D. altissima	To 2.5 m tall	Dark blue	Lime soil, full sun, warm or mild climate.
D. cuneata = *D. linearis*			
D. diversifolia	Prostrate	Deep purple to pale blue	Widely grown, very adaptable, prefers some shade.
D. eriocephala	0.3 x 0.4 m	Purple	Excellent drainage.
D. hederacea	Up to 1 m tall	Dark to light blue	Moisture, filtered sun, good drainage.
D. incana	0.3 x 1 m	Blue, yellow throat	Good drainage, full sun.
D. lavandulacea	Up to 0.5 m tall to 3 m wide	Blue, pink or lilac with yellow throat	Good drainage, part or full sun.
D. linearis	0.2–0.5 m tall to 2 m wide	Shades of blue or purple, light throat	Generally adaptable, but not all forms.
D. rosmarinifolia	Up to 0.4 m tall, suckering	Purple, pink or white	Plenty of sunlight.
D. stricta	Up to 0.7 m tall	Shades of blue	Very adaptable.
D. teres	To 0.5 m tall	Mauve or pink with pale throat	Good drainage and full sun.
D. trigona	0.5 x 0.8 m	Blue, light throat	Good drainage.

- Best in filtered sun or shade but not too dark.
- Propagate by divisions or cuttings.

DANTHONIA ❧ Wallaby Grass ❧
Poaceae

At a glance
NUMBER OF SPECIES 33; found throughout Australia.
NATURAL HABITAT Grasslands and open forests.
FLOWERING Spring to summer.
HARDINESS Very hardy.
HABIT Grassy tussock.
FOLIAGE Long grass leaf.
GROWTH RATE Generally fast.
LIFESPAN Medium.
COMMENTS Native pasture species; also has ornamental value in landscaping.

Culture
- Prefers semi-shade under tall trees.
- Avoid overcrowding with dense shrubs.
- Normally propagate by division, disturbing roots as little as possible.
- Seed is difficult to get, and needs to be stored for at least 1 year before planting to achieve good germination.

Species
D. caespitosa
- Perhaps the most common species, occurs across most of southern Australia. Soft, light-coloured seed heads look very attractive set against a dark background of foliage or stone.

D. longifolia
- Hardy, forming a clump to 0.7 m tall, prefers good light and drainage, avoid feeding, prefers infertile soil.

D. nivicola

- Reddish stems make it an attractive ornamental grass, forms clumps 0.1–0.3 cm tall, tolerates frost and snow.

DARWINIA ✻ Myrtaceae

At a glance

NUMBER OF SPECIES About 70; all endemic to Australia, most from south WA.
NATURAL HABITAT Sandy coastal heaths.
FLOWERING Mainly spring.
HARDINESS Species from WA not hardy in eastern states.
HABIT Small- to medium-sized shrubs.
FOLIAGE Leaves occur in four rows up the stem and are scented.
GROWTH RATE Usually moderate.
LIFESPAN Medium.
COMMENTS Eastern states' species are less showy, but hardier than WA species. WA species have better flowers but are harder to grow. Grafting WA types onto hardier species has promise.

Culture

- Needs excellent drainage.
- Prefers moist soil but many tolerate dry periods.
- Avoid alkaline soils.
- Prefers full sun, will take filtered sun in a well-lit position.
- Propagate by cuttings

DAVIDSONIA ✻ Davidsoniaceae

At a glance

NUMBER OF SPECIES 3; all endemic to eastern Australia.
NATURAL HABITAT Rainforests of NSW and Qld.
FLOWERING Spring to summer.
GROWTH RATE Slow.
HARDINESS Semi-hardy.
HABIT Small- to medium-sized trees.
FOLIAGE Toothed foliage.
COMMENTS Commonly known as Davidson's plum, the trees produce edible, burgundy-coloured sour fruits which somewhat resemble the unrelated European plum; grown commercially as gourmet bush-food.

Species

D. jerseyana

- 5–10 m. Slender sparsely branched tree with

DARWINIA SPECIES	HEIGHT	WIDTH	FLOWERS	PREFERRED CONDITIONS
D. citriodora	0.5–2 m	to 1.5 m	Yellow-orange	Very adaptable
D. collina	0.3–1 m	0.5–1 m	Yellow-green	Excellent drainage
D. homoranthoides	0.1 m	3 m	Cream and green	Very adaptable
D. leiostyla	0.2–1 m	0.5–1 m	Pink and white	Not too wet or shaded
D. macrostegia	1–1.5 m	1 m	Cream and red	Excellent drainage and light shade
D. neildiana	0.2–1 m	0.5–1 m	Green changing to red	Excellent drainage, keep roots cool
D. oldfeldii	0.5–1 m	1.5 m	Green changing to rich red	Part to full sun
D. oxylepis	0.8 m	0.5–0.9 m	Crimson	Constant soil moisture, grows best in a container
D. rhadinophylla	0.2 m	1–2 m	Bright rich red	Part to full sun, mild climate
D. taxifolia	0.1 m	1.5 m	Dark pink-red	Very adaptable

tufts of hairy leaves that irritate the skin.

D. johnsonii

- 5–10 m. Small, smooth-leafed spreading tree. Fruit is infertile, plants must be propagated through cuttings.

D. pruriens

- 5–10 m. Usually a bit taller than the previous species. Produces larger fruit, from the trunk, in large clusters.

DAVIESIA Fabaceae

At a glance

NUMBER OF SPECIES About 200; all endemic to Australia, mainly from south-western WA, but some from all states.
NATURAL HABITAT Usually sandy heath country.
FLOWERING Pea-like flowers, flowering periods and times vary, often large quantities of flowers but sometimes only for a short period.
HARDINESS Generally hardy.
HABIT Tiny to medium shrubs.
FOLIAGE Normally rigid, sometimes thorny.
GROWTH RATE Fast.
LIFESPAN Short to medium.

Culture

- Requires well-drained sands or loams, not clay.
- Prefers full sun or filtered sun.
- Has no major pest or disease problems.
- Propagate easily from hot-water-treated seed.
- Some will grow from cuttings.

Species

D. alata

- Up to 1.5 m. Hardy shrub that adapts to semi–shade, withstands frost, often has weak branches, needs regular pruning to keep in shape and has orange and red pea flowers in spring.

D. brevifolia

- Up to about 1.5 m tall. A thorny bush with greyish stems, few leaves, and apricot to maroon flowers in spring. It needs well-drained soil and filtered sun, and is best in a warm spot.

D. cordata

- Up to 1.5 m. Hardy shrub, heart-shaped leaves with 'book leaf' bracts, red and yellow spring flowers.

D. incrassata

- Up to 1 m tall. A spreading shrub with red and orange flowers. It adapts to most conditions if soil is well drained.

DECASPERMUM Myrtaceae

At a glance

NUMBER OF SPECIES 1; endemic to Australia.
NATURAL HABITAT Drier rainforests of NSW and Qld.
FLOWERING March to August.
HARDINESS Very hardy.
HABIT Small tree in natural habitat with weeping foliage.
FOLIAGE Shiny green. New shoots are silky and pink.
LIFESPAN Long-lived.
GROWTH RATE Slow to establish.
COMMENTS Fragrant ornamental flowers. Berries attractive to birds. Large demand as a landscape plant in south-eastern Qld.

Culture

- Protection needed when young.
- Prefers slightly acid, well-drained soils.
- Light pruning will improve shape.
- Propagate by fresh seed.

Species

D. humile (silky myrtle).

- Highly ornamental shrub in the garden, 3–4 m in cultivation. Attractive bark. Can tolerate cool conditions.

DIANELLA ❧ Liliaceae

At a glance

NUMBER OF SPECIES About 30; 8 species occur in Australia.
NATURAL HABITAT Extremely variable, from rainforests to semi-arid areas.
FLOWERING Spring to summer; white, blue or purple flowers.
HARDINESS Adaptable depending on species.
HABIT Tuft-forming or spreading perennial herbs.
FOLIAGE Strap-like deep green foliage.
LIFESPAN Long-lived.
GROWTH RATE Medium.
COMMENTS Well suited to cultivation; very hardy due to underground rhizomes and root systems. Decorative berries follow the flowers.

Culture

- Full sun to part shade.
- Additional watering and fertilising will encourage healthier specimens.
- Adaptable to a range of soils.
- Propagation by seed or division.

Species

D. caerulea (paroo lily)
- Wiry flower stems. Blue flowers and globular berries.

D. odorata (flax lily)
- Wiry flower stems. Flowers may be white, pale or deep blue. Berries are blue and oblong.

DICHONDRA ❧ Kidney Weed ❧ Convolvulaceae

At a glance

NUMBER OF SPECIES 4; 1 endemic to Australia.
NATURAL HABITAT Tropical and subtropical areas.
FLOWERING Inconspicuous flowers in spring.
HARDINESS Tolerates some people traffic, but not abuse. Generally hardy.
HABIT Creeping mat-like growth.
FOLIAGE Bright green kidney-shaped leaves.
GROWTH RATE Rapid.
LIFESPAN Can be long-lived.
COMMENTS Is used as a lawn alternative, providing foot traffic is not heavy, particularly in moist, shaded places.

Culture

- Requires ample moisture.
- Prefers shade.
- Propagation by seed or division.

Species

Dichondra repens is the Australian species commonly used in lawns.

DILLWYNIA ❧ Fabaceae

At a glance

NUMBER OF SPECIES About 20; all endemic to Australia.
NATURAL HABITAT Sandy heaths, open forests.
FLOWERING Spring.
HARDINESS Very susceptible to cinnamon fungus.
HABIT Small to medium shrubs.
FOLIAGE Generally small, undivided and elongated.
GROWTH RATE Moderate to fast.
LIFESPAN Short to medium.

Culture

- Prefers well-mulched sandy soil.
- Most will not tolerate waterlogging.
- Scale and root rots can sometimes be a problem.
- Needs filtered sunlight or semi-shade.
- Propagate from hot-water-treated seed.

DILLWYNIA SPECIES	HEIGHT	FLOWERS	PREFERRED POSITION
D. cinerascens	0.5–2 m	Yellow and orange	Filtered sun, good drainage
D. dillwynoides	Up to 2 m	Yellow and orange with red	Filtered sun, well-drained soil
D. floribunda	Up to 2 m	Yellow and orange or just yellow	Full or filtered sun, reasonable drainage
D. glaberrima	1–3 m	Yellow and red	Partial sun, sandy soil
D. hispida	0.5 m	Red to orange-red	Partial sun, most soils
D. pungens	0.5–1.5 m	Yellow and red	Filtered sunlight
D. sericea	0.5–1.5 m	Various shades: yellow, red, pink, orange etc	Under tall trees, very adaptable.

DIPLOGLOTTIS ⁂ Sapindaceae

At a glance

NUMBER OF SPECIES 10
NATURAL HABITAT Predominantly rainforests.
FLOWERING Almost all year depending on species.
HARDINESS Sensitive to frosts and strong winds when young.
HABIT Large spreading trees.
FOLIAGE Large pinnate leaves. Attractive foliage and new growth.
LIFESPAN Long-lived.
GROWTH RATE Vigorous in growing season. Slow growing when young.
COMMENTS Excellent shade trees or for protecting other plants. Fleshy aril (a membrane-like covering of the seed) in the fruits are acidic but can be made into jams. Do not eat the seeds.

Culture

- Grows best in full sun.
- Responds to additional watering and fertilising.
- Most species are frost sensitive.
- Propagate by fresh seed.

Species

D. campbellii (small-leaved tamarind)
- 10 m tall. Red juicy acidic aril. Sheltered site with part-shade preferred.

D. cunninghamii (native tamarind) (syn *D. australis*)
- 10 m tall. Orange-yellow acidic fruit.

D. diphyllostegia (northern tamarind)
- 5–8 m tall. Yellow sour fruit.

D. smithii (Smith's tamarind)
- 4–8 m tall. Yellow sour fruit. Silver new foliage.

DIPLOLAENA ⁂ Rutaceae

At a glance

NUMBER OF SPECIES 6; all endemic to south-western WA.
NATURAL HABITAT Mainly coastal areas.
FLOWERING Very showy.
HARDINESS Hardy.
HABIT Medium woody shrubs.
FOLIAGE Undivided, usually soft green.
GROWTH RATE Usually moderate.
LIFESPAN Medium.

Culture

- Most prefer filtered sunlight or partial shading.
- Pruning regularly from when young will encourage flowering.
- Propagates easily from cuttings.

Species

D. angustifolia

- Up to 1.5 m tall
- Shrub with crimson to orange flowers winter to spring. Needs perfect drainage and some shade, best as a tub plant.

D. dampieri

- Up to 2 m tall
- Dense shrub, red or yellow flowers, widely cultivated in WA, does not like heavy competition from other plant roots, otherwise adapts to a wide range of conditions.

D. grandiflora

- Up to 3 m tall
- Shrub, pink to red flowers are the largest of any Diplolaena, requires good drainage, alkaline soil, light shade and a protected warm position.

DODONAEA ✻ Hop Bush ✻
Sapindaceae

At a glance

NUMBER OF SPECIES 69; 60 endemic to Australia.
NATURAL HABITAT Mainly open forests and low-rainfall areas, but there are exceptions.
FLOWERING Generally insignificant, but the winged hop-like fruits are often colourful and mistaken for flowers.
HARDINESS Hardy to very hardy.
HABIT Normally shrubs.
FOLIAGE Usually sticky, often scented.
LIFESPAN Can be short-lived.
GROWTH RATE Rapid.

Culture

- Adapts to a wide range of soils and climates.
- Scale and sooty mould can be serious problems.
- Only tip-prune. Heavy cutting can cause dieback.
- They react well to slow-release fertiliser.
- Seed propagation is fairly successful provided male and female plants are in the area.
- Cutting propagation is successful for most species.

Species

D. adenophora

- Up to 1–2 m tall and 1–2 m wide
- An upright shrub with small green fruit. It prefers full sun and needs well-drained soil. It is a hardy plant that is frost and drought tolerant.

D. humifusa

- Up to 2 m spread
- Prostrate plant, attractive brown to pink fruits, very hardy, withstands frost and drought.

D. larreoides

- 1–4 m tall
- Upright shrub, very attractive purple-brown to red-coloured fruits, requires an alkaline soil and semi-arid climate.

D. procumbens

- Prostrate plant up to 3 m wide
- Grows well in full sun or shade, and is frost and drought tolerant.

D. viscosa

- Up to 4 m tall and 3 m wide
- An upright shrub found in all states. It is well suited to coastal and inland sites. A purple-leaved form (var. *purpurea*) is very popular.

DORYANTHES

At a glance

NUMBER OF SPECIES 2; both endemic to Australia.
NATURAL HABITAT Coastal, eastern Australia.
FLOWERING Mainly spring–summer, on very long flower spikes.
HARDINESS Hardy.
HABIT Large clump.
FOLIAGE Sword-like to 3 m long.
LIFESPAN Medium to long.
GROWTH RATE Slow.

COMMENTS Flowers are rich in nectar. Seedling-grown plants may require 5 years or more before first producing flowers.

Culture

- Prefers well-drained, fertile soil.
- Clumps can be transplanted at any age with care.
- Prefers filtered sunlight but tolerates full sun.
- Flowers can be damaged by frost otherwise the plants are frost hardy.
- Propagates readily by seed. Clumps can sometimes be divided with care.

Species

D. excelsa (Gymea lily)

- Leaves up to 2 m tall and flower spikes up to 4 m with large red flowers in spring. Occurs widely in the sandstone country around Sydney.

D. palmeri

- Leaves up to 3 m tall, with red-brown flowers on spikes up to 5 m tall. The hardiest of the two species, it grows well from Vic to Qld.

DROSERA Droseraceae

At a glance

NUMBER OF SPECIES 160; about 65 endemic to Australia.
NATURAL HABITAT Wet areas.
FLOWERING Varies but often very showy.
HARDINESS Not hardy – good for pot culture.
HABIT Herbaceous, small, insectivorous plants that are summer dormant when they die back to their roots.
FOLIAGE Sticky, hairy leaves vary in shape according to species.
LIFESPAN Short, but plants often re-grow after a dormant period.
COMMENTS Commonly known as 'sundews', this genus trap insects on their sticky, hairy leaves by curling the leaves around the insect

DROSERA SPECIES	COMMENTS
D. adelae	Narrow leaves up to 7 cm in a rosette. Brownish-red small flowers. Qld.
D. auriculata	Central stem up to 50 cm on a basal rosette. Leaves are round on a long petiole. 1.5 cm flowers; pink or white. Spring and summer. ACT, Qld, SA, Tas, Vic.
D. binata	Erect plant 20–80 cm high. Leaves are forked, narrow and pale green to reddish. White flowers on 80 cm stems in spring, summer, mid-autumn. Soils damp/peat. All states.
D. gigantea	Tallest drosera, grows to 100 cm tall, with a tree-like shape (the sturdy main stem has many smaller branching stems). White flowers in spring. WA.
D. macrantha	40–80 cm tall, somewhat climbing plant on a tuberous rootstock. Yellowish-green cup-shaped leaves. White or pink perfumed flowers appear in terminal clusters in winter–mid-spring. SA, Tas, Vic, WA.
D. peltata ssp. *peltata*	Similar to *D. auriculata* but with hairy buds. All states except NT.
D. pygmaea	Round tiny bronze leaves up to 2 cm long on 8 mm stalks. Moist, sandy soil. All states.
D. shizandra	Large 6 cm reddish leaves in a rosette. Greenish-white flowers on 8 cm stems. Qld.
D. spatulata	5–10 x 2 cm, tuberous basal rosette. Many reddish spathulate 10 mm leaves. Flowers red, pink or white on 20 cm stems, year-round. NSW, Qld, Tas, Vic.
D. whittakeri	3 x 3 cm flat basal rosette, tuberous. 25 mm leaves green-bronze to red. Single perfumed white flower on 40 mm stalk, late winter–mid-spring. SA, Vic.

when it lands. Secretions of fluid digest the insects, which are in turn used, along with photosynthesis, to feed the plant.

Culture

- Damp soils for the growing part of the year (winter), and dry soils during the dormant summer period.
- Plenty of light.
- Can be grown in bog gardens or pots – add commercial peat to the soil or potting mix.
- Propagate by seed in spring or leaf cuttings.

DRYANDRA Proteaceae

At a glance

NUMBER OF SPECIES About 92; all endemic to south-west Australia.
NATURAL HABITAT Mainly gravel soils in south-western WA.
FLOWERING Varies.
HARDINESS Hardy if soil is well drained.
HABIT Shrubs and small trees.
FOLIAGE Varies, generally toothed, often sharp-tipped.
GROWTH RATE Usually medium.
LIFESPAN Generally long-lived but may die in an abnormally wet year.

Culture

- Highly susceptible to *Phytophthora* (cinnamon fungus).
- Most prefer full sun.
- Avoid fluctuations in soil temperature by mulching.
- Young plants may need watering in dry months.
- Avoid the use of fertilisers containing phosphorus.
- Tip-prune when young to shape, but do not prune hard.
- Propagation: Sow seed in autumn or spring in 75% coarse sand and 25% peat mix. Keep moist but not too wet for 3–4 weeks. To germinate, the seed needs cold nights and warm days (too much heat can be a problem). Young seedlings should be potted

DRYANDRA SPECIES	SIZE	COMMENTS
D. arborea	8 x 8 m	Susceptible to damage by excess water.
D. arctotidis	1 x 1 m	Red-yellow flowers, hardy.
D. cirsiodes	1.5 x 1 m	Yellow flowers late winter or early spring, very hardy if in well-drained soil.
D. comosa	1.7 x 2 m	Prickly leaves, yellow flowers.
D. concinna	1.5 x 0.7 m	Small yellow flowers, hardy in well-drained sunny spot.
D. falcata	1.5 x 2 m	Prickly foliage, yellow flowers in spring. Hardy.
D. formosa	3 x 4 m	Yellow flowers in spring–summer. One of the hardiest, and tolerates semi-shade.
D. nivea	0.2 x 1 m	Red flowers over winter. Hardy if soil is cool and well drained.
D. obtusa	0.2 x 1 m	Reddish flowers in mid-spring. It needs good drainage and a sunny spot.
D. plumosa	1.3 x 1.5 m	Very hardy in a well-drained sunny spot.
D. praemorsa	3 x 3 m	Long wavy leaves and large yellow flowers. The foliage thins and plants become woody after 5–10 years.
D. quercifolia	2 x 2 m	Yellow flowers with brown bracts in winter and prickly leaves. It is frost and drought tolerant.
D. tenuifolia	1 x 1 m	Red-yellow flowers and narrow leaves. Hardy.

when small to minimise root damage. Plants are best planted into a permanent position as young as possible. Difficult varieties are sometimes grown by grafting onto hardy seedling species. Some success has been had with cuttings.

DYSOXYLUM Meliaceae

At a glance

NUMBER OF SPECIES 70; 15 endemic to Australia in NSW, Qld, NT, WA.
NATURAL HABITAT Subtropical–tropical and dry rainforests.
FLOWERING Insignificant.
HABIT Medium to tall trees.
HARDINESS Reasonably hardy once established in preferred conditions.
FOLIAGE Glossy green, slightly hairy depending on species.
GROWTH RATE Often slow at first.
LIFESPAN Long-lived.

Culture

- Ample moisture required.
- Rich well-drained soils.
- Shade to part-shade, will tolerate full sun when mature.

Species

D. fraserianum (rosewood)
- 20–40 x 15–20 m. Dense crown of dark glossy leaves, creamy white to pale mauve fragrant flowers followed by decorative round pinky-grey fruit year-round. Well-drained rich soils. Needs frost and sun protection when young. Rose-coloured timber is prized for carpentry work.

D. mollisimum **syn.** ***D. meulleri*** (red bean)
- Up to 30 x 5 m. Glossy, deep green, fern-like leaves up to 60 cm with up to 20 leaflets, prefers deep moist soils.

D. rufum
- Up to 20 m. Dull to dark grey-green leaves up to 20 cm, with lighter hairy undersides, 11–21 leaflets. White 5-petal flowers in mid-summer. Timber smells like onions.

ELAEOCARPUS Elaeocarpaceae

At a glance

NUMBER OF SPECIES Over 200; 28 endemic to Australia.
NATURAL HABITAT Rainforests in eastern Australia.
FLOWERING Bell-shaped, both flowers and berries can be attractive.
HARDINESS Hardy once established.
HABIT Trees with spreading canopies.
FOLIAGE Undivided leaves, sometimes with toothed margins.
GROWTH RATE Some can be fast in ideal climate.
LIFESPAN Medium- to long-lived.

Culture

- Prefer moist soil with high organic content.

ELAEOCARPUS SPECIES	HEIGHT	FLOWERS	FRUITS	REQUIREMENTS
E. angustifolius (quandong)	15–30 m	Green-white, autumn–winter	Blue, edible	Good drainage, filtered sun, feed and water regularly.
E. eumundi	to 25 m	Cream and scented	Dark blue	Mulch, feed and water well.
E. grandis	to 12 m	White bell-shaped	Blue, edible	Adaptable but growth is encouraged with extra water.
E. obovatus	15–20 m	White–cream	Rich blue	Adaptable species.
E. reticulatus	10–15 m	White or pink	Dark blue	Hardy and adaptable.

- Requires lots of water in dry weather.
- Most prefer cool position in a mild to warm climate, though some will grow in Tasmania.
- Propagate from cuttings, or from seed which has been scarified or stored in moist peat for several months.

EPACRIS ❧ Native Heath ❧ Epacridaceae

At a glance

NUMBER OF SPECIES 40; most are endemic to Australia.
NATURAL HABITAT Varied.
FLOWERING Variable, many flower for months, some flower most of the year.
HARDINESS Hardy.
HABIT Small, generally upright shrubs.
FOLIAGE Heath-like (i.e. small leaves on long stems)
LIFESPAN Short to medium.

Culture

- Generally prefers well-drained but moist positions.
- Filtered sun or semi-shade preferred.
- Propagate by cuttings.

Species

E. brevifolia

- Shrub 0.5 to 1 m tall, up to 0.6 m spread, scented white flowers in spring, grow in full or filtered sunlight, prune after flowering.

E. impressa (pink heath)

- Small upright shrub to 0.75 m that grows best in semi-shade. Pink, red or white flowers mainly in winter. The Victorian state floral emblem.

E. longiflora

- An adaptable shrub, grows between 0.5 and 2 m tall and up to 2 m wide but generally much narrower. It has red flowers with white tips, mainly in August–November. Very adaptable in cultivation.

E. microphylla

- Clump-like, upright small shrub 0.5–1 m tall, with small white flowers mainly in winter. It is best in partial shade, and is frost and snow hardy.

E. pulchella

- Small clump grows to 0.5 m tall with white- to rose-coloured flowers.

EREMAEA ❧ Myrtaceae

At a glance

NUMBER OF SPECIES 8; all endemic to south-western Australia.
NATURAL HABITAT Sandy heathlands.
FLOWERING Usually orange or purple.
HARDINESS Not hardy in eastern states.
HABIT Small shrubs.
FOLIAGE Small, heath-like, narrow or broad leaves.
GROWTH RATE Usually moderate.
LIFESPAN Medium.

Culture

- Require full sun, warmth and good drainage.
- Most need pruning after flowering to keep bushy.
- Root rot in wet soils can be a problem.
- Propagates easily from seed or cuttings. Sometimes grafted onto *Kunzea ambigua* to help control root rot problems.

EREMOPHILA ❧ Emu Bush ❧ Myoporaceae

At a glance

NUMBER OF SPECIES About 260; all endemic to Australia.
NATURAL HABITAT Mainly arid areas.
FLOWERING Colour varies but normally red, cream, pink or purple.
HARDINESS Very hardy, especially in dry areas.

EREMAEA SPECIES	SIZE	FLOWERS	PREFERRED CONDITIONS
E. beaufortioides	1–3 x 1–2 m	Orange	Open, airy position, full sun.
E. ebracteata	0.5–1.5 x 1–2.5 m	Orange-red	Full sun, perfect drainage, good in tub.
E. fimbriata	0.5–1 x 0.5–1.5 m	Pink	Full or filtered sun, sandy soil.
E. pauciflora	1–2.5 x 0.5–2.5 m	Pale orange or yellow	Good drainage and light, best in containers.
E. violacea	0.4 x 0.5–2 m	Violet blue to pale red	Needs full sun to flower well, good drainage.

HABIT Variable shrubs.
FOLIAGE Variable, often with a waxy or hairy surface.
GROWTH RATE Usually moderate to fast.
LIFESPAN Medium in cultivation but variable in the wild.

Culture

- Needs good drainage and warm sunny position.
- Needs open uncrowded position to minimise fungal problems.
- Aphis, caterpillars and beetles are occasional problems.
- Most are drought and frost hardy.
- Most respond well to pruning.
- Propagate by cuttings, seed germination is difficult.
- Can be grafted onto *Myoporum* rootstocks to increase hardiness.

ERIOSTEMON Wax Flowers
Rutaceae

At a glance

NUMBER OF SPECIES 39; endemic to Australia.
NATURAL HABITAT Sub-alpine to semi-arid areas.
FLOWERING Late winter to spring.
HARDINESS Many are very hardy in a suitable climate (e.g. *E. myoporoides* [syn. *Philotheca myoporoides*] withstands most adverse conditions in Melbourne).
HABIT Shrubs.
FOLIAGE Scented, often sticky.
LIFESPAN Medium.
COMMENTS All Eriostemons other than *E. australasius* and *E. banksii* (which is sometimes classified as a subspecies of *E. australis*) were recently transferred to *Philotheca*.

EREMOPHILA SPECIES	HEIGHT	FLOWERS	LEAVES	PREFERRED CONDITIONS
E. brevifolia	1–4 m	White to pale mauve	Smooth surface	Adaptable, not too shaded though
E. cuneifolia	to 1.5 m	Pale blue	Sticky	Good in containers
E. densifolia	to 0.4 m	Purple to blue	Hairy and crowded	Tolerates semi-shade and salt winds
E. divaricata	1–2 m	Lilac or blue	Smooth surface	Tolerates some shade and heavy soils
E. gibbifolia	0.5–1 m	White or mauve	Warty but hairless	Adapts to most soils
E. glabra	Prostrate or to 1.5 m	Yellow to red or green	Very hairy or hairless	Very adaptable in full or filtered sun
E. maculata	0.5–3 m	Variable	Grey-green	Heavy but drained soil

ERIOSTEMON SPECIES	SIZE	COMMENTS
E. angustifolius syn. *Philotheca angustifolius*	Up to 1.5 x 1.5 m	Shrub with pink or red buds opening to white flowers with pink markings. Best as a container plant.
E. australasius	1–2.5 m tall	Shrub with pink or mauve to white flowers, one of the most attractive species, but difficult without perfect drainage, and a cool constantly moist root system. Excellent cut flower.
E. buxifolius syn. *Philotheca buxifolius*	0.5–1.5 m tall	Shrub with pink buds opening to white or pink flowers.
E. myoporoides syn. *Philotheca myoporoides*	Up to 2 x 2 m	A variable shrub with oval-shaped light green leaves, and white star–shaped flowers mainly in winter and spring. Best grown in filtered sunlight. Several forms of this species are available varying in flower and size characteristics.
E. nodiflorus syn. *Philotheca nodiflorus*	Up to 1 x 0.7 m	Mauve flowers, must have shade and excellent drainage to do well.
E. obovalis syn. *Philotheca obovalis*	Up to 1 m tall	Shrub with white flowers, reasonably hardy.
E. pungens syn. *Philotheca pungens*	0.3 x 1 m	Prostrate or low compact shrub with attractive small, white flowers.
E. spicatus syn. *Philotheca spicatus*	0.3–1 m tall	Small shrub with mauve flowers, needs good drainage and full sun or light shade.
E. verrucosus syn. *Philotheca verrucosus*	Up to 1.5 m tall	Has white flowers that develop from pink buds, mainly in spring. This species is hardy in most soils but does not tolerate waterlogging.

Culture

- Most prefer moist but well-drained soils.
- Prefers semi-shade or filtered sun.
- Scale and sooty mould are common problems.
- Collar rot can be a problem if mulch is too thick around base of plant.
- Responds to medium (but not heavy) pruning.
- Responds to regular feeding.
- Propagates easily from cuttings, although they can be slow.

EUCALYPTUS ❧ Gum Tree ❧
Myrtaceae ❧ *See also Corymbia*

At a glance

NUMBER OF SPECIES Approximately 600, almost all Australian.
NATURAL HABITAT All situations in all states.
FLOWERING Varies greatly.
HARDINESS Generally very hardy.
HABIT Mainly trees, some shrubs.
FOLIAGE Tough, leathery, undivided leaves, often aromatic.
LIFESPAN Generally long-lived.
GROWTH Fast to very fast.
COMMENTS Includes some of our most important commercial timbers and ornamental tree species. Some species of *Eucalyptus* have been renamed as *Corymbia*.

Culture

- Root systems generally deep and vigorous.
- Should not be transplanted as large plants.
- If pollarded (i.e. the top cut out to reduce height etc.) once, then this must be redone at least every 2–3 years to avoid branches falling.
- Established trees respond to feeding and deep watering in dry seasons.
- Leaf-eating insects, such as caterpillars and borers, can be serious pests.
- Most species respond well to a variety of soil and climatic conditions.
- Propagation: Almost always from seed, though limited success has been achieved in recent years with other methods, such as cuttings and grafting. Seeds germinate readily and are easy to obtain.
- Forestry departments direct-sow eucalypt seed in the field to establish forests. Nurserymen generally germinate the seed in a well-drained potting mix, then transplant when the seedling has its second or third pair of 'true' leaves into tubes. There can be great variation within a species, hence the characteristics of the parent plant the seed came from can influence the success or otherwise of the seedling. Eucalypts are not generally suited to growing on as advanced plants in containers. They are best planted in their permanent position as young as possible.

Types of eucalypts

Most people call eucalypts 'gum trees'; however, the gum is only one of several distinct subgroups in this genus.

- Gums are eucalypts that shed a layer of bark from most or all of the trunk and branches, leaving a smooth, usually light coloured trunk (e.g. *E. citriodora*, *E. pauciflora*, *E. papuana*).
- Stringybarks are eucalypts that have bark made up of long string-like fibres. The bark is usually grey to reddish-brown. The trunks are normally long and straight (e.g. *E. obliqua*, *E. macrorhyncha*, *E. muelleriana*).
- Peppermints have a fine, interlaced bark. It may be fibrous, but the fibres are very fine and crumble when rubbed. The leaves have a characteristic peppermint odour when crushed (e.g. *E. nicholii*, *E. radiata*, *E. dives*).
- Boxes have flaky scale-like bark that persists over the trunk and all branches. Leaves and buds tend to be smaller than on other eucalypts, and their wood is generally close-grained, durable and an excellent timber (e.g. *E. melliodora*, *E. goniocalyx*).
- Ironbarks have a hard, deeply ridged bark (e.g. *E. sideroxylon*).
- Yates are smaller eucalypts, bushy in habit, with very large nobbly gum nuts (e.g. *E. lehmannii* has gum nuts the size of a tennis ball).
- Mallees are small-growing eucalypts (usually no more than 5–8 m) with several or many main trunks coming from close to ground level. They tend to come mainly from semi-arid to arid areas (e.g. *E. preissiana*, *E. forrestiana*).

Hybrid eucalypts

Different eucalypt species sometimes crossbreed to form hybrids. Many seedlings found growing both in home gardens and in the wild may be difficult to identify because they are in fact a cross between two different species. If you can identify other eucalypts growing nearby you might be able to make an educated guess as to the hybrid's parentage and what characteristics the plant will have as it matures. Some eucalypt hybrids are highly ornamental and well worth trying in your garden although plants grown from seedlings can be quite variable. Noted examples are:

- *E.* 'Torwood' which is a cross between *E. torquata* and *E. woodwardii*.
- *E.* 'Augusta Wonder', a cross between *E. torquata* and possibly *E. erythronema* var. *erythronema*.

EUCALYPTUS SPECIES	COMMON NAME	COMMENTS
E. alpina	Grampians gum	4–7 m tall, sometimes to 15 m. Medium to high rainfall, well-drained soil.
E. alba	White gum	Up to 12 m. Accepts wet conditions. Brittle wood.
E. astringens	Brown mallet	12–18 m tall. Medium to high rainfall. Well drained clay soils.
E. botryoides	Mahogany gum	20–25 m tall. Medium to high rainfall. Poor sandy soil on a clay base, tolerates wet soils. Prone to insect damage.
E. caesia	Gungurru	A weeping tree up to 7 m tall with pink flowers. Low to medium rainfall. Some forms have attractive foliage.
E. caesia subsp. *magna* syn. *E. caesia* 'Silver Princess'	'Silver Princess'	A weeping tree up to 7 m tall with pink flowers. Low to medium rainfall. Some forms have attractive foliage. Habit is more pendant, and fruit and flowers larger than above species.
E. calophylla 'rosea' (now known as *Corymbia calophylla*)	Pink marri	Up to 10 m tall with pink flowers in summer and autumn. Medium to high rainfall, avoid heavy soils.
E. camaldulensis	River red gum	A large spreading tree up to 40 m tall and 30 m wide with a smooth white-grey trunk. It grows in a wide range of conditions and tolerates waterlogging and drought.
E. campaspe	Silver top gimlet	A slim-trunked tree up to 8 m tall with whitish stems. It grows in heavy soils and is drought tolerant.
E. citriodora (now known as *Corymbia citriodora*)	Lemon scented gum	An open smooth–barked tree up to 25 m tall and 12–15 m wide. It grows on a wide variety of soils and is frost tender when young. Aromatic foliage.
E. cladocalyx	Sugar gum	A hardy tree, up to 35 m tall and 15 m wide, that tends to drop lower branches. It grows in most soils in low to high rainfall. A dwarf form that grows up to 8 m is popular as a street tree.
E. coccifera	Tasmanian snow gum	Small, hardy shrub-like tree, up to 7 m tall. Compact habit. Withstands windy conditions.
E. cornuta	Yate	An upright to spreading tree, up to 20 m tall and 10 m wide, that grows naturally on poorly drained loams and clays. It tolerates lime, frost, waterlogging and drought.
E. crebra	Narrow-leaved iron bark	Slow-growing erect tree, up to 25 m tall. Important timber tree in Qld. Narrow, drooping leaves. Suitable for heavy soils.
E. crenulata	Silver gum	Small tree, up to 8 m tall, that is very adaptable to a wide range of conditions except for alkaline soils. Juvenile foliage popular for floral work.
E. curtisii	Plunkett mallee	Multi-trunked shrub, 2–6 m tall. Profuse pure white flowers in November. Very adapted to poor sandstone soils.
E. elata	River peppermint	A smooth white-barked tree, up to 30 m tall, with narrow, pendulous leaves. Cool to warm, humid to sub-humid climate. Grows along riverbanks but also in open fields and rocky outcrops.

EUCALYPTUS SPECIES	COMMON NAME	COMMENTS
E. erythrocorys	Red cap gum	Bushy upright or spreading mallee-type tree, up to 8 m tall and 3–8 m wide. It will grow in most soils but prefers slightly alkaline ones. It is frost tender when young. Red buds burst into vibrant yellow flowers in spring.
E. ficifolia (now known as *Corymbia ficifolia*)	Red flowering gum	Widely cultivated ornamental small tree, up to 15 m tall and 5–20 m wide. Medium to high rainfall, and good drainage. Frost tender when young. Flowers up to 4 cm, varied colour.
E. forrestiana	Fuchsia mallee	Upright to spreading shrub or small tree, usually 4–5 m tall and 3–5 m wide. Adaptable to a wide range of conditions. Tolerates dry, frosts and short periods of waterlogging. In summer red buds burst into yellow flowers.
E. globules	Blue gum	Blue leaves on young plants turning green on older plants, up to 60 m tall. Prefers high rainfall but highly adaptable.
E. grandis	Rose gum	Straight tree to 30 m. Attractive smooth white bark. Grows very rapidly.
E. gummifera (now known as *Corymbia gummifera*)	Red bloodwood	Up to 35 m tall, tolerant of most soils.
E. gunnii	Cider gum	A smooth-barked shade tree, up to 25 m tall. Wind tolerant and prefers medium to light soils.
E. intermedia	Red bloodwood	Medium tree to 30 m. White-cream flowers 2 cm in January to March.
E. lehmannii	Bushy yate	Mallee-type shrub, up to 5 m tall and 5 m wide. Dry to medium rainfall, sandy soil or clay loam. Large decorative buds and nuts, yellow flowers. Tends to blow over if not planted in clumps.
E. leucoxylon	Yellow gum	Tree up to 12 m tall with smooth whitish bark. Moderate to dry rainfall, most soils. Several forms which vary in height and flower colour.
E. macrocarpa	Mottlecah	Bushy shrub up to 4 m tall with large red flowers in spring and attractive silver leaves. Prefers low to medium rainfall in well-drained, even poor, soils.
E. maculata (now known as *Corymbia maculata*)	Spotted gum	Tree up to 30 m tall with smooth cream spotted trunk. Medium to high rainfall in most soils. Frost tender when young.
E. mannifera	Brittle gum	A white-trunk tree, up to 20 m tall. It is often coppiced to display multiple trunks. Most soils. Branches tend to drop easily.
E. marginata	Jarrah	Up to 60 m tall. An important timber tree from WA. Performs well on gravel soil or sandy loams.
E. microcorys	Tallowwood	Large tree, up to 30 m tall, with fibrous bark and small leaves. Produces a dense crown.
E. melliodora	Yellow box	Up to 30 m tall. Hardy on most soil types but slow to establish. It grows best on soils that are acidic and well drained. It will grow poorly if soils are alkaline and struggle if waterlogged.

EUCALYPTUS SPECIES	COMMON NAME	COMMENTS
E. microcorys	Tallow-wood	Large tree, up to 30 m tall, with fibrous bark and small leaves. Produces a dense crown. Grows in tall, open forest on the fringe of rainforests of NSW and Qld.
E. muelleriana	Yellow stringybark	Adaptable tree, up to 50 m tall and 15–30 m wide. Prefers high rainfall and medium to heavy soils. Good timber tree.
E. nicholii	Narrow leaved peppermint	Medium tree up to 15 m tall with spreading crown up to 12 m wide and narrow blue-green drooping leaves. Adaptable in most temperate areas, medium to high rainfall.
E. niphophila	Snow gum	A twisted (or mallee-type) sub-alpine tree, up to 10 m tall, with red or grey patches on a white trunk. The only tree species able to withstand alpine winds, prolonged snowfalls, and the chilling cold of Australia's sub-alpine regions.
E. oblique	Messmate	Up to 80 m tall. A moisture-loving tree, grown for timber. Prefers cool sub-humid to humid conditions, ranging to warmer climates.
E. occidentalis	Flat-topped yate	A WA species, up to 20 m tall, which can thrive in saline soils or saline irrigation water.
E. ovata	Swamp gum	Medium to tall tree, 10–30 m tall and 10–20 m wide, with light-coloured deciduous bark. Adaptable to a wide range of conditions. Useful for poorly drained soils.
E. papuana (now known as *Corymbia papuana*)	Ghost gum	Medium tree, up to 15 m tall and 12 m wide, with striking white smooth-barked trunk and stems. For dry-arid to northern inland tropical areas, usually sandy or rocky soil, sometimes poorly drained or wet soils.
E. pauciflora	Snow gum	Small to medium tree from 8–20 m tall and 5–12 m wide with often twisted trunks, and striking light-coloured bark often with orange, pink or other coloured splotches. Adapts to most soils. Moderate to high rainfall.
E. platypus	Round leaved moort	Dense mallee-type bush or small tree, up to 8 m tall and 5–10 m wide, with glossy foliage. Buds red and large yellow flowers. Adaptable to most conditions except tropical. Good in smog-prone areas.
E. preissiana	Bell fruit mallee	Small to medium mallee, up to 5 m tall and 8 m wide, with spectacular yellow winter flowers and attractive gum nuts. Most well-drained soils, may be frost tender when young. Smog resistant.
E. ptychocarpa	Swamp bloodwood	Small spreading tree to 10 m. Spectacular red/pink/white large blooms. Large glossy pendulous foliage. Ornamental nuts.
E. radiate	Grey peppermint	Medium tree to 30 m by 10–20 m with grey-brown bark and aromatic foliage. Adaptable except for tropical areas.
E. regnans	Mountain ash	Very tall tree up to 100 m high and 30 m wide. Prefers moist but well-drained loams and clay loams, and high rainfall. Prized timber species.

EUCALYPTUS SPECIES	COMMON NAME	COMMENTS
E. robusta	Swamp mahogany	Medium tree with a spreading crown, up to 20 m tall by 10–20 m wide, with attractive red-brown bark. Very adaptable, good in wet soils and coastal areas.
E. rubida	Candlebark	Medium tree, up to 25 m tall by 20 m wide, with attractive white trunk with pink-red stripes in spring–summer. Hardy and adaptable in well-drained soils.
E. saligna	Sydney blue gum	Medium to tall tree, up to 50 m high, with a tall straight trunk and long deciduous white to blue-grey bark. Fertile, well-drained soil, and medium to high rainfall. Fast growing and ornamental.
E. sideroxylon	Red ironbark	Medium tree with rounded or spreading crown, up to 30 m tall by 20 m wide, with deep furrowed red-brown to black bark. Hardy, adaptable ornamental if drainage is good. Yellow or red flowers.
E. spathulata	Swamp mallee	Hardy, ornamental small tree, up to 10 m tall by 8 m wide, with coppery coloured bark and fine leaves. Adaptable to a wide range of conditions. Best planted in clumps.
E. teretocornis	Forest red gum	30 m tall, with a thick attractive trunk. Excellent for heavy soils. White flowers in June–Nov.
E. tessellaris	Carbeen Moreton Bay ash	Very attractive gum, grows to 25 m. Decorative trunk. Willow-like leaves. Suitable for shallow soils and tolerates salt spray.
E. tetraptera	Four wing mallee	Spreading mallee-type shrub, up to 6 m tall by 8 m wide, with large leathery leaves and attractive red buds and pink-red flowers in spring. Low rainfall, warm conditions, well-drained soils best. Not for windbreaks.
E. torelliana	Cadaga	Large tree, up to 30 m tall. Regarded as a pest in many areas. Dense crown and attractive trunk. Bird attracting. Prone to sooty mould infections.
E. torquata	Coral gum	Very ornamental, long-flowering small tree, 5–10 m tall by 5–10 m wide, with large pink-red, white-cream flowers. Adaptable and hardy in most conditions, particularly semi-arid. May be frost tender when young.
E. viminalis	Manna gum	Ornamental upright variable tree, 10–50 m tall by 10–20 m wide, with ribbon-like bark. Hardy and adaptable, preferring moist, well-drained soils. Important commercial species, and food source for koalas.
E. viridis	Green mallee	Hardy, attractive multi-trunked shrub or small tree, 5–12 m tall by 5 m wide, with fine dark green leaves, and often profuse white flowers. Low–medium rainfall, most soils, adaptable. Good nectar- and oil-production species.
E. woodwardii	Lemon flowered gum	Up to 12 m tall. Suited to arid sites and most soils. Does not tolerate salt. Lovely specimen tree with white to pale pink or greenish bark that sheds in ribbons.

EUCHRYPHIA

At a glance

NUMBER OF SPECIES 8; 5 endemic to Australia from rainforests in Qld, Vic, NSW and Tasmania.
NATURAL HABITAT Rainforest in Qld and rainforest or sub-alpine shrubberies throughout Tasmania.
FLOWERING Large, usually white (or pale pink) flowers in spring–summer.
HABIT Medium to straight tall tree with an open-canopy crown.
HARDINESS Medium.
FOLIAGE Shiny, oblong leaves.
GROWTH RATE Medium.
LIFESPAN Medium- to long-lived.
COMMENTS Important in Tasmania for the production of leatherwood honey.

Culture

- Needs a sheltered position in semi-shade or full sun.
- Grows in moist, well-drained acid to neutral soils.
- Prune to maintain compact shape.
- Propagate from seed or cuttings.

Species

E. lucida (Tasmanian leatherwood)

- 2–10 m tall shrubby tree, higher in favourable conditions. Young leaves and buds covered in a sticky gum-like substance. Large white, pink-tinged flowers in spring and summer. Rich soils and high rainfall.

E. moorei (pink bloodwood)

- Small tree to tall shrub, bright green oblong leaves and white flowers. Grows on acidic, organic soils. NSW and Vic. Coastal areas.

E. wilkiei

- Shrubby tree with creamy saucer-shaped flowers. Qld.

E. jinksii

- Large tree, up to 25 m tall, with 5–10 cm long, green simple leaves, sometimes appearing as three leaflets. Qld.

EUGENIA ❧ Myrtaceae

At a glance

NUMBER OF SPECIES About 1000; 1 endemic to Australia.
NATURAL HABITAT Qld rainforests.
FLOWERING Mainly in summer.
HABIT Large shrubs to large trees.
HARDINESS Generally hardy.
FOLIAGE Glossy, undivided leaves.
GROWTH RATE Can be fast under good conditions.
LIFESPAN Long-lived.
COMMENTS Many Australian species formerly listed in the genus *Eugenia* are now included in the *Acmena*, *Acmenosperma*, *Syzygium* and *Waterhousea* genera.

Culture

- Prefers moist, well-mulched soil.
- Propagate by seed.
- Will tolerate full sun.

Species

E. reinwardtiana

- Up to 3 m tall, bushy, white flowers, shiny red berries up to 1.5 cm, from coastal rainforests of Qld.

E. smithii

- Now known as *Acmena smithii*.

EUTAXIA ❧ Fabaceae

At a glance

NUMBER OF SPECIES About 9; all endemic to WA except for *E. microphylla* which is widespread.
NATURAL HABITAT Mainly near the coast in open forest and heathlands.
FLOWERING Yellow and red pea flowers mainly in spring.
HABIT Mainly small or dwarf woody shrubs, sometimes prostrate.
HARDINESS Generally hardy.

FOLIAGE Usually small, simple leaves arranged oppositely.
GROWTH RATE Medium to quick.

Culture

- Most prefer partial or filtered sunlight.
- Most prefer well-drained light to medium soils.
- *E. microphylla* will tolerate poorer drainage.
- Propagate by seed (treat with hot water first) or semi-hardwood cuttings.

Species

E. microphylla

- Variable shrub, 30–50 cm tall, spreading to 1.5 m wide. It withstands dry periods and prefers well-drained acid soil, semi-shade. It is salt tolerant and has reddish-yellow flowers in spring and summer. It responds well to pruning. Prostrate forms make good rockery plants.

E. obovata

- A bushy variable shrub, up to 1–2 m tall with a spread of 0.5–3 m with yellow and red flowers in spring. It prefers semi-shade and well-drained soils. Heavy frosts may cause damage. Regular tip pruning will help keep it bushy.

EVODIELLA Rubiaceae

At a glance

NUMBER OF SPECIES About 5; 1 endemic to northern Australia.
NATURAL HABITAT North-eastern Qld, rainforests and wet-sclerophyll forests.
FLOWERING Small pink flowers in clusters borne December to May.
HABIT Medium shrub.
HARDINESS Hardy in most gardens.
FOLIAGE Glossy green trifoliate.
GROWTH RATE Slow in the early stages.
COMMENTS Bird- and butterfly-attractive.

Culture

- Full shade to full sun.
- Prefers rich organic moist soils.
- Water in dry periods for improved results.
- Pruning will produce a thicker specimen.
- Propagate from seed.

Species

E. muelleri (little Evodia)

- 3–4 m tall in domestic gardens. Very popular in south-eastern Qld.

FICUS Moraceae

At a glance

NUMBER OF SPECIES About 800 with around 40 in Australia, mostly in Qld.
NATURAL HABITAT Generally high-rainfall areas, particularly in the tropics; one as far south as East Gippsland in Victoria.
FLOWERING Generally insignificant flowers at variable times, followed by edible fig-like fruits varying in size and colour.
HABIT Mainly trees and shrubs. Some are epiphytic, growing on and eventually strangling other trees.
HARDINESS Generally hardy. Lerps and fig-leaf beetles may sometimes be a problem.
GROWTH RATE Generally fast under good conditions.
COMMENTS Can have damaging root systems, particularly near drains. Their white sap can irritate the skin. They are generally excellent shelter trees, and the edible figs are an excellent source of food for wildlife. Most are unsuitable for the average suburban garden.

Culture

- Most tolerate a wide range of soils and some waterlogging.
- Generally hardy in full sun.
- Generally long-lived.
- Most species are normally frost tender.
- Propagate mainly by cuttings, seed is

FICUS SPECIES	COMMENTS
F. benjamina (weeping fig)	Up to 30 m tall, from Qld, small shiny leaves, very hardy in subtropics, often grown as an indoor plant.
F. coronata (sandpaper fig)	A small to medium tree with dark green leaves that have rough, sandpaper-like upper surfaces, and masses of hairy edible fruit. Grows well in cultivation in moist, well-drained soils.
F. crassipes (round-leafed banana fig)	Medium to large spreading tree, up to 30 m tall. Leaves glossy and leathery up to 20 cm long. Fruit is finger-shaped, spotted and 6 cm long. Loam soils in full sun. Qld.
F. fraseri	Small to medium tree, 10–15 x 3–5 m, with a sparse, spreading crown of rough leaves. Bird-attracting bright orange-red fruit, which ripens between May and February. NT, Qld, NSW.
F. hillii	A very popular tree, 6–14 m tall, grown in most major Australian cities both as an indoor container plant and an outdoor tree. Commonly considered to be a variety of *F. macrocarpa.*
F. macrophylla (Moreton Bay fig)	Used as a feature tree in large gardens from Qld to Melbourne. Up to 40 m tall and 30 m wide. Large dark green oval leaves, edible fruits, hardy to some frost once established.
F. obliqua (small-leaved fig)	Tall tree, 15–3 x 15–30 m, with a dense spreading crown. Small 6 cm elliptical leaves. Excellent shade tree. Fleshy, small yellow-orange bird-attracting fruit. NSW, Qld.
F. opposita	A sandpaper fig. Tall shrub or small tree, 3–8 m x 2–3 m, with sandpaper-like leaves, sometimes deciduous. Globular reddish-brown fruit eaten by birds. Qld.
F. platypoda (small-leaved Moreton Bay fig)	Small tree, often with multi-trunks of smooth grey bark, 6–8 x 5–10 m. Bears bright orange to red fruit, attractive to birds and other wildlife. Excellent for bonsai. NT, Qld, WA.
F. pleurocarpa (banana fig)	A large spreading tree with a dense canopy, 10–15 m tall. Leaves are large, shiny and leathery. Fruits are banana-shaped, yellow and edible. Adventitious roots descending from the branches make this an interesting tree.
F. racemosa (cluster fig)	A medium to large tree, height 8–15 m, with a spreading crown. Edible fruits are borne in clusters on the trunk and branches. Bird attracting. NT, Qld, WA.
F. rubiginosa (Port Jackson fig)	Medium to large bushy tree, 10–20 m tall. Leaves are dark green and hairy underneath. Yellowish fleshy fruit. autumn-winter-spring. Moist, well-drained soils. Will tolerate light frosts. NSW, Qld.
F. superba (cedar fig)	Large tree, 6–25 x 10–20 m, dense, shady, bright green crown with smooth grey bark. Purple edible fruit that matures Jan–Aug. Tree has short deciduous period. Suits parks and large gardens. NSW, NT Qld.
F. triradiata (red stipule fig)	A large bushy tree, 10–20 m tall, with a rounded or spreading crown. Young shoots have bright red stipules. Qld.
F. variegata	From northern Qld, a good shade tree in the subtropics, used as an indoor plant or protected shrub in the south.
F. virens (banyan fig)	Large tree, 15–30 x 15–40 m, widely spreading, shady canopy. Trunk often forms flanges and buttresses for wind resistance. Edible, bird-attracting fruit. Northern Australia, also found in Asia.
F. watkinsiana (strangler fig)	Medium-sized tree, up to 15 x 5–10 m, with an irregularly buttressed trunk and long strangling roots. Edible fleshy fruit is dark purple and spotted.

unreliable. Aerial layering is generally successful.
- Smaller species can be used as indoor plants. Some have been successful in bonsai.

FLINDERSIA Flindersiaceae

At a glance

NUMBER OF SPECIES 15; all endemic to Australia.
NATURAL HABITAT Most are rainforests species.
FLOWERING Small flowers clustered together to produce a large head.
HABIT Small to large spreading trees.
HARDINESS Very hardy and adaptable to cultivation. Best suited to high-rainfall areas.
FOLIAGE Dark green compound leaves.
GROWTH RATE Generally fast-growing trees.
LIFESPAN Long-lived.
COMMENTS Interesting woody fruit capsules. Good timber trees.

Culture

- Full sun encourages a better-shaped tree.
- Early protection desirable.
- Additional irrigation required in dry periods.
- Propagate by fresh seed.

Species

F. australis (crows ash)
- 15 x 7 m. Provides good shade. Does well in dry areas.

F. bennettiana (Bennett's ash)
- 15 x 10 m. Ornamental shade tree. Tolerates poor soils.

F. brayleyana (Queensland maple)
- 10 x 4 m. Produces an excellent shade tree.

F. schottiana (bumpy ash)
- 25 x 15 m. Attractive tree when in flower. Good street tree.

FRANKENIA Frankeniaceae

At a glance

NUMBER OF SPECIES 80 worldwide; 50 endemic to Australia, in all mainland states.
NATURAL HABITAT Coastal areas or near salt lakes.
FLOWERING Small but profuse flowers sporadically produced in spring and summer.
HABIT Low-growing to prostrate or small sub-shrubs.
HARDINESS Hardy.
GROWTH RATE Medium.
FOLIAGE Leaves are usually crowded on the stem, hairy on some species, appearing silver mainly due to salt deposits.

FRANKENIA SPECIES	SIZE	COMMENTS
F. cinerea	0.1–0.3 x to 0.45 m	Shrub with white or pink flowers in late winter to mid-spring. WA salt lakes etc.
F. crispa	0.3 x 0.5 m	Shrub with short stems, rounded crown and grey-green leaves. Open, 5-pink-petal flowers appear in spring. Prefers light, well-drained soil in an open sunny position. NSW, Vic, SA.
F. gracilis	0.30 x 0.50 m	Low prostrate shrub with thin branches. Pink-red flowers in spring and summer. NT, Qld, SA.
F. latior	0.30 x 0.50 m	Small shrub with prostrate hairy branches, flowers in spring or autumn.
F. serpyllifolia	0.30 x 0.50 m	Low spreading, hairy herb or shrub. Flowers in spring. NT, Qld, SA.
F. pauciflora	0.30 x 0.30 m	Light to medium soils in an open semi-shaded position, drought and frost resistant. Pink or white flowers. NSW, SA, TAS, Vic, WA, NT.

Culture

- Grows in full sun to light shade.
- Needs well-drained to dry soil.
- Tolerates saline soils.
- Good rockery plants.

GASTROLOBIUM ❧ Fabaceae

At a glance

NUMBER OF SPECIES About 60, mainly from south-western WA. These include all the *Brachysema* species which have been transferred to *Gastrolobium*.
NATURAL HABITAT Varied, mainly south-western WA.
FLOWERING Showy yellow and red pea flowers.
HARDINESS Generally very hardy, especially in dry areas.
HABIT Groundcovers and shrubs.
FOLIAGE Variable in both shape and colour.
GROWTH RATE Medium to fast.
LIFESPAN Long-lived under good conditions.
COMMENTS The foliage of many species is toxic, containing a poison similar to '1080', deadly to both stock and humans.

Culture

- Tolerate most soils and conditions.
- Prune after flowering but take care with poisonous species.
- Resistant to most pests and diseases. Scale is the most likely pest problem.
- Propagate from hot-water-treated or scarified seeds, and by cuttings in late summer.

Species

G. bilobum

- 1–4 x 1–4 m, showy clusters of yellow and red pea flowers in spring. Prefers some shade and moist, well-drained soils. One of the more toxic Gastrolobiums.

G. calycinum

- 1–3 x 1–3 m, bright orange-red flowers and green to grey-green foliage. Adaptable species but grows best in warm and sunny positions.

G. truncatum

- Prostrate, spreading habit. Profuse flowering and hardy in most conditions. Non-toxic.

GOMPHOLOBIUM ❧ Fabaceae

At a glance

NUMBER OF SPECIES 26; 25 endemic to Australia, most found in south-western WA.
NATURAL HABITAT Coastal heaths and open forests mainly in sandy or gravelly soils.
FLOWERING Pea-shaped flowers, most have yellow, orange or red flowers in spring.
HABIT Shrubs.
HARDINESS Generally hardy once established but can be difficult to establish.
FOLIAGE Normally divided, most pinnate.
GROWTH RATE Normally fast.
COMMENTS Leaves are poisonous.

Culture

- Prefers light, well-drained soils in a protected position.
- Sun in cool climates or semi-shade, and even full shade may be needed in hot areas.
- Keep soil reasonably dry. (A few species will tolerate wet periods.)
- Tip-prune after flowering.
- White fly, scale and sooty mould can be a problem.
- Some species are susceptible to Phytophthora root rot in the eastern states.
- Propagate from late summer cuttings or hot-water-treated seed.

Species

G. grandiflorum

- An upright shrub to 1–2 m tall with spectacular yellow flowers up to 2.5 cm. It needs some shade.

G. latifolium

- A small shrub from 1–2 m tall with large

yellow flowers up to 3 cm. It requires good drainage and partial or filtered sun. Will withstand most frosts.

GOODENIA ❧ Fabaceae

At a glance

NUMBER OF SPECIES Over 170; most native to Australia. They are distributed in all states, although most are found in the west.
NATURAL HABITAT Distribution ranges from coastal heaths and arid deserts to moist forests.
FLOWERING Most common colour is yellow, although a few species have shades of blue and mauve. Generally long-flowering.
HABIT Herbs and shrubs.
HARDINESS Variable, some very hardy.
FOLIAGE Variable in size, shape and texture.
GROWTH RATE Fast.
LIFESPAN Often short-lived in cultivation.

Culture

- Most varieties prefer full sun and good drainage.
- Some tolerate light shade.
- Scale, white fly and botrytis (grey mould) are sometimes a problem.
- Propagate from stem cuttings and division of rooted stolons. Some can also be grown successfully from seed.

Species

G. amplexans

- Shrub, 0.5–1 m tall, large yellow flowers, prefers full sun, susceptible to root rot, short-lived.

G. hederacea

- Variable, prostrate plant which sends out roots at nodal points. Fairly dense covering of rounded leaves that are dark green on top and whitish below. Bright yellow flowers are borne in spring and summer. Adaptable and ornamental species.

G. humilis

- Prostrate, suckering habit. Profuse yellow flowers are borne in spring. Will adapt to a wide range of conditions but grows best in moist soil in a sunny position.

G. lanata

- Adaptable and responds to hard pruning.

G. ovata

- Shrubby habit, 1–2 m x 1–2 m. Commonly grows in forest understorey in south-eastern Australia, especially in areas which have been recently disturbed. Will tolerate shade, wet soil and frosts.

GOODIA ❧ Fabaceae

At a glance

NUMBER OF SPECIES 2; both endemic to Australia.
NATURAL HABITAT Widespread along the coast and on the tablelands of southern and eastern Australia as well as southern WA.
FLOWERING Pea-shaped yellow flowers with purplish-red markings from winter to spring.
HABIT Open to moderately dense shrubs.
HARDINESS Hardy.
FOLIAGE Soft pinnate leaves comprising 3 blue-green to grey-green leaflets on long petioles.
GROWTH RATE Fast.
LIFESPAN Short- to medium-lived.

Culture

- Prefers moist soil but will tolerate dry periods.
- Avoid alkaline soils.
- Prefers reasonable drainage and a good mulch.
- Semi-shade best but will tolerate full sun.
- Regular pruning is beneficial.
- Propagate from hot-water-treated seed or by cuttings

Species

G. lotifolia

- A variable, quick-growing shrub to 5 m tall and 3 m spread. It prefers semi-shade, is best grown in coastal or mountain areas and is generally frost hardy.

G. medicaginea

- A shrub from 1 to 4 m tall and up to 4 m spread, similar to *G. lotifolia* but often occurs naturally in drier, more exposed conditions such as rocky hillsides.

G. pubescens* = *G. lotifolia var. pubescens

GREVILLEA ✲ Spider Flower ✲
Proteaceae

At a glance

NUMBER OF SPECIES At least 300 species; all but 7 are endemic to Australia. About half occur in south-western WA. A large number of cultivars are also available.

NATURAL HABITAT Widespread in a variety of habitats across Australia.

FLOWERING Wide variety of colours and flowering times. Grevilleas are usually long flowering.

HABIT Ranges from prostrate groundcovers, through small and medium shrubs up to large trees.

HARDINESS Variable according to species. Some of the easiest to grow, most popular Australian natives.

FOLIAGE Very variable, ranging from small, entire leaves to lobed or pinnate leaves. All are arranged alternately on the stems and some have hairy under-surfaces.

GROWTH RATE Generally medium to quick.

Culture

- Generally adapt to most soils, some prefer acid, many prefer clay; all require good drainage.
- Many varieties are difficult to grow in Adelaide.
- Lightly tip-prune several times each year.
- Most tolerate frost and some drought.
- Most flower for long periods, off and on all year round.
- Most prefer full sun but will tolerate some shade.
- Propagation best done by semi-hardwood cuttings. Seed should be avoided unless it is from isolated parents, or is to be used for breeding new cultivars, as grevilleas hybridise readily.

GREVILLEA SPECIES	SIZE (METRES)	FLOWER COLOUR	FOLIAGE
G. acanthifolia	1 x 2	Mauve-pink	Prickly
G. acerosa	0.5 x 0.6	Cream	Dense, prickly
G. alpina	Variable, many forms, often less than 0.3	Variable	Relatively small, not prickly
G. alpina 'Beechworth'	0.6 x 0.6	Orange, red and yellow	Relatively small, not prickly
G. alpina 'Grampians'	0.3 x 0.6	Red and yellow	Relatively small, not prickly
G. apiciloba	2 x 2	Green toothbrush	Prickly, to 7 cm
G. aquifolium	1.5 x 2	Red toothbrush	Prickly, holly-shaped
G. aquifolium 'prostrate'	Creeping x 2	Red toothbrush	Prickly
G. arenaria	2 x 2	Red or yellow	Dense, soft grey
G. aspera	1.5 x 1.5	Cream–red	Oblong

GREVILLEA SPECIES	SIZE (METRES)	FLOWER COLOUR	FOLIAGE
G. asplenifolia	2.5 x 2.5	Mauve toothbrush	Slender grey leaf
G. asteriscosa	2 x 3	Bright red	Prickly, star-shaped
G. australis	0.2 x 2	White, small	Small leaves
G. baileyana	6 x 4	White	Bronze underside
G. banksii	2.5 x 2	Red or cream	Grey to dark green
G. banksii 'Forsteri'	2.5 x 2	Red	Grey to dark green
G. barklyana	3 x 2.5	Pale pink	Lobed leaf, open
G. baueri	0.6 x 1.2	Deep red	Rusty tips
G. bipinnatifida	1 x 1	Orange-red	Stiff and divided
G. brevicupsis	1.5 x 2	White	Prickly
G. brownii	0.3 x 1	Orange-red	Dense
G. buxifolia	1.5 x 2	Grey	Rusty new growth
G. 'Carrington Falls' (syn *G. rivularis*)	2.5 x 3	White	Divided, prickly
G. capitellata	1 x 1.5	Red	Soft greyish
G. chrysophaea	0.8 x 1.2	Gold-red	Round, soft
G. cinerea	0.8 x 1.2	Green	Soft
G. Clearview Hybrids – see separate table			
G. confertifolia	0.3 x 2	Pink	Prickly and fine
G. 'Crosbie Morrison'	1.2 X 2	Pink-red	Grey, dense
G. curvilobia subsp. *incurva* (syn. *G. biternat*)	1 x 4	White	Prickly, pale green, creeping with tall upright shoots
G. dielsiana	2 x 1	Pink and yellow	Fine, prickly
G. diminuta	0.5 x 2	Pink-red	Broad and oval
G. endlicheriana	3 x 2	Light pink	Fine, greyish
G. fasciculata	1 x 2	Orange or scarlet	Silver, narrow
G. formosa	0.7 x 4	Gold	Silver-green
G. X *gaudichaudi*	0.3 x 2	Red	Lobed, red tips
G. glabrata	3 x 3	White	Blue, prickly
G. hookeriana	3 x 3.5	Scarlet toothbrush	Dense, ferny leaf
G. 'Ivanhoe'	2.5 x 3	Red toothbrush	Deeply serrated
G. juniperina	2 x 2	Red	Dark green needles
G. juniperina 'prostrate'	0.1 X 2	Red or yellow	Prickly needles
G. lanigera	1 x 1.5	Red or cream	Grey, soft
G. laurifolia	0.2 x 3	Dark red	Large, brown-tipped
G. lavandulaceae	1 x 1.5	Red masses	Soft grey needles

GREVILLEA SPECIES	SIZE (METRES)	FLOWER COLOUR	FOLIAGE
G. nudiflora	1 x 2	Scarlet	Very fine
G. obtusifolia	0.2 x 2	Scarlet	Light green
G. parviflora	1 x 1	Soft pink	Delicate needles
G. pinaster	2 x 3	Scarlet	Woolly, dense
G. pteridifolia	8 x 6	Yellow-gold	Grey-green
G. repens	2 x 2.5	Dark red	Holly shape, not prickly, green
G. robusta	15–20 x 8	Orange	Divided, young growth rust colour
G. rosmarinifolia	2 x 3	Red	Green, prickly
G. sericea	1 x 2	Pink	Oval
G. sessilis	2-5 x 4	White to cream	Similar to *G. banksii*
G. speciosa subsp. *dimorpha*	12 x 2	Brilliant red	Fine or broad types
G. speciosa subsp. *oleoides*	2 x 1.5	Scarlet	Dark green
G. thelmanniana	0.2 x 3	Red	Fine, green or grey
G. victoriae	2.5 x 3	Large red	Oval to short oval
G. 'White Wings'	2.5 x 3	White	Divided and prickly

VARIETIES OF *G. ROSMARINIFOLIA*

GREVILLEA SPECIES	SIZE (METRES)	FLOWER COLOUR	FOLIAGE
G. 'Jenkinsii'	1 x 1	Red flowers	Woolly green needles
G. 'Pink Pearl'	1.5 x 1	Bright pink flowers	Deep green needles
G. 'Pink Pixie'	1 x 1	Spectacular pink flowers	Light green needles
G. rosmarinifolia 'Whipstick'	2 x 1	Red flowers	Open upright habit

GREVILLEA CLEARVIEW HYBRIDS Hybrids from the nursery of Mr W. Cane of Maffra in Victoria

GREVILLEA SPECIES	SIZE (METRES)	FLOWER COLOUR	FOLIAGE
G. 'Clearview David' *G. rosmarinifolia* X *G.* 'Crosbie Morrison'	0.3 x 1.2	Rich red	Prickly green needle-like foliage
G. 'Clearview Dwarf' *G. lanigera* x *G. lavandulacea*	0.3 x 1	Red	Greyish leaves
G. 'Clearview Robin' Same origin as *G* 'Clearview David'	2.5 x 1	Red and cream	Greyish leaves

GREVILLEA POORINDA HYBRIDS			
Hybrids which occurred naturally in the garden of Mr Leo Hodge, at Poorinda, near Buchan in eastern Victoria			
GREVILLEA SPECIES	**SIZE (METRES)**	**FLOWER COLOUR**	**FOLIAGE**
G. 'Poorinda Beauty' *G. juniperina* x *G. alpina*	1 x 1	Orange-red	Needle leaves
G. 'Poorinda Constance' *G. juniperina* x *G. victoriae*	2 x 2.5	Red	Soft linear leaves
G. 'Poorinda Elegance' *G. alpina/obtusifolia* x *G. juniperina*	2.5 x 2.5	Yellow and red	Linear-oval leaves
G. 'Poorinda Firebird' *G. oleoides* x *G. speciosa*	2 x 2.5	Brilliant red	Grey-green leaf
G. 'Poorinda Peter' *G. acanthifolia* x *G. asplenifolia*	3 x 2	Red toothbrush	Serrated bronze leaf
G. 'Poorinda Queen' *G. juniperina* x *G. victoriae*	2 x 2.5	Orange	Soft pointed oval leaves

Grevilleas for warm climates (including *G. banksii* hybrids)

The most commonly grown grevilleas in the subtropics and tropics are hybrids produced by crossbreeding *G. banksii* with various other species. Sometimes known as 'northern hybrids', these plants have large colourful flowers. Generally these have divided leaves and large cylinder-type flowers.

They are grown in both the north and south of Australia, but are particularly suited to warmer climates.

The following are most commonly grown in warm parts of Australia:

GREVILLEA HYBRID	SIZE	COMMENTS
G. 'Caloundra Gem'	3–5 x 3 m	A hybrid between *G. banksii* and *G.* 'Honeycomb'. Foliage extends to ground level. Pink and yellow flowers up to 20 cm long, all year. Prefers sunny, average position, and responds well.
G. 'Coconut Ice'	1.5 x 1.5 m	Parents are *G. banksii* and *G. bipinnatifida.* Pink- and orange-coloured flowers up to 20 cm long, all year. Prefers full sun. Very hardy, tolerating wind and frost. Prune regularly to keep healthy and in good shape.
G. 'Golden Yul-lo'	4 x 2.5 m	Similar in habit to *G.* 'Honey Gem' but with lemon-coloured flowers.
G. 'Honeycomb'	3–4 x 2 m	This is a form of the species *G. whiteana*, a native of southern Qld. Cream-yellow flowers up to 12 cm long in winter and spring. Relatively frost hardy.
G. 'Honey Gem'	4 x 2.5 m	One of the most popular plants in south-eastern Queensland, a hybrid between *G. banksii* and *G. pteridifolia.* Orange flowers with some pink, up to 20 cm long. Very fast growing, hardy, new growth tips are bronze colour.
G. 'Masons Hybrid'	2 x 1.5 m	A hybrid of *G. banksii* and the orange form of *G. bipinnatifida.* The correct botanical name is *G.* 'Masons Hybrid', but it is also sold as *G.* 'Ned Kelly'. Covered in orange and red flowers all year. Very hardy, tolerates frost, grows well in most soils.

GREVILLEA HYBRID	SIZE	COMMENTS
G. 'Misty Pink'	3 x 2 m	A hybrid of *G. banksii* and *G. sessilis.* Originated on Mt Tamborine, near the Gold Coast in Qld. Hardy, vigorous, with greyish leaves. Flowers are pink with cream styles, and occur all year, but in greater profusion during spring and autumn. Prune regularly and remove seed pods after flowering to increase flowers.
G. 'Moonlight'	4 x 1.5 m	Selected from a seedling of *G. whiteana*; a rapid-growing shrub. Large white flowers all year. Prefers full sun and good drainage. Prune regularly to keep bushy.
G. 'Cherry Brandy'	2–3 x 2 m	Another hybrid of *G.* 'Misty Pink'. Flowers are mid-pink to deep pink, produced for most of the year.
G.'Pink Parfait'	3.5 x 1.5 m	A hybrid bred from *G.* 'Misty Pink'. Leaves are more silvery-coloured than 'Misty Pink'. Flowers are a rich, shiny watermelon pink with gold tips, up to 18 cm long. Frost tender, but otherwise hardy. Regular pruning encourages flowering.
G. 'Pink Surprise'	3–6 x 2 m	A hybrid, probably between *G. banksii* 'Forsters' and *G. whiteana.* Flowers are bright pink with white-cream styles up to 22 cm long, all year. Sensitive to root infections and wind damage. Prune regularly to avoid wind damage. Tolerates moderate frosts. Grows as far south as Melbourne, but generally more suited to warm climates.
G. banksii 'Prostrate alba'		A white-flowered form of the species *G. banksii.*
G. 'Robyn Gordon'	1.5 x 2 m	A hybrid of *G. bipinnatifida* x *G. banksii.* Huge red flowers, bright green foliage. Hardy and adaptable to a wide variety of climates and soils, but more susceptible to disease than most other *banksii* hybrids. Best in open, sunny, well-drained position. Flowers all year but heavier in mild to warm weather (usually spring and autumn). Responds well to pruning.
G. 'Sandra Gordon'	3–4 x 6 m	A hybrid of *G. sessilis* and *G. pteridifolia.* Yellow flowers up to 20 cm long for up to 8 months of the year starting late summer. There are few if any flowers over summer. Prune annually after flowering in winter or spring. Susceptible to wind, but frost hardy.
G. 'Starfire'	4 x 2 m	A hybrid of *G.* 'Honey Gem'. Flowers have a dark red striped centre and pink styles are tipped with gold. Flowers all year. Best pruned.
G. 'Superb'	1.5 x 1.5 m	A hybrid of *G. bipinnatifida* and the white form of *G. banksii.* Dense foliage. Orange and pink flowers are tipped with gold. Very hardy, and a better plant than *G.* 'Robyn Gordon', often having denser foliage. Regular pruning encourages better flowering.

Scented grevilleas

The following grevilleas are scented. Some have very sweet scents, others have unattractive odours.

ATTRACTIVE SCENTS

G. argyrophylla
G. australis strong sweet scent
G. buxifolia honey scent
G. costata sweet scent
G. curviloba honey scent
G. polybotrya caramel scent
G. umbellulata spicy scent

UNATTRACTIVE SCENTS

G. leucopteris
G. manglesoides
G. prostrata

GUICHENOTIA Sterculiaceae

At a glance

NUMBER OF SPECIES 6; all endemic to WA.
FLOWERING Pink or mauve cup-shaped flowers in late winter to spring.
HABIT Small shrubs.
FOLIAGE Leaves generally long (linear or lanceolate) and undivided.
GROWTH RATE Normally fast.
HARDINESS Usually hardy.
LIFESPAN Short to medium.

Culture

- Most prefer a position in full sun with good drainage.
- Propagate from cuttings.

Species

G. ledifolia

- Shrub 0.7 x 0.8 m. Mauve flowers, 1 cm in diameter, in clusters of 4 or 5.

G. macrantha

- Small shrub up to 1 m with narrow silvery-green leaves and showy mauve flowers in late winter. Tolerates light frosts.

G. sarotes

- Shrub 0.5 x 0.7 m, pink to blue flowers 1.5 cm diameter.

HAKEA Proteaceae

At a glance

NUMBER OF SPECIES About 130; 70 endemic to WA, others from other states.
NATURAL HABITAT Widespread; open forest to arid plains, not rainforests.
HARDINESS Hardy to most conditions. Most require good drainage with a few, however, growing naturally in swampy or moist conditions.
FLOWERING Often attractive, many flower over cooler months when few other plants are flowering. Wide variety in size, shape and colour.
HABIT Small woody shrubs up to small trees.
FOLIAGE Leaves highly variable in shape and colour, many prickly.
GROWTH RATE Fast growing in well-drained soils.
LIFESPAN Medium.

Culture

- Many Hakeas will suffer toxicity problems when fed with fertiliser containing phosphorus (P).
- Do not prune hard.
- Plant on slopes, in raised beds or in sandy soils.

HAKEA SPECIES	SIZE	COMMENTS
H. ambigua	1–2 x 1–1.8 m	Compact shrub, stiff linear grey-green leaves. White or pink flowers in spring.
H. baxteri	Up to 3 x to 1.8 m	Open, upright shrub with rigid fan-shaped, toothed foliage. White flowers in small clusters in spring.
H. bucculenta	2–4 x to 2.5 m	Erect shrub, long narrow leaves and showy spikes of red-pink flowers in winter. Full sun to part shade.
H. ceratophylla	To 1 m x 80 cm	Upright shrub with lobed leaves, brown-rust clusters of flowers in summer.
H. clavate	1 x to 1 m	Low-growing shrub with stiff club-shaped leaves. Small clusters of white flowers.
H. conchifolia	To 1.5 m x 90 cm	Upright shrub, leaves are folded and shell-shaped to enclose clusters of pink-white flowers in winter.
H. coriacea	4 x 3 m	Erect shrub, grey linear leaves; flowers are bright pink long spikes from winter to spring.

HAKEA SPECIES	SIZE	COMMENTS
H. corymbosa	1.5 x to 2 m	Compact dense shrub, linear pointy leaves. Showy display, large clusters of white flowers in spring.
H. costata	1.8 x to 2 m	Upright shrub, small rigid narrow elliptical-shaped leaves, small white showy flowers on upper stems in spring.
H. dactyloides	4 x 3 m	Lanceolate leaves up to 10 cm long, fragrant cream flowers, sometimes pink and white, clustered along the stem in spring.
H. drupacea (syn *H. suaveolens*)	4 x 3 m	Dense large shrub to small tree, rigid divided foliage. Creamy white flowers autumn to winter.
H. elliptica	3.5 x 4 m	New growth golden, large elliptical leaves, cream-white flowers appear in clusters in winter–spring. Hardy fast-growing plant suited as a screen. Avoid lime.
H. laurina	3–5 x 3 m	Red rose-pink and cream ball flowers, broad eucalyptus-like leaves. Prone to blowing over.
H. leucoptera	3 x 1.5 m	Spreading or upright shrub with narrow leaves up to 7 cm long. White flowers in clusters in summer, best in dry climates.
H. microcarpa	1–2 x 1.5 m	Rounded alpine shrub with white flowers in clusters in early summer.
H. multilineata	4 x 2 m	Erect shrub with narrow-oblong leaves and pink-red flowers in winter–spring.
H. nodosa	3 x 1.5 m	Upright or sometimes rounded shrub with dense grey-green prickly needle foliage. White lemon-yellow flowers in summer–autumn.
H. petiolaris	5 x 3 m	Grey-green pointed, broadly ovate leaves, purple-red and cream flowers in autumn–winter.
H. prostrata	1–1.5 x to 3 m	Compact sometimes prostrate shrub, with narrowly divided oval, toothed leaves. White flowers in spring.
H. purpurea	2 x 1 m	Rounded shrub, with narrow divided leaves. Red flowers in winter–spring, very hardy plant.
H. rostrate	1 x to 1.5 m	Compact shrub with long narrow leaves, white flower clusters in spring.
H. salicifolia (syn. *H. saligna*)	5 x 3 m	Large shrub to small tree. White-cream perfumed flowers in spring, young leaves red-bronze.
H. scoparia	2–3 x to 2.5 m	Upright shrub with long, fine-channelled leaves. Pinkish-red flowers appear in clusters in late winter to spring.
H. sericea	3 x 1.5 m	Upright shrub. Stiff prickly needle leaves, cream to pink flowers in late winter–spring. Hardy plant, excellent for bird habitat.
H. teretefolia	To 1.5 x to 1.5 m	Open shrub with long, prickly needle foliage. White flowers spring–summer.
H. undulata	1–3 x 1–2.2 m	Dense upright shrub, variable in height. Oval leaves with prickly, wavy margins. White flowers in spring.
H. verrucosa	50 cm–2 m x 1–2 m	Compact shrub of variable height. Dense needle foliage, white to purple red flowers in clusters in winter.
H. victoriae	4 x 3 m	Erect imposing shrub with large prickly-edged shell-like leaves ranging from green to gold to red. Flowers white to yellow in spring.

- Some are susceptible to wind damage.
- Propagate by seed, similar to banksias. Some hard to grow. West Australian species have been successfully grafted onto *H. salicifolia* rootstock in an attempt to grow them in the eastern states.

HALGANIA Boraginaceae

At a glance

NUMBER OF SPECIES 18; all endemic to Australia.
NATURAL HABITAT Dry areas, such as sand plains and mallees.
FLOWERING Round blue or white tubular.
HABIT Perennial shrubs or sub-shrubs.
FOLIAGE Alternate, entire toothed.
HARDINESS Moderate.
GROWTH RATE Fast.
LIFESPAN Short to medium.

Culture

- Dry sunny position.
- Will tolerate damper soils as long as they are well drained.
- Germinates well from seed.

Species

H. andromedifolia

- Up to 1.3 m. Narrow elliptical leaves with entire margins, deep blue flowers in spring. NSW, SA, Vic, WA.

H. brachyryncha

- 0.3–0.6 m. Spreading sub-shrub. Leaves hairy with coarsely toothed margins, deep blue flowers in summer. NSW, Qld.

H. cyanea

- Up to 40 cm. Soft, dull green, 25 mm linear to narrow elliptical leaves with dark blue flowers occur singly on the ends of branches mainly in summer. NSW, Vic, WA, SA, NT.

H. preissiana

- 0.3 x 0.4 m. Small, often suckering shrub with dull green prickly leaves and small bright blue flowers in spring.

HARDENBERGIA Fabaceae

At a glance

NUMBER OF SPECIES 3; all endemic to Australia.
NATURAL HABITAT Sclerophyll forests.
FLOWERING Generally mauve pea-shaped flowers in spring.
HARDINESS Hardy.
HABIT Sprawling and twining growth, upright shrubby forms also available.
FOLIAGE Trifoliate (leaf divided into three).
GROWTH RATE Can be very fast, but not always.
LIFESPAN Medium to long.

Culture

- Do not tolerate waterlogging.
- Adapts to most soils.
- Prefers filtered sun, not too dark or light.
- Some frost sensitive, others not depending on where they naturally occur.
- Propagates easily from hot-water-treated seed.
- Superior forms such as *H.* 'Happy Wanderer' are grown by cuttings in a heated propagation bed.
- Few pests apart from grubs attacking seed.

Species

H. comptoniana (native wisteria)

- Normally a creeper, leaves in groups of 3, blue or purple flowers in spring, best in well-drained soil.

H. violacea (false sarsaparilla)

- Larger leaves, not in threes but single, climber, creeper or small shrub about 1 x 1 m, white, pink, mauve or purple flowers.

***H.* 'Happy Wanderer'**

- A vigorous, excellent flowering form of *H. violacea*.

HARPULLIA Sapindaceae

At a glance

NUMBER OF SPECIES 8 found in Australia.
NATURAL HABITAT Rainforest, warm districts.

FLOWERING White, green or yellow. Individually insignificant.
HABIT Large shrubs to small trees.
HARDINESS Very hardy.
FOLIAGE Light or deep green glossy pinnate leaves.
GROWTH RATE Generally medium.
COMMENTS Useful timber from some species.

Culture

- Protect from frost in early stages.
- Tolerates full sun.
- Keep moist in dry periods.

Species

H. alata (winged tulip)

- 4 m tall. Winged and toothed leaves. Yellow capsules, brown seeds, yellow aril.

H. hillii (blunt-leaved tulip)

- 10 m tall. Smooth leaves. Tolerates exposed sites. Yellow capsule, brown seed, yellow or red aril.

H. pendula (tulipwood)

- 10 m tall. Smooth leaves. Common street tree. Orange capsules, black seeds, lacking aril.

HELICHRYSUM ❧ Strawflower or Everlasting Daisy ❧ Asteraceae

(Some helichrysums have recently been listed in the genera *Bracteantha*, *Chrysocephalum*, *Ozothamnus* and *Xerochrysum*.)

At a glance

NUMBER OF SPECIES About 500 worldwide, although many are being reclassified. Currently about 100 Australian species.
NATURAL HABITAT Occurs in wide range of soils and climates.
FLOWERING Mostly in warm weather, dry, straw-like petals, daisy-like flowers, most flower for extended periods.
HABIT Small herbaceous plants (including annuals) and small shrubs.
FOLIAGE Generally soft, often covered with hairs.
GROWTH RATE Fast.
LIFESPAN Frequently short-lived.
COMMENTS Flowers commonly used as cut flowers and for dried arrangements. Some of the herbaceous perennial species can be treated as annuals. The widely cultivated *H. bracteatum* has been named *Bracteantha bracteata*.

HELICHRYSUM SPECIES	COMMENTS
H. apiculatum (now known as *Chrysocephalum apiculatum*) (common everlasting)	Spreads to 1 m diameter, soft grey leaves, flowers are small yellow clusters in spring and autumn.
H. baxteri (white everlasting)	Small bush 0.3 x 0.4 m with thin leaves, dark green on top, white underneath. Masses of white daisy flowers in spring–summer.
H. bracteatum (now known as *Xerochrysum bracteatum*) (golden everlasting)	Small bush, 0.5 m tall with 1 m spread. Woolly grey-green leaves, large yellow flowers. Several forms are available.
H. 'Dargen Hill Monarch'	1 m x 1 m, gold flowers all year, blue-grey leaves. Prefers full sun.
H. 'Diamond Head' (form of *H. bracteatum*)	Creeper with a 0.6 m spread. Gold flowers above green hairy leaves in summer.
H. diosmifolium (now known as *Ozothamnus diosmifolium*)	Shrub 2.5 m tall, 1 m spread, white or pink flowers, spring and summer.
H. paralium	Shrub 2 m tall with 1.5 m spread. Linear grey woolly leaves become green with age and small white flower clusters.
H. ramosissima (now also known as *Chrysocephalum apiculatum*)	Creeper with a 1 m spread. Soft grey leaves with golden flowers all year.

Culture

- Prune when young to shape the plant.
- Adapt to most soils, but prefers good drainage.
- Many do not tolerate severe waterlogging or prolonged drought.
- Few pests and diseases, apart from occasional caterpillars.
- Propagate easily from cuttings in standard propagating mix, or often straight into open ground. Annuals generally propagate readily from seed.

HELIPTERUM *see Rhodanthe*

HEMIANDRA Lamiaceae

At a glance

NUMBER OF SPECIES About 8; all endemic to WA.
NATURAL HABITAT South-western WA.
FLOWERING Flowers similar to *Westringia*.
HABIT Low shrubs or ground cover.
FOLIAGE Leaves needle-like or linear and in most cases sharp.
HARDINESS Moderate.
GROWTH RATE Can be fast, but often short-lived.

Culture

- Needs excellent drainage and full sun.
- Propagates easily from cuttings. May be grafted onto *Westringia fruticosa* to improve hardiness and lifespan.

Species

H. pungens

- Shrub to 1.5 m tall or creeper with pink to mauve flowers in spring.

HIBBERTIA Guinea Flowers Dilleniaceae

At a glance

NUMBER OF SPECIES 150; most occur in Australia, about 60 are endemic to south-western WA.
NATURAL HABITAT Widespread, except in arid areas.

HIBBERTIA SPECIES	COMMENTS
H. astrotricha = *H. empetrifolia*	
H. cuneiformis	Up to 2 x 1.5 m. Yellow flowers and glossy dark green foliage.
H. dentata	Climber with bright yellow flowers and reddish tones in stems and young shoots.
H. empetrifolia	0.1–0.6 x 2 m. Sprawling shrub or creeper, coarse foliage, bright yellow flowers for long periods in spring.
H. longifolia	0.5 x 0.7 m. Purple to grey-green foliage, large bright yellow flowers.
H. microphylla	0.4 x 1 m. Small leaves, masses of tiny yellow flowers in spring and summer.
H. montana	1 x 1 m, attractive and variable. Large yellow flowers in spring, prefers open sunny position.
H. obtusifolia	Creeper with 1 m spread. Fleshy thick leaves, bright yellow flowers, responds to watering.
H. scandens	Climber or creeper with large fleshy, glossy leaves, large flowers in spring and summer. Best in open sandy soils, slightly frost tender.
H. stellaris	Creeper or small shrub up to 0.6 m spread. Orange flowers spring and autumn. Appreciates moist soil.

FLOWERING Showy gold flowers with 5 delicate petals.
HABIT Creepers or small shrubs.
HARDINESS Many are hardy once established.
FOLIAGE Variable.
GROWTH RATE Fast.
LIFESPAN Medium.

Culture

- Prefers moist soil and full sun.
- Only a few tolerate dryness.
- Withstands pruning.
- Most will survive frost but will burn to some degree.
- Most are difficult to propagate by seed or cuttings. *H. scandens* is easy to grow from cuttings.

HIBISCUS ❧ Malvaceae

At a glance

NUMBER OF SPECIES 300 in tropical and subtropical regions; about 30 native to Australia.
NATURAL HABITAT Mostly tropical or subtropical areas, some grow in mild temperate regions.
FLOWERING Large showy flowers from spring to autumn.
HABIT Shrubs.
FOLIAGE Normally toothed or lobed leaves, often prickly.
GROWTH RATE Very fast.
LIFESPAN Long-lived.
HARDINESS Moderate but can be damaged by frost.

Culture

- Prune annually after flowering.
- Susceptible to aphis, scale, caterpillars, sooty mould.
- Prefers well-drained position.
- Requires sun to flower.
- Most are frost tender to some degree.
- Grows best when placed against the wall of a building or fence, where they will be protected from frost and severe winds.
- Responds well to feeding with slow-release fertiliser or manure, and regular watering.

Species

H. diversifolius

- 3 x 3 m. Heart-shaped or rounded leaves, stiff hairs or prickles on stems. Flowers pink with large crimson throat, generally hardy, but frost and drought tender.

H. heterophyllus

- 3 x 3 m. Large lobed green leaves. Flowers white with purple throat but sometimes yellow.

H. tileaceus

- 4 x 3 m. Heart-shaped leaves, green on top, whitish underneath. Large yellow flowers in summer, best suited to coastal areas.

HOMORANTHUS ❧ Myrtaceae

At a glance

NUMBER OF SPECIES 19; all endemic to Australia.
NATURAL HABITAT Open woodlands and heaths.
FLOWERING Cream and dull red-yellow fringed flowers.
HABIT Small-growing, erect or spreading shrubs.
FOLIAGE Fine grey-green leaves.
GROWTH RATE Medium to fast in good conditions.
LIFESPAN Medium.
COMMENTS Useful small landscaping plants, featuring attractive foliage and habit.
HARDINESS Generally very hardy.

Culture

- Likes full or filtered sun.
- Adapts to most soils provided well drained.
- Does not like heavy shade or badly drained soils.
- Propagate easily from cuttings.

HOMORANTHUS SPECIES	SIZE	COMMENTS
H. biflorus	1–1.2 m	Erect shrub. Yellow-greenish yellow or red flowers in spring–mid-summer
H. binghiensis	To 3 m	Erect shrub that is endangered (NSW). Yellow-green or red flowers in late spring to early summer.
H. bornhardtiensis	30 cm x 1 m	Endangered species of NSW. Yellow flowers in mid- to late spring.
H. cernuus	Up to 60 x 60 cm	Erect and slender shrub. Flowers cream-pink at base, mid-winter–mid-spring.
H. croftianus	2 m x 1.5 m	Endangered species of NSW. Greenish-cream flowers in winter.
H. darwinioides	Up to 80 cm x 1 m.	Open shrub with grey-green leaves and pendulous yellow-fringed flowers in summer and autumn.
H. flavescens	0.4 or more x up to 1.5 m	Attractive spreading and layering habit. Erect clusters of cream. Foliage can be red in winter. Prior to 1981 this species was often confused and grouped together with *H. papillatus*.
H. floydii	1.5 x 1 m	Erect shrub with yellow-red flowers in late winter to early spring. A rare and threatened species.
H. lunatus	1 x 1 m or more	Spreading shrub with yellow flowers from mid-winter to mid-spring. Distribution narrowly confined to parts of NSW. A threatened species.
H. melanostictus	10 cm tall spreading	Low-growing, prostrate, spreading shrub. Flowering in midwinter–mid-spring.
H. pappilatus	Up to 2 x 2.5 m	Erect clusters of cream to green-yellow flowers in spring and summer with red bracts, and strongly scented.
H. porteri	60 x 60 cm	Low-growing shrub found only in Qld. Pink flowers appear in summer.
H. proxilus	30 cm tall spreading	A low-growing spreading shrub. Yellow to red flowers in mid-spring.
H. virgatus	80 cm x 80 cm	Erect shrub with white to pink insignificant flowers from late spring–summer.

HOVEA Fabaceae

At a glance

NUMBER OF SPECIES 12; all endemic to Australia, widely distributed.
NATURAL HABITAT Open forests and woodlands.
FLOWERING Blue or purple pea flowers.
HARDINESS Most are relatively hardy, tolerate dry or wet soils and resistant to frost and drought.
HABIT Shrubs and creepers.
FOLIAGE Simple (undivided) and often hairy.
GROWTH RATE Medium.
LIFESPAN Medium.

Culture

- Generally prefers filtered light.
- Roots should not overheat, keep well mulched, or plant where roots can grow under rocks or in shade.
- Propagate from hot-water-treated seed.

Species

H. elliptica

- 2–3 x 1.5 m. Slender shrub with elliptical leaves, deep pale blue flowers in spring. Best on sandy soils in a warm and shaded spot, ideal on coast.

H. lanceolata

- 2 x 1.5 m. Blue-purple flowers, open shrub.

H. pungens

- 1 x 1 m. Narrow prickly leaves, brilliant purple flowers in winter–spring.

H. rosmarinifolia

- 2 x 1 m. Narrow leaves, hairy underneath, purple flowers in summer. Prefers open, moist spot.

HYMENOSPORUM ✻ Native Frangipani ✻ Pittosporaceae

At a glance

NUMBER OF SPECIES 1 (*H. flavum*); occurs in Australia and New Guinea.
NATURAL HABITAT Rainforests in NSW and north-eastern Qld.
FLOWERING Large clusters of scented cream to yellow flowers in spring.
HABIT Tree up to 10 m.
FOLIAGE Large glossy leaves.
GROWTH RATE Fast in warm, moist climates.
LIFESPAN Long-lived.
HARDINESS Moderate – needs adequate water and protection from frost.

Culture

- Frost tender, particularly when young.
- Flowers best in full sun, in a sheltered position.
- Propagate by seed or cuttings.

Species

H. flavum

- Grows to 10 x 3 m, has glossy leaves, sparse branches, and yellow, fragrant flowers in summer.

HYPOCALYMMA ✻ Myrtaceae

At a glance

NUMBER OF SPECIES About 29; all endemic to WA.
NATURAL HABITAT South-western WA:
FLOWERING Generally has a fluffy appearance, normally flowers from winter to early spring. Flowers are generally profuse.
HABIT Small shrubs.
HARDINESS Most hardy.
FOLIAGE Small.
GROWTH RATE Medium to fast.
LIFESPAN Medium.

Culture

- Prefers moist but well-drained soil, full sun or at least sun for part of the day.
- Generally frost tolerant, also drought tolerant; however, varies with species.
- Generally propagate by semi-hardwood cuttings.

Species

H. angustifolium

- 1 x 1 m. Fine, soft, needle-like foliage. Masses of white and pink flowers completely cover bush in spring and summer.

H. cordifolium

- 1 x 1.5 m. Reddish stems, attractive foliage plant, small white flowers in spring. Water well in summer, tolerates some overwatering. Variegated form also available.

H. robustum

- 1 x 0.6 m. Elegant small shrub with fine branches. Deep pink flowers with gold tips in spring.

INDIGOFERA ✻ Fabaceae

At a glance

NUMBER OF SPECIES Over 700 species; approximately 25 Australian.
NATURAL HABITAT Most from warmer parts of eastern and northern Australia, but extending to northern Tasmania.
FLOWERING Sprays of purple pea flowers.
HABIT Shrubs, often straggly.
HARDINESS Generally hardy.

FOLIAGE Normally pinnate (divided).
GROWTH RATE Some very fast.
LIFESPAN Medium.

Culture

- Prefers well-drained, partly shaded position.
- Many are frost tender.
- Propagate by hot-water-treated seed.

Species

I. australis

- 1 to 2 m tall with 1 m spread. Black to purple buds in spring open to rich mauve pea flowers. Soft blue-green leaves. Grows best under canopy of trees, but with room to spread, very hardy and drought resistant, but can be frost tender (particularly young shoots).

I. linifolia

- Long narrow leaves covered by fine white hairs, purple-red flowers.

ISOPOGON ❧ Drumsticks or Coneflowers ❧ Proteaceae

At a glance

NUMBER OF SPECIES 35; most endemic to south-western WA.
NATURAL HABITAT Heaths and open forests.
FLOWERING Showy terminal flower heads in late winter and spring. Colours include cream, yellow, pink and mauve. Flowers are followed by large woody seed pods.
HARDINESS Eastern species are very hardy; western species may be, once established, on most well-drained soils.
FOLIAGE Divided, often prickly leaves.
HABIT Small shrubs, rarely over 2 m.
GROWTH RATE Slow-growing.
LIFESPAN Medium.

Culture

- Avoid phosphorus fertilisers.
- Always provide good drainage.
- No major pests.
- Tip-prune only.
- Propagate normally by seed, or, in some cases, cuttings.

Species

I. anemonifolius

- Up to 1.2 m tall. Light green leaves. Yellow flowers in spring.

I. anethifolius

- Up to 2 m tall. Stems and growing tips reddish and yellow flowers in December.

I. buxifolius

- Up to 0.6 m tall. Small woolly pink flowers in August–September.

I. dawsonii

- Up to 1 m tall. Cream-white flowers, fine foliage.

I. dubius

- Up to 1.8 m tall. Rose flowers in late winter and spring.

I. formosus

- Up to 2 m tall. Soft pink flowers in spring.

I. latifolius

- Up to 2 m tall. Light green elliptical leaves and pink flowers in spring.

JACKSONIA ❧ Fabaceae

At a glance

NUMBER OF SPECIES 46; all endemic to Australia, and distributed in all states except Tas.
NATURAL HABITAT Mainly sclerophyl forests or open woodland.
FLOWERING Yellow or orange flowers.
HABIT Shrubs with greyish-green stems.
FOLIAGE Generally branches appear leafless.
GROWTH RATE Medium- to fast-growing.
HARDINESS Moderate to hardy.
LIFESPAN Medium.

Culture

- Prefers well-drained soils.
- Propagate from hot-water-treated seed.

Species

J. floribunda

- Grey-green, flattened stems, prickly leaves, purple and yellow flowers.

J. scoparia

- Upright shrub or small tree with grey-green stems and yellow flowers.

JAGERA ❧ Foambark ❧ Sapindaceae

At a glance

NUMBER OF SPECIES 3 found in Australia.
NATURAL HABITAT Rainforest.
FLOWERING Small insignificant flowers.
HABIT Small spreading trees.
HARDINESS Very hardy.
FOLIAGE Delicate-looking foliage. Colour tones when young.
GROWTH RATE Medium.
LIFESPAN Long-lived.
COMMENTS Most parts of the plant, especially the fruits, are covered in fine stiff bristles which can cause irritation. Aborigines produced a poisonous foam by agitating the plant in water, which they used to catch fish. They are attractive trees worth cultivation.

Culture

- Full sun.
- Provide ample moisture and nutrients.
- Propagation by fresh seed.

Species

J. discolor (red foambark)

- Large tree up to 18 m. Spreading canopy. From northern Qld. Ornamental new red flushes.

J. pseudorhus (foambark)

- Small tree up to 6 m. Umbrella-shaped crown with fern-like foliage. From NSW and Qld. Very hardy to light frosts.

J. serrata (pink foambark)

- Large tree up to 12 m. Not frost tolerant.

JUNCUS ❧ Juncaceae

At a glance

NUMBER OF SPECIES 300; 8 endemic to Australia.
NATURAL HABITAT Moist areas, wet swamps, alpine and sub-alpine areas. Some are tolerant of saline conditions.
FLOWERING Flowers appear on one side of the stem, greenish-brown, pale brown rust, or brownish-purple; spring and summer.
HABIT Annual or perennial rushes, with creeping rhizomes.
HARDINESS Hardy.
FOLIAGE Leaves are smooth and arranged in basal rosettes.
GROWTH RATE Fast.
COMMENTS Some species may become invasive under certain conditions.

Culture

- Full sun to semi-shade.
- Moist–wet soils but some species tolerate short dry periods.
- Propagate by fresh seed or division of rhizomes.

KENNEDIA ❧ Fabaceae

At a glance

NUMBER OF SPECIES 15; all endemic to Australia.
NATURAL HABITAT A wide variety of soils and climates across all states.
FLOWERING Red, pink or purple pea flowers.
HABIT Creepers, some climbers; non-suckering.
HARDINESS Frost hardiness and drought tolerance varies between species.
FOLIAGE Leaves generally divided (similar to clover) into three parts.
GROWTH RATE Very rapid growing.
LIFESPAN Often short-lived (3–4 years). If they live longer, they often become leggy.

Culture

- Generally adaptable, preferring full or

JUNCUS SPECIES	SIZE	COMMENTS
J. amabilis	0.2–1.2 x to 0.5 m	Tufted perennial rhizomatous rush, blue-green stems. Light brown flowers from mid-spring to mid-summer. NSW, SA, Tas, Vic.
J. australis	0.6–1.2 x 0.5–1 m	Perennial rush with short creeping rhizome. Shiny blue-green stems and pale brown flowers throughout the year. NSW, SA, Tas, Vic and also NZ.
J. caespiticius	10–40 x 20–50 cm	Tufted rhizomatous perennial, flat curved narrow leaves. Brownish flowers throughout the year. NSW, Tas, Vic, WA.
J. filicaulis	0.4–0.7 x 0.3– 0.5 m	Tufted rhizomatous perennial herb. Narrow blue-green stems. Straw-coloured flowers in clusters all year round. NSW, Tas, Vic, WA.
J. flavidus	0.4–1.2 x 0.2–1 m	Tufted rhizomatous perennial, yellow-green stems with clusters of pale yellow flowers in mid-spring–mid-autumn. All states excluding NT.
J. gregiflorus	0.5–1.4 x 0.6–1.5 m	Shiny bright green stems above purplish-brown basal sheaths. Pale brown panicles, flowers mid-spring to mid-autumn. NSW, Tas, Vic.
J. holoschoenus	20–45 x 10–40 cm	Clumping rhizomatous leafy perennial. Clusters of pale green flowers from mid-spring to mid-autumn. All states excluding NT.
J. homalocaulis	2–15 x 5–30 cm	Slender, perennial rhizomatous rush with reddish-brown flowers in mid-spring to mid-autumn. All states excluding NT.
J. krausii	0.6–2.1 x 0.5–1.5 m	Sparse dark green pointed leaves. Dark brown flowers in loose clusters mid-spring to mid-autumn. Grows in saline conditions. All states excluding NT.
J. pallidus	0.5–2.1 x 0.3–1 m	Rhizomatous tufted perennial with pale green stems and brown basal sheaths. Pale yellow flowers in numerous clusters from summer to mid-autumn. NSW, SA, Tas, Vic, WA.
J. pauciflorus	0.3–1 x 0.2–0.6 m	Bright green rhizomatous perennial with arching tussocks and reddish flowers from summer to mid-autumn. NSW, SA, Tas, Vic, WA.
J. procerus	1–2 x 0.5–1.5 m	Perennial tufted herb with thick soft stems and large broad basal sheaths. Single brown flowers from mid-spring to mid-summer. NSW, SA, Tas, Vic, WA.
J. radula	0.3–0.7 x 0.2–0.6 m	Rough-stemmed tufted rhizomatous perennial with branches of single pale brown flowers on narrow grey stems. Flowers mid-spring to mid-autumn. NSW, Tas, Vic.
J. revolutus	5–30 cm x 0.5–1 m	Perennial rush with creeping rhizomes and flat thin leaves, grows in salt marshes. Pale brown flowers from mid-spring to mid-autumn. NSW, Vic, Tas.
J. sarophorus	0.6–2 x 0.5–1 m	Perennial rush with tufting reddish-brown basal sheaths and hard blue-green stems. White to pale brown flowers on a fan-shaped panicle from mid-spring to mid-autumn. NSW, SA, Tas, Vic.
J. subsecundus	0.5–1 x 0.5–1 m	Perennial tufted rhizomatous rush with pale brown basal sheaths and blue-green stems. Clusters of pale brown flowers from mid-spring to mid-summer and again in autumn. All states excluding NT.
J. usitatus	0.3–1.2 x 0.3–1.2 m	Perennial tufted rush with yellowish-green slender stems and reddish-brown basal sheaths. Fan-shaped panicles of pale brown flowers from mid-spring to mid-autumn. NSW, Qld, Vic.
J. vaginatus	0.3–1 x 0.5–1 m	Perennial rhizomatous rush with solid stems and yellow-green to grey basal sheaths and pale brown through to deep orange flowers from mid-spring to mid-autumn. NSW, Qld, Tas, Vic.

filtered sun (not heavy shade).
- Responds to moist mulched soil.
- Adapts to most soil types provided not waterlogged.
- Various insect pests can occasionally be a problem.
- Normally propagate by seed, though cuttings have been successful on some species.

Species

K. beckxiana
- Climber or groundcover, up to 4 m spread. Pink-scarlet flowers with green blotch in throat, and green leaves.

K. coccinea
- Climber or groundcover, up to 3 m spread. Red flowers with yellowish throat and dull green leaves.

K. microphylla
- Creeper up to 0.6 m spread. Small leaves and brick-red pea flowers in spring.

K. nigricans
- Vigorous climber or creeper up to 5 m or more spread. Large black and yellow pea flowers in winter and spring. One of the hardiest and most rampant species.

K. prostrata (running postman)
- Creeper up to 2.5 m spread. Blue-green leaves with bright red flowers mainly in spring.

K. rubicunda (dusky coral pea)
- As vigorous and hardy as *K. nigricans*, but slightly smaller leaves and red flowers.

KINGIA ✻ Xanthorrhoeaceae

(Note: Common names 'blackboy' and 'black gin' have been widely used in the past and are still well known; however, due to racist connotations, their use is increasingly discouraged.)

At a glance

NUMBER OF SPECIES 1 (*K. australis*); endemic to WA.

NATURAL HABITAT Heath and open forest in south WA.

FLOWERING Similar to *Xanthorrhoea* except flower spike ends with a ball atop a short spear.

HABIT Grassy clump on top of a thick trunk or stump.

HARDINESS Hardy once established.

GROWTH RATE Very slow.

LIFESPAN Very long-lived, up to several hundred years.

Culture

- Full sun.
- Needs excellent drainage.
- Can be very difficult to establish.
- Propagation is by seed, which can be slow to germinate, or by transplanting mature specimens 'rescued' from land clearing.

Species

K. australis
- Up to 5 m tall on a solid stem with a grass skirt on top. Flowers turn into drumsticks which persist for a long time.

KUNZEA ✻ Myrtaceae

At a glance

NUMBER OF SPECIES About 30 species; all endemic to Australia, distributed in all states.

NATURAL HABITAT Varies greatly.

FLOWERING Fluffy white, pink, mauve or red flowers.

HABIT Shrubs and some groundcovers.

FOLIAGE Small, undivided leaves.

GROWTH RATE Medium to fast.

LIFESPAN Long-lived.

HARDINESS Generally hardy.

Culture

- Generally as for *Callistemon* or *Melaleuca*.
- Propagate by seed or cuttings (late summer).

KUNZEA SPECIES	SIZE	COMMENTS
K. acuminata	2 x 1–2 m	Pink flowers in early spring. WA.
K. affinis	30 cm–2 m	Erect shrub, variable in height and width. Pink-red-purple flowers in late winter to late spring.
K. ambigua	1–3 x 2–3 m	White or pink flowers in late spring to early summer.
K. baxteri	3 x 3 m	Bright red flowers which are similar in appearance to *Callistemon* (bottlebrush) flowers.
K. bracteolata	1.5 x 1 m	Erect shrub. Cream flowers from spring to early summer.
K. cambagei	50 cm x 1 m	Spreading shrub with cream-white flowers in summer.
K. capitata	1 x 1 m	Mauve flowers in spring and summer.
K. ciliata	0.3–0.5 x to 2.5 m	Variable spreading shrub. Pink flowers mid- to late spring.
K. cincinnata	0.6 x to 2 m	Low-growing spreading shrub with red-pink-purple flowers in early to mid-spring.
K. clavata	2.5 x 4 m	Tree-like shrub with yellow flowers early to mid-spring.
K. ericifolia	3 x 2 m	Open shrub with slightly pendulous habit. Cream-yellow flowers in spring.
K. ericoides (syn. *Leptospermum ericioides*)	5 x 4 m	Large round shrub. White flowers in summer.
K. flavescens	2.5 x 1.5 m	Erect shrub with yellow-cream flowers in summer.
K. glabrescens	Up to 4 x to 3 m	Tree-like shrub, variable in height and width. Yellow flowers from mid- to late spring.
K. graniticola	4 x 3 m	Branching shrub. White flowers in late winter–early spring.
K. jucunda	Up to 1.2 x up to 2 m	Variable erect and open shrub. Pinkish-purple flowers in late winter to mid-spring.
K. micrantha	0.35–1.5 x up to 3 m	Erect shrub of variable size. Pinkish-purple, purple, white or cream flowers from spring to early summer.
K. micromera	0.3–1.5 m	Variable shrub with sparse habit. Pink-purple flowers in late winter to mid-spring.
K. montana	Up to 1.5 x 4 m	Variable shrub or tree. Yellow-cream flowers in spring.
K. newbeyii	0.6–1.5 x to 2 m	Variable strongly growing shrub. Pink flowers from mid- to late spring.
K. opposita	1.5 x 1.5 m	Erect shrub with open habit. Pink flowers in spring.
K. parvifolia	1.5 x 3 m	Spreading shrub. Profuse pink flowers in late spring to early summer.
K. pauciflora	1 x 0.8 m	Erect shrub with deep pink flowers in spring.
K. praestans	0.3–2 x 0.3–2 m	Erect shrub of variable growth. Pinkish-purple flowers in early spring.
K. preissiana	0.5–1.2 x to 1.8 m	Erect shrub. Pinkish-purple flowers in late August to mid-spring.
K. pulchella	1 x 1.5 m	Red flowers in spring. Small tea-tree-like leaves. A less vigorous species than *K. baxteri*.
K. recurva	2 x 1.5 m	Erect shrub with pinkish-mauve flowers in spring–summer.
K. rostrata	3 x 2 m	Large shrub. Pink flowers from mid- to late spring.
K. similis	0.5–1 x to 1.5 m	Rare species exhibiting pink flowers from mid-spring.
K. spathulata	4.5 x 3 m	Erect shrub. Yellow-green flowers mid- to late spring.
K. sulphurea	Up to 3.5 x to 6 m	Compact, erect sometimes tree-like shrub. Yellow flowers in spring.

LACHNOSTACHYS ❧ Lamb's Tails ❧ Verbenaceae

At a glance

NUMBER OF SPECIES 6; all endemic to WA.
NATURAL HABITAT Yellow sand to alluvial and gravel soils of WA.
FLOWERING Spikes of woolly flowers.
HABIT Small shrubs.
FOLIAGE Soft and thick, downy leaves.
HARDINESS Can be difficult to cultivate.
GROWTH RATE Can be fast.
LIFESPAN Short.

Culture

- Open sunny position with well-drained soil.
- Mild or warm dry climate.
- Propagate from cuttings without mist spray.

Species

L. eriobotyra

- 1 x 1 m. Woolly purple-centred flowers. Woolly narrow–linear leaves.

L. verbascifolia

- Up to 0.5 m. Woolly purple-centred flowers. Woolly broad–elliptical leaves.

LAMBERTIA ❧ Proteaceae

At a glance

NUMBER OF SPECIES 11; all endemic to WA, except *L. formosa* from NSW.
NATURAL HABITAT Mainly sclerophyll woodland, often in sands or gravels.
FLOWERING Showy tube-like flowers.
HABIT Shrubs to small trees.
FOLIAGE Stiff, often prickly leaves.
GROWTH RATE Medium.
LIFESPAN Medium to long.
HARDINESS Moderate, can be difficult to establish.

Culture

- Prefers well-drained soil in sunny position.
- Seed germinates easily, but seedlings are very susceptible to damping off.

LAGUNARIA ❧ Malvaceae

At a glance

NUMBER OF SPECIES 1; (*L. patersonii* [the pyramid tree]) endemic to Australia and Norfolk Island.
NATURAL HABITAT Temperate coastal.
FLOWERING Pink flowers in spring.
HARDINESS Salt tolerant, tolerates some water-logging, frost, smog and other adverse conditions.
HABIT Well-formed tree to 8 m tall.
FOLIAGE Attractive blue-green leaves.
GROWTH RATE Medium to fast growth rate.
LIFESPAN Long-lived.

Culture

- Does well on coast or as windbreak.
- Major disadvantage is the hairs released from the fruit are a bad skin irritant.

LAMBERTIA SPECIES	SIZE	FLOWERS	LEAVES
L. formosa (mountain devil)	1.8 x 1.4 m	Red and pink	Linear, prickly
L. ilicifolia	1.5 x 1 m	Yellow	Very prickly
L. inermis	3 x 3 m	Yellow or red	Smooth, elliptical
L. multiflora	1.5 x 1 m	Pink or yellow	Broadly linear
L. orbifolia	4 x 2 m	Red	Round, cupped
L. propinqua	1.5 x 1 m	Yellow	Small, lobed, prickly
L. uniflora	2 x 3 m	Red, solitary	Prickly, green, up to 3 cm long

Because they are so fine, they carry in the wind and can settle on clothing, etc. For this reason, the tree should be avoided in highly populated areas.

LASIOPETALUM Sterculiaceae

At a glance

NUMBER OF SPECIES About 30; found in all states except Qld.
NATURAL HABITAT Temperate climates.
FLOWERING Small flowers normally winter or spring, covered with hairs.
HABIT Shrubs.
HARDINESS Hardy.
FOLIAGE Leathery leaves, upper surface smooth, lower surface hairy.
GROWTH RATE Medium growth rate.
LIFESPAN Medium- to long-lived.

Culture

- Prefers full sun, well-drained soil.
- Prefers dry conditions.
- Propagate from cuttings or seed.

Species

L. behrii

- Up to 0.8 m. Pink flowers. Very hardy and adaptable.

L. dasyphyllum

- 0.3–2 m. Rusty cream flowers. Not showy, but hardy.

L. ferrugineum

- Up to 1.5 m or prostrate. Brown with cream-centre flowers. Prostrate form is best.

L. floribundum

- Pink and black flowers. Tolerates wet conditions.

LEPTORHYNCHOS Asteraceae

At a glance

NUMBER OF SPECIES 10; endemic to Australia.
NATURAL HABITAT Plains grassland, dry forests, woodland and valley forests.
FLOWERING Daisy flowers, white or yellow, held singly above the foliage.
HABIT Perennials or sub-shrubs.
HARDINESS Hardy.

LEPTORHYNCHOS SPECIES	SIZE	COMMENTS
L. baileyi	Up to 30 cm	Annual, branched slightly woolly herb with small linear leaves, yellow flowers in spring.
L. elongatus	Up to 50 x 60 cm	Annual or perennial herb with linear leaves up to 75 mm long and white or pale yellow flowers from mid-spring to early summer. All states except WA. Rare.
L. nitidulus	10–25 cm high	Slender herb spreading by stolons with pale cobweb stems, small linear leaves 2–4 cm long. Yellow flowers from summer to autumn.
L. squamatus	Up to 30 x 40 cm	Low-growing, spreading herb. Dark green leaves up to 20 mm with white woolly undersides, situated on one side of the stem. Yellow, small flowers from spring to mid-summer.
L. tenuifolius	30 x 30 cm	Branched, wiry perennial, dark green narrow leaves with woolly white undersides and rolled margins. Yellow flowers from spring to mid-summer.
L. tetrachaetus	Up to 15 cm	Slender annual herb with wiry red stems, linear leaves 8–20 mm long have woolly undersides. Bright yellow florets from spring to early summer.
L. waitzia	Up to 20 cm	Annual prostrate herb, with hairy oblong leaves up to 20 mm long, bright yellow flowers in spring.

FOLIAGE Linear or lanceolate leaves varying in size and colour.
GROWTH RATE Fast.

Culture

- Well-drained soils with some moisture.
- Propagation by seed or cutting.

LEPTOSPERMUM ✤ Tea-Tree ✤ Myrtaceae

At a glance

NUMBER OF SPECIES About 40; mainly in Australia, a few from New Zealand.
NATURAL HABITAT Variable.
FLOWERING Most are very showy.
HABIT Trees and shrubs.
HARDINESS Most are very hardy. New Zealand hybrids (mostly *L. scoparium* hybrids) are less hardy in Australia although the flowers are generally showier.
FOLIAGE Generally aromatic, leaves not divided.
HARDINESS Mostly hardy.
GROWTH RATE Fast.
LIFESPAN Variable, most have a medium lifespan.

Culture

- Most species like moist but well-drained soil.
- Some will tolerate dryness and others waterlogging.
- Some species are susceptible to scale, sooty mould, web-weaving caterpillars, and stem borers.
- Propagate by cuttings or seed. Hybrids propagate by cuttings.

LESCHENAULTIA ✤ Goodeniaceae

Leschenaultia is sometimes spelt without an 's' (i.e. *Lechenaultia*). Different experts vary on how they choose to spell this name.

At a glance

NUMBER OF SPECIES About 25; all endemic, most in south-west Australia.
NATURAL HABITAT WA.
FLOWERING Quick to flower, flowering over extended periods, often most of the year.
HABIT They are small shrubs, generally below 0.8 m.
FOLIAGE Fine, soft and feathery.
GROWTH RATE Fast growing.
HARDINESS Generally not hardy in cultivation.
LIFESPAN Frequently short-lived (i.e. 1–4 years).

Culture

- Must have well-drained situation, ideal as tub plants, or in sandy soil.
- Grows better in low-rainfall areas. In medium to wet climates it may do better if protected from rain and grown in a container.
- Responds to frequent light pruning.
- Propagates easily and quickly from cuttings.

Species

L. biloba

- Up to 0.5 m tall. Blue-green soft needle foliage, brilliant blue flowers. Common in cultivation.

L. formosa

- Many forms available from creeping plants to 0.4 m tall sprawling shrub. Generally red, yellow or combinations of red and yellow flowers. Foliage generally light green. Dozens of different named varieties exist.

***L. formosa* 'Brownii'**

- Form of *L. formosa* up to 0.3 m tall, with brown-orange flowers.

***L. formosa* 'Prostrate Red'**

- Creeping form of *L. formosa* with bright red flowers.

***L. formosa* 'Scarlet O'Hara'**

- Form of *L. formosa* up to 0.3 m with red flowers.

***L. formosa* 'Tango'**

- Creeping form of *L. formosa* with yellow and orange flowers.

LEPTOSPERMUM SPECIES	SIZE	COMMENTS
L. amboiniensis	3 x 2.5 m	Grey-green leaves and white flowers in summer. Hardy in subtropics or tropics.
L. arachnoides	1 x 1.5 m	White flowers in spring–early summer. Hardy, tolerates wet soil and dense shade.
L. brachyandrum	4 x 3 m	Green narrow leaves, grey-pinkish bark, white flowers in spring and summer. Suited to poorly drained soil, frost hardy and tolerates heavy shade.
L. brevipes	4 x 3 m	Small oblong green leaves, white flowers in spring and summer. Frost hardy, hardy and fast growing. Suitable as a hedge.
L. citratum (lemon-scented tea-tree)	3 x 2 m	Light green, soft lemon-scented leaves, white flowers in summer. Tolerates dry periods but not waterlogging. Also known as *L. petersonii*.
L. continentale	2 x 2 m	Small lance-shaped leaves, white and occasionally pink flowers from spring to summer. Good screening plant. Tolerates poorly drained soil.
L. coriaceum	2 x 2 m	Grey-green elliptical small leaves with white flowers in spring. A good, hardy screen or windbreak plant for semi-arid climates. Full sun — most soils are suitable.
L. deuense	1.5 x 1.5 m	Elliptical green leaves up to 3 cm long, white flowers in summer. Suited to most situations. Frost hardy.
L. epacridoideum	2 x 2 m	Small round leaves. White flowers in summer. Tolerates shade and frost, and is resistant to salt spray.
L. juniperinum	2 x 1 m	White flowers in spring. Very hardy, suited to poorly drained soils and tolerates frost.
L. laevigatum (coastal tea-tree)	4 x 3 m	White flowers in spring and summer. Heavily ridged papery bark, grey-green leaves, very hardy, resistant to frost, drought and salt, good for windbreaks
L. lanigerum (woolly tea-tree)	3 x 1 m	Young hairy growth, sometimes pinkish. White flowers in summer. Hardy, prefers semi-shade and damp soil.
L. liversidgei	2 x 1 m	Bright green, narrow lemon-scented leaves. Small white flowers, occasionally pink, in summer.
L. leuhmanii	5 x 5 m	Shiny dark green elliptical leaves up to 5 mm. White flowers in summer. Well-drained soil and full sun, in semitropical to tropical areas.
L. longifolium	3 x 3 m	Attractive bright green weeping habit and long, narrow leaves. Grows along river banks.
L. macrocarpum (syn. *L. lanigerum* var. *macrocarpum*)	1.5 x 1.5 m	Leaves are oblong up to 2 cm. Large 3 cm flowers are white, pink or red, with prominent green centres in summer and autumn.
L. madidum subsp. *sativum*	3 x 3 m	Narrow grey-green leaves to about 5 cm long with tiny white flowers. Good feature plant or hedge. Tolerant of most soils. Semi-tropical to tropical areas.
L. minutifolium	2 x 2 m	Tiny attractive leaves. White flowers 1.2 cm in diameter in spring and early summer. Suited to semi-shade. Frost hardy.
L. muticaule	1 x 2 m	Leaves are elliptical up to 1 cm. Small white flowers, needs good drainage, otherwise hardy.

LEPTOSPERMUM SPECIES	SIZE	COMMENTS
L. myrsinoides	2 x 1 m	Small dark green leaves up to 1 cm. White to pink flowers spring to early summer. Frost hardy.
L. nitidum 'Copper Sheen'	1.5 x 2 m	Bronze leaves, spreading bush, green-yellow flowers in spring. Hardy.
L. obvatum	3 x 1.5 m	Small dark green leaves up to 1.2 cm. White flowers in summer. Frost hardy, good screening plant, suited to heavy shade.
L. oligandrum	1 x 2 m	Small grey-green obovate leaves, white flowers in spring. Hardy.
L. parvifolium	1.5 x 1.5	Obovate 5 mm leaves. White or pale pink flowers in late winter and early spring. Very hardy.
L. petersonii	4 x 3 m	Narrow, dark green, lemon-scented, lance-shaped leaves up to 4 cm. White (lemon-scented tea-tree) flowers in spring and early summer. Fast-growing plant suited for screening, slightly frost tender. Suited to tropics.
L. polygalifolium (syn. *L. flavescens*)	1–4 x 1–4 m	Oblong leaves 5–20 mm, light green. Flowers are white and profuse in late spring and summer. Frost hardy feature plant suited to tropics.
L. purpurascens	4 x 3 m	Leaves are light green, broad and lance-shaped, up to 2 cm long. Tiny white flowers in winter. Frost tender and moisture-loving. Suited to tropics.
L. rotundifolium (syn. *L. scoparium* var. *rotundifolium*)	2 x 3 m	Leaves shiny and rounded. White to deep pink flowers in spring and early summer. Resistant to salt spray, frost hardy, suited as hedge.
L. scoparium (manuka)	1–3 x 2 m	Variable in size, shape and flower colour. Many forms and hybrids are widely cultivated for their spectacular flowers of pinks, whites, reds, doubles and singles. This species is relatively hardy, but normally short-lived (5–7 years) and susceptible to scale and sooty mould.
L. sericeum	1.3 x 3 m	Bush with drooping branches, silky-smooth leaves, pink flowers in spring, hardy, slightly frost tender.
L. specatabile	2–3 x 2 m	Narrow leaves to 3.5 cm long. Red 2 cm flowers in late spring. Well-drained soil, full sun, frost hardy.
L. speciosum	2 x 3 m	Broad, lance-shaped 2.5 cm leaves. Small white flowers. Useful screening plant, tolerant of damp soil conditions.
L. spinescens	1 x 1 m	Bright green leaves, white spring flowers, prickly foliage and corky bark. Good drainage required. Frost hardy.
L. squarrosum	2.5 x 1.5 m	Lance-shaped leaves up to 1.5 cm. Pale to deep pink flowers produced on old wood in autumn and winter. Frost hardy, resistant to salt spray.
L. trinervium	4 x 3 m	Light green oblong leaves up to 2 cm. White flowers in spring and throughout the year. Bird attracting. Frost hardy.
L. turbinatum	2 x 2.5	Leaves 2 cm long, glossy, dark green. Large 2.5 cm white flowers in late spring. Frost hardy, grows in heavy shade.
L. variabile	1–2 x 1–2m	Dark green narrow leaves 2 cm long. White round-petalled flowers in late spring. Tolerant of most soils and aspects, frost hardy.

L. tubiflora

- Creeping or upright to 0.5 m tall, sometimes suckering, flower colour is variable, may be anything from white through yellow to red.

LEUCOPHYTA Asteraceae

At a glance

NUMBER OF SPECIES 1; endemic to Australia; previously classified as *Calocephalus brownii*.
NATURAL HABITAT Coastal areas in southern Australia.
FLOWERING Pale yellow insignificant flowers.
HABIT Low-growing, densely branched shrub.
FOLIAGE Silver-grey, wiry branches.
GROWTH RATE Moderate to fast.
LIFESPAN Short.
HARDINESS Moderately hardy.
COMMENTS A popular landscape specimen grown for its striking silver foliage and compact cushion shape.

Culture

- Full sun.
- Grows in most soil types.
- Resistant to salt spray.
- Tolerates moderate frosts.
- Prune regularly to maintain compact shape.
- Propagated by cuttings.

Species

***L. brownii* (syn. *Calocephalus brownii*)**

- Cultivars include *L. brownii* 'nana', a dwarf compact form of the species.
- Densely branched shrub, 0.2–0.7–1 m high. Yellow flowers year-round.

LEUCOPOGON Epacridaceae

At a glance

NUMBER OF SPECIES About 160; most endemic to Australia, some from NZ and South-East Asia.
NATURAL HABITAT Generally forests or woodlands, widespread in Australia.
FLOWERING Small white or pink flowers.
HABIT Small or medium-size bushes.
FOLIAGE Leaves often small with pointed tips.
GROWTH RATE Can be slow.
HARDINESS Not hardy; difficult to propagate and establish in cultivation.

Culture

- Well-drained, high-organic content soil.
- Roots need to be cool in summer, mulching is beneficial.
- Difficult to pot up, their fine roots damage easily.
- Propagated by cuttings with difficulty. Seed generally does not germinate.

Species

L. ericoides

- 1 x 0.7 m. White flowers in late winter to spring.

L. lanceolatus

- 3 x 1 m. White bearded spring flowers, easier than others to cultivate, suited to pot culture.

L. verticillatus

- 3 x 1.5 m. Pink flowers in spring, cultivate in acid soil over limestone underlay.

LOBELIA Lobeliaceae

At a glance

NUMBER OF SPECIES 300; 20 endemic to Australia, distributed throughout all states.
NATURAL HABITAT Varied but often grows in damp depressions.
FLOWERING Blue, white, mauve or purple.
HABIT Annual or perennial herbs with erect branched or prostrate stems.
FOLIAGE Alternate, usually toothed leaves.
GROWTH RATE Moderate.
LIFESPAN Varies.
HARDINESS Moderate.

LOBELIA SPECIES	SIZE	COMMENTS
L. alata	Up to 30 cm	Perennial layering herb. Narrow toothed leaves, lower ones broader. Pale blue, small fan-shaped flowers appear singly year-round.
L. dentata	Up to 40 cm	Slender erect herb with reddish stems, numerous leaves have deeply incised margins. Deep royal blue flowers from mid-autumn to mid-spring.
L. gibbosa	0.10–0.50 x 0.10 m	Annual herb, slender and erect. Narrow leaves up to 30 mm long, deep blue flowers with white markings on the lower lobes appear mid-spring–mid-autumn.
L. gracilis	Up to 30 cm	Erect to prostrate herb. Deeply incised leaves up to 5 cm long. Dark violet-blue flowers from mid-spring to late winter.
L. heterophylla	Up to 60 cm	Erect annual herb, blue-purple flowers in late winter to mid-summer.
L. pratiodes	Spreading	Prostrate matting herb, with dull green incised leaves up to 50 mm long. Single blue or white flowers from mid-spring to mid-summer. Requires moist shade.
L. rhombifolia	10–40 cm	Branched, spreading annual herb, light purple to dark blue flowers with a white and yellow throat in early to mid-spring.
L. simplicicaulis	Up to 0.8 m	Large lanceolate lower leaves up to 20 mm long, deep blue flowers from mid-spring to mid-autumn.

Culture

- Moist, well-drained soils.
- Sun to part shade depending on species.
- Propagated by division.

LOMANDRA ❧ Xanthorrhoeaceae Dasypogonaceae

At a glance

NUMBER OF SPECIES 50; all endemic to Australia.
NATURAL HABITAT Very variable in distribution.
FLOWERING Short-lived single-sexed flowers borne in tight clusters within the tussock. Male and female flowers on separate spikes.
HABIT Tussock-forming plant.
HARDINESS Very hardy. Many adapted to cultivation.
FOLIAGE Lineal green leaves.
GROWTH RATE Generally fast growing.
COMMENTS Extremely reliable in the garden. As flower spikes mature, spines may be developed. This depends on the species.

Culture

- Full sun to shade.
- Plenty of moisture preferred.
- Propagate by seed, division and stem cuttings.

LOMATIA ❧ Protaceae

At a glance

NUMBER OF SPECIES 12; 9 endemic to Australia, 3 endemic to Chile.
NATURAL HABITAT Mostly in damp or dry forests and scrub.
FLOWERING White to cream, fragrant.
HABIT Shrubs or small trees.
FOLIAGE Varies.
GROWTH RATE Slow.
HARDINESS Medium.
LIFESPAN Usually medium.

Culture

- Deep, moist, well-drained soils, some tolerate wetness.
- Tolerate both shade and sun.

LOMANDRA SPECIES	SIZE	COMMENTS
L. banksii (tropical mat rush)	0.5–3 m tall	Fragrant cream flowers in December to March. Frost sensitive, good for subtropics and tropics.
L. filiformis spp. *filiformis*	0.15–0.50 x 0.15–0.20 m	Bluish grey-green to green leaves, sparsely tufted grassy perennial. Numerous, small globe-shaped yellow flowers from spring to early summer.
L. longifolia (long mat rush)	1 m tall	Fragrant cream or yellow flowers from August to December. Frost-hardened. Highly ornamental specimen.
L. multiflora	Up to 0.50 x 0.50 m	Rigid greyish narrow leaves up to 3 mm wide. Flowers with yellow petals and purplish sepals appear in early winter to mid-summer. Well-drained soils, tolerates some dryness.
L. nana	Up to 0.15 x to 0.10 m	Dense tufts of flat bluish-green slender rough leaves. Creamy-white flowers appear from mid-spring to early summer.

LOMATIA SPECIES	SIZE	COMMENTS
L. fraseri	2–7 x 1–4 m	Small rounded shrub to small tree. Leaves are stiff, leathery with silvery hairs on the underside. Cream, hairy flowers in summer.
L. ilicifolia	0.5–2 x 1 m	Erect shrub with dark green crinkly leaves similar to holly. Cream flowers in summer.
L. myrcrioides	2–5 x 1–3 m	Rounded shrub or open tree. Narrow lance-shaped dull green leaves up to 20 cm long. Cream flowers in summer.
L. polymorpha	2.5–4 x 1–3 m	Shrub or small tree. Simple linear, narrowly ovate leaves, white-green or cream flowers in late summer–autumn.
L. tasmanica	2–8 x 1–4 m	Small tree. Buds densely covered with small hairs. Glossy green alternate leaves crowded at the ends of branches. Crimson flowers with yellow pollen sacs occur generally in late summer but often does not flower every year. Endangered species of Tas.
L. tinctoria	Up to 2 x 1 m	Small shrub with dark green leaves up to 80 cm long comprising many small pinnate leaflets. Cream or white flowers in summer.

- Tip-prune to encourage bushiness.
- Propagation by seeds and cuttings.

LOPHOSTEMON Myrtaceae

This genus was formerly included under *Tristania*.

At a glance

NUMBER OF SPECIES 6; all endemic to tropical eastern Australia and New Guinea.
NATURAL HABITAT Tropics to temperate areas.
FLOWERING Similar to eucalyptus.
HABIT Small to large trees.
FOLIAGE Similar to eucalypt leaves.
GROWTH RATE Can be rapid.
HARDINESS Generally hardy.
LIFESPAN Long-lived.

Culture

- Needs adequate water.
- Propagated easily from seed.

Species

L. confertus

- Known as brush box, a tall tree commonly growing to 35 m in moist tropical to subtropical rainforests of Qld, up to 10 m in Melbourne. Some specimens in south-eastern Qld are much larger with butts more than 10 m in diameter, claimed to be over 1000 years old. In southern states it develops into a well-shaped, hardy tree that adapts to a wide range of conditions; however, it does not tolerate extended dry periods. Fast growing if watered in dry seasons.

MACADAMIA ❧ Proteaceae

At a glance

NUMBER OF SPECIES 8; 7 endemic to eastern Australia, 1 endemic to Indonesia.
NATURAL HABITAT Warm rainforests.
FLOWERING Small white to pink flowers, similar to *Grevillea*.
HABIT Trees.
FOLIAGE Dark green leaves, thick and leathery.
GROWTH RATE Medium to fast in good conditions.
HARDINESS Moderate.
LIFESPAN Long-lived.
COMMENTS Fruits yield an edible nut.

Culture

- Excellent drainage.
- Grows best in sheltered positions.
- Propagate by grafting onto seedlings.
- Seeds need to be cracked open before sowing.

MACROPIDIA ❧ Haemodoraceae

At a glance

NUMBER OF SPECIES 1; *M. fuliginosa*, endemic to WA.
NATURAL HABITAT Semi-arid areas, WA.
FLOWERING Black kangaroo paw-like flowers in spring.
HABIT Low clump-forming perennials.
FOLIAGE Strap-like leaves.
GROWTH RATE Medium to fast.
LIFESPAN Short.
HARDINESS Not hardy in eastern states.

Culture

- Prefers well-drained soil.
- Don't over water.
- Susceptible to fungal diseases. Regular spraying is often necessary in cultivation.
- Propagation by division. Propagating by seed is difficult.

MALLOTUS ❧ Euphorbiaceae

At a glance

NUMBER OF SPECIES 12 species found in Australia; 6 endemic.
NATURAL HABITAT Rainforest fringe plant.
FLOWERING Small insignificant flowers in clusters.
HABIT Woody shrubs and trees.
HARDINESS Very hardy, especially to drought.
FOLIAGE Smooth green foliage.

MACADAMIA SPECIES	SIZE	LEAVES	COMMENTS
M. heyana	Up to 6 m tall	Lanceolate to wedge-shaped	Gold-brown flowers, fruits are unknown.
M. integrifolia	Up to 20 m tall	Slightly wavy margins	White flowers, slightly hairy, used for commercial nut growing.
M. ternifolia	Up to 20 x 12 m	Long narrow leaves with stiff teeth	Rough bark.
M. tetraphylla	Up to 20 x 12 m	Serrated leaf margins	White or pink, very hairy flowers, used for commercial crops.
M. whelani	Up to 12 m	10–15 cm long	Smooth bark, reddish young stems.

GROWTH RATE Medium growth.
LIFESPAN Medium- to long-lived.
COMMENTS Used for land reclamation works in some areas.

Culture

- Full sun to part shade.
- Adaptable to a range of soils.
- Pruning will improve shape of the plants.
- Tolerates light frosts.
- Propagation by fresh seed and by cuttings.

Species

M. claoxyloides (smell of the bush)
- 6 m. Straggly shrub, leaves release a distinctive smell.

M. discolor (yellow kamala)
- 10 m. Rounded small tree, fast growing. A yellow dye can be made from the powder covering the fruit.

M. philippensis (red kamala)
- 8 m. Dense bushy tree for screening. A red dye can be made from the powder covering the fruit.

MAZUS ❧ Scrophulariaceae

At a glance

NUMBER OF SPECIES About 30; from Australia, Pacific and Asia.
NATURAL HABITAT Widespread, mainly alpine, not arid areas.
FLOWERING Blue or white terminal on one-sided racemes.
HABIT Clump- or mat-forming.
FOLIAGE Leaves with toothed or cut margins.
GROWTH RATE Medium to fast.
HARDINESS Needs adequate water.
LIFESPAN Short.

Culture

- Prefers moist soil.
- Suited to rockeries.
- Propagate by division or seed.

Species

M. pumilo is the only widely grown native species.

MELALEUCA ❧ Paperbark ❧ Myrtaceae

At a glance

NUMBER OF SPECIES About 200; most endemic to Australia, a few from South-East Asia and New Guinea.
NATURAL HABITAT Varies greatly.
HARDINESS Generally very hardy.
HABIT Small shrubs, small and large trees.
FOLIAGE Mainly fine undivided leaves.
GROWTH RATE Very fast.
LIFESPAN Medium- to long-lived.

Culture

- Generally tolerates most soils and some waterlogging.
- Most are drought tolerant.
- Feed only with organic or slow-release foods.
- Respond to light pruning in spring and autumn.
- All propagate easily from seed. Most propagate from cuttings.

The difference between *Callistemon* and *Melaleuca*

- Both have bottlebrush-like flowers of varying lengths.
- *Callistemon* flowers have long stamens (i.e. the stalks which bear the pollen).
- *Melaleuca* flowers have stamens generally less than 2.5 cm long.
- *Melaleuca* filaments of the flowers are fused together, whereas *Callistemon* has separate filaments.
- Though there are many exceptions, the bark on *Melaleuca* is often more papery than on *Callistemon*.

MELALEUCA SPECIES	SIZE	TOLERATES DROUGHT	TOLERATES WET	TOLERATES FROST	FLOWERS
M. acerosa	2.5 x 2.5 m	Yes	No	No	Cream
M. acuminata	2 x 1 m	Yes	No	Yes	Cream
M. adnata	2 x 2 m	Yes	Yes	Yes	White
M. alternifolia	6 x 4 m	No	Yes	Yes	White
M. argentea	25 x 15 m	No	Part	No	Cream
M. armillaris	5–8 x 3–5 m	Yes	No	Part	White
M. biconvexa	6 x 2 m	Yes	Yes	Yes	White
M. brachystachya = *M. subfalcata*					
M. bracteata	2–5 x 4 m	Yes	Yes	Yes	White
M. bracteata 'Golden Gem'	2 x 1 m	Yes	Yes	Part	White (golden and compact)
M. bracteata 'Revolution Gold'	4 x 1.5 m	Yes	Yes	Part	White (golden foliage)
M. bracteata 'Revolution Green'	2–6 x 2–3 m	Yes	Yes	Part	White (green foliage)
M. brevifolia	3 x 1.5 m	Yes	No	Yes	White
M. calothamnoides	3 x 1 m	Yes	Part	Yes	Red or green
M. capitata	3 x 2.5 m	Yes	Part	Yes	Cream
M. cardiophylla	1–1.5 x 2 m	Yes	Part	Part	White
M. cheelii	6 x 3 m	Part	Part	Yes	Pale cream
M. citrina = *M. pungens*					
M. coccinea	2 x 1 m	No	No	*	Bright red
M. conothamnoides	1–2 x 1–3 m	Yes	No	Part	Red or purple
M. cordata	1 x 1.5 m	Yes	No	*	Purple
M. corrugata	1 x 1.5 m	Yes	No	No	White
M. crassifolia = *M. laxiflora*					
M. cuneata	1.5 x 2 m	Part	No	Yes	Purple
M. cuticularis	3–4 x 1 m	Yes	Yes	Yes	White
M. decora	4–6 x 2 m	No	Yes	Yes	White
M. decussata	3 x 3 m	No	Yes	Yes	Mauve
M. densa	2 x 2.5 m	Yes	No	Yes	Yellow
M. depauperata	1.5 x 2 m	Part	No	*	Cream or mauve
M. depressa	1 x 1 m	Part	No	Yes	Yellow
M. diosmifolia	2–4 x 2–3 m	Yes	No	No	Yellow-green
M. dissitiflora	4 x 2 m	Yes	No	*	White
M. elliptica	2–3 x 2.5 m	Yes	Part	Yes	Red

* Insufficient data

MELALEUCA SPECIES	SIZE	TOLERATES DROUGHT	TOLERATES WET	TOLERATES FROST	FLOWERS
M. ericifolia	5 x 3 m	No	Yes	Yes	White
M. erubescens = (*M. diosmatifolia*)	2 x 1.2 m	Part	No	Yes	Mauve
M. exarata = *M. suberosa*					
M. filifolia	2 x 2 m	Yes	No	Part	Pink and gold
M. fulgens	2 x 2 m	Yes	No	No	Red or pink
M. gibbosa	1.5 x 2 m	No	Yes	Part	Mauve
M. glaberrima	0.8 x 1.5 m	Part	*	Yes	Mauve
M. glomerata	5 x 2 m	Yes	No	Part	Cream
M. groveana	3 x 1.5 m	*	Part	Yes	White
M. hakeoides = *M. glomerata*					
M. halmaturorum	3–6 x 4 m	No	Yes	Yes	White
M. hamulosa	2–3 x 2 m	Yes	Yes	Yes	White or pink
M. huegelii	2–3 x 3 m	Yes	No	Yes	Pink to cream
M. hypericifolia	3 x 4 m	Yes	Part	Part	Red
M. incana	2.5 x 2 m	Part	Yes	Yes	Yellow
M. incana 'Velvet Cushion'	0.5 x 0.6 m	Part	Yes	Yes	Cream
M. irbyana	8 m	Yes	*	*	White or cream
M. lanceolata	7 x 3 m	No	Part	Yes	Creamy-white
M. lateralis	Up to 1 x 2 m	No	No	Yes	Mauve
M. lateritia	2 x 2.5 m	Part	Part	Yes	Red to orange
M. laxiflora	1.5 x 1.5 m	Yes	No	Part	Pink or red
M. leptoclada = *M. pauciflora*					
M. leptospermoides	1 x 1 m	Yes	No	Part	Purple or red
M. leucadendron and *M. linariifolia* are similar and often confused with each other. *M. leaucadendron* has leaves to 15 cm long, *M. linariifolia* has leaves up to 4 cm long, *M. viridiflora* has leaves up to 9 cm long.					
M. leucadendron	25 x 15 m	Yes	Yes	Yes	Cream
M. linariifolia Note: *M. linariifolia* can grow to a much larger tree in northern rainforests.	7 x 5 m	Yes	Yes	Yes	White
M. longicoma = *M. macronychia*					
M. macronychia	2 x 2 m	Yes	Part	Yes	Red
M. megacephala	1–3 x 3 m	Part	Part	Yes	Yellow
M. micromera	1 x 1 m	Yes	No	Yes	Fluffy yellow
M. microphylla	3 x 2 m	Part	Part	Yes	Cream
M. minutifolia	5 x 4 m	Yes	No	*	White
M. neglecta	1.5 x 1.5 m	Part	Part	Yes	White

MELALEUCA SPECIES	SIZE	TOLERATES DROUGHT	TOLERATES WET	TOLERATES FROST	FLOWERS
M. nesophila	2.5 x 3 m	Yes	Yes	Part	Mauve
M. nodosa	2–3 x 2–3 m	Yes	Yes	Yes	Yellow
M. oldfieldii	1 x 0.5 m	Part	No	*	Mauve
M. oraria = *M. neglecta*					
M. pauciflora	0.3 x 2 m	Yes	Part	Yes	Light purple
M. pauperiflora	3 x 1.5 m	Yes	Part	Yes	White
M. Paynes Hybrid	1–2 x 2 m	Yes	No	Part	Crimson
M. pentagona	1.5–2 m	Yes	Part	Yes	Mauve
M. platycalyx	0.8 x 1 m	Part	No	Yes	Mauve
M. polygaloides	1–1.5 x 2 m	Yes	Part	Yes	Yellow
M. preissiana	6–13 x 4–5 m	No	Yes	*	White
M. pubescens = *M. lanceolata*					
M. pulchella	1 x 1.2 m	Yes	Yes	Yes	Pink
M. pungens	1.2 x 1.3 m	Yes	No	Part	Yellow
M. quadrifaria	3 x 3 m	Part	Part	No	Cream-white
M. radula	2.5 x 2 m	Yes	No	Part	Pink-mauve
M. rhaphiophylla	8–15 x 4–6 m	No	Yes	Yes	Cream
M. scabra	1–1.5 x 1 m	Yes	No	Yes	Purple-red
M. seriata	2.5 x 1.5 m	Yes	No	Part	Red or purple
M. sheathiana = *M. pauperiflora*					
M. sieberi	3 x 3 m	No	Yes	Yes	White
M. 'Snowflake'	2 x 1.5 m	No	Part	No	White
M. sparsiflora	2 x 1.5 m	Part	No	Yes	White
M. spathulata	1–2 x 1.2 m	No	Yes	No	Mauve-red
M. spicigera	1.5 x 1 m	Part	No	*	Purple-pink
M. squamea	1–2.5 x 2 m	No	Yes	Part	Red-purple
M. squarrosa	2–3 x 1–2	No	Yes	No	Cream
M. steedmanni	1–1.5 x 1.5 m	Yes	No	Yes	Orange or red
M. striata	1.5 x 2 m	Yes	No	Part	Pink or white
M. stypheloides	5–8 x 5 m	No	Yes	Yes	White
M. suberosa	0.3–1 x 1.2 m	Part	No	Yes	Mauve
M. subfalcata	0.5 x 3 m	Yes	Yes	Yes	Pink-purple
M. symphyocarpa	7 x 2 m	No	Yes	No	Orange-red
M. tasmariscina	5 x 3 m	No	Part	Yes	Mauve to white
M. tenella	1–2 x 1 m	Part	No	Part	Mauve

* Insufficient data

MELALEUCA SPECIES	SIZE	TOLERATES DROUGHT	TOLERATES WET	TOLERATES FROST	FLOWERS
M. teretifolia	2.5 x 1 m	Part	Part	Yes	White
M. thymifolia	0.8 x 1.2 m	Yes	Yes	Part	Purple
M. thymoides	1–2 x 2 m	Yes	No	Part	Light yellow
M. uncinata	3 x 2 m	Yes	No	Yes	Cream
M. undulata	1 x 2 m	Part	Part	Yes	Cream-white
M. urceolaris	1.5 x 1.5 m	Part	No	*	Yellow
M. viminea	1.5–3 x 3 m	Part	Yes	Part	White
M. viridiflora var. *viridiflora*	18 x varies	No	Yes	No	White-green-red
M. viridiflora var. *rubriflora*	25 x varies	No	Yes	No	White
M. violacea	1.5 x 1.5 m	Yes	Yes	Part	Purple or red
M. wilsonii	2–3 x 2–3 m	Yes	Yes	Yes	Purple
M. wilsonii prostrate	0.5 x 2 m	Yes	Yes	Yes	Purple

Where to grow melaleucas

MEDIUM OR HIGH RAINFALL IN SUBTROPICS

M. bracteata, calothamnoides, cardiophylla, decussata, densa, diosmifolia, erubescens, exarata, filifolia, fulgens, gibbosa, halmaturorum, huegelii, hypericifolia, incana, lateritia, laxiflora, leptospermoides, leucadendron, linariifolia, macronycha, megacephala, micromera, nematophylla, nesophila, nodosa, Paynes Hybrid, *pulchella, radula, scabra, seriata, spathulata, steedmanii, striata, suberosa, tenella, thymifolia, violacea, wilsonii.*

MEDIUM OR HIGH RAINFALL IN TEMPERATE AREAS

M. armillaris, calothamnoides, cardiophylla, decussata, densa, diosmifolia, elliptica, ericifolia, erubescens, fulgens, gibbosa, huegelii, hypericifolia, incana, lateritia, leptospermoides, linariifolia, micromera, nesophila, nodosa, Paynes Hybrid, *pulchella, scabra, steedmanii, styphelioides, thymifolia, thymoides, violacea, wilsonii.*

WILL GROW IN ARID INLAND

M. acuminata, adnata, calothamnoides, cardiophylla, conothamnoides, decussata, densa, diosmifolia, elliptica, exarata, filifolia, fulgens, halmaturorum, hamulosa, hypericifolia, incana, lateritia, macronycha, micromera, neglecta, nematophylla, nesophila, Paynes Hybrid, *polygaloides, pulchella, pungens, scabra, spathulata, squamea, steedmanii, suberosa, thymoides, viminea, violacea, wilsonii.*

SUITED TO SALT-AFFECTED SOILS

M. cutticularis, rhaphiophylla, lanceolata.

SUITABLE FOR WINDBREAKS

M. acuminata, armillaris, bracteata, conothamnoides, decussata, diosmifolia, ericifolia, hamulosa, huegelii, hypericifolia, linariifolia, nesophila, styphelioides, wilsonii.

Types of foliage

GREEN FINE NEEDLES

M. armillaris, calothamnoides, ericifolia, erubescens, lateritia.

PRICKLY OR STIFF LEAVES

M. styphelioides, tenella, thymioides.

BROADER LEAVES

M. linariifolia, hypericifolia, megacephala, nesophila, polygalioides, spathulata, squarrosa, steedmanii, violacea.

GREY OR BLUE-GREEN

M. conothamnoides, elliptica, fulgens, incana, Paynes Hybrid, *pulchella, seriata, thymifolia, wilsonii.*

MELIA ❧ White Cedar ❧ Meliaceae

At a glance

NUMBER OF SPECIES About 10; 1 endemic to Australia (*M. azaderach*).
NATURAL HABITAT Warm rainforest.
FLOWERING Purplish flowers in winter or spring followed by yellow berry-like fruits.
HABIT Deciduous tree.
FOLIAGE Bipinnate leaves (similar to an ash tree).
GROWTH RATE Medium in cool climates, fast in warm climates.
HARDINESS Very hardy in most situations.
LIFESPAN Medium- to long-lived.

Culture

- Adaptable to most parts of Australia.
- Respond to fertile, moist soil.
- Prone to attack by skeletonising beetles which defoliate the tree.
- Propagate by fresh seed or occasionally cuttings.

Species

M. azedarach (white cedar)

- Grows up to 40 m tall in warm, wet climates, smaller in drier cool climates (sometimes no more than 5 m). Purple and white flowers, highly scented. Round yellow fruits, which can be poisonous. Deciduous.

MELICOPE ❧ Rutaceae

At a glance

NUMBER OF SPECIES About 150; 8 endemic to tropical Australia.
NATURAL HABITAT Rainforests.
FLOWERING Mainly in summer.
HABIT Small to medium trees.
HARDINESS Generally hardy in subtropics.
FOLIAGE Glossy divided leaves.
GROWTH RATE Generally a very fast grower.
LIFESPAN Long-lived.
COMMENTS This genus was previously known as *Euodia*.

Culture

- Prefer moist, well-mulched soil.
- Tolerate full sun.
- Propagate by seed.

Species

M. elleryana (syn. *Euodia elleryana*) (butterfly tree)

- Medium tree of 6–9 m tall and 5 m wide. Bears pale pink flowers in clusters on the stems. Attractive to birds. Host tree of the blue Ulysses butterfly. Propagate by seed.

M. erythrococca (tingle tongue)

- Similar to *M. elleryana* except with white flowers and bright red fruit. Tolerates cool conditions.

M. micrococca (white euodia)

- Similar to *E. elleryana* except flowers are white and leaflets are smaller. Better suited to cooler districts like Sydney and Melbourne.

MICROMYRTUS ❧ Myrtaceae

At a glance

NUMBER OF SPECIES About 22; all endemic to Australia.
NATURAL HABITAT Open forests.
FLOWERING Small profuse flowers in winter and spring.
HABIT Low-growing, spreading shrubs.
HARDINESS Moderate to hardy in well-drained soils.
FOLIAGE Small dark green leaves.
GROWTH RATE Medium.
LIFESPAN Medium.

Culture

- Drought tolerant.
- Do not tolerate waterlogging.
- Frost tolerant.

MICROMYRTUS SPECIES	SIZE	COMMENTS
M. ciliata	0.5 x 1 m	Small heath-like shrub with pink buds opening to white flowers which change to red.
M. drummondii	0.8 x 1 m	White flowers in spring, only takes light frosts.
M. flaviflora	1.5 x 1 m	Pink to pinkish-yellow flowers, suited to gravel or sandy soils in arid climates.
M. leptocalyx	1–2 m tall	White flowers, suits warm climates.
M. minutiflora	Up to 1 m tall	Pale pink flowers.
M. obovata	Up to 1.5 x 1 m	Erect shrub with white flowers in mid-winter–early spring.
M. racemosa	Up to 2 x 1.5 m	White, cream, yellow or pink flowers in late autumn to early spring.
M. rosea	1 x 1 m	White to pink flowers, prefers full sun.
M. sessilis	Up to 1.5 x to 1 m	Dense shrub. White to pink flowers in spring.
M. striata	Up to 1.2 x to 1.5 m	Erect to spreading shrub. Whitish-pink flowers in late winter–spring.
M. stricta	0.7 x 0.3 m	White flowers, can be difficult to grow.
M. sulphurea	50 cm to 1.5 m x 1.5 m	Widely spreading shrub that is sometimes stunted. Yellow flowers in mid-winter–mid-spring.

Note: *Thyptomene* and *Micromyrtus* are very similar and often confused. Stamens and petals are opposite each other in the *Micromyrtus* flower.

- Prefer sun at least part of the day.
- Propagate by cuttings.

MYOPORUM ❧ Myoporaceae

At a glance

NUMBER OF SPECIES About 30; 16 endemic to Australia.
NATURAL HABITAT Usually dry inland, some coastal.
FLOWERING Small, usually white, clustered in large numbers. Often attractive berries.
HABIT Creepers, small and large shrubs.
FOLIAGE Thick, fleshy, resistant to salt winds, fire and drought.
GROWTH RATE Fast.
HARDINESS Hardy in most conditions.
LIFESPAN Medium.
COMMENTS Good firebreak plant.

Culture

- Most don't tolerate waterlogging.
- Prefer full sun.
- Propagate fast and easily from cuttings.

NEOLITSEA

At a glance

NUMBER OF SPECIES 80; 3 endemic to Australia, occurring in NT, Qld and NSW.
NATURAL HABITAT Understorey trees in tropical to subtropical rainforest and eucalypt forests.
FLOWERING Insignificant flowers followed by black globular fruit.
HABIT Evergreen trees with erect branching stems.
FOLIAGE Green, elliptical, with a grey undersurface.
GROWTH RATE Medium to fast.
HARDINESS Moderate.

MYOPORUM SPECIES	SIZE	COMMENTS
M. acuminatum	4 x 3 m	White flowers, light green foliage, needs good drainage and full sun, bluish berries.
M. debile (now known as *Eremophila debilis*)	Prostrate x 1.5 m	White flowers, pink berries, adaptable.
M. deserti	3 x 4 m	Small white flowers, yellow fruits, best in arid areas.
M. ellipticum	0.8 x 3 m	Large leaves, white flowers, dark purple berries.
M. floribundum	3 x 3 m	Long narrow leaves, white spring flowers.
M. insulare (boobialla)	4 x 3 m	White flowers, very hardy windbreak plant.
M. montanum	3 x 3 m	White and purple flowers, long narrow leaves, best in arid areas.
M. parvifolium	0.3 x 1 m	White flowers, very hardy groundcover.
M. platycarpum	2–10 m tall	White flowers, suits dry climates.
M. tetrandrum	2 x 2 m	White flowers, must have good drainage.
M. viscosum	1 x 1.5 m	White flowers, needs good drainage.

LIFESPAN Medium- to long-lived.

Culture

- Light to medium well-composted soils.
- Filtered sun to open sunny position.
- Propagation by cuttings.

Species

N. australiensis

- 6–15 m x 3 m. Small tree with smooth dark brown bark. Glossy green leaves, cream flowers in summer followed by black fruit.

N. dealbata

- Up to 10 m x 3 m. Small tree with ovate-elliptical green leaves that are grey underneath and drooping new growth. Insignificant flowers are followed by round black fruit.

NOTHOFAGUS ❧ Beech ❧ Fagaceae

At a glance

NUMBER OF SPECIES 40; 3 occurring in Australia.
NATURAL HABITAT Rainforests at high altitudes.
FLOWERING Catkin-like, generally not significant.
HABIT Tall trees.
FOLIAGE Simple leaves.
GROWTH RATE Slow.
HARDINESS Moderate once established.
LIFESPAN Very long-lived, can live hundreds if not thousands of years.
COMMENTS Plants are suitable for bonsai.

Culture

- Needs moist, fertile soil.
- Avoid waterlogging.
- Generally prefers cool to mild climates.
- Protect from wind.
- Propagate by seed or hardwood cuttings.

Species

N. cunninghamii

- 12–35 m. Attractive reddish tinge to young foliage.

N. gunnii

- 3 x 3 m. Deciduous shrub from Tasmania, very slow growing.

N. moorei

- 18 m. Young leaves are green, old leaves red.

NUYTSIA ❧ West Australian Christmas Tree ❧ Loranthaceae

At a glance

NUMBER OF SPECIES 1, endemic to WA (*N. floribunda*).
NATURAL HABITAT Open woodland.
FLOWERING Spectacular deep orange flowers in early to mid-summer.
HABIT Parasitic tree (roots attach to other tree roots).
FOLIAGE Variable coarse dark green growth.
GROWTH RATE Very slow for first 5–10 years.
HARDINESS Can be difficult to establish and maintain.

Culture

- Full sun.
- Soil must be well drained.
- Tolerates light to moderate frosts.
- Best if grown alongside another plant which it can attach to.
- Difficult to propagate due to gelatinous exude from cut wood. Cuttings may be successful if stored cold to slow down exudation before planting.

Species

N. floribunda

- Tree 5–7 m tall, with spectacular masses of golden flowers in early summer.

OLEARIA ❧ Daisy Bush ❧ Asteraceae

At a glance

NUMBER OF SPECIES About 130; 80 endemic to Australia.
NATURAL HABITAT Woodland and alpine areas.
FLOWERING Daisy-like in large numbers.
HABIT Mainly shrubs.
FOLIAGE Often an attractive grey to grey-green.
GROWTH RATE Can be fast.
HARDINESS Generally hardy.
LIFESPAN Often found to be short-lived (i.e. less than 5 years).

Culture

- Prefers moist soil.
- Some are drought tolerant.
- Most tolerate light frosts.
- Withstands pruning.
- Generally prefer semi-shade or filtered sun.

OLEARIA SPECIES	SIZE	FLOWERS	COMMENTS
O. adenophora	1 x 1.5 m	White to mauve	Scented. Can become untidy, prune after flowering to maintain shape.
O. asterotricha	1 x 1.5 m	Purple	Tolerates drought and frost.
O. axillaris	2 x 1.5 m	Cream	Suits coastal areas. Has silver foliage.
O. ciliata	0.2 x 0.2 m	Rich purple	Tolerates full sun.
O. erubescens	1.5 x 1 m	White	Untidy if not pruned, best in full sun.
O. glandulosa	1.5 x 1.5 m	White or blue	Likes full sun or part shade and well-drained soil.
O. gunniana = *O. phlogopappa*			
O. lirata	2 x 2 m	Purple	Very hardy, slightly frost tender.
O. pannosa	1.5 x 1.5 m	White	Large grey-green leaves.
O. phlogopappa	1.5–2 m tall	Lavender or white	Tolerates frost and drought, moderately hardy.
O. pimeleoides	1 x 1 m	White	Easy to keep tidy.
O. tomentosa	0.5–1 x 1 m	White or blue	Very hardy, frost and drought tolerant.

- Propagate by semi-hardwood cuttings or seed.
- Some have been successfully grafted to hardy seedlings.

OPISTHIOLEPIS ✻ Proteaceae

At a glance

NUMBER OF SPECIES 1; *O. heterophyllus* endemic to north-eastern Qld.
NATURAL HABITAT Rainforests.
FLOWERING Small flowers borne on 15 cm-long racemes.
HABIT Bushy tree.
HARDINESS Hardy in warm areas of Australia.
FOLIAGE Striking bronze undersides. Leaf shape changes with maturity.
GROWTH RATE Medium to fast.
COMMENTS Highly prized ornamental tree due to foliage colour. Full sun encourages thick growth habit.

Culture

- Will tolerate sun from an early age.
- Additional irrigation required in dry periods.
- Well-drained loamy soil preferred.
- Responds to fertiliser.
- Propagation by seed.

Species

O. heterophylla (blush silky oak)

- Grows to 15 m. White flowers on 10–15 cm-long racemes in spring. Leaves change shape as the tree matures: juvenile leaves are entire and toothed, adult leaves are pinnate.

ORTHOSIPHON ✻ Lamiaceae

At a glance

NUMBER OF SPECIES 1 known of in Australia.
NATURAL HABITAT Understorey rainforests of north Qld.
FLOWERING Summer flowers of terminal spikes.
HABIT Small bushy shrub.
HARDINESS Frost sensitive. White-flower form is more cold tolerant.
FOLIAGE Deep green.
GROWTH RATE Very fast.
COMMENTS Can easily be used in warm frost-free sites in domestic gardens due to its versatility.

Culture

- Part-shade to full sun.
- Moist soils.
- Not for frost areas.
- Pruning will encourage thick growth habit.
- Propagation is by cuttings.

Species

O. aristatus (cat's whiskers)

- Small bushy understorey plant grows to 1 m. Has attractive white or mauve flowers in a terminal spray. Very ornamental when pruned to a hedge.

ORTHROSANTHUS ✻ Iridaceae

At a glance

NUMBER OF SPECIES 7
NATURAL HABITAT Sandy plains of southern Australia.
FLOWERING Star-shaped flowers in spring.
HABIT Small, iris-like clumps.
FOLIAGE Grass-like clumping leaves.
GROWTH RATE Fast.
HARDINESS Hardy.
LIFESPAN Short-lived.
COMMENTS Ideal for rockeries and garden edging.

Culture

- Full sun.
- Well-drained soil.
- Propagate by seed; seedlings flower in first year.

Species

O. laxus

- 0.4 x 0.6 m. Light blue flowers on stalks to 0.6 m.

O. multiflorus

- 0.6 x 1 m. Stems to 1 m bearing deep blue flowers in spring.

OXYLOBIUM ❧ Fabaceae

At a glance

NUMBER OF SPECIES About 35; all endemic to Australia.

NATURAL HABITAT Occur in all states, mainly in south-western WA.

FLOWERING Yellow or yellow and red pea flowers.

HABIT Creepers to medium-height trees.

FOLIAGE Varies in shape.

GROWTH RATE Fast under good conditions.

HARDINESS Generally hardy.

LIFESPAN Short to medium.

Culture

- Needs well-drained soil.
- Prefers full sun and a thick mulch.
- Propagate by cuttings or hot-water-treated seed.

Species

O. alpestre

- 1 x 1.5 m. Orange-red flower
- Alpine plant, adaptable.

O. ellipticum

- 0.2–2 m tall. Yellow flowers
- Prostrate forms are best.

O. tricuspidatum

- 0.1 x 0.7 m. Orange-yellow flowers
- Excellent in a rockery.

OZOTHAMNUS ❧ Asteraceae

At a glance

NUMBER OF SPECIES 53; 44 endemic to Australia, occurring in NSW, Qld, Tas and Vic.

NATURAL HABITAT Open forests.

FLOWERING Daisy flowers belonging to the group known as everlastings.

HABIT Shrubs.

FOLIAGE Stem-clasping, alternate, entire,

OZOTHAMNUS SPECIES	SIZE	COMMENTS
O. ferrugineus	2–6 x 1–3 m	Small tree or open rounded shrub, narrow dark green leaves to 70 mm long, undersides white. White, broad-clustered flowers heads from mid-spring to mid-summer.
O. diosmifolius syn. *Helichrysum diosmofolium*	2.5 x 2 m	Erect shrub with linear-shaped aromatic leaves, dense clusters of white flowers (sometimes pink) in spring and summer.
O. hookeri syn. *Helichrysum hookeri*	Up to 60 cm	Compact, conifer-like shrub with tiny leaves up to 3 mm long. Cream flowers in summer.
O. obcordatus	1–2 x 1 m	Erect, slender shrub with shiny, dark green, wedge-shaped leaves, undersides white. Numerous dense clusters of yellow tubular flowers mid-spring to mid-summer.
O. rosmarinifolius	1.5–3 x 1–2 m	Narrow, rough, erect dark green leaves with white undersides. Cream tubular flowers in dense clusters in late summer to late autumn. Needs well-drained but moist soil.
O. turbinatus	1–3 x 1.5 m	Upright, rounded hairy shrub of coastal areas. Narrow, stiff grey-green leaves with woolly white undersides. Cream tubular flowers in dense clusters, late summer to late autumn.

varying in size and colour.
GROWTH RATE Fast.
HARDINESS Usually hardy.
LIFESPAN Usually short to medium.
COMMENTS All Australian species were formerly classified as *Helichrysum*.

Culture
- Adaptable to many soil conditions.
- Full sun.
- Prune after flowering.
- Propagation by seed or cuttings.

PANDANUS ❧ Screw Pine ❧ Pandanaceae

At a glance
NUMBER OF SPECIES About 600, occurring in East Africa, Malaysia, Australia and the Pacific.
NATURAL HABITAT Warm or hot climates.
FLOWERING Very small flowers, followed by pineapple-like fruits.
HABIT Palm-like or clump-forming.
FOLIAGE Strap-like, spiny-edged.
GROWTH RATE Medium to fast in good conditions.
HARDINESS Usually hardy once established in suitable conditions.
LIFESPAN Long-lived.
COMMENTS Suitable for seaside plantings.

Culture
- Good drainage.
- Full or filtered sun.
- Some species can be invasive.
- Propagate by seed.

Species
P. aquitus
- Yellow-green foliage. Suits hot climates.

P. fosteri
- Green foliage. Hardier than most in cool climates.

P. pedunculatus
- Green or variegated foliage. Ideal as coastal or container plant.

P. spiralis
- Blue-green foliage. Suits subtropics.

P. tectorius
- Light green foliage. Suits tropics, prickly leaves, 3–6 m tall.

PANDOREA ❧ Bignoniaceae

At a glance
NUMBER OF SPECIES 6; 3 endemic to Australia.
NATURAL HABITAT Rainforests of north-eastern NSW and south-eastern Qld.
FLOWERING Bell- or trumpet-shaped tubular flowers.
HABIT Twining plants.
FOLIAGE Dark green pinnate leaves.
GROWTH RATE Medium to fast.
HARDINESS Moderate.
LIFESPAN Medium.
COMMENTS Useful plants for covering pergolas and fences.

Culture
- Suited to full sun or filtered sun.
- Must have moist but drained soil.
- Susceptible to frost and in most cases drought.
- Propagate by cuttings.

Species
P. baileyana
- Climber, flowers cream with a pink throat, not widely available.

P. jasminoides
- Vigorous climber from Qld and NSW rainforests with large pink trumpet flowers in summer and autumn. White-flowering form also available.

P. nervosa
- Climber, flowers white with a yellow throat, dark green leaves and purple stems.

P. pandorana (wonga vine)
- Vigorous climber, occuring naturally from

Qld to Tas, hardier than *P. jasminoides*, white, cream or gold flowers in winter and spring, often with red or purple throat.

PARAHEBE ✤ *see Veronica*

PASSIFLORA ✤ Passifloraceae

At a glance

NUMBER OF SPECIES About 400; 9 occur in Australia.
NATURAL HABITAT Rainforests and other woodlands.
FLOWERING Often spectacular, feathery flowers with 5 petals, in spring.
HABIT Vines.
FOLIAGE Leaves commonly lobed.
GROWTH RATE Generally fast.
HARDINESS Moderate to hardy once established.
LIFESPAN Medium.

Culture

- Prefers moist, drained, fertile soils.
- Frost-tender.
- Some are extremely vigorous to the point of being invasive.
- Propagate by seed, cuttings or occasionally grafting onto seedlings.

Species

P. aurantia
- Pink or red flowers. Dark green leaves.
- Very attractive, not invasive.

P. cinnabarina
- Red flowers. Green leaves.
- Adaptable, showy, can damage walls or fences it grows on.

P. herbertiana
- Red-yellow flowers. Dark green or green lobed leaves.
- Frost hardy, tolerates some shade.

PATERSONIA ✤ Iridaceae

At a glance

NUMBER OF SPECIES 20; most endemic to south WA.
NATURAL HABITAT Grassland, woodland and open forest
FLOWERING Three-petalled iris-like flowers, usually in spring and summer.
HABIT Upright grassy clumps.
GROWTH RATE Moderate to fast.
HARDINESS Medium.
LIFESPAN Short.

Culture

- Needs moist soil and filtered sunlight.
- Few pests or diseases.
- Propagate readily from seed.

Species

P. longifolia
- 0.5 x 0.6 m. Mauve flowers in spring, more tolerant of wet soil than others.

P. occidentalis
- 0.5 x 0.6 m. Purple or white flowers in October–November.

P. sericea
- 0.4 x 0.3 m. Blue-purple flowers in spring–summer.

P. xanthina
- 0.4 x 0.4. The only yellow-flowering *Patersonia*.

PELARGONIUM ✤ Geraniaceae

At a glance

NUMBER OF SPECIES 250; 6 endemic to Australia.
NATURAL HABITAT Varies.
FLOWERING White to deep pink, often with darker veins.
HABIT Annual or perennial low shrubs or herbs.
FOLIAGE Often aromatic. Leaf shape varies with species.
GROWTH RATE Fast.

HARDINESS Usually hardy.
LIFESPAN Short.

Culture

- Damp, well-drained soils. Some species tolerate dryness once established.
- Cut back plants after flowering to prolong life.
- Propagate from seeds or cuttings.

Species

P. asperum

- Up to 1 m. Aromatic hairy shrub with palmate-shaped, dissected leaves. Flowers pink with purple markings from spring to mid-summer.

P. australe

- Up to 0.60 x to 0.70 m. Clump-forming, soft, hairy perennial herb. Round, lobed velvety leaves. Pink or white flowers with purple markings. May be herbaceous in summer.

P. inodorum

- Up to 0.35 x to 0.70 m. Annual or short-lived sprawling perennial herb. Light green, round, lobed leaves. Deep pink flowers, with dark veins in clusters, from mid-spring to mid-autumn.

P. rodneyanum

- Up to 0.30 x to 0.50 m. Perennial herb with tuberous rootstock from which leaves arise in a loose rosette. Tiny deep pink flowers with dark veins in clusters in late spring to late summer.

PERSICARIA ❧ Polygonaceae

At a glance

NUMBER OF SPECIES 150; 15 endemic to Australia.
NATURAL HABITAT Permanently or seasonally wet sites.
FLOWERING Spikes of many small flowers occur on the ends of branches.
HABIT Annual or perennial herbs.
FOLIAGE Lanceolate leaves variable in size according to species.
GROWTH RATE Fast.

PERSICARIA SPECIES	SIZE	COMMENTS
P. attenuata syn. *Polygonum attenuata*	60–100 cm	Thick prostrate herb that grows along waterways. White flowers in late autumn to early summer.
P. decipiens syn. *Polygonum minimus*	60–100 cm	Prostrate hairy herb, semi-aquatic to aquatic, 15 cm lance-shaped leaves with dark brown-purple blotches. Small pink flowers in narrow 50 mm spikes throughout the year.
P. hydropiper syn. *Polygonum hydropiper*	60–100 cm	Upright, annual smooth herb grows in shallow waters and swamps in woodland areas. Small green-white flowers on pendulous spikes in summer. Leaves have a peppery taste. Stems used as food by Aborigines.
P. lapathifolia syn. *P. lapathifolia*	50–150 cm	Erect annual plant with large 20 cm leaves that often have a brown blotch in the centre. Thick dense spikes of pink flowers throughout the year.
P. praetermissa syn. *Polygonum strigosum*	Variable	Creeping, prostrate, slender perennial herb with lance-shaped leaves, lobed at the base and with hairy mid-ribs. Pink flowers appear in the leaf axils in short spikes from summer to autumn.
P. prostrata syn. *Polygonum prostrata*	Up to 1 m	Prostrate, matt-forming, perennial herb, with 55 mm-long smooth leaves with hairy stalks. Green flowers on dense, oval spikes from mid-spring to mid-winter.

HARDINESS Medium.
LIFESPAN Short.

Culture

- Prefers damp areas.
- Propagation by seed or division.

PERSOONIA Geebungs
Proteaceae

At a glance

NUMBER OF SPECIES Over 60, only one not occuring in Australia.
NATURAL HABITAT Variable (heaths, wet and dry forests).
FLOWERING Yellow with four petals.
HABIT Groundcovers to medium-size shrubs.
FOLIAGE Often attractive.
GROWTH RATE Medium to fast.
HARDINESS Hardy.
LIFESPAN Medium.

Culture

- Hardy in well-drained position.
- Needs full sun or only light shade.
- Propagation is difficult, best by cuttings with hormone powder.
- Root cuttings are successful with some species.

Species

P. elliptica

- Up to 6 x 5 m. Bright yellow
- Close-grained hard bark, elliptical leaves, rare plant.

P. longifolia

- 1–5 x 1 m. Yellow flowers.
- Rough dark brown bark peels to become red-bronze underneath.

P. pinifolia

- 3 x 3 m. Bright yellow flowers.
- Most commonly grown variety.

PETROPHILE Proteaceae

At a glance

NUMBER OF SPECIES About 40; all endemic to Australia.
NATURAL HABITAT Open sclerophyll woodland, mainly south-western WA.
FLOWERING Pink, cream or yellow flower clusters followed by woody cone-shaped fruits.
HABIT Small- to medium-size bushes.
FOLIAGE Heavily divided leaves.
GROWTH RATE Medium.

PETROPHILE SPECIES	SIZE	FLOWER	COMMENTS
P. biloba	1.5 x 1 m	Pink and grey	Grey leaves, prune after flowering.
P. divaricata	1–2 x 1 m	Bright yellow	Full to filtered sun; well drained, moist sand–gravel soils
P. diversifolia	1–3 x 2 m	Cream-pink	Best in full sun.
P. ericifolia	1 x 1 m	Yellow	Needs full sun, is prickly, flowers heavily.
P. linearis	0.5 x 0.3 m	Pink and woolly	Grey, good in a container, a particularly hardy species.
P. media	Up to 0.8 m tall	Yellow	Very attractive but variable.
P. pulchella	2.5 x 2 m	Cream	Relatively easy to grow.
P. seminuda	1.2 x 1 m	Yellow	Bright green foliage.
P. serruriae	1–3 x 2 m	Cream to yellow	Frost hardy, good in a container, quite prickly.
P. sessilis	1–2 x 1 m	Yellow and white	Excellent container plant, needs reasonable drainage.
P. squamata	1.5 x 1 m	Yellow	Very adaptable.

HARDINESS Species from WA difficult to grow in the eastern states.
LIFESPAN Medium.

Culture

- Full or filtered sun (not heavy shade).
- Good drainage.
- Propagate from seed, germination can be irregular.

PHALERIA ❧ Thymelaeaceae

At a glance

NUMBER OF SPECIES About 20; 5–6 species in Australia.
NATURAL HABITAT Rainforests in warm districts.
FLOWERING Highly scented white flowers in small clusters.
HABIT Open shrub.
HARDINESS Delicate to full sun.
FOLIAGE Deep green thick-textured leaves.
GROWTH RATE Medium growth.
LIFESPAN Medium.
COMMENTS After long dry periods, flowers will virtually explode from the tree after the first rains.

Culture

- Semi-shaded position.
- Protect from strong dry winds.
- Keep moist in dry periods.
- Propagation by fresh seed.

Species

P. chermsideana

- Up to 4 m tall in the garden. White and pink flowers in leaf axils. Good for full sun and part shade. From NSW and Qld.

P. clerodendron

- 3–5 m tall in the garden. Flowers from spring to autumn especially after rain showers. Flowers are borne directly on the trunk. Large red attractive fruits. From northern Qld.

PHEBALIUM ❧ Rutaceae

At a glance

NUMBER OF SPECIES About 45; all endemic to Australia except 1 from New Zealand.
NATURAL HABITAT Open woodlands.
FLOWERING White, yellow or pink, fluffy appearance, occurs in spring.
HABIT Small to large shrubs.
FOLIAGE Undivided leaves.
GROWTH RATE Can be fast.
HARDINESS Some difficult to grow in cultivation.
LIFESPAN Medium.

Culture

- Most prefer good drainage, some shade and a thick organic mulch.
- Some tolerate wet soils.
- Propagate by cuttings. Difficult-to-grow varieties can be grafted onto hardier species.

The difference between Phebalium and Eriostemon

- In *Eriostemon* the flower petals do not overlap in the bud.
- In *Phebalium* the flower petals do overlap in the bud.

PHILOTHECA ❧ *See also Eriostemon*

PIMELEA ❧ Thymelaceae

At a glance

NUMBER OF SPECIES About 80; mainly from Australia, some from New Zealand.
NATURAL HABITAT Varies.
FLOWERING White, pink, yellow or red. Most flower for long periods.
HABIT Generally small- to medium-size woody shrubs, some are annuals.
FOLIAGE Simple, undivided leaves.
GROWTH RATE Can be fast.

PHEBALIUM SPECIES	HEIGHT	FLOWERS	LEAVES
P. ambiens (now known as *Leionema ambiens*)	Up to 2.5 m	White	Broad, smooth margins
P. bilobum	1 m	Yellow	Long, narrow, curving upwards
P. carruthersii	1 m	Yellow or red	Triangular
P. coxii	2 m	White	Narrow elliptical, dark green
P. dentatum	2 m	Pale yellow	Narrow, toothed
P. diosmeum	1.5 m	Yellow	Long, narrow
P. elatius spp. *beckleri*	2 m	White	Glossy
P. glandulosum	1 m	Cream-yellow	Wedge-shaped
P. lamprophylum	2 m	White	Elliptical, 1 cm long
P. microphyllum		Pale yellow	Small, narrow
P. nottii	To 1 m	Rich pink	Small, narrow
P. obcordatum	1 m	Cream	Broad, oval-shaped
P. phylicifolium (now known as *Leionema dentatum*)	1 m	Cream	Narrow oblong
P. ralstonii	To 0.6 m	Pink and green	Elongated oval shape
P. squamulosum	1–3 m	Yellow	Lanceolate

HARDINESS Variable, some are difficult to grow, others easy.
LIFESPAN Variable, often short- to medium-lived.

Culture

- Vary in cultural requirements.
- Propagated mostly by cuttings.

Species

See table on next page.

PITTOSPORUM ❧ Pittosporaceae

At a glance

NUMBER OF SPECIES About 150; 9 endemic to Australia.
NATURAL HABITAT Occur naturally in both deserts and rainforests.
FLOWERING Sometimes scented.
HABIT Trees or large shrubs.
FOLIAGE Glossy undivided leaves.
GROWTH RATE Can be spasmodic.
HARDINESS Generally very hardy once established.
LIFESPAN Medium- to long-lived.

Culture

- Scale, aphis, and sooty mould can be a problem.
- Propagate from seed or cuttings.
- Cuttings should be taken as terminal buds swell for a flush of growth (before they burst), irrespective of time of year. Bottom heat and hormone treatments are essential for cuttings. Cuttings taken this way root quickly; cuttings taken at other times can take up to 12 months to form roots.

Species

See table on next page.

PIMELIA SPECIES	SIZE	COMMENTS
P. ammocharis	1.5 x 0.7 m	Yellow flowers, requires dry soil, tolerates heavy clays, prefers a lime soil, very hardy.
P. angustifolia	to 0.8 m tall	Variable habit, cream or yellow flowers.
P. argentea	to 1.5 m tall	Cream flowers, grey foliage.
P. brachyphylla	0.3 x 0.2 m	White flowers, needs dry soil, hardy.
P. brevifolia	0.6 x 0.3 m	White flowers, prefers well-drained soil.
P. clavata	to 6 m tall	Cream flowers, prefers sandy soil, tolerates some waterlogging.
P. concreta	0.5 x 0.3 m	White flowers.
P. cornucopiae	0.5 x 0.3 m	White autumn flowers.
P. ferruginea	0.5–1 x 1.5 m	Oval glossy green leaves, heavy pink flowering in spring, frost hardy, requires moist soil.
P. flava	2 x 1 m	Yellow flowers.
P. floribunda	0.8 x 0.3 m	White, scented flowers, best on well-drained lime soils.
P. forrestiana	1 x 1.5 m	Yellow flowers.
P. hispida	1.5 x 0.5 m	Pink to cream flowers, prefers sandy soils.
P. imbricata	1 x 0.7 m	White flowers.
P. lanata	2.5 x 1. 5 m	Pink to white flowers over warm season.
P. lehmanniana	1 x 0.5 m	Cream or white flowers, prefers sandy soil.
P. linifolia	0.6 x 0.3 m	Grey-green foliage, white flowers.
P. longiflora	1 x 0.5 m	White flowers.
P. microcephala	2 x 2 m	Yellow flowers.
P. nervosa	0.6 x 0.3 m	White flowers.
P. rosea	0.5 x 1 m	More drought tolerant than *P. ferruginea*, pink or white flowers in spring.
P. spectabilis	1 x 0.5 m	White to pink flowers.
P. suaveolens	1 x 0.6 m	Yellow flowers.
P. sulphurea	1 x 0.4 m	Yellow flowers.
P. villifera	1 x 0.7 m	Grey foliage, white flowers.

PLECTRANTHUS ❧ Lamiaceae

At a glance

NUMBER OF SPECIES 250; 22 endemic to Australia.

NATURAL HABITAT Subtropical to tropical, warm temperate.

FLOWERING Small two-lipped flowers distinctive of the Lamiaceae family, usually mauve, purple, blue or white.

HABIT Erect or prostrate herbs, sub-shrubs and shrubs.

FOLIAGE Slightly aromatic. Varies with species, some have thick almost succulent leaves.

GROWTH RATE Fast.

HARDINESS Medium once established.

LIFESPAN Medium.

PITTOSPORUM SPECIES	COMMENTS
P. bicolor	Shrub or tree 3–10 m tall, grey bark, yellow flowers with red markings, from south-eastern Australia.
P. bracteolatum	Tree to 7 m tall, dark green foliage, yellow-green flowers, from Norfolk Island.
P. ferrugineum (kamut)	Tree or shrub 10–20 m tall, grey bark, leathery leaves, yellow to cream flowers, green to orange fruits, from coastal Qld.
P. moluccanum	Up to 4 m tall, glossy green leaves, cream flowers, orange fruits, from northern Australia.
P. phillyreoides	Weeping upright tree up to 6 m tall, open foliage, scented cream flowers in summer, orange fruits in autumn; drought tolerant.
P. revolutum (wild yellow jasmine)	Shrub or tree up to 6 m tall, yellow flowers, green fruits change colour to brown, occurs from NT to Vic.
P. rhombifolium	Tree 15–25 m tall, cream flowers in summer and orange fruits from autumn to winter, roots must not dry out.
P. rubiginosum (rusty pittosporum)	Tree up to 5 m tall, pale green foliage, yellow to cream flowers.
P. undulatum (native daphne)	Bushy tree up to 10 m tall with dense rich green foliage, scented cream flowers in spring and orange berries, very hardy, has become a weed in some areas.
P. venulosum	Tree to 12 m tall. White or yellow flowers, from coastal Queensland.

PLECTRANTHUS SPECIES	SIZE	COMMENTS
P. alloplectus	To 70 cm	Not aromatic, yellow-whitish hair covered branches. Narrowly ovate leaves with hairy undersides. Violet-purple flowers, mid-summer to mid-autumn. Not a common plant. NSW, NT, Qld.
P. argentatus	To 1 m	Slightly aromatic shrub, broadly round leaves narrower at the tip. Silver-green woolly leaves, bluish-white flowers early summer to late autumn.
P. congestus	To 2 m	Annual or perennial, herb or shrub, Flowers blue, purple, pink, mid-autumn to mid-winter. Grows along watercourses in northern WA.
P. graveolens	To 1 m	Prostrate to partially erect shrub with unpleasant aroma. Leaves are broad elliptical to ovate. Blue-violet flowers year-round. NSW, Qld.
P. intraterraneous	To 1.5 m	Perennial herb or shrub. Flowers blue, purple, mid-summer to autumn and again in spring. Grows on poor rocky sites, hillsides and gorges of WA.
P. parviflorus	To 70 cm	Non-aromatic herbaceous shrub with hairy branches. Round to oblong slightly hairy leaves. Violet/blue flowers year-round. NSW, Qld, Vic.
P. sauveolens	To 80 cm	Sub-shrub with either prostrate or erect branches. Hairy ovate leaves. Blue-violet flowers year-round. NSW, NT, Qld.

Culture

- Most soils are suitable.
- Frost-free position.
- Shade to part sun or under protection of trees.
- Propagate from cuttings. Plants tend to take root at the nodes.

PLEIOGYNIUM Anacardiaceae

At a glance

NUMBER OF SPECIES 2; 1 endemic to Australia.

NATURAL HABITAT Rainforest fringes throughout Qld.

FLOWERING August to October with fruit ripening from February onwards.
HABIT Large trees.
HARDINESS Very hardy to a range of climates. Tolerate mild frosts.
FOLIAGE Attractive pinnate foliage with velvety reddish new growth.
GROWTH RATE Normally deciduous in winter.
LIFESPAN Long-lived.
COMMENTS Large purple-black edible fruit. Popular street tree and bush tucker tree.

Culture

- Adaptable to a wide range of soil types, but good drainage important.
- Handles dry periods very well.
- Full sun.
- Seeds germinate erratically.

Species

P. timoriense (Burdekin plum)

- Rounded tree up to 25 m tall but less in domestic gardens. May develop a buttress root system.

POA Poaceae

At a glance

NUMBER OF SPECIES 200; 34 endemic to Australia.
NATURAL HABITAT Grassland, woodlands, open dry or damp forest.
FLOWERING Solitary spikes comprising several florets.
HABIT Loose or dense tussocks.
FOLIAGE Grass-like.
HARDINESS Hardy.
GROWTH RATE Fast.
LIFESPAN Varies.

Culture

- Moist to slightly dry soils.
- Shade or sun depending on species.
- Propagate by seed.

POA SPECIES	SIZE	COMMENTS
P. annua	Up to 30 cm	Annual with light green smooth leaves, flowers in winter–spring.
P. clelandii	Up to 25 cm	Creeping rhizomes, dense or loose tussocks. Flowering stems up to 75 cm; purple-, green- or straw-coloured spikes from spring to mid-summer.
P. ensiformis	Up to 75 cm	Flat, narrow, dark green leaves with purple sheaths. Vigorous. Flowers from mid-spring to mid-autumn. Ideal in erosion control.
P. labillardieri	Up to 80 cm	Variable vigorous grass forming large dense tussocks of greyish-green to blue-green coarse leaves. Tall flowering stems up to 1.2 m tall from mid-spring to mid-autumn.
P. morrisii	Up to 30 cm	Dense tufts of soft, angular greyish-green leaves. Flowering mid-spring to mid-summer.
P. poiformis var. *poiformis*	Up to 1 x 1 m	Rigid, erect, dense tufts of bluish leaves. Pale green to straw-coloured spikes, same height as the grass, in spring to mid-summer.
P. sieberiana var. *hirtella*	Up to 30 x 90 cm	Similar to above but leaves hairy.
P. sieberiana var. *sieberiana*	Up to 30 x 90 cm	Tufts of greyish-green smooth leaves; green-, purple- or straw-coloured spikes in pairs.
P. tenera	5–20 cm	Trailing (stolons), bright green soft leaves, pale green spikes from mid-spring to mid-summer.

POLYSCIAS ❧ Aralaceae

At a glance

NUMBER OF SPECIES 125; 9 or 10 endemic to Australia.
NATURAL HABITAT Tropical and subtropical, and damp, wet, valley sclerophyll forests. ACT, Qld, NSW, Vic.
FLOWERING Clusters of flowers, colour varies with species, followed by purple fruit.
HABIT Variable, small to large trees or shrubs.
FOLIAGE Varies according to species and geographical regions, but usually 2 pinnate.
GROWTH RATE Can be very fast.
HARDINESS Medium in suitable conditions.
LIFESPAN Medium- to long-lived.

Culture

- Moist, well-drained soil.
- Propagation from roots or by cuttings.

Species

P. elegans (elderberry panax)
- Up to 25 m. Palm-like tall tree with large 1 m leaves. Insignificant flowers followed by attractive purple fruit. NSW, Qld and PNG.

P. murrayi (pencil cedar)
- Up to 15 m. Open, slender tree with large young leaves up to 1 m long. Insignificant flowers followed by small purple fruit. NSW, Qld.

P. sambucifolius (celery wood)
- 1–6 x 1–3 m
- Variable shrub or small tree, leaves dark green with paler undersides. Clusters of small yellow-green flowers from mid-spring to mid-summer followed by blue berries. Soil needs to be well composted. Shady position. Attractive foliage, suited as an indoor plant. NSW, Qld, Vic. ACT.

POMADERRIS ❧ Rhamnaceae

At a glance

NUMBER OF SPECIES About 40; most endemic to Australia, some in New Zealand.
NATURAL HABITAT Widespread throughout southern Australia.
FLOWERING Yellow or cream flowers clustered into large heads, often insignificant in appearance.
HABIT Small to large woody shrubs.
FOLIAGE Undivided leaves, often soft appearance.
GROWTH RATE Medium to fast.
HARDINESS Hardy.
LIFESPAN Medium.

Culture

- Prefer good drainage.
- Full or filtered sun.
- Propagate by cuttings.

PRATIA ❧ Lobeliaceae

At a glance

NUMBER OF SPECIES 20; occurring in Australia, NZ, Africa, South America and Asia.
NATURAL HABITAT Grasslands and swamps.
FLOWERING Tiny star flowers in spring and summer.
HABIT Ground-hugging, creeping plants.
FOLIAGE Small, dark green, suckering.
GROWTH RATE Fast.
HARDINESS Moderate to hardy in suitable conditions.
LIFESPAN Short.
COMMENTS Some species can be invasive in wet areas.

Culture

- Must have moist soil.
- Some are frost tolerant.
- Propagates easily by division.

POMADERRIS SPECIES	SIZE	COMMENTS
P. aspera	3 x 1.5 m	Hardy in shaded sites, insignificant flowers.
P. bilobum	1–2 x 2 m	White flowers, good in heavy shade.
P. elachophylla	2–3 x 2 m	Tiny flower clusters, attractive fine foliage, prefers shaded site.
P. ferruginea	3 x 1 m	Large showy yellow flower heads, prefers full sun, attractive foliage.
P. grandis	1–2 x 1 m	Small heads of white silky flowers.
P. lanigera	2 x 2 m	Large golden flowers, attractive velvet foliage.
P. ligustrina	2 x 2 m	Pale flowers but attractive foliage.
P. multiflora	3–5 m tall	Yellow flowers, attractive shade plant.
P. phylicifolium	0.5–1 x 1 m	White flowers, hardy in dry, shady site.
P. pilifera	3 x 2 m	Large yellow flowers, prefers full sun.
P. squamulosum	0.3–3 x 2 m	Cream or yellow, compact, attractive shrub.
P. velutina	1–2 x 2 m	Golden flowers, attractive greyish foliage.

Species

P. pendunculata

- Blue-white flowers in spring

P. purpurescens

- Suckering, purple-mauve flowers in Feb-April.

PROSTANTHERA ❧ Mint Bush ❧
Lamiaceae

At a glance

NUMBER OF SPECIES About 65; all endemic to Australia.

NATURAL HABITAT Widespread except in the tropical north; normally under canopy of trees or larger shrubs.

FLOWERING Bell-shaped with a prominent lip.

HABIT Small or medium shrubs.

FOLIAGE Generally soft, undivided scented leaves.

GROWTH RATE Generally fast.

HARDINESS Medium.

LIFESPAN Short to medium.

Culture

- Provide some protection from full sun and wind.
- Keep soil moist during dry months for best results.
- Most are drought tolerant to some degree.
- Most are at least tolerant of light frosts.
- Over-watering can shorten lifespan, otherwise most are long-lived.
- Highly susceptible to cinnamon fungus. In affected areas it may be grafted onto *Westringia* rootstock to resist the effect of this root rot disease.
- Generally propagate by softwood cuttings.

PROSTANTHERAS WITH GREYISH FOLIAGE

P. cruciflora, nivea var. *induta, staurophylla, teretifolia.*

PROSTANTHERAS SUITED TO HEAVILY SHADED AREAS

P. prunelloides, most others will grow in shade but may not develop such dense foliage in heavy shade.

PROSTANTHERAS WITH PARTICULARLY STRONGLY SCENTED FOLIAGE

P. cineolifera, cuneata, incisa, melissifolia, odoratissima, ovalifolia, sieberi.

PROSTANTHERA SPECIES	SIZE	TOLERATES DROUGHT	TOLERATES DIRECT SUN	FLOWERS
P. aspalathoides	0.3 x 1 m	Yes	Part	Red or yellow
P. baxteri	0.7 x 0.7 m	Part	No	Pale mauve
P. behriana	2 x 1.5 m	Part	Part	White-purple
P. calycina	0.5 x 0.5 m	No	No	Red
P. chlorantha	0.6 x 0.6 m	Yes	No	Greenish
P. cineolifera	2 x 1 m	Part	Part	Mauve
P. cruciflora	1 x 0.5 m	Yes	Part	Mauve
P. cryptandroides	0.8 x 0.8 m	Yes	Part	Mauve
P. cuneata	0.5 x 1 m	Part	No	White-mauve
P. denticulata	0.3 x 2 m	Yes	No	Purple
P. euphrasioides	1 x 0.7 m	No	No	Mauve
P. eurybioides	1 x 0.5 m	*	*	Mauve
P. grylloana	0.8 x 0.5 m	Yes	*	Red
P. hirtula	2 x 1 m	No	No	Mauve
P. incana	1.5 x 1–2 m	Yes	Yes	White or mauve
P. incisa	1.5 x 1.5 m	Yes	Part	Violet
P. lasianthos	2–10 x 1.5 m	No	No	Large white
P. leichhardtii	1.5 x 0.8 m	*	*	Mauve
P. linearis	1.5 x 1 m	Yes	No	Violet
P. magnifica	1.5 x 1 m	*	*	Pale mauve
P. marifolia	0.6 x 0.4 m	*	*	Mauve-blue
P. megacalyx	1 x 0.5 m	No	No	Light purple
P. melissifolia	3 x 3 m	Part	No	Pink or purple
P. nivea	3 x 2 m	No	No	White or blue
P. odoratissima	1 x 1.5 m	*	*	Purple
P. ovalifolia	3 x 3 m	Part	No	Purple
P. phylicifolia	1.5 x 1.5 m	*	*	White or violet
P. prunelloides	2 x 1 m	No	No	Blue
P. rhombea	1 x 0.5 m	Part	Part	*
P. rotundifolia	2 x 1.5 m	Part	No	Purple
P. rugosa	1 x 1 m	*	*	Violet
P. saxicola montana	0.3 x 1 m	Part	No	White
P. scutellarioides	1.5 x 1 m	No	No	Purple
P. sieberi	1.5 x 1.5 m	Part	No	Purple

* Insufficient data

PROSTANTHERA SPECIES	SIZE	TOLERATES DROUGHT	TOLERATES DIRECT SUN	FLOWERS
P. spinosa (very susceptible to root rot)	0.6 x 1 m	Yes	Part	Blue or white
P. staurophylla	1 x 1 m	*	*	Blue-violet
P. striatiflora	1.5 x 1.5 m	Yes	Part	White
P. stricta	1.3 x 1 m	Yes	Yes	Deep violet
P. teretifolia	2 x 2 m	*	*	Blue
P. violaceae	1 x 1 m	*	*	Purple
P. walteri	1 x 1 m	Yes	Yes	Green

PTILOTUS ✲ Amaranthaceae

At a glance

NUMBER OF SPECIES About 100; all but one endemic to Australia.
NATURAL HABITAT Mainly from semi-arid north.
FLOWERING Dense, brightly coloured conical heads in winter to spring.
HABIT Low-growing herbs.
FOLIAGE Thick leaves, often stemless.
GROWTH RATE Medium to fast.
HARDINESS Not reliable in cultivation; not suited to humid or coastal conditions.
LIFESPAN Short.
COMMENTS Some species have potential as cut flowers.

Culture

- Full sun.
- Excellent drainage.
- Propagation is normally by seed but low germination rates have restricted introduction of the genus into culture.

Species

P. drummondii

- Herb up to 0.3 m
- Fluffy pink cylindrical flowers; must have perfect drainage.

P. manglesii

- Low herb with creeping flower stems
- Flowers pink and white cylinders up to 5 cm long and 3 cm wide; grows as pot plant or rockery plant on well-drained site in temperate climate.

PULTENAEA ✲ Bush Pea ✲ Fabaceae

At a glance

NUMBER OF SPECIES Over 100; all from Australia.
NATURAL HABITAT Mainly temperate regions, sclerophyll woodlands and rainforests.
FLOWERING Normally red and yellow pea flowers in large numbers.
HABIT Small bushes and ground covers.
FOLIAGE Variable, often medium to light green.
HARDINESS Moderately hardy in well-drained soils.
GROWTH RATE Medium to fast.
LIFESPAN Short to medium.

Culture

- Relatively hardy and adaptable to most soils, provided there is good drainage and some leaf litter covering the ground surface.
- Most prefer light filtered sunlight, some withstand full sun.
- Generally frost hardy.
- Flowering normally extends over a 1–2 month period.

PULTANAEA SPECIES	SIZE	FOLIAGE	FLOWERS
P. cunninghamii	2–3 x 2–3 m	Drooping, grey-green	Yellow
P. daphnoides	1–1.5 x 2 m	Pale underneath	Red and yellow
P. flexilis	3–4 x 2 m	Drooping, dark under	Yellow
P. gunnii	1 x 1 m	Hairy branches	Deep yellow
P. humilis	0.4 x 1 m	Woolly	Orange and apricot
P. microphylla	0.1–1 x 1 m	Small narrow leaves	Yellow and red
P. pendunculata	0.1 x 2 m	Green	Orange, yellow and red
P. polifolia mucronata	0.3 x 1 m	Cascading	Orange-yellow
P. scabra	1–1.5 x 1 m	Hairy underneath	Yellow-brown
P. villosa	1–2 x 1 m	Soft	Yellow

- Some propagate by cuttings, others by hot-water-treated seed.

RANDIA ❧ Native Gardenia ❧ Rubiaceae

At a glance

NUMBER OF SPECIES 9 species in Australia.
NATURAL HABITAT Rainforest margins along watercourses.
FLOWERING Fragrant white flowers.
HABIT Tall bushy shrubs, attractive juvenile foliage.
HARDINESS Generally hardy in warm conditions.
FOLIAGE Dark shiny leaves.
GROWTH RATE Some fairly slow, others moderately fast.
LIFESPAN Medium- to long-lived.
COMMENTS Several species (e.g. *R. chartacea* and *R. fitzalanii*) make interesting indoor plants.

Culture

- Shaded conditions required in early stages.
- Will tolerate full sun although leaves may go slightly yellow.
- Well-drained soil with an abundance of water.
- Scale can occasionally be a problem on some species.
- Propagation by fresh seed or by cuttings.

Species

R. benthamiana
- Small tree up to 6 m. Qld and NSW.

R. chartacea
- 2–3 m shrub, suitable in most situations. Good for boggy soils and rocky soils.

R. fitzalanii
- 3–6 m in cultivation, up to 12 m in natural habitat. Edible fruit developed in autumn. Qld. Frost sensitive.

R. hirta
- 5 m straggly shrub with large 5 cm flowers. A good shrub for gardens.

REGELIA ❧ Myrtaceae

At a glance

NUMBER OF SPECIES 6; all endemic to Australia, mainly south WA.
NATURAL HABITAT WA.
FLOWERING Similar to *Melaleuca*, most flower for long periods.
HABIT Woody shrubs.
FOLIAGE Leaves are small and opposite.

GROWTH RATE Can be fast.
HARDINESS Medium.
LIFESPAN Medium.

Culture

- Needs a well-drained soil.
- Tolerates very dry soils.
- Propagate by seed or cuttings.

Species

R. ciliata

- 1.3 x 2 m. Mauve flowers, all year.
- Hairy oval-shaped leaves.

R. inops

- 1 x 1 m. Mauve flowers, spring-summer.
- Small oval-shaped leaves.

R. megacephala

- 2–4 x 3 m. Red-purple flowers, summer.
- Small ovate leaves.

R. velutina

- 3 x 1.5 m. Red flowers, spring–summer.
- Greyish elliptical leaves.

RESTIO ✤ Restioniaceae

At a glance

NUMBER OF SPECIES 4 currently; some previous species in this genus have undergone name changes.
Restio complanatus = *Eurychorda complanata*
Restio fastigiatus = *Saropsis fastigiata*
Restio pallens = *Baloskion pallens*
Restio stenocoleus = *Baloskion stenocoleum*
Restio tenuiculmis = *Baloskion tenuiculme*
Restio tetraphyllus = *Baloskion tetraphyllum*
Restio tetraphyllus spp. *meiostachyus* = *Baloskion tetraphyllum* spp. *meiostachyus*
NATURAL HABITAT Varies from damp sandy heathlands to sub-alpine areas.
FLOWERING Usually brown, small, insignificant.
HABIT Rush-like perennial.
FOLIAGE Rush-like varying in colour.
GROWTH RATE Medium in damp conditions.
HARDINESS Hardy in suitable moist conditions.
LIFESPAN Medium.

Culture

- Damp sandy or peaty soils, depending on species.
- Propagate by division.
- Sun to part-shade.
- Drought tender.

Species

R. australis

- 1 x 1 m. Erect cylindrical unbranched, straight slightly glaucous stems; rush-like leaves are finely divided. Sub-alpine plant, peaty gravelly soils and moist conditions in full sun. Drought tender but frost-resistant native of NSW.

R. dimorphus

- 1 x 0.50 m. Erect slender un-branching stems and rush-like leaves with sheathing bases. Brown flowers. Native of NSW.

R. fimbriatus

- 0.80 x 0.50 m. Erect un-branching stems, rush-like leaves with sheathing bases. Flowers brown. Moist, well-drained soils and open sunny position. Native of WA.

R. gracilis

- 0.50 x 0.50 m. Narrow rush-like leaves closely sheathing at the base. Flowers occur in small spikelets 1.6 cm long. Wet sandy soils. All states except WA.

RHAGODIA ✤ Chenopodiaceae

At a glance

NUMBER OF SPECIES 11; all endemic to Australia.
NATURAL HABITAT Coastal and dryland areas.
FLOWERING Usually insignificant flowers.
HABIT Prostrate spreading shrubs or small to medium bushes.
FOLIAGE Silver-blue or dark green leaves.
GROWTH RATE Fast.
HARDINESS Very hardy; some species resistant to salt spray.
LIFESPAN Short to medium.

Culture

- Full sun and good drainage.
- Drought tolerant.
- Tolerant of saline conditions.
- Propagate by cuttings.

Species

R. baccata **(coastal saltbush)**

- 1.5 x 1.5 m; native to coastal sand dunes throughout southern Australia from WA to Tas. Red berries most of the year, hardy on coast or inland.

R. spinescens

- 0.3 x 0.6 m, hardy shrub, red or yellow berries in summer.

RHODANTHE ❧ Paper Daisies ❧

Asteraceae

(formerly this genus was called *Helipterum*)

At a glance

NUMBER OF SPECIES About 100, approximately 60 in Australia.
NATURAL HABITAT Inland areas of all states.
FLOWERING Can occur for extended periods over warm months, flowers similar to Helichrysums.
HARDINESS Most moderately hardy to hardy.
HABIT Small herbaceous clumping plants with flowers on tall stems emerging above the main clump. Some perennial, some annuals.
FOLIAGE Undivided, generally elongated and hairy to a varying degree.
GROWTH RATE Fast.
LIFESPAN Short-lived, treat as annuals.

Culture

- Good drainage.

RHODANTHE SPECIES	SIZE	COMMENTS
R. albicans	0.2 x 0.3 m	Several forms available, tall thin flower stems, cream flowers in summer.
R. anthemoides (syn. *Helipterum anthemioides*)	0.5 x 0.3 m	White flowers in summer.
R. chlorocephalum	0.3 x 0.3 m	White flowers late winter to spring.
R. corymbiflorum	0.3 x 0.2 m	White flowers winter to spring.
R. craspedioides	0.3 x 0.4 m	Yellow flowers.
R. fitzgibbonii	0.3 x 0.3 m	White flowers with rust-coloured bracts.
R. floribundum	0.4 x 0.6 m	White flowers profuse in spring.
R. jessenii	0.1 x 0.1 m	Yellow 1 cm-diameter flowers.
R. manglesii (syn. *Helipterum manglesii*)	0.4 x 0.2 m	Grey-green leaves, pink or white spring flowers.
R. polygalifolium	Up to 0.4 m	Yellow flowers up to 3 cm diameter.
R. roseum	0.5 x 0.3 m	Pink or white flowers with yellow or black centres in late winter through to spring. This is the most popular variety.
R. stipitatum	0.4 x 0.3 m	Woolly greyish foliage, yellow flowers.
R. stuartianum	0.2 x 0.2 m	White flowers.
R. tenellum	0.3 x 0.3 m	Golden yellow flowers.

- Cutting flowers will extend the flowering season.
- Prune back after flowering.
- Propagate by seed or cuttings.
- Good in baskets or tubs.

RHODODENDERON ❧ Ericaceae

At a glance

NUMBER OF SPECIES 1 (*R. lochiae*), possibly 2 (validity of the second species *R. notiale* is not yet widely accepted by botanists).
NATURAL HABITAT Temperate areas. Grows on cliff faces, in crevices and rocks and sometimes on trees as an epiphyte.
FLOWERING Deep red in spring and summer, dependent on the geographical area.
HABIT Small shrub.
FOLIAGE Glossy green 75 mm-long leaves.
HARDINESS Medium in suitable conditions.
GROWTH RATE Slow.
LIFESPAN Medium- to long-lived.

Culture

- Moist, well-drained soils.
- Shaded position.
- Propagation from seeds or cuttings.

RHODOSPHAERA ❧ Anarcardiaceae

At a glance

NUMBER OF SPECIES 1; *R. rhodanthema* endemic to Australia.
NATURAL HABITAT Dry rainforests from NSW to Qld.
FLOWERING Insignificant flowers.
HABIT Small to medium tree.
HARDINESS Very hardy and adaptable to garden cultivation.
FOLIAGE Dark green pinnate foliage.
GROWTH RATE Fast growing.
LIFESPAN Medium- to long-lived.
COMMENTS Flowers are attractive to birds. Attractive shiny brown fruit are retained on the tree.

Culture

- Full sun.
- Easy-care plant.
- Pruning may encourage bushy habit.
- Propagation — seed coat needs to be broken.

Species

R. rhodanthema (tulip satinwood)

- Flowers from September to October. Bushy tree to 15 m. Excellent street and garden tree for south-eastern Qld.

RICHEA ❧ Epacridaceae

At a glance

NUMBER OF SPECIES 10; 9 from Tas., 1 from alpine areas of Vic and NSW.
NATURAL HABITAT Mainly moist organic soils.
FLOWERING Normally pink on a terminal spike.
HABIT Woody shrubs and small trees; larger varieties look more like a palm than a dicotyledon (which it is).
FOLIAGE Leaves vary from 1 cm to more than 1 m long.
HARDINESS Medium in suitable conditions.
GROWTH RATE Slow to fast growth rates, depending on species and location, have been reported.
LIFESPAN Can be long-lived.

Culture

- Requires fertile moist soil and cool climate.
- Soil should have high organic content and be well mulched.
- Strikes from cuttings with difficulty. Seed propagation also difficult.

Species

R. continentis

- 1 x 1 m. Cream flowers in summer on red stems.

R. dracophylla
- 3 x 2 m. White summer flowers.

R. pandanifolia
- 1–15 m tall. Pink or white summer flowers.

R. scoparia
- 1.5 x 1 m. Interesting foliage, attractive red or pink flower spikes in spring or summer.

RULINGIA ❧ Sterculiaceae

At a glance

NUMBER OF SPECIES 25; 20 endemic to Australia.
NATURAL HABITAT Varies.
FLOWERING White with 5 petals often fading to pink.
HABIT Erect or prostrate sub-shrubs or shrubs.
FOLIAGE Varies according to species.
HARDINESS Most hardy to dry conditions but some species are frost tender.
GROWTH RATE Medium.
LIFESPAN Short to medium.

Culture

- Well-drained soil.
- Open sunny position.
- Easily propagated from semi-hard cuttings or seeds.

SCAEVOLA ❧ Goodeniaceae

At a glance

NUMBER OF SPECIES 70; most occurring in south WA.
NATURAL HABITAT Variable, ranges from coastal areas to semi-arid and cold areas.
FLOWERING Fan-shaped flowers.
HABIT Mostly small herbaceous plants.
FOLIAGE Small, often sparse leaves.
GROWTH RATE Fast.
HARDINESS Variable.
LIFESPAN Short-lived.

Culture

- Full sun.
- Good drainage.
- Propagation by cuttings.

Species

- ***S. enantophylla*** is the only yellow-flowering species.
- ***S.* 'Mauve Clusters'**, prostrate, soft-wooded, to 1 m diameter, blue flowers in spring and summer, propagate by cuttings.

RULINGIA SPECIES	SIZE	COMMENTS
R. densiflora	1 x 1.5 m	Erect branching stems. Pinnate divided leaves with 5 cm leaflets. White flowers in spring. Frost tender. Native to WA.
R. grandiflora	1 x 1.5 m	Erect stems, spreading branches with white, velvet-like bark. Leaves are also white with serrate margins. Dense white flowers in loose heads, flowers in spring. Open sunny position, drought resistant but frost tender. Native to WA.
R. hermannifolia	0.30 x 1.5 m	Mat-forming stiff stems, branches spreading. Leaves are lance-shaped with in-rolled margins. Small terminal heads of white flowers in spring.
R. pannosa	2 x 3 m	Erect stems with spreading branches and soft velvet-like bark. 10 cm heart-shaped leaves with serrate margins, and a rough, woolly underside. Drought and frost resistant. Native to NSW, Qld. Vic.
R. prostrata	2.5 x 2.5 m	Erect and branching stems. The ovate leaves up to 30 cm long have serrate and recurved margins, arranged in spirals. Tolerates most soils. NSW.

SCHEFFLERA ❧ Araliaceae

At a glance

NUMBER OF SPECIES About 150; 2 endemic to Australia, occurring in Qld rainforests.
NATURAL HABITAT Mainly warm, moist rainforests in Qld.
FLOWERING 5 to 7 small petals, flowers clustered on a long stalk.
HABIT Small trees or shrubs.
FOLIAGE Divided leaves soft but palm-like in appearance.
GROWTH RATE Generally fast.
HARDINESS Moderate.
LIFESPAN Medium- to long-lived.

Culture

- Requires moist soil.
- Generally frost tender.
- Suited to pot culture.
- Scale and sooty mould can be a problem.
- Propagate from fresh seed.

Species

***S. actinophylla* (umbrella tree)**

- Commonly grown as an indoor plant, both in Australia and overseas. In the ground it can reach 7 x 4 m if in a warm, moist, well-drained and protected environment. Can be invasive in some areas.

SCHOLTZIA ❧ Myrtaceae

At a glance

NUMBER OF SPECIES 13; endemic to WA.
NATURAL HABITAT Often arid to semi-arid areas.
FLOWERING Similar to *Thryptomene*, large quantities of small flowers, often flowering all year.

SCHOLTZIA SPECIES	SIZE	FLOWERS	COMMENTS
S. capitata	2.5 x 2 m	Light pink	Tolerates full sun and drought periods.
S. chapmanii	0.3 x 1 m	Pink, late spring to mid-summer	Sand, clay, limestone soils on seasonal wetlands.
S. ciliate	Up to 1.5 x to 2 m	White-pink, late winter to early summer	Sand or clay soils.
S. drummondii	Up to 1.5 x up to 1 m	Pinkish white in late autumn–mid-spring	Gravelly sands.
S. involucrate	1 x 1.5 m	White or pink	Flowers all year round.
S. laxiflora	Up to 2 x up to 2 m	Pale pink	Compact heath-like plant.
S. leptantha	Up to 2 x 3 m	White from winter to mid-spring.	Sands and coastal dunes.
S. oligandra	0.5 x 1 m	Pink in spring	Prefers gravel soil.
S. parviflora	1–3 x 2 m	White-pink	Sands and laterite. Will grow in wet conditions.
S. spatulata	0.3–1.5 m x up to 1.5 m	Pinkish-white	Sandy soils on sand plains.
S. teretifolia	Up to 0.5 x 1.5 m	Whitish pink in mid-spring–midsummer	Sands and river flats.
S. uberiflora	2 x 2 m	Pale pink	Sand plains and river flats.
S. umbellifera	0.4 – 2 m tall	Pink, white in late winter to early summer	Grows on limestone.

HABIT Small and medium heath-like shrubs.
FOLIAGE Small and undivided, heath-like.
HARDINESS Hardy in well-drained soils.
GROWTH RATE Fast.
LIFESPAN Short.

Culture

- Most need good drainage and prefer full sun.
- Drought tolerant.
- Propagate from cuttings.
- Respond well to regular pruning and clipping.

SCLERANTHUS ❧ Caryophyllaceae

At a glance

NUMBER OF SPECIES 12; 9 native to Australia.
NATURAL HABITAT Alpine to semi-arid, depending on species.
FLOWERING Small to very small whitish or greenish flowers, 4-5 sepals, petals absent.
HABIT Small clumping or mounding perennial herbs.
FOLIAGE Small and linear to subulate, margins fringed or faintly toothed.
GROWTH RATE Medium.
HARDINESS Moderate in suitable conditions.
LIFESPAN Short to medium.

Culture

- Rarely cultivated except for *S. biflorus*.
- Most need good drainage and prefer full sun, may tolerate some shade.
- Drought tolerant.
- Propagate from cuttings.

Species

S. biflorus

- Moss-like cushion plant, bright green, tiny green flowers, propagate by division or seed, prefers full sun and soil which is always moist but never waterlogged. If patches of a clump die, they should be cut out and the area sprayed with Fongarid.

SENECIO

At a glance

NUMBER OF SPECIES 2000; 50 native to Australia.
NATURAL HABITAT Understorey plants that can tend to be invasive.
FLOWERING Yellow flower heads occur in terminal clusters and have either tubular florets or both tubular and ligulate florets. Flower heads are surrounded by a row of bracts.
HABIT Herbaceous plants.
FOLIAGE Varies according to species.
HARDINESS Hardy.
GROWTH RATE Fast, particularly after fires.
LIFESPAN Annuals or short-lived perennials.

Culture

- Moist soils, some species tolerate wet soils.
- Salt and wind tolerant.

SENNA ❧ Caesalpiniaceae

At a glance

NUMBER OF SPECIES 350; 33 endemic to Australia.
NATURAL HABITAT Tropical and warm temperate regions.
FLOWERING Open yellow, 5 petals, flowers over an extended period.
HABIT Erect, rounded or spreading shrubs.
FOLIAGE Most have attractive pinnate leaves.
HARDINESS Hardy in well-drained soils.
GROWTH RATE Medium to fast.
LIFESPAN Short to medium.

Culture

- Well-drained soil.
- Frost-free area.
- Warm sunny position.
- Light prune after flowering.
- Propagate from scarified seed.

SENECIO SPECIES	HEIGHT	COMMENTS
S. biserratus	0.6–1 m	Erect annual herb with prominently veined, toothed leaves, dense clusters of flower heads with tubular florets, with some narrow green bracts. Flowers in late winter to mid-autumn. NSW, SA, Tas, Vic.
S. glomeratus	0.5–1.2 m	Soft, hairy, erect annual. Lance to ovate lobed leaves to 12 cm long, dense clusters of disks with tubular florets which are surrounded by woolly bracts. Flowers in mid-spring to mid-summer. NSW, SA, Tas, Vic, WA.
S. lautus	Up to 0.5 m	Variable, sprawling or sometimes erect perennial herb or sub-shrub. Tubular and ligulate flower heads in loose clusters. Flowers from spring to autumn. All states.
S. linearifolius	Up to 1.5 m	Erect perennial herb. Dark green, toothed, linear 15 cm leaves. Large flat-topped clusters of tubular and ligulate flower heads. Flowers from mid-spring to mid-summer. NSW, Tas, Vic.
S. macrocarpus	Up to 0.4 m	Erect to straggling perennial herb. Narrow, downy, grey 6 cm leaves. Large, but few flower heads with tubular florets. Flowers from early to mid-spring. SA, Tas, Vic.
S. minimus	Up to 1 m	Erect annual herb. Ridged stems branching at the base or just below the flower heads. Lance-shaped, toothed 9 cm leaves. Many flower heads with tubular florets and narrow green bracts. Flowers from summer to mid-autumn. All states except NT.
S. odoratus	0.6–1.5 m	Erect, perennial sub-shrub. Bluish, coarse, toothed, broadly lance-shaped leaves up to 12 cm. Large clusters of flat-topped flower heads with tubular florets, with 8 bracts. Flowers from mid-spring to mid-summer. SA, Tas, Vic.
S. tenuiflorus	Up to 0.60 m	Biennial or annual herb branching at the base or just below the flower heads. Many rough, lance-shaped leaves, broadening in the middle, with hair, purplish undersides. Small flower heads with tubular florets from mid-spring to mid-summer. All states except NT.
S .velleioides	0.5–1 m	Showy, perennial, soft, branched herb, stem-clasping and heart-shaped leaves, lower leaves are toothed, upper are entire. Clusters of large flower heads with tubular and ligulate florets, from mid-spring to late summer.

SENNA SPECIES	SIZE	COMMENTS
S. aciphylla	1 x 1.5 m	Pinnate dark green leaves, with pointy leaftlets. Flowers in spring. NSW, Qld, Vic.
S. barclayana	0.60 x 1.5 m	Perennial herb or shrub. Flowers appear from mid- to late autumn. North-western WA floodplains.
S. coronilloides	Up to 3 m	Sprawling shrub. Leaves are 5–7cm long with 9–12 leaflets. Qld, NSW.
S. magnifolia	2 x 1–2 m	Leaves pinnate and large up to 30 cm with oval leaflets. Large terminal flowers, beautiful spikes up to 40 cm. Prune after flowering.
S. odorata (syn. *Cassia odorata*)	Up to 2.5 m	Variable prostrate or sprawling shrub. Dark green pinnate leaves with 8–13 pairs of leaflets. Prolific flowers in spring. Tolerates mild frosts. NSW, Qld.
S. pleurocarpa	1–3 m	Spreading shrub. Leaves up to 15 cm long with 5–7 pairs of leaflets. Flowers all year round. Qld, NT, SA, WA.
S. venusta	Up to 2 m	Beautiful spreading shrub with 25 cm-long pinnate leaves, 6–15 pairs of ovate leaflets. Stiff stems produce terminal heads of closely packed flowers. Qld, NT, WA.

Note: *S. artemisioides* has been subdivided into many subspecies which hybridise freely causing confusion when identifying and naming.

SOLANUM Solanaceae

At a glance

NUMBER OF SPECIES 1700; 80 endemic to Australia.
NATURAL HABITAT Varied but often occurs in dry areas.
FLOWERING White, purple or blue.
HABIT Herbaceous shrubs.
FOLIAGE Often poisonous, often have spines on stems.
GROWTH RATE Usually fast.
HARDINESS Generally hardy.
LIFESPAN Often short-lived.

Culture

- Most are hardy, some are weeds.
- Prefers full sun and good drainage.
- Most grow easily from cuttings.

SOLLYA Pittosporaceae

At a glance

NUMBER OF SPECIES 3; endemic to WA.
NATURAL HABITAT Mainly climbers.
FLOWERING Bell-like, white, pink, blue.
HABIT Climbers or shrubs.
FOLIAGE Linear, lanceolate, narrow to oblong.
HARDINESS Most are hardy.
GROWTH RATE Fast, some become a weed.
LIFESPAN Medium.

Culture

- Some can become weeds, especially near bushland areas.
- Prefers full sun and good drainage.
- Most grow easily from seeds after soaking, or cuttings.

Species

S. heterophylla

- Climber, scented leaves, drought tolerant once established. Blue-, white- or pink-flowering forms are available. Frost hardy.

S. parviflora

- Climber with deep blue flowers. Frost sensitive.

STENOCARPUS Proteaceae

At a glance

NUMBER OF SPECIES About 22; 4 endemic to Australia, others from South-East Asia and New Caledonia.
NATURAL HABITAT Rainforests.
FLOWERING Usually autumn to winter, white

SOLANUM SPECIES	HEIGHT	FLOWERS	COMMENTS
S. aviculare (kangaroo apple)	1–2.5 m	Blue-mauve	Needs moist drained soil and prefers semi-shade.
S. brownii	3 m	Purple	Prefers sunny, well-drained spot.
S. campanulatum	0.8 m	Blue	Full or filtered sunlight.
S. cinereum	0.5–1 m	Blue-purple	Greyish leaves, prickly stems.
S. ellipticum	0.2 m	Purple	Groundcover for arid areas.
S. laciniatum	1–2.5 m	Rich mauve	From wet temperate climate.
S. petrophilum	0.5 m	Purple	Prickly, prefers arid conditions.
S. simile	2 m	Purple	Similar to *S. aviculare*, but slower growth rate.
S. stelligerum	0.8–2.5 m	Blue	Prickly branches.
S. sturtianum	1 m	Purple	Well-drained sunny position.

to orange or red, similar to *Grevillea*.
HABIT Trees or shrubs.
FOLIAGE Simple or pinnate.
HARDINESS Moderate to hardy in the subtropics.
GROWTH RATE Can be slow when young.
LIFESPAN Long-lived.

Culture

- Many are frost tender.
- Require good drainage.
- Propagates easily from seed.

Species

S. salignus (scrub beefwood)

- 15–30 m tall, greenish-white flowers. Needs moist soil and cool shaded position preferably in a warm to mild climate.

S. sinuatus (firewheel tree)

- Attractive tree up to 20 m tall. Spectacular large red flowers, grows well in cool or warm areas but can be sensitive to severe cold, particularly when young.

STIPA Poaceae (syn. *Austrostipa*)

At a glance

NUMBER OF SPECIES 300; 58 (or more) endemic to Australia.
NATURAL HABITAT Grasslands, woodlands, wetlands.
FLOWERING Feathery flowering panicles of oat-like flowers.
HABIT Perennial tufted grasses.
FOLIAGE Overlapping hairy leaves.
HARDINESS Moderate to hardy.
GROWTH RATE Fast.
LIFESPAN Short.

Culture

- Full sun to semi-shade.
- Moist, heavy soils, some prefer well-drained gravels.
- Prune back hard after flowering.

STIPA SPECIES	SIZE	COMMENTS
S. blackii (syn. *Austristipa blackii*)	20 cm	Flowering stems 0.5–1 m high. Erect densely tufted grass, with rough, stiff leaves, lower leaves being hairy, bracts enclosing the flowers are yellow-orange, with a tuft of hairs. Flowers early to mid-spring. NSW, SA, Vic, WA.
S. elegantissima (syn. *Austrostipa elagantissima*)	Up to 80 cm	Cane-like stems up to 1 m tall in tussocks. Leaves are rough, narrow and in-rolled. Bracts purple, black when mature. Large panicles of flowers up to 25 cm long. Flowers mid-winter to mid-summer. NSW, SA, Vic, WA.
S. mollis (syn. *Austrostipa mollis*)	Up to 30 cm	Erect, tufted, robust grass with downy, in-rolled, limp leaves. Rigid stems up to 1.5 m high produce narrow panicles of flowers from mid-spring to mid-summer. NSW, SA, Tas, Vic, WA.
S. pubinodis (syn. *Austrostipa pubinodis*)	Up to 35 cm	Leaves are ridged, rough and tightly in-rolled. Stems up to 1.5 m, bracts enclosing flowers are white. Flowers from early spring to mid-summer. SA, Tas, Vic.
S. stipoides (syn. *Austrostipa stipoides*)	Up to 1 m	Rush-like tussock of densely tufted grass with prickly, hairless, cylindrical leaves up to 70 cm long. Panicles of flowers up to 25 cm long are held inside the tussocks, bracts enclosing flowers have white to yellow hairs. Flowering from mid-spring to mid-autumn.
S. stuposa (syn. *Austrostipa stuposa*)	Up to 40 cm	Perennial, robust tufted grass with either smooth or hairy leaves. Panicles vary from sparsely flowering to many-flowering, bracts are covered in yellowish-white hairs. Flowering in mid-spring.

STYLIDIUM ❧ Trigger Plants ❧ Stylidiaceae

At a glance

NUMBER OF SPECIES About 130; around 100 endemic to Australia.
NATURAL HABITAT Widespread, frequently forests and woodland.
FLOWERING 5 petals, one much smaller than others; white, pink or red.
HABIT Clump-forming.
FOLIAGE Normally linear.
HARDINESS Some hardy; others difficult to grow in gardens.
GROWTH RATE Fast.
LIFESPAN Short.

Culture

- Some need well-drained soils, others tolerate wet situations.
- Transplants easily.
- Most are well suited to rockeries or containers.
- Seed germinates easily.

Species

S. bulbiferum
- Spreading to 0.5 m diameter, 0.1 m tall, rich pink flowers.

S. graminifolium
- Occurs from Qld to SA, pink flowers.

S. laricifolium
- Tall upright species with pink flowers.

S. linare
- Small clump-forming species, pink flowers.

S. soboliferum
- Grey foliage and pink flowers, up to 5 cm tall.

S. spathulatum
- Up to 0.1 m tall with cream flowers.

STYPANDRA ❧ Liliaceae

At a glance

NUMBER OF SPECIES 6; endemic to Australia.
NATURAL HABITAT Wide distribution.
FLOWERING Small lily-like blue flowers with yellow conspicuous stamens.
HABIT Small tufted grass-like plants.
FOLIAGE Lanceolate alternate.
GROWTH RATE Fast.
HARDINESS Hardy.

Culture

- Prefers sunny or semi-shade positions and well-drained soils.
- Most grow easily from seeds or division.

Species

S. caespitosum (now known as *Thelionema caespitosum*)
- Up to 0.5 m tall, grey foliage, white or rich blue flowers.

S. glauca
- Up to 1 m tall, blue and yellow flowers, requires good drainage (preferably sandy soil) and filtered sunlight.

SWAINSONA ❧ Fabaceae

At a glance

NUMBER OF SPECIES About 50; all endemic to Australia and New Zealand.
NATURAL HABITAT Mainly arid areas.
FLOWERING Mainly in spring, very colourful pea flowers.
HABIT Small shrubs, mainly perennials but some annuals.
FOLIAGE Pinnate, soft and hairy.
HARDINESS Generally hardy but *S. formosa* is not hardy in moist or humid conditions.
GROWTH RATE Medium to fast.
LIFESPAN Short, often treated as annuals.
COMMENTS *Swainsona formosa*, Sturt's Desert Pea, was formerly classified in the genus *Clianthus*.

SWAINSONA SPECIES	SIZE	FLOWERS	FOLIAGE	PREFERRED CONDITIONS
S. burkittii	0.3 x 0.6 m	Purple-red	Woolly	Extra drought hardy
S. canescens	0.5 x 0.6 m	Purple or yellow	Soft grey-green	Arid areas, sandy soils
S. formosa	0.3 x 2 m	Red	Green-grey	Arid areas, sandy soils
S. galegifolia	1 x to 1 m	White, pink to red	Bright green	Dry well-drained soil
S. greyana	1 x 1 m	White to pink	Grey-green	Good drainage
S. macullochiana	2 x 2 m	Red-purple	Hairy	Hot, exposed sites
S. microphylla	Varies	Blue to white or yellow	Smooth or hairy	Variable
S. phacoides	0.1 x 0.4 m	Purple, white or yellow	Grey-green	Arid areas
S. procumbens	0.3 x 0.6 m	Blue tones	Mid-green	Extra frost hardy
S. swainsonoides	0.6 x 1 m	Blue-purple	Grey-green	Arid areas, clay or loam

Culture

- Prefers dry, sunny and warm position. Susceptible to fungal diseases in humid and moist areas (and particularly during propagation).
- Most need excellent drainage and are drought resistant.
- Most are frost tender.
- Prune hard each year to promote flowering and keep from becoming leggy.
- Propagate from hot-water-treated seed or cuttings. *S. formosa* is sometimes grafted onto the New Zealand species *Colutea puniceus* (formerly *Swainsona puniceus*) which is hardier.
- *S. formosa* has been grown successfully in containers or hydroponics where drainage can be improved.

SYZYGIUM ✻ Lillipilly ✻ Myrtaceae

At a glance

NUMBER OF SPECIES About 450; about 50 occurring in Australia.
NATURAL HABITAT East-coast rainforests.
FLOWERING Four or five petals, red to blueish fruit.
HABIT Evergreen trees, mainly warm climates.
FOLIAGE Glossy dark green leaves with attractive flushes of new red growth.
HARDINESS Hardy in suitable conditions.
GROWTH RATE Medium to fast in ideal conditions.
LIFESPAN Medium- to long-lived.
COMMENTS *S. australe* and *S. paniculatum* are frequentlyy considered to be the same species. There are, however, differences between the two. *S. paniculatum* has green stems and seeds that separate into distinctive embryos. *S. australe* has red young stems and a single seed.

Culture

- Mainly prefer shade.
- Moist, well-drained soil.
- Responds to mulching.
- Some susceptible to scale and pysillid attack.
- Many new cultivars and varieties have been developed recently. The new forms are generally smaller and more compact, making them better suited to the home garden. They are widely used as hedging and topiary plants in mild climates.
- Propagate easily from fresh seed, but sometimes slowly. Cultivars are also grown from cuttings.

SYZYGIUM SPECIES	HEIGHT	FLOWERS	FRUITS	COMMENTS
S. alatoramulum	Up to 6 m	White	Pale purple	—
S. australe (syn. *Eugenia australis*)	Up to 8 m	White	Dark red	New cultivars are much smaller and widely grown in home gardens.
S. cormiflorum	Up to 10 m	White	Pink	Fruit occurs on trunk.
S. crebrinerve	Up to 30 m	White or pink	Red-purple	—
S. fibrosum	4–8 m	Apricot	Bright red	—
S. francisii	Up to 30 m	White	Blue-purple	Good shade tree.
S. hodgkinsoniae	Up to 4 m	Cream	Red	Fragrant flowers.
S. luehmannii	5–30 m	White	Red	Weeping foliage.
S. moorei	10–20 m	Pink	White	Very attractive tree.
S. oleosum (syn *S. coolminianum*)	10 m	White	Blue	Highly scented leaves.
S. paniculatum	To 8 m	White	Magenta	Edible magenta-coloured fruits.
S. papyraceum	to 10 m	Mauve scented	Purple	—
S. wilsonii	3 m	Rich red	White	Weeping foliage.

TASMANNIA Pepper Bush
Winteraceae

At a glance
NUMBER OF SPECIES 9: 6 endemic to Australia. Also found in New Zealand and New Guinea.
NATURAL HABITAT Generally rainforests or alpine areas.
FLOWERING Normally cream to white.
HABIT Shrubs and trees.
FOLIAGE Glossy dark green leaves and reddish stems.
HARDINESS Variable, depending on species and growing conditions.
GROWTH RATE Medium to fast.
LIFESPAN Medium.

Culture
- Relatively hardy if kept moist and shaded.
- Prefers half to heavy shade.
- Requires high organic soil and thick mulch.
- Propagate by cuttings.

Species
T. insipida
- Shrub up to 5 x 3 m. Cream flowers, purple fruits.

T. lanceolata
- Shrub up to 2 x 2 m. Cream flowers, black fruits, red stems, hot-flavoured fruits sometimes dried and used as a spice.

T. membranea
- Up to 3 m. From tropical rainforests, suited to container growing.

T. purpurescens
- Up to 3 x 1.5 m. Occasionally taller, cream flowers in spring or summer.

T. stipitate
- Shrub up to 4 m. White flowers.

T. xerophila
- Shrub up to 1.5 m. Thick leaves, white flowers, very dark fruits, a particularly hardy species.

TELOPEA ❧ Waratah ❧ Proteaceae

At a glance

NUMBER OF SPECIES 5; all endemic to Australia.
NATURAL HABITAT Sandy loam plateaus and ridges on the east coast of NSW and in cool temperate rainforest in Tasmania.
FLOWERING Spectacular large terminal flowers.
HABIT Large shrubs.
FOLIAGE Leathery leaves, either entire or with a serrated margin.
GROWTH RATE Medium to fast under good conditions.
LIFESPAN Short to medium.

Culture

- Deep soil.
- Friable topsoil.
- Minimal competition in root zone.
- Constant moisture level in soil.
- Do not apply phosphorus at all!
- Semi-shade or some protection.
- Propagate by seed (no special treatment).

Species

T. mongaensis
- 3 x 3 m. Hardy, red flowers, acid soil, tolerates full sun or shade, prune to keep compact.

T. oreades (Gippsland waratah)
- 4 x 3 m. Relatively hardy, red flowers.

T. speciosissima (NSW waratah)
- 3 x 1.5 m. Red flowers up to 15 cm across, surrounded by large red bracts.

T. truncata (Tasmanian waratah)
- 3 x 3 m. Red flowers.

T. truncata* var. *lutea
- 3 x 3 m. Yellow-flowering form, found only in cool temperate rainforest in Tasmania.

TEMPLETONIA ❧ Fabaceae

At a glance

NUMBER OF SPECIES 11; all endemic to Australia.
NATURAL HABITAT Varies from woodland to sand plains.
FLOWERING Pea-shaped flowers representative of the genus.
HABIT Erect to sprawling or prostrate shrubs.
HARDINESS Moderate.
FOLIAGE Usually narrow or leaves reduced to dark green scales.
GROWTH RATE Fast.
LIFESPAN Medium to short.

TEMPLETONIA SPECIES	SIZE	COMMENTS
T. aculeata	20–50 cm	Erect, open multi-stemmed shrub with yellow, brown and red flowers in late winter to early spring. WA, SA, NSW.
T. egena	0.5–1.3 m	Multi-stemmed, erect leafless shrub similar to broom. Yellow, brown, purple and red flowers in late winter to mid-spring. Qld, Vic, WA, SA, NT.
T. hookeri	2 x 2 m	Pendulous, open shrub with narrow linear-shaped leaves, often pinnate. Cream pea flowers with flat pods in late summer to mid-spring. WA, NT, Qld.
T. retusa	2 x 3 m	Round spreading shrub with egg-shaped leaves up to 4 cm, wider at the top than at the base. Red pea flowers in winter and early spring. SA, WA.
T. stenophylla	30 x 20–50 cm	Shrub of trailing or arching habit. Linear upper leaves up to 6 cm long. Stems quadrangular. Yellow and red pea flowers in pairs or singly in late winter to late spring. NSW, Qld, SA, Vic.
T. sulcata	0.3–3.2 m	Variable, multi-stemmed leafless shrub with yellow, purple and brown flowers in late autumn to early spring. Vic, WA, SA, NSW.

Culture

- Well-drained soils.
- Tolerates dry periods once established.
- Propagate by scarified seeds.

TETRATHECA ❧ Black Eyed Susan ❧ Tremandraceae

At a glance

NUMBER OF SPECIES About 20; all endemic to Australia.
NATURAL HABITAT Woodland and forests.
FLOWERING Pink, lilac or purple bell-like flowers with black centres.
HABIT Shrubs.
FOLIAGE Heath-like.
HARDINESS Moderate to hardy.
GROWTH RATE Sometimes slow at first, then fast.
LIFESPAN Short to medium.

Culture

- Prefers well-drained soil and half shade.
- Avoid full sun in the middle of the day.
- Responds well to annual pruning, grows back fast.
- Propagate by cuttings in late summer.

THEMEDA ❧ Poaceae

At a glance

NUMBER OF SPECIES About 50 from Africa, Asia and Australia; none endemic.
NATURAL HABITAT Grasslands and open woodland, beside watercourses in arid climates.
FLOWERING Loose attractive seed heads.
HABIT Clump-forming perennial.
FOLIAGE Grass.
HARDINESS Hardy.
GROWTH RATE Very fast.

Culture

- Drought resistant.
- Seed often needs to be stored for 6 months or more after collecting before it will germinate.

Species

T. triandra (kangaroo grass)

- Grows to 0.5 m tall, clump-forming, is widespread and commonly grown.

TETRATHECA SPECIES	SIZE	FLOWERS	COMMENTS
T. bauerifolia	0.2 x 0.2 m	Pink	Broad dark leaves.
T. ciliata	0.3 x 0.5 m	White to pink or purple	Perfumed flowers.
T. ericifolia	0.3 x 0.3 m	Pink on red stalks	Suits drier climates. Narrow leaves.
T. glanduosa	0.6 x 0.6 m	Pale mauve	Ovate leaves.
T. hirstua	0.4 x 0.6 m	Pale pink	–
T. juncea	0.2 x 0.3 m	Mauve in spring	–
T. pilosa	Up to 0.5 m tall	Purple	Almost leafless. Long-flowering.
T. setigera	Up to 0.5 x 0.4 m	Pink and scented	–
T. shiressii	0.6 x 0.7 m	Deep lilac-pink	Leaves in whorls of 3 or 4.
T. subapphylla	Up to 0.3 x 1 m	Fragrant pink	Almost leafless.
T. thymifolia	0.5 x 0.6 m	Mauve or white	Hardier species.
T. viminea	Up to 0.5 m tall	Mauve flowers	From south-eastern WA.

THOMASIA ✻ Sterculiaceae

At a glance:

NUMBER OF SPECIES 32; all endemic to Australia, with 31 endemic to WA.
NATURAL HABITAT Open plains and gravelly soils in south-western Australia.
FLOWERING Pink, mauve or white flowers.
HABIT Mostly small woody shrubs.
FOLIAGE Dark green heart-shaped or narrow eliptical leaves.
GROWTH RATE Medium to fast.
HARDINESS Generally very hardy.
LIFESPAN Short to medium.

Culture

- Grow in full sun or part shade.
- Requires well-drained soil.
- Due to success with cutting grown plants, this has become more popular in recent years, particularly as a rockery plant.
- Propagate easily by cuttings.

Species

T. glutinosa
- 1 x 1 m. Sticky soft leaves, pink-mauve drooping flowers in spring.

T. pauciflora
- 1.3 x 1 m. Lance-shaped leaves, pink-mauve flowers in spring.

T. pygmea
- 0.3 x 0.8 m. Freckled leaves, pink flowers in spring and summer.

T. quercifolia
- 1 x 1.3 m. Oak-shaped (lobed) leaves, mauve flowers in spring.

THRYPTOMENE ✻ Myrtaceae

At a glance

NUMBER OF SPECIES 35; all endemic to Australia.
NATURAL HABITAT From both tropical and temperate climates.
HABIT Small and large woody shrubs.
FLOWERING Masses of small pink or white flowers.
FOLIAGE Tiny fragrant leaves.
HARDINESS Hardy and drought tolerant.
GROWTH RATE Fast.
LIFESPAN Short to medium.

Culture

- Generally prefers good drainage, though some tolerate wet conditions.
- Harvested from the wild and sold as a cut flower.
- Increasingly being grown by cut-flower growers.
- Propagate by cuttings.

THYRPTOMENE SPECIES	SIZE	COMMENTS
T. baeckeacea	1–2 x 1 m	Pink flowers in spring, full sun preferred.
T. calycina	1–2 x 1–2 m	Pink and white flowers turn red as they age, tolerates dryness and frost, hardy species.
T. denticulata	0.7 x 1 m	Rich pink flowers, suits coastal areas.
T. hyporhytis	0.7 x 2 m	Pink flowers.
T. oligandra	4 x 3 m	White flowers, slightly frost tender.
T. Paynes Hybrid	0.5 x 1 m	Pink flowers Sept-Oct, hardy.
T. saxicola	0.8 x 1.3 m	Drought and frost hardy, pink flowers all year.
T. stenophylla	0.7 x 1 m	Deep pink flowers.
T. strongylophyla	0.6 x 1.5 m	Rich purple flowers.

TOONA ❧ Meliaceae

At a glance

NUMBER OF SPECIES 20; 1 endemic to Australia (*Toona australis*).
NATURAL HABITAT Tropical and subtropical rainforests.
HABIT Large deciduous trees. Often develop buttress roots.
FLOWERING Flowers small, sweet-scented, cream-whitish, in drooping terminal panicles.
FOLIAGE Large pinnate leaves with 5-15 leaflets.
HARDINESS Hardy once established in suitable growing conditions.
GROWTH RATE Very fast in warmer climates, slower in temperate areas.
LIFESPAN Long-lived.

Culture

- Prefers fertile, moist soil.
- Additional fertiliser will improve growth.
- Tolerates full sun.
- Protect from frosts.
- Propagation is by seed which germinates easily, but can be difficult to obtain. Also grown from cuttings and root cuttings.

Species

Toona ciliata (syn. *T. australis*) (red cedar)

- Large tree up to 40 m tall in NSW and Qld rainforests, grows successfully but smaller in southern states. In cooler climates young spring growth is white-pink, changing to green towards the end of spring or early summer.

TRISTANIOPSIS ❧ Myrtaceae

At a glance

NUMBER OF SPECIES About 40; 16 endemic to Australia.
NATURAL HABITAT Commonly beside creeks.
FLOWERING Small yellow or white clusters.
HABIT Evergreen trees and shrubs.
FOLIAGE Simple, often glossy leaves which, from a distance, appear similar to Eucalypt leaves.
GROWTH RATE Medium to fast in warm climates. Can be slow in less-than-perfect conditions.
HARDINESS Generally hardy.
LIFESPAN Long-lived.
COMMENTS Formerly included in the genus *Tristania*, along with *Lophostemon*.

Culture

- Prefers moist, fertile soil, otherwise generally adaptable.
- Do not transplant easily.

Species

Tristaniopsis laurina

- Known as water gum, a medium-sized tree up to 15 m tall. Leaves reddish in southern states, green in warmer conditions, requires moist soil.

VERONICA ❧ Scrophulariaceae

At a glance

NUMBER OF SPECIES About 250; around 20 occurring in Australia but the genus is currently under review.
NATURAL HABITAT Varies, generally temperate areas in eastern Australia.
FLOWERING White-pink to shades of blue in spring.
HABIT Small herbs and shrubs.
FOLIAGE Undivided opposite leaves.
HARDINESS Moderate to hardy, depending on species and growing conditions.
GROWTH RATE Fast.
LIFESPAN Generally short.
COMMENTS The genus *Parahebe* is sometimes considered to be synonymous with some Veronicas. Strictly speaking, Parahebes are those species which have soft wood and Veronicas are those with hard wood.

Culture

- Prefers moist, well-mulched positions.
- Can become invasive.
- Most prefer some shade.
- Prune in winter to stimulate flowering and shape.
- Propagate by cuttings or division.

Species

V. calycina

- Suckering; blue flowers.

V. formosa

- Normally to 0.7 m, occasionally up to 2 m tall. Pale blue flowers from spring to early summer, requires more sun than most.

V. gracilis

- Up to 0.2 m, suckering, pale blue flowers.

VERTICORDIA ❧ Myrtaceae

At a glance

NUMBER OF SPECIES About 99; most endemic to south-western WA.
NATURAL HABITAT Shrublands and sandy heaths in WA.
HABIT Small bushy shrubs.
FLOWERING The flowers are 10–15 mm wide and come in various colours, ranging from white to dark pink, with feathery calyces.
FOLIAGE Small, usually rounded leaves.
HARDINESS Not hardy in eastern states, but can grow well in dry climates.
GROWTH RATE Medium.
LIFESPAN Tends to be short-lived in eastern states, longer in WA.

Culture

- Perfect drainage and a good mulch are essential.
- Full sun.
- Grows well in 50% compost and 50% coarse sand.
- Harvested commercially from the bush for cut-flower market.
- Propagate by seed or cuttings with some species being difficult.

VIMINARIA ❧ Fabaceae

At a glance

NUMBER OF SPECIES 1; endemic to Australia (*V. juncea*).
NATURAL HABITAT Woodlands, forests and heathlands in all states except NT.
FLOWERING Yellow or orange pea flowers.
HABIT Small trees or shrubs.
FOLIAGE Leafless.
HARDINESS Very hardy.
GROWTH RATE Can be fast.
LIFESPAN Medium.

Culture

- Prefers wet soils.
- Full or filtered sunlight (not heavy shade).
- Propagate by hot-water-treated seed.

Species

V. denudata* = *V. juncea

V. juncea Small tree or tall shrub up to 6 m tall, leafless branches, yellow spring flowers.

VIOLA ❧ Native Violet ❧ Violaceae

At a glance

NUMBER OF SPECIES Over 500; about 2 are endemic to Australia.
NATURAL HABITAT Forests.
FLOWERING Violet-like unscented flowers in shades of white, purple and pink.
HABIT Creeping or tuft-forming plants.
FOLIAGE Green, entire.
HARDINESS Usually hardy in a range of growing conditions but grows best in moist soils.
GROWTH Medium to fast in moist, semi-shaded conditions.
LIFESPAN Medium.

VERTICORDIA SPECIES	SIZE	COMMENTS
V. acerosa	To 0.6 x 0.5 m	Small yellow flowers.
V. brownii	0.6 x 0.6 m	Spectacular cream flowers in spring.
V. chysantha	60 x 50 cm	Erect shrub with linear leaves and heads of feathery yellow flowers in spring. WA.
V. densiflora	0.5 x 0.3 m	Mauve to white flowers from spring to summer; one of the hardiest Verticordias.
V. drummondii	50 x 30 cm	Erect, narrow shrub with small oblong to egg-shaped leaves. Pink flowers in summer and autumn.
V. eriocephala (syn. *V. brownie*)	60 x 60 cm	Small round shrub with 3 mm oblong leaves and white-cream flowers that cover the entire shrub in spring.
V. grandiflora	0.8 x 0.8 m	Light green foliage, yellow flowers become darkened with age.
V. grandis	1 x 1 m	Rich red flowers, grey foliage.
V. insignis	To 1 x 1.2 m	Pink to purple flowers.
V. mitchelliana	0.5 x 1 m	Brilliant red flowers in December, silver leaves, drought tolerant.
V. monodelpha	To 2 m tall	Pink to purple flowers, very attractive.
V. muelleriana	Up to 1 m	Small shrub with small round leaves and mauve-purple flowers in spring. WA.
V. nitens	To 1.2 m tall	Yellow-orange flowers.
V. ovalifolia	To 1.5 m tall	White flowers, best in gravel soils.
V. oxylepis	0.6 x 1 m	Cream flowers.
V. picta	To 1 m tall	Pink flowers, suits hot, dry areas.
V. plumosa	1 x 1 m	Blue-green leaves, pink flowers.
V. preissii	To 0.9 m tall	Soft foliage, bright yellow flowers.
V. serrata	To 0.9 m tall	Yellow flowers, tolerates semi-shade.
V. spicata	0.3–0.8 m tall	Purple flowers, tiny leaves.
V. staminosa	0.6 x 0.3 m	Yellow-red flowers.
V. subulata	0.2–1 m	Small variable shrub with dark green round leaves and yellow-red flowers in spring.

Culture

- Needs moist soil at all times.
- Prefers mulch and semi-shade.
- Responds to feeding, mulching and watering in dry periods.
- Propagate by division or seed.

Species

***V. banksii* (syn. *V. hederacea*)**

- Creeping, ground-hugging plant, blue and white flowers most of the year.

V. betonicifolia

- Purple flowers on 6 to 8 cm stems rising above small tufts.

V. sieberana

- Like *V. hederacea* but smaller, denser foliage.

VITEX ❧ Verbenaceae

At a glance

NUMBER OF SPECIES 250; 8 endemic to Australia.
NATURAL HABITAT Interior tropics, sandstone rocky hills and gullies, Qld, WA, NSW, NT.
FLOWERING Many-flowered inflorescences.
HABIT Evergreen or deciduous shrubs or trees that bear essential oils.
FOLIAGE Leaves are usually compound and palmate in shape.
GROWTH RATE Slow to medium, slower in temperate areas.
HARDINESS Hardy.
LIFESPAN Medium- to long-lived.

Culture

- Frost-free areas.
- Well-drained soils.

Species

V. acuminata

- 3–15 m. Shrub to small tree with blue, purple, white or cream flowers most of the year.

V. glabrata

- 3–20 m. Small to medium tree with white, blue or purple flowers from winter to summer.

V. rotundifolia

- 1 x 1.5 m. Low-growing to prostrate shrub with round 4 cm leaves. Flowers are white or pale blue. Tolerates salt-laden winds.

V. trifolia* var. *trifolia

- 3 x 3 m. Bushy shrub with trifoliate leaves and blue to purple flowers in autumn and again in mid-spring.

WAHLENBERGIA ❧ Campanulaceae

At a glance

NUMBER OF SPECIES 13 endemic to Australia; others in South Africa, South America and NZ.
NATURAL HABITAT Varies.
FLOWERING Blue or white with 5 lobes, on long stalks.
HABIT Small clump-forming herbaceous perennials.
FOLIAGE Small undivided leaves, sometimes toothed margins.
GROWTH RATE Fast.
HARDINESS Hardy.
LIFESPAN Short.

Culture

- Prefers well-drained soil.
- Full sun or filtered sunlight.
- Has been propagated by division, cuttings and seed.

Species

W. communis

- Slender foliage, blue to white flowers, suits arid climates.

W. gloriosa (austral or royal bluebell)

- Up to 0.3 m tall, dark blue flowers.

W. gracilis

- As for *W. communis* but smaller.

W. stricta (bluebell)

- Up to 0.4 m tall, light blue spring or summer flowers.

WATERHOUSEA ❧ Myrtaceae

At a glance

NUMBER OF SPECIES 4; all endemic to Australia.
NATURAL HABITAT Rainforests of Qld and NSW, often along streams.
FLOWERING Panicles of many small flowers.
HABIT Trees.
FOLIAGE Dark green glossy foliage similar in shape to eucalypt leaves.
GROWTH RATE Medium to slow.
HARDINESS Hardy once established in suitable conditions.

Culture

- Moist, well-drained soils but tolerates dry periods once established.
- Frost-free areas.
- Scale insects can be a problem.

Species

***W. floribunda* (syn. *Eugenia ventenatii, Syzygium floribundrum*)**

- Up to 30 m.
- Small to medium pendulous tree, with dark grey bark and narrow, green shiny leaves with pale undersides. Small white flowers are followed by green fruit. Good screening plant.

W. unipunctata

- Up to 8 m
- Small tree with soft, small, lance- to egg-shaped leaves that are limp and pink when young. Small white flowers are followed by pink to purple fruit.

WESTRINGIA ❧ Lamiaceae

At a glance

NUMBER OF SPECIES About 30; all endemic to Australia.

NATURAL HABITAT A wide variety of climates and soils.

FLOWERING White or blue, similar to *Prostanthera*.

HABIT Small to medium woody shrubs.

FOLIAGE Leaves occur in fours encircling the stem.

HARDINESS Most are hardy.

GROWTH RATE Can be fast.

Culture

- Prefers semi-shade and reasonable drainage.
- Needs pruning to shape.
- Propagate by cuttings.
- Varieties requiring very good drainage can be grafted onto *W. fruticosa*.

Difference between Prostanthera and Westringia

- *Westringia* flowers are solitary (i.e. each attached singly to the stem).
- *Prostanthera* flowers occur in clusters.

WESTRINGIA SPECIES	SIZE	COMMENTS
W. blakeana	2 x 2 m	White spring flowers, prefers warm climate and semi-shade.
W. cheelii	1 x 1 m	White or mauve flowers, requires good drainage, prefers full sun.
W. eremicola	1.5 x 1 m	White or mauve flowers in spring and summer, hardy, flowers not as spectacular as others.
W. fruticosa	2 x 4 m	White flowers sporadic throughout all months, extremely hardy, resists frost, drought and salt but not waterlogging, blue-grey leaves.
W. glabra	1.5 x 2 m	Mauve or white flowers, requires better drainage than *W. fruticosa*.
W. grandiflora	1.5 x 2 m	Large mauve or white flowers, needs very good drainage.
W. longifolia	2 x 1.5 m	White or pale blue flowers in spring. Very hardy but sensitive to frost, wet soils and waterlogging. Blue-grey leaves.
W. lucida	0.6 x 1 m	Blue to mauve summer flowers. Attractive foliage.
W. rigida	0.5 x 0.5 m	White flowers all year. Good drainage essential.
W. rosmariniformis = *W. fruticosa*		
W. rubiifolia	1 x 1 m	White or blue flowers spring to summer, good drainage is important, full or filtered sun.

XANTHORRHOEA ❀ Blackboy or Grass Tree ❀ Xanthorrhoeceae

(Note: The name 'blackboy' is discouraged due to racist overtones; however, it is still the most widely used and recognisable name for these popular plants.)

At a glance

NUMBER OF SPECIES About 15; all endemic to Australia.
NATURAL HABITAT Varies, widespread throughout Australia.
FLOWERING Tall spike covered with small flowers, often cream or white.
HABIT Palm-like growth generally consisting of a trunk with a grass-like tussock on top.
FOLIAGE Normally long and thin (needle-like).
HARDINESS Moderate established but many professionals in the horticulture industry claim that plants transplanted from the bush are difficult to establish and will, over a long period of time (up to 10 years), gradually die.
GROWTH RATE Slow to medium.
LIFESPAN Very long-lived.

Culture

- They require well-drained conditions and grow best in sandy soils. They are particularly susceptible to root rot, so drainage is important.
- Drought tolerant.
- Fresh seed germinates very easily. Spray seedlings with fungicide to control root rot, and keep plants well spaced for good ventilation. A deep taproot makes transplanting very difficult.

Species

X. australis
- Sunny or semi-shaded position, frost tolerant, responds to moist soil, tolerates dry soil, shorter thick spike with white flowers in spring but they may not occur annually.

X. minor
- Smaller species, white flowers on a short spike in spring and summer.

X. preissii
- Tall, rough stem, long, narrow, upright leaves, white flowers on tall spike.

XANTHOSTEMON ❀ Myrtaceae

At a glance

NUMBER OF SPECIES About 25; 13 occur in Australia.
NATURAL HABITAT Rainforests.
FLOWERING Large clusters of bright flowers.
HABIT Large trees to small trees.
HARDINESS Mostly hardy and adaptable to cultivation.
FOLIAGE Glossy green elliptical foliage. New growth may be reddish or hairy.
GROWTH Normally vigorous.
LIFESPAN Usually long-lived.
COMMENTS Very attractive to birds. There is a dwarf variety of *X. chrysanthus* available.

Culture

- Full sun.
- Prefers moist fertile loam soils.
- May be pruned to obtain thicker specimens.
- Propagation by fresh seed or cuttings.

Species

X. chrysanthus (golden penda)
- Small tree up to 10 m. If propagated by cutting it may only grow to 3–5 m. Brilliant large clusters of gold-yellow flowers. Pink-red new foliage flushes. Well established in the ornamental industry.

X. whitei (red-brown penda)
- 15 m tree with large clusters of golden flowers. Young shoots are hairy. Likes an abundance of water.

X. youngii (red penda)
- 2–5 m shrub. Small red cluster flowers in spring and summer. Note: this species is too hard to acquire and grow in domestic gardens.

Glossary

ANGIOSPERMS Flowering plants

ANNUAL A plant that completes its life cycle in one year

AXIL The angle between the upper part of the stem and the leaf, petiole or branch

BASAL Pertaining to the base

BERRY A fruit in which the entire ovary wall matures into an edible fleshy pericarp wherein the seeds are contained

BIPINNATE Pinnately compound leaves with pinnately-compound leaflets; twice-pinnate (*see* page 4 diagram)

BRACT Reduced leaf structure associated with the flower or cone

CLADODES A stem that looks like a leaf

CLIMBER A plant that grows long shoots that cling to other surfaces (walls, poles, trees) to grow upwards

CREEPER A plant that grows long shoots along the soil surface

COMPOUND LEAF A leaf made up of two or more leaflets attached to the leaf stalk (*see* page 4 diagram)

CONE Reproductive structure with (mostly) woody scales organised around a central stalk, and seeds located and protected by the scales. It characterises conifers

CULTIVAR A group of cultivated plants that are distinguished from others by a particular characteristic (for example, variegated leaves) that is passed on to the offspring

CYCADS Primitive seed plants with a large crown of compound leaves and a stout trunk that make the order Cycadales

DIVISION Breaking of the plant roots into smaller portions that have roots, stems and leaves

ENDEMIC Plant or animal species found only in a particular location in the world

EPIPHYTE Plant that grows on top of other plants. It doesn't root on soil

FAMILY Taxonomically, a group of related genera (plural of *Genus*)

FERN Non-flowering vascular plants with rhizomes and fronds as leaves

FRONDS Foliage of a plant that shows many divisions, as in ferns and palms

GALL Proliferation or growth of plant cells induced by insects, bacteria, fungus or virus, which create an external structure protecting the offspring

GENUS A group of related species according to genetic or morphological characteristics that are not present in other groups

GRAFTING Attaching a piece of stem from one plant to the stem of another plant so that they grow together

GYMNOSPERMS Seed-bearing plants that don't produce flowers. Represented by conifers and cycads

INFLORESCENCE A flower cluster arranged in a particular way on a stem or a system of branches; spikes, racemes, umbels, whorls, panicles, cymes and corymbs are common types of inflorescences (*see* page 4 diagram)

LANCEOLATE Leaf shape with a broad base and pointed terminal end, like a lance

LINEAR An object shaped as a straight line

NATIVE Those plants originally evolved in and adapted to a specific location, genetically unaltered by humans

NUTRIENT Chemical element or compound that a living being absorbs and metabolises for growth and maintenance

OBOVATE Leaf shape where the base is pointed and the tip rounded, as an inversed water drop

OVATE Oval-shaped leaf with a slightly pointed tip

PALMATE Palm-like leaf, divided into three or more lobes

POLLARDED Tree that has been pruned to produce a uniform close head with young shoots

PANICLES Branched grouping of raceme inflorescences (*see* page 4 diagram)

PINNATE A leaf divided into many leaflets organised in two opposing rows along the axis (*see* page 4 diagram)

PEDICEL The tiny stalk of an individual flower

PEDUNCLES stalk that attach flowers to the stem, or where the individual pedicels arise

PERENNIAL A plant that completes its life cycle in more than two years

PETIOLE Leaf stalk

PHYLLODE Leaf with enlarged midrib and no blades; the blade is replaced by the enlarged petiole

PINNAE (plural **pinna**) A leaflet of a compound leaf that lies on each side of a common axis (the rachis) as seen in ferns (*see* page 4 diagram)

POD Elongated two-sided seed-bearing structure that opens once the seeds are mature, releasing them to the ground

PROSTRATE Plants whose branches extend horizontally near the ground, forming groundcovers or low wide shrubs

RACEMES Inflorescence that grows continuously at the end of the axis (shoot), with pedicel attached flowers (*see* page 4 diagram)

RECURVED MARGINS Curved margins as in wave-like margin shapes

RHIZOME An underground stem that forms shoots and roots at intervals

RHIZOMATOUS Rhizome-like shape or function

SCARIFY Break the seed surface with knife or sandpaper to speed up germination

SEED Small plant embryo covered by a coat, occurring in gymnosperms and angiosperms as the ovary ripens after fertilisation.

SEPALS Small leaves at the base of the flower

SERRATE MARGINS A margin of a leaf that is jagged, like many pointed teeth

SHRUB A woody plant with multiple stems and in general lower than 6 m in height

SPATHULATE Spoon-shaped leaf

SPECIES A group of organisms that can interbreed freely

SPIKE Inflorescence where the flowers are attached to the main stem without stalks (peduncles) (*see* page 4 diagram)

SPORES Single-celled and hard-shelled propagating units resistant to environmental factors.

STAMENS Masculine part of the flower made up of filament (stalk) and anther or pollen-bearing top

STIPULE Paired appendages located at the base of leaf petioles; they may be shaped like tiny leaves

STOLONS An above-ground stem that forms new shoots and roots at intervals, as in strawberries

SUB-SHRUB A low-growing, ground-hugging, partly woody, party herbaceous plant

SUBSPECIES A wild or naturally occurring variant of a species (differing in colour, size or habit), often occurring within a distinct geographical area

SUCKERS A shoot growing from a horizontal root

VARIETY A plant that can interbreed with other plants of the same species, but shows one or more differences, like flower or leaf shape or colour

Appendix

DISTANCE LEARNING AND ONLINE COURSES

The authors of this book conduct a wide range of distance learning courses, online, on CD or by correspondence, through the Australian Correspondence Schools and ACS Distance Education. These courses include:

Australian Native Plants I

Australia has one of the oldest and most diverse communities of plants of any country. It also has the most diverse climate, from tropical to hot and dry arid landscapes, from snowy mountains to Mediterranean climates. This climatic variation reflects in the flora, producing many endemic plants. This course is designed to develop your ability to identify, select and cultivate Australian native plants, in a wide variety of situations. This course is relevant to any part of Australia, and equally to most parts of the world. It is now available online, on CD and by correspondence.

Australian Natives Plants II

This course covers both woody (hard-wooded) and herbaceous (soft-wooded) low-growing Australian native plants that bear showy flowers. It is an in-depth study of small native shrubs, ground covers and clump-forming perennials. An excellent course for anyone wanting to know and grow Australian native wildflowers.

Nature Park Management I & II

This course has been specifically designed for people working or wishing to work in nature parks and reserves, in managerial or technical positions. Learn about natural environments, and the management of zoos, wildlife parks and nature reserves. Develop an understanding of the natural environment and basic ecological principles, and learn a variety of skills ranging from basic gardening and nature-park design, to erosion control, weed control and tree surgery. The course covers many of the fundamental tasks which people who work in such parks need to do; including weed control, soil management, land rehabilitation, landscape construction etc.

Natural Garden Design

Create a garden following nature's laws. This course builds your knowledge of natural environments and how to create innovative plans for low-maintenance bush gardens. It develops your ability to design a bush garden — either totally native or a mix of indigenous and exotic plants. The course consists of eight lessons covering information about native plants, how to mix them together in a balanced way to create desired effects, how to build rockeries, ponds, paths, and lots more.

Certificate in Horticulture (VHT002)

If you want a career in horticulture, this is one of the best starting points. This Certificate was developed with a great deal of industry input throughout the 1990s then reviewed and upgraded in 2004 to ensure international relevance. Graduates from this 600–700 hour certificate course have a history of outstanding career success. The course provides a very strong foundation in general horticulture (up to 350 hours) as well as specialisation in a chosen area such as Grounds Management, Ornamental Horticulture, Horticultural Technology, Horticultural Science, Plant Protection, Propagation, Landscaping and Garden Design, Organics and Permaculture, Turf, Arboriculture, Herbs, and Nature Park Management.

Advanced Diploma in Horticulture (VHT009) — Nursery Management or Parks and Recreation or Ornamental Horticulture

Take a leap forward into a career in applied horticulture. Do you work in a nursery and want to advance to a managerial position? If so, then this course is the best for you. It has been specifically designed to provide excellent and applied training for people wishing to work at a high technician or management level; in positions such as nursery managers, parks manager, technical representatives or consultants.

This Advanced Diploma can be taken also in other specialisations such as: Parks and Recreation and Ornamental Horticulture.

Rhs (Level 2) Certificate in Horticulture

This vocationally oriented course comprises core studies in general horticulture plus specialised elective studies. The course is designed to lay a foundation for a long-term career in horticulture by developing the ability to identify a large range of plants, knowledge of essential horticultural principles and practices and practical skills in plant propagation, growth and care. This course provides certification from the Royal Horticultural Society (RHS) UK.

Other courses

More than 120 certificates, diplomas, higher level education and individual specialised courses in horticulture are also available. The school also conducts a range of highly specialised courses, such as Eucalypts, Acacias, Australian Native Trees, Australian Native Ferns, Grevilleas, Trees for Rehabilitation, and various other specialised courses.

For further information please visit:
www.acs.edu.au
www.acsedu.co.uk
www.acseduonline.com
www.acsgarden.com
www.hortcourses.com

Or contact us:
ACS Distance Education
Email: admin@acs.edu.au
Fax: (07) 5562 1099
PO Box 2092
Nerang East Qld 4211

AUSTRALIAN NATIVE NURSERIES

A very comprehensive web page to look for Australian native nurseries is Nurseries Online web page: www.nurseriesonline.com.au, menu 'Mail Order and Specialists Nurseries', then click over 'Natives'.

Retail Seed Nurseries

Most of the nurseries will send all over Australia and some also to overseas.

Australian Native Seeds Online
www.australiannativeseeds.com.au/OnlineShop.aspx

Bushland Flora
17 Trotman Crescent
Yanchep WA 6053
Phone: (08) 9561 1636

Traditional Seeds
PO Box 715
Busselton WA 6280
Phone: (08) 9754 1919
Fax: (08) 9752 1399
Email: abbeycon@iinet.net

Vaughans Wildflower Seeds
RMB 642
Donnybrook WA 6239
Phone: (08) 9732 1152
email:vaughanseeds@bigpond.com

Australian Capital Territory

Rodney's Plant Plus
24 Beltana Road
Pialligo ACT 2609
Phone: (02) 6248 6156
Fax: (02) 6257 6203
Email: nursery@rodneys.com.au

New South Wales

Cranebrook Native Nursery
175 Cranebrook Road
Cranebrook NSW 2749
Phone: (02) 4777 4256

Dingo Creek Rainforest Nursery
Bulga Road
Bobin (via Wingham) NSW 2429
Phone: (02) 6550 5167
Fax (02) 6550 5086
Email: dingock@mideast.com.au

Eastcoast Perennials
PO Box 323A
Wauchope NSW 2446
Website: www.nurseriesonline.com.au/eastcoast/eastcoast.html

Forest Native Nursery
210 Wattamolla Road
Berry NSW 2535
Phone: (02) 4464 2275

Illawambra Native Growers
PO Box 89
Cobrago NSW 2550
Phone/Fax: (02) 6493 7398

Kanget Native Nursery
929 Gloucester Road
Wingham NSW 2429
Phone: (02) 6553 5561

Muswellbrook State Forest Nursery
New England Highway
Muswellbrook NSW 2333
Phone: (02) 6543 2622

The Ragged Blossom Native Nursery Bangalow
Bangalow NSW 2479
Phone: (02) 6687 1309
Mobile: 0403 720 950
Email: plants@raggedblossom.com.au
Website: www.raggedblossom.com.au

Terania Rainforest Nursery
299 Main Arm Road
Mullumbimby NSW 2482
Phone: (02) 6684 3100
Fax: (02) 6684 3660
Email: info@terania.com.au

Northern Territory

Alice Springs (Garden) Nursery
PO Box 3210
Alice Springs NT 0871
Phone: (08) 8952 5055
Fax: (08) 8952 2716
Email: mackamob@bigpond.com

Heavitree Nursery
PO Box 2412
Alice Springs NT 0870

Ironstone Lagoon Nursery
2849 Lagoon Road
Knuckey Lagoon NT 0801
Phone: (08) 8984 3186

Queensland

A comprehensive list of native plants nurseries in Queensland can be seen at the SGAP web page Queensland chapter: www.sgapQld.org.au/growers.html

Fairhill Native Plants & Botanic Gardens
Fairhill Road
Yandina Qld 4561
Phone: (07) 5446 7088
Fax: (07) 5446 7379

Rons Rare Palms and Cycads
404 Browns Creek Road
Yandida Qld 4561
Phone: (07) 5446 7573

Shenandoah Nursery
142 Arnolds Road
Byfield Qld 4703
Phone/Fax: (07) 4935 1134

Simpson Orchids
29 Gannon Street
Mount Mee Qld 4521
Phone: (07) 5498 2185

South Australia

Berri Native Plants
Sturt Highway
Berri SA 5343
Phone: (08) 8582 1599

Carawatha Native Garden & Brenton Tucker Native Plants
Placid Estates Road
Wellington East (near Tailem Bend) SA 5259
Phone: (08) 8572 7104

Corinne Hampel-Mallee Native Plants Nursery
Murray Bridge SA 5253
Phone: (08) 8532 3701 for an appointment
Email: corinne@hampel.com.au
Website: www.malleenativeplants.com.au

Coromandel Native Nursery
RMB 840 Star and Arrow Road
Coromandel Valley SA 5051
Phone: (08) 8388 2777 for opening times

The Daisy Patch
Cnr George and Richmond Terraces
Coonalpyn SA 5265
Phone: (08) 8571 1172 for opening times
Website: http://lm.net.au/~daisyp/

Daryl Kinnane—Native Rainforest Flora
PO Box 239
Summertown SA 5141
Phone: (08) 8390 1155

Dealtry Native Plants
Lot 2 Trevilla Road
One Tree Hill SA 5114
Phone: (08) 8280 7079 for opening times

Goodwinii Eremophila Nursery
Lot 4 Bowman Road
Stirling North (via Port Augusta) SA 5710
Phone: (08) 8643 6541
Website: www.goodwinii.com.au

Mid-North Native Plants
PO Box 767, Clare SA 5453
Phone/Fax: (08) 8842 1874
Email: utegrehn@hotmail.com

Mt Barker Woodlots & Wildflower Nursery
2 Fletcher Road
Mt Barker SA 5251
Phone: (08) 8391 1971 for opening times

Natural State
Second Avenue
Tailem Bend SA 5260
Phone/Fax: (08) 8572 3049
Mobile: 0439 727 057
Website: www.naturalstate.com.au

Nellie's Native Nursery
Randell Street
Mannum SA 5238
Phone: (08) 8569 1762

Northside Native Plants
Cnr Diagonal & Goldsborough Roads
Cavan SA 5094
Phone: (08) 8262 6509
Fax: (08) 8260 6501
Email: nornat@esc.net.au

Pavy Saunders Native Plant Nursery and Ecology Restoration
PO Box 62, Ardrossan SA 5571
Mobile: 0418 802 636
Email: pavysaunders@bigpond.com.

Poolman's Native Plant Nursery
Oliver's Road
McLaren Vale SA 5171
Phone: (08) 8323 8155

Southern Native Plant Nursery
Chalk Hill Road
McLaren Vale SA 5171
Phone: (08) 8323 8259

State Flora, Belair
Queens Jubilee Drive
Belair National Park
Belair SA 5052
Phone: (08) 8278 7777
Website: www.stateflora.com.au

State Flora, Murray Bridge
Bremer Road
Murray Bridge SA 5253
Phone: (08) 8351 1420
Website: www.stateflora.com.au

Williamstown Native Plant Nursery
PO Box 1136
Gawler SA 5118
Mobile: 0419 246 687

Tasmania

Allans Garden Centre Prospect
285 Westbury Road
Prospect Tas. 7250
Phone: (03) 6344 6257
Email: allansprospect@bigpond.com.au

Allan's Garden Centre
East Tamar Highway
Rocherlea Tas. 7248
Phone: (03) 6326 3668

Brown's Mountain Nursery
Browns Mountain Road
Underwood Tas. 7254

Habitat Plants
240 Jones Road
Liffey Tas. 7302
Phone: (03) 6397 3400
Fax: (03) 6397 3074
Email: habitatplants@our.net.au

Redbreast Nurseries
1709 Channel Highway
Margate Tas. 7054
Phone: (03) 6267 2871
Fax: (03) 6267 1077

Victoria

Australian Ecosystems Nursery
Eastern Treatment Plant
Alan Bird Drive
Bangholme Vic. 3175
Phone: (03) 9775 0612
Fax: (03) 9775 0614
Email: nursery@australianecosystems.com.au

Australian Orchid Nursery
58 Mornington Tyabb Road
Tyabb Vic. 3913
Phone: (03) 5977 3122
Fax: (03) 5977 3350
Email: wto@peninsula.hotkey.net.au
Website: www.australianorchids.com.au

Browns Wildflower Gardens & Handcraft
340 One Chain Road
Kardella Vic. 3951
Phone: (03) 5659 8219

The Bush-House Nursery
18 Hermitage Drive
Allansford Vic. 3277
Phone: (03) 5565 1665
Mobile: 0429 862 184

Codrington Nursery
RMB 2480
Codrington Vic. 3285
Phone: 5568 4344
Fax: 5568 4306
Email: info@codringtonnursery.com.au

Fern Acres Nursery
1052 Whittlesea-Kinglake Road
Kinglake West, Vic. 3757
Phone: (03) 5786 5031
Email: sales@fernacres.com.au
Website: www.ferns.com.au

Glenleith
275 Whites Road
Mount Duneed Vic. 3216
Phone: (03) 5264 1091
Fax: (03) 5264 1012

Goldfields Revegetation
230 Tannery Lane
Mandurang Vic. 3551
Phone: (03) 5439 5384
Email: goldrevg@netcon.net.au

Green Planet Nursery
355 Lancefield Road
Sunbury Vic. 3429
Phone: (03) 9740 8144

Kooringa Native Plants
743 Warby Range Road
Wangaratta South Vic. 3678
Phone: (03) 5725 7238
Fax: (03) 5725 7218
Mobile: 0427 573 659
Email: john@warbyrange.com.au
Website: www.warbyrange.com.au/kooringahome.htm

Kuranga Native Nursery
118 York Road
Mt Evelyn Vic. 3796
Phone: (03) 9760 8100
Website: www.kuranga.com.au

Lang's Native Plant Nursery
564 11th Street
Mildura West Vic. 3500
Phone/Fax: (03) 5023 2551
Email: langsnursery@hotkey.net.au

Lovers Leap Nursery & Garden
Egertoon-Ballark Road
Ballark Vic. 3342
Phone: (03) 5368 9474
Website: www.ballarat.com/gordon/loversleap.htm

Mildura Native Nursery Pty Ltd
Phone: (03) 5021 4117
Fax: (03) 5023 0607
Email: tim@nativenursery.com.au
Website: www.nativenursery.com.au

Montburg Gardens
1620 Hamilton Highway
Murgheboluc Vic. 3221
Phone: (03) 5265 1198
Fax: (03) 5265 1218
Mobile: 0417 428 689
Email: order@montburggardens.com.au
Website: www.montburggardens.com.au

Mt Cassel Native Plants
Phone: (03) 5356 6351
Email: jbm.malligan@bigpond.com

The Native Shop
Native Growth Holdings
6/15 Marine Parade
St Kilda Victoria 3182
Phone: (03) 9593 9665
Fax: (03) 9593 9071
Email: tim@nativenursery.com.au
Website: www.nativenursery.com.au/shop

Pomonal Wildflower Nursery
Phone: (03) 5356 6250

Quamby Nursery
Phone: (03) 5455 1367
Fax: (03) 5455 1368
Website: www.quambynursery.com.au

Ronneby Trees
Phone: (03) 5627 6327
Fax: (03) 5627 6421
Email: ronnebytrees@iprimus.com.au
Website: www.ronnebytrees.com.au

Smartgraft
PO Box 464
Stawell Vic. 3380
Phone: (03) 5358 4445 after hours

Suntuff Natives
(Telephone first)
1220 Bacchus Marsh Road
Bullengarook, near Gisborne, Vic. 3437
Phone: (03) 5428 9369
Website: www.users.ssc.net.au/pyesplants

Tall Trees
Phone: (03) 5983 0166
Fax: (03) 5983 0188
Email: info@talltrees.com.au
Website: www.talltrees.com.au

Tambo Vale Nursery & Gardens
Princes Highway
Nicholson Vic. 3882
Phone: (03) 5156 8310

Terraflora Nursery & Gardens
South Gippsland Highway
Leongatha Vic. 3953
Phone: (03) 5662 4124

Treeplanters Nursery
530 Springvale Road
Springvale South Vic. 3172
Phone: (03) 9546 9668
Fax: (03) 9547 1719

Vaughan's Australian Plants
1060 Portarlington Road
Curlewis Vic. 3222
Phone: (03) 5250 5592
Mobile: 0403 403 871

Weeping Grevillea Nursery
(On appointment only)
Bartletts Lane
Kangaroo Ground (Melway) Vic.3097
Phone: (03) 9719 7505

Wimmera Native Nursery
Phone: (03) 5389 1193
Fax: (03) 5389 1458
Email: tim@nativenursery.com.au
Website: www.nativenursery.com.au/wimmera

Western Australia

APT Nursery
Lot 12 South Western Highway
Boyanup WA 6237
Phone: (08) 9731 5470

Bushland Flora (Native seed specialists)
17 Trotman Crescent
Yanchep WA 6053
Phone: (08) 9561 1636

Hamel Nursery Greening Australia
PO Box 329
Waroona WA 6215
Phone: (08) 9733 1241
Fax: (08) 9733 1417
Website: www.aoi.com.au/atcros/A1231P.htm

Lullfitz Nursery
PO Box 34
Wanneroo WA 6949
Phone: (08) 9405 1607
Fax: (08) 9306 2933
Email: sales@lullfitz.com.au
Website: www@lullftiz.com.au

Nindethana Seed Service Pty Ltd
PO Box 2121
Albany WA 6331
Phone: (08) 9844 3533
Fax: (08) 9844 3573
Email: nindseed@iinet.net.au

Traditional Seeds
PO Box 715
Busselton WA 6280
Phone: (08) 9754919
Fax: (08) 97521399
Email: abbeycon@iinet.net

WA Wildflower Seed Company
PO Box 804
Canning Bridge WA 6152
Phone: (08) 9313 3090
Fax: (08) 9313 3091

Zanthorrea Nursery
155 Watsonia Road
Maida Vale WA 6057
Phone: (08) 9454 6260
Fax: (08) 9454 4540
Email: jackie@zanthorrea.com.au
Website: www.zanthorrea.com.au

ORGANISATIONS

Association of Societies for Growing Australian Plants

The Association of Societies for Growing Australian Plants (ASGAP) caters for people interested in Australia's native flora whether that interest is simple appreciation of the beauty and diversity of the flora or whether it extends to propagation, cultivation and conservation. ASGAP is made up of seven independent, non-profit, regional societies:
CANBERRA http://nativeplants-canberra.asn.au
NEW SOUTH WALES www.austplants-nsw.org.au
QUEENSLAND www.sgapqld.org.au
SOUTH AUSTRALIA (INCLUDING ALICE SPRINGS)
www.australianplantssa.asn.au
TASMANIA www.apstas.com
VICTORIA http://home.vicnet.net.au/~sgapvic
WESTERN AUSTRALIA
http://members.ozemail.com.au/~wildflowers

Within these state societies there are further regional societies.

The association conducts meetings, shows and research activities into Australian native plants. The ASGAP produces an online magazine, a printed magazine and other publications that are particularly valuable resources.
Email: asgaponline@yahoo.com.au
Web: http://asgap.org.au

Australian National Botanic Gardens

The Australian National Botanic Gardens maintains a scientific collection of native plants from all parts of Australia. The plants are displayed for the enjoyment and education of visitors and are used for research into plant classification and biology. A herbarium of preserved plant specimens is closely associated with the living collection.

The ANBG have a web page full of information on Australian flora, worth visiting at: www.anbg.gov.au

Further reading

Australian plants have only been in cultivation since settlement. Callistemons, grevilleas, melaleucas and similar natives have been in cultivation for a long time but many other natives have only entered cultivation in the past few years and, as such, there is little knowledge about their ideal cultivation conditions. Other natives are only grown in their original location and are not known to other areas.

The Society for Growing Australian Plants (SGAP) (http://asgap.org.au) publishes guides, books and booklets on Australian natives which are worth consulting.

GENERAL BIBLIOGRAPHY

Brock, J. (1988), *Top End Native Plants* John Brock, Northern Territory Botanical Bulletin

Brooker, I. & D. Kleinig (2006, 3rd edn), *Field Guide to Eucalypts Vol. 1* South-eastern Australia Bloomings Books, Sydney

Brooker, M.I.H & D.A. Kleinig (1990), *Field Guide to Eucalypts Vol.2* Inkata Press, Melbourne

Brooker, M.I.H & D.A.Kleinig (1994), *Field Guide to Eucalypts Vol.3* Butterworth-Heinemann, Sydney

Centre for Plant Biodiversity Research (2006, 3rd edn), EUCLID – *Eucalypts of Australia* CSIRO Publishing, Victoria

Elliot, G. & R. Elliot (1996), *The Kuranga Handbook of Australian Plants* Lothian Books, Melbourne

Elliot, W.R. & D.L. Jones, *Encyclopedia of Australian Plants* Lothian, Melbourne
At this stage, only the first six of volumes have been published:
Vol 1 1980; Vol 2 (A-Ca), 1982; Vol 3 (Ce-Er), 1984; Vol 4 (Eu-Go), 1986; Vol 5 (Gr-J), 1990; Vol 6 (K-M), 1993: A-Z Supplement, 1994

Elliot, R. (2003), *Australian Plants for Mediterranean Climate Gardens* Rosenberg Publ. Dural, NSW

Fagg, M. & J.W. Wrigley (2003, 5th edn), *Australian Native Plants* New Holland Publishers, Sydney

Holliday, I. (2004, 2nd edn), *Melaleucas: A Field and Garden Guide* New Holland Publishers, Sydney

Lamp, C & F. Collet (2004), *Field Guide to Weeds in Australia* Inkata Press, Melbourne

McGillivray, D.J. (1993), *Grevillea, Proteaceae: A taxonomic revision* Melbourne University Press, Melbourne

Molineaux, B & S. Forrester (2004), *The Australflora A-Z of Australian Plants* Reed New Holland Publishers, Sydney

Nicholson, N & H. Nicholson (1985), *Australian Rainforest Plants Vol.1* self-published, The Channon, NSW

Nicholson, N & H. Nicholson (1988), *Australian Rainforest Plants Vol.2* self-published, The Channon, NSW

Nicholson, N & H. Nicholson (1991), *Australian Rainforest Plants Vol.3* self-published, The Channon, NSW

INDEX